ONCE WERE LIONS

ONCE WERE LIONS

Jeff Connor & Martin Hannan

HarperSport
An Imprint of HarperCollinsPublishers

First published in 2009 by
HarperSport
an imprint of HarperCollins
77–85 Fulham Palace Rd
London W6 8JB
www.harpercollins.co.uk

1

A CIP catalogue record for this book is
available from the British Library

ISBN 978-0-00-724152-1

Printed and bound in Great Britain
by Clays Ltd, St Ives plc

Photographs courtesy of: **Action Images** 14t and inset, 14bl; **Colorsport** 4,
5bl, 7, 8t, 12c, 16b; **David Moir/Scotsman Publications** 15c; **Family of Rob
Howie** 1t, 1c; **Fotosport** 13b; **Getty Images** 3tr, 3b, 5tl, 5br, 6t, 6c, 6b, 8br,
9tr, 9b, 10tl, 10b, 11tl, 11tr, 11b, 12t, 12br, 13t, 14br, 16tl, 16tr; **Harlequin
Events** 15t; **Hugh McLeod** 3tl; **Jack Crombie/Scotsman Publications** 3c;
Ken Scotland 2bl; **PA Photos** 15b; **Peter Burns/Fairfax newspapers** 5tl;
Rugbyrelics.com 2t, 2br, 8bl, 9tl, 10tr, 12bl

Mixed Sources
Product group from well-managed
forests and other controlled sources
www.fsc.org Cert no. SW-COC-1806
© 1996 Forest Stewardship Council
FSC

FSC is a non-profit international organisation established to promote the
responsible management of the world's forests. Products carrying the FSC
label are independently certified to assure consumers that they come
from forests that are managed to meet the social, economic and
ecological needs of present and future generations.

Find out more about HarperCollins and the environment at
www.harpercollins.co.uk/green

CONTENTS

FOREWORD

By Finlay Calder OBE
Captain, the British and Irish Lions in Australia, 1989

On 15 July 2006, I sat in the Caledonian Club in London, surrounded by friends from the British and Irish Lions who had toured Australia with me some seventeen years previously.

Rory Underwood apart, the rest of us had long given up on our youthful looks, and much water had passed beneath the bridge since those wonderful days back then. It was a night of great warmth, more than a few drams: an evening of mutual respect, trust and friendship. Before we said Grace, I suggested that in the intervening years, probably not one of us has escaped the passing of time. In truth, most of us at some stage must have trod a pretty uncomfortable path, whether that had been in terms of health, wealth or indeed happiness.

But why should a British Lion be different from anyone else? The truth is of course, he is not, and just like everyone else, they are burdened with the trials that come along in this life of ours.

To quote Max Ehrmann:

Take kindly the counsel of the years, gracefully surrendering the things of youth.

Nurture strength of spirit to shield you in sudden misfortune. But do not distress yourself with dark imaginings. Many fears are born out of fatigue and loneliness. Beyond a wholesome discipline, be gentle with yourself.

A night like that in London reminded us all just how privileged we had been in our lives to have come in contact with this wonderful pastime.

This book, *Once were Lions* by Jeff Connor and Martin Hannan, perhaps underlines that although some may have suffered at times, all Lions, I'm sure, will have felt privileged to at least have been given the chance to have worn the famous red jersey in their rugby lives.

Finlay Calder,
January 2009

PREFACE

THE MEN WHO ONCE
WERE LIONS

There is no such thing as a 'former' British and Irish Lion. Like the kings and queens of Britain, once you are a Lion you always stay a Lion, except that you can never abdicate Lionship. That is entirely fitting, for to be a Lion means to be a king, if only of the wonderful, glorious, many-hued jungle that is rugby union.

In this book you will find no references to 'former' or 'ex'-Lions. To us, the men who once were Lions on the field have stayed Lions in name and status ever since. Since the day they pulled on the Lions jersey, through the many vicissitudes of life – in this book you will read of some who have suffered – they have carried the title of Lion. It is an honoured name, revered indeed. It marks out every one of those who once were Lions as a breed apart, special men, and no one can ever take the name away from them.

Let us say at the outset that this is not a definitive history of the British and Irish Lions, nor is it meant to be. Works such as *The History of the British Lions* by Clem Thomas and his son Greg, and *British Lions* by

John Griffiths, are the standard Lions histories and we are not trying to compete with them. Indeed we are indebted to Clem, Greg, John and all the many, many writers, journalists, biographers and memorialists who have chronicled the Lions in the past 120 years.

This book is a history of a kind, though. It is the story of extraordinary men in circumstances which for many of them happened just once. It is tale of happy and sad experiences, all of them life-changing in a way, because once a man becomes a Lion, he is altered and exalted, and joins a roll of honour bedecked by comparatively few in rugby. There is no going back to being ordinary once you are a Lion.

For that reason we have ignored an old convention that a person only really becomes a Lion when he plays in an international Test Match. For us, to be named a Lion it is enough that a player pulled on the jersey no matter the opposition – W.S. Gainsford was injured in the very first training session of the 1924 tour to South Africa, and never played for the Lions, but he was deemed worthy of selection for the tour so his name is on the Roll of Honour at the end of this book. Gerald Davies, who will manage the Lions on their forthcoming tour to South Africa, put it succinctly: 'The Lions are the best of the best, and those who are selected for the Tests are the best of the best of the best.'

This account is in great part the players' own history of the Lions. It is very much their first-hand story, told by the Lions themselves in a series of interviews given over the past few years to Jeff Connor and in 2008/09 to Martin Hannan. We conceived of this book as a written record of history provided by the Lions themselves, and that is why we mention the views of administrators, coaches and commentators, such as rugby correspondents, only when they are relevant to what happened to the players.

It stands to reason that we have been unable to interview any Lion from before the Second World War. Where necessary – for instance in the first and second chapters – we have augmented their recorded views with contemporaneous reports. We have also taken on board the views and thoughts of some relatives of the Lions, on the entirely justifiable grounds that the men themselves are sadly no longer with us.

For some of the Lions, assisting the authors of this book has been the first chance they have taken to talk about their experiences. Whether or not their words are controversial, let no one doubt the sincerity of their views.

We are greatly indebted to Finlay Calder OBE for his support for this project from the outset. He has been a great friend over the years to Jeff Connor in particular, and you simply could not meet a more honest, modest and loyal a man. Almost twenty years on from his magnificent captaincy of the Lions in Australia, he remains one of the few men to bring back a winning series from the Antipodes.

We are also indebted to all those Lions who agreed to be interviewed for this book. We know it brought back happy memories for the majority, and less happy thoughts for others. To them all, we extend our sincere thanks.

We should say that no Lion has been paid for their contribution to this book. Instead, we are making a donation from the royalties to the Lions Trust, the excellent charity which works to look after the interests of all the British and Irish Lions. The more books that are sold, the bigger the donation, so please recommend this book to your friends.

We trust that the players give some insight into the importance of the British and Irish Lions in world rugby. At first sight, the efforts of teams drawn from five nations in the islands of Great Britain and Ireland against the representatives of three English-speaking lands in the southern hemisphere might seem unimportant in the great sporting scheme of things. And more than a few misguided people have described the Lions in terms of an outmoded concept in this era of professionalism, the World Cup and annual tours by individual nations. If that is so, why do the Lions still matter to so many people?

Touring to other countries is still very much a practice of rugby clubs everywhere, and perhaps the best experience an ordinary club member will enjoy. The Lions are the ultimate tourists, and as the players say, it is their great tradition and history which has made the Lions tours something of massive importance to millions of people, not least the thousands who follow them on their travels. There is also the small matter of bragging rights in world rugby, and as anyone who has ever played the glorious game will tell you, such rights count for much more than Mammon or trophies.

In recent decades, apart from England's World Cup triumph in 2003, long-term precedence in world rugby has lain south of the equator, which is possibly another reason why the performances of the British Lions against the might of New Zealand, Australia and South Africa still count for so much. The World Cup may now bring the greatest accolades, but for many people in these islands and among our southern cousins, the ultimate trial in rugby will always be one of the three main southern hemisphere teams against the Lions, that unique touring side that represents the best in British and Irish rugby. It is also why the International Rugby Board considers the Tests played by the Lions to be full 'cap' internationals and recognizes them as such in the record books. Anyone who doubts the importance of the Lions need only read the views of the players themselves to realize what it means to be involved in what they variously describe as the 'ultimate' or the 'crowning moment' of a career.

We have also compiled some thoughts on the future of the British and Irish Lions. Based on our discussions with the Lions, we make suggestions as to how the great traditions can be carried on for another century. At the time of writing in 2008, the next tour to South Africa is already in the advanced stages of planning, and in Ian McGeechan and Gerald Davies we feel that the Lions Committee has found the perfect combination to coach and manage the tour. We wish them every success.

We have also asked every Lion to whom we have spoken to nominate their choice of the best Lion in their own position and the person they consider as embodying the spirit of the Lions – the greatest Lion of them all. Obviously, very few people alive, never mind Lions, saw the early tours, so the choice was restricted from the first post-war tour in 1950 to the latest tour to New Zealand in 2005. Apologies to any claimants from before then.

We are well aware that rugby people in different countries prefer to give different names to the various positions. For sake of convenience, we have used the English style of description, such as fly-half rather than stand-off, outside-half or first five-eighth.

The form British and Irish Lions is also used throughout this book, even though that name was not formally adopted until 2001. Similarly, although the name 'Lions' was not minted until 1924, we have adopted the custom of referring to earlier tourists as Lions. It may not be historically accurate for the pedants, but it is now accepted usage.

As is convention, we have referred to the various touring parties down the years by the name of the squad captain, thus Finlay Calder's 1989 side. No doubt some coaches might think in terms of Carwyn James's 1991 team or Ian McGeechan's 2009 squad, but this is one book where players are given precedence.

In similar fashion we have stuck to the official Lions Committee's definition of what were formal Lions tours, although we make mention of 'non-tour' matches, such as the 1986 one-off game against the Rest of the World, and give details of the tours before 1910 when the first fully representative official tour recognized by the four home unions took place. In common with most authorities and historians, we do not recognize pre-war matches played in Argentina as being tours by the Lions, though the pre-2005 tour match against the Pumas is recognized as a full Lions Test and after their Herculean efforts in the World Cup, we do strongly feel that some way should be found of including the South American side in future Lions itineraries.

It will not have escaped the notice of Lions fans that the 2009 tour to South Africa comes 99 years after that first official tour to the same country. The number 99 has become part of Lions folklore, and in this book you will learn precisely why.

We would particularly like to thank everyone at HarperCollins for their unstinting support and professionalism, especially Tom Whiting who commissioned the book and Nick Fawcett and Colin Hall who edited and designed it.

In the course of our joint researches, it is remarkable how many times we heard one word used to describe the Lions, both individually and as teams. That word was indomitable, and as Lions, many have displayed that quality both on the field and off it.

These men once were Lions. To us, they still are Lions and always will be.

Jeff Connor and Martin Hannan
January 2009

CHAPTER ONE

FIRST TWENTY YEARS OF THE LIONS

1888–1908

The British Isles gave rugby to the world. Of that there is no doubt. The trouble is that, as with so many sports invented or codified in these islands, the world insisted on taking 'our' ball and running away with it. It happened fairly early in rugby union, when it soon became clear that France and a few Empire countries had mastered rugby and the pupils were only too anxious to teach the 'masters' a thing or two.

Despite the present ascendancy of the southern hemisphere countries, the number of British and Irish 'firsts' in rugby constitutes a history to be proud of, including William Webb Ellis's glorious disdain for the rules in 1833 which marked the beginning of the sport of rugby union; the first international played in 1871 at Raeburn Place in Edinburgh with Scotland beating England; both those nations competing for the first international trophy, the Calcutta Cup, in 1879 and ever since; the foundation of the first Unions; and the first schism over professionalism which led to the establishment of rugby league in 1895 in the guise of the Northern Rugby Football Union.

The honour of being the first truly international 'tourists' did not go to any of the home unions, however. In 1882, a team from New South Wales in Australia crossed the Tasman Sea and played seven games against club and provincial sides in New Zealand. The concept of the rugby 'tour' was born.

Six years later, in 1888, what has become recognized as the first Lions tour took place. It is remarkable to reflect that in that long gone heyday of amateurism, it was two professional cricket players doubling as sporting entrepreneurs, Arthur Shrewsbury and Alfred Shaw, who proposed and organized the first ever tour by a team from the British Isles. They had seen in Australia how popular matches against the England cricketing side had proved, and proposed to the Rugby Football Union that a similar exercise should be tried with rugby players from the British Isles.

The latter part of Queen Victoria's long reign saw the British Empire at its zenith. Migration to the Colonies by entire families was a regular feature of life in Britain, and certainly the nabobs of the Colonial Service and the various armed forces loved nothing better than to take their British traditions with them. So it was natural that the fast-developing and already very popular sport of rugby football should be exported to countries like South Africa, Australia and New Zealand where the climate suited the game. Attempts to establish rugby in other warmer colonies such as India largely failed – the Calcutta Cup is made of the melted-down silver rupees of the Calcutta Rugby Club which disbanded in 1878 after just five years of existence.

The colonials, both immigrants and natives, considered themselves equal subjects of the Queen Empress, and liked nothing better than to prove their prowess against the 'old country' on the cricket pitch in particular. In retrospect, the two entrepreneurs were knocking at an open door when they decided to try and repeat the success of touring cricket teams with a rugby side.

To promote their case, Shrewsbury and Shaw enlisted the help of a very popular sportsman, Andrew Ernest 'A.E.' Stoddart of Middlesex County Cricket Club and Blackheath Rugby Football Club, who was with them in the English cricket side in Australia and who would go on to captain England at both rugby and cricket. He was, by all accounts, a born leader of men.

The politics of rugby organization at that time explain why the RFU's permission was sought, rather than the International Board which had been formed by the then Scottish Football Union and their Irish and Welsh counterparts in 1886. The RFU haughtily refused to join the Board until 1890 and still saw themselves as the supreme body of world rugby. In truth, so did most people in the fledgling sport.

Perhaps surprisingly, given its reputation for extreme conservatism at that period, the RFU gave a sort of tacit approval for the first tour, in so far as they did not try to ban it. They stopped well short of fully sanctioning the tour, however, and issued stern warnings about the issue of payment to the players – the promoters could make a profit, but the participants could not. Many Lions will tell you things have not changed.

The RFU's overriding concern about any such tour was a perceived threat to the amateur status of players. Driven by class considerations as much as anything, at that time the rules on combating professionalism were incredibly strict as the various rugby unions fought against even those who wanted to at least compensate players for loss of earnings. Anyone who took so much as petty expenses for playing rugby was summarily banned *sine die*, while a player could be deemed professional, and thus expelled from rugby, if he even took part in a game where any one of the other 29 players was being paid. It was massive discrimination against working people in an age when club and Union officials were uniformly middle or upper class and could afford their time off work. Politics, professionalism, arguments over expenses, debates going back and forth with the sport's administrators – these themes will recur again in this book.

Shrewsbury, Shaw and Stoddart employed an agent to find players in the then heartlands of the game, the Scottish Borders and the northern counties of England. Some 22 men signed up from 'working class' clubs such as Swinton, Salford and Hawick.

Since the tour was going to last eight months, it is inconceivable that some form of compensation was not paid to men who, in some cases, surrendered jobs to take part.

From the outset, an important principle was established. The tourists would be 'British' with, initially, players from England, Scotland and Wales. Shrewsbury and Shaw had realized that a team of such a nature would appeal to the large expatriate community in both Australia and New Zealand, Scots being particularly prevalent in the latter country. In the end, the party consisted of sixteen players from English clubs, four from clubs in Scotland, and one each from Wales and the Isle of Man, W.H. Thomas and A.P. Penketh respectively. Two of the Scots, the Burnetts of Hawick, became the first brothers to tour together for the Lions, while among the 'English' players were Irish-born Arthur Paul and Dewsbury's Scottish exile Angus Stuart, so from the start the tourists really were British and Irish, though not yet known as 'Lions'.

At the last minute the RFU put the whole tour in doubt when one of the 22 tourists, J.P. Clowes of Halifax, was declared a professional and thus cast into the rugby wilderness. His 'crime' was to accept £15 in expenses for his kit for the tour. And given the draconian 'catch all' nature of the rules on professionalism, every player who played with him or against him would face a similar sentence.

The RFU Committee made their point clear in a statement recorded for posterity in the minutes: 'The Rugby Football Union has decided, on the evidence before them, that J.P. Clowes is a professional within the meaning of the laws. On the same evidence they have formed a very strong opinion that other players composing the Australian team have also infringed those laws and they will require from them such explanation as they think fit on their return to England.' That decision was announced just one day before the party was due to sail. The British and Irish Lions were almost strangled at birth by officialdom, and the whole affair heightened feelings on the issue of 'broken time' payments, among other things, which would lead to the foundation of professional rugby league just seven years later. Not for the last time, the world's most famous rugby tourists had sparked controversy.

Anxious not to slay their golden goose, Shaw and Shrewsbury reacted by pacifying the RFU while honouring their commitment to Clowes, who went Down Under with the party but did not play in a single match under rugby football rules – nice work if you can get it.

The touring party left Britain on 8 March 1888, and returned on 11 November. In their time in Australia and New Zealand, the first Lions played 35 rugby matches, winning 27, drawing 6 and losing 2, scoring 300 points for the loss of 101. The tour was split into three sections, the first sojourn of 9 matches in New Zealand followed by 16 in Australia and then back to New Zealand for 10 games.

The first ever match played by the Lions was against Otago in Dunedin on 28 April 1888, the score being 8–3 to the visitors. The honour of being the first team to beat the tourists went to the Taranaki Clubs of New Zealand, victors by a single point. Auckland was the only other home side to triumph, in the final match of the first leg of the tour. From then until they embarked for home, the tourists were unbeaten. It was a fine record, but much more important was the effect the tourists had on rugby in those faraway lands.

The rules of the game were somewhat different in those days. A try, originally known as a touchdown, only gave a team the right to 'try' a conversion, which could earn the scoring side two or three points and was known as a goal. The confusion over scoring was because there were differences in the scoring system between various countries, with a penalty goal worth two or three points in some countries, and a drop goal worth up to four depending on where you were playing. The first standardized scoring across the rugby world did not arrive until 1891 after England's RFU joined the International Board, when a try was set at two points; a 'goal', i.e. try and conversion, earned five points; a penalty was worth four; and a drop goal also scored four.

There were also variations in the rules and refereeing standards and practices between north and south – another constant refrain that still bedevils rugby. In the early tours, the home sides made the adjustments to accommodate the tourists, who had developed forms of play which the other countries considered as breaches of the offside law. It was the Lions heeling from the scrummage that proved most controversial on the first tour, but the New Zealanders in particular soon became masters of this imported art.

The first tourists had expected that Australia would prove the tougher part of the tour, but in the end it was New Zealand, where immigrants and natives alike had taken to the sport with great gusto, that proved a far more difficult territory. Their provincial sides in particular learned quickly from the visitors, not least the marvellous passing game among the backs. This was a revelation to the New Zealand teams, which had concentrated on the 'dribbling' game involving gangs of players moving the ball forward with their feet or with the ball 'up the jumper'.

Opinions vary as to how much the tourists imparted to their hosts – 'I challenge anyone to tell me what the 1888 side taught us' wrote subsequent New Zealand captain T.R. Ellison, though one of his successors as captain, Dave Gallaher, wrote 'the exhibitions of passing which they gave were most fascinating and impressive to the New Zealander, who was not slow to realise the advantages of these methods. One may safely say that, from that season, dates the era of high-class rugby in the colony.'

If Gallaher is to be believed, then the first tourists accomplished something wonderful for world rugby, as they played their part in helping to create the passion for good rugby which still permeates the sport in New Zealand. For their role in bringing about the players who became the All Blacks, those first tourists deserve our thanks, though not many of New Zealand's humbled opponents over the years might agree.

A triumphal progress, then, but one tinged with tragedy. In August, the captain of the side, Bob Seddon of Lancashire, was out rowing on the Hunter River in New South Wales when his scull capsized and he was drowned. He was by all accounts a popular figure, and his loss was deeply felt both by the tourists and their hosts – a memorial was erected to him in the nearby town of Maitland. Some 120 years later, it is well maintained by local enthusiasts.

Seddon's place as captain was taken by A.E. Stoddart, who went on to become the star of the tour with his all-round skills. As one of the triumvirate who had put together this first tour, Stoddart may well have made some money, but if so, he was not saying. When some of the tourists tired of their schedule, he also invited a friend from the cricket world to come and play for the Lions – which is how C. Aubrey Smith, the gentlemanly actor of *Prisoner of Zenda* fame, otherwise known as Sir Charles Aubrey Smith KBE, a future captain of England's cricket side, became the only Hollywood star ever to turn out for the Lions.

After all the travel – it took six weeks to sail there and back – the tourists returned to some plaudits for their pioneering efforts but also a strict ruling by the RFU. Every player who came back to Britain was forced to swear an affidavit on their return stating that they had not been paid for playing on the tour. The RFU were satisfied though suspicious, and one player did not have to sign – Angus Stuart stayed on in New Zealand and played for its national side in 1893 before returning to Britain and taking up rugby league as a coach.

One final element of controversy emerged from that first tour, and the RFU at last found something to get really angry about. While in Victoria, the players took part in exhibition matches of football played under Victorian or what we now call Australian Rules. It was in these matches that C. Aubrey Smith made his appearances for the Lions, never having actually played rugby before. The surprising thing is how well the visitors managed, winning 6, drawing 1 and losing 11 of the 18 matches which undoubtedly lined the pockets of Shrewsbury and Shaw and may well have enriched some of the players. No one really knows what went on in the background, but as a touring entity, the side from Britain and Ireland was undoubtedly a profitable enterprise – for some.

The seeds had been sown by these first tourists, and the full flowering of the touring concept did not take long to emerge. In 1891, with the full approval of the RFU, a second tour was planned, this time to South Africa at the invitation of the Western Province Union, the South African Rugby Board being still in its infancy.

As before, it was a previous visit by an England cricket side which inspired the thought of a rugby tour, but in those days South Africa was probably bottom of the rugby heap. The matches were not expected to be close as South African rugby was so far behind that of Britain and Ireland. It was feared no one would want to see a mismatch, and Cecil Rhodes, one of the richest men in Africa and Prime Minister of the Cape Colony as well as an ardent imperialist, had to step in to underwrite the whole tour. The exercise thus became something of a missionary outing, with the tourists keen to show the colonials just how the game should be played, in the hope they would learn quickly and become stiffer opposition in years ahead. They certainly did that.

With official sanction, and former RFU Secretary Edwin 'Daddy' Ash as manager, this time most of the tourists were better exponents of the game than their predecessors. Drawn entirely from England and Scotland, there were 9 internationalists in the squad of 21 players, with the remainder all from big clubs and a sizeable contingent from Cambridge University's then dazzling squad. Students could also usually afford to take a long break from their studies, and it is obvious from the fact that so few 'northerners' appeared in the squad that the bitter struggle over 'broken time' payments – compensation for lost wages – was already affecting the selection policies.

This tour introduced a new concept to world rugby – the international Test series. A team representing all of South Africa – though this technically was not an independent country in its own right – would play the Lions three times in the course of the tour, losing all three Test Matches.

Despite the fears of disparity between the teams, large numbers came out to support the home sides, with 6,000 reported to have attended the first Test. There was also great excitement about the tour across South Africa, with the considerable political differences between the various regions such as the Cape Colony and the Transvaal being set aside for the duration.

The statistics do not lie. The Lions went unbeaten through all 20 matches, notching 226 points for the loss of just 1, and that in the opening match against the Cape Town Club. It remains the most one-sided tour to date.

Captained by Bill Maclagan, who had played 26 times for Scotland, the visitors were just too big and strong, too skilful and experienced, for the willing but technically unsound South Africans. In only one match, on brick-hard ground in Kimberley against Griqualand West, did the visitors feel in any real danger, the Lions eventually winning 3–0, though Stellenbosch in the final match actually held the visitors to just 2–0.

A bigger problem for the tourists was the many days of backbreaking travel in horse-drawn vehicles between the various venues, as well as the generous hospitality of their hosts. Centre Paul Clauss described the tour as 'champagne and travel', and some fans would say that this succinct description of Lions tours has never been bettered.

Without a doubt, the tour transformed South African rugby, not least because of a gift made by a shipping magnate. The party had travelled on the *Dunottar Castle* of the Union Castle Line, and its owner donated a magnificent trophy to be presented to the province that performed best against the Lions. The tourists selected Griqualand West, who became the first proud owners of the cup competed for by the South African provinces to this day and named after the man who donated it, Sir Donald Currie.

More importantly, the South African rugby players took to heart all the lessons they had learned from the 1891 Lions. One of the Lions, the Rev. H. Marshall, wrote that the tourists had 'initiated the colonists of South Africa into the fine points and science of the rugby game'. Maclagan and his men did their missionary work all too well, as subsequent touring parties would find to their cost.

The third tour was again to South Africa, which could be reached in 16 to 17 days by boat rather than the 6 weeks it took to sail to Australia or New Zealand. Well organized and funded by the various provincial unions across South Africa, the 1896 tour was memorable for several reasons – it featured a sizeable contingent from Ireland for the first time, it included the first defeat of the Lions in an international Test, and the whole exercise officially made a profit, showing that the Lions were by now welcome visitors wherever they went.

The touring party featured players only from English and Irish clubs and was missing those players from the northern English clubs who had 'defected' to rugby league on its formation in 1895. The choice of players for touring also reflected the massive infighting that had split the RFU from the SFU – the name Scottish Rugby Union was not adopted until 1924 – and the Welsh Union over issues related to professionalism.

The squad was captained by Johnny Hammond of Blackheath and Cambridge University, who at 36 was the oldest Lions captain to date. Irish vice-captain Tom Crean, already an internationalist with nine caps, actually led the side on more occasions, age presumably having withered Hammond. Though we will learn more about his heroic nature, Crean, it should be said, must not be confused with his contemporary fellow Irishman of the same name, who accompanied both Scott of the Antarctic and Ernest Shackleton on their Polar expeditions. One of the Lions tourists, Cuthbert Mullins of Oxford University, was actually a native of South Africa, and he later went back home to practise as a doctor.

It is perhaps an insight into the inclusive nature of the Lions as representing all of Britain and Ireland that, on arrival in South Africa, the three Roman Catholics in the party – Crean, and Louis and Eddie Magee – wanted to attend Sunday mass rather than take part in an excursion. The management decreed that all religious people would be able to attend their various churches that morning and the excursion would start later. The Lions, it seemed, happily answered to a Higher Power.

That Power looked kindly on them. The Lions went undefeated through the tour until the final game. They had beaten South Africa in three Tests, and won against every provincial side except one, Western Province, which gained a 0–0 draw. They had scored 320 points for the loss of 45, yet such apparently one-sided statistics hid the fact that South African rugby had vastly improved.

In their final match in Cape Town, the Lions found out just how much the sport had moved on in South Africa. Wearing their famous green jerseys for the first time, South Africa were led by Barrie Heatlie, who rejoiced in the nickname 'Fairy' – it is not known why. His side had developed their forward play to such an extent that the Lions buckled, and when the referee, Alf Richards, who just happened to be a former South African internationalist, ruled against the Lions' favourite tactic of wheeling the scrummage, things began to look bad for the visitors.

South Africa then gained a controversial try, not least because the scorer, Alf Larard, had been reinstated as an amateur on immigrating to the country from England where he had been involved in the row over 'broken time' payments which had led to the establishment of rugby

11

league the previous year. Also, by a strict interpretation of the rules, the ball had been won from an offside position before being passed to Larard for his try, which was converted.

The visitors mounted a late rally, but could not score. South Africa had beaten the Lions 5–0, and the victory caused a sensation across that country. The row over the debatable score rumbled on for days, and some would say has never stopped, as the northern hemisphere and southern hemisphere nations still disagree over the laws of the game and their interpretations.

We are indebted to Walter Carey, one of the tour party, for an insider's account of the 1896 tour. He would eventually make his home in South Africa as Bishop of Bloemfontein and is most famous for coining the motto of the Barbarians: 'Rugby is a game for gentleman in any class, but no bad sportsman in any class.'

Carey wrote that the tour had been 'very happy' and praised the 'scrupulously fair' play of the host teams. He added: 'I hope and pray that South African teams will always play like gentlemen.' His missionary zeal is perhaps understandable, given that he did become a clergyman.

Carey also described the tour's star player Tom Crean in glowing terms as 'the most Irish, the most inconsequent, the most gallant, the most lovable personality one could ever imagine and made the centre of the whole tour'. Over the years the Lions have featured many such personalities, and a goodly number of them have been Irish.

Sadly, within a few years of that happy tour in 1896, South Africa was torn apart by the Boer War. It seems almost incredible that so soon after their tour as Lions, several of the 1896 touring party were back as combatants. Two of them, Tom Crean and Robert Johnston, both won the Victoria Cross for acts of gallantry in that conflict – it was not just on the rugby battlefield that Lions were heroic.

Crean in particular appears to have been practically born heroic. Blessed with good looks and a magnificent physique, Crean was what the Irish call a 'broth of a boy', who loved nothing better than good wine, good company of both sexes and plenty of singing. In short, an ideal Lions tourist. From Dublin, he had just qualified as a doctor in 1896 and he had already been decorated for heroism. At the age of 18, he received a Royal Humane Society award for saving the life of a 20-year-old student who had got into difficulties in the sea off Blackrock in Co. Dublin. He enjoyed South Africa so much he stayed on in Johannesburg and, in 1899, joined up as an ordinary trooper, seeing action at the Relief of Mafeking and being wounded in battle.

Serving as a surgeon captain in 1901, Crean won his VC for continuing to attend to the wounded under fire. Presented with the medal in 1902 by King Edward VII, his citation read:

Thomas Joseph Crean, Surgeon Captain, 1st Imperial Light Horse. During the action with De Wet at Tygerskloof on the 18th December 1901, this officer continued to attend to the wounded in the firing line under a heavy fire at only 150 yards range, after he himself had been wounded, and only desisted when he was hit a second time, and as it was first thought, mortally wounded.

As if that wasn't enough, Crean went on to win the Distinguished Service Order and commanded the 44th Field Ambulance brigade which served in the trenches in the First World War. He was again wounded several times.

Sadly, his health failed as a result of his wartime injuries, and he began to drink heavily and developed diabetes. His private practice in London failed, and he was declared bankrupt shortly before his death in 1923, aged just 49. You will read in this book of how life after the Lions has often been an anti-climax for individual players, but that could not be said of war hero Crean.

It was said at one time that the two most famous men in South Africa were Cecil Rhodes and Tom Crean. Crean's heroism as a player and in combat were not forgotten – in the third of their special Boer War centenary commemorative stamps issued by the South African Post Office in 2001, he was one of two people honoured with their own stamp.

Amazingly, the other Lion to win a VC, Robert Johnston, was a member of the same club as Crean, Wanderers. Born in Donegal, Johnston celebrated his 24th birthday on the Lions tour and he and Crean became fast friends. Indeed, they joined the Imperial Light Horse together, and served through various battles including Elandslaagte. It was there that Johnston won his VC. The citation read that at a critical moment when the advance was checked, Johnston 'moved forward under heavy fire at point blank range to enable a decisive flanking movement to be carried out'.

After initial treatment to his wounds, Johnston was transferred to a field hospital where the doctor who treated him was none other than Tom Crean. His friend's treatment proved successful, as Johnston made a full recovery and after serving as a prisoner of war camp commandant, he lived until 1950.

The unexpectedly long duration of the Boer War did not prevent a fourth tour taking place, though in 1899 the venue was Australia rather than South Africa. The squad was captained and managed by the Rev. Matthew Mullineux who had toured in 1896 and was then a member at Blackheath.

Reverend Mullineux was perhaps not the best player around, never receiving an England cap, but he was at least a modest realist. In the first Test against Australia in Sydney, he could not perform to the same level as those around him, and having seen his team soundly beaten by 13–3, Mullineux promptly dropped himself. England international Frank Stout took over as on-field captain for the remaining three Tests, all of which were won by the Lions to give them the first Test series victory in Australia.

The touring party featured representatives from all four home nations, but the star of the side was the sole Welsh international, Gwyn Nicholls of Cardiff, who brought a new dynamism to the position of centre. He ended the tour as top try scorer, with C. Y. Adamson of Durham gaining the most points thanks to his prodigious kicking. On a tour where the Lions won 18 of their 21 matches, scoring 333 points for the loss of 90, Adamson amassed 135 points by himself, a tour record that would stand for many years.

It might seem incredible to modern sensitivities, but just a year after the cessation of hostilities in the Boer War, a Lions squad toured South Africa. The war may have split South Africa asunder, but it wasn't going to get in the way of the national passion for rugby. And just as the spectacular victory of South Africa in the 1995 World Cup did much to heal wounds in the post-apartheid era, so did the 1903 tour help the normalization process after the Boer War. It also helped that, for the first time, a host country defeated the Lions in a Test series.

Captained by Mark Morrison of Scotland, the 1903 Lions featured internationalists from Scotland, Ireland and Wales, but none from England. Led by Morrison, the forwards gave a good account of themselves, though South Africa's scrummaging power was beginning to become a mighty weapon. In the backs, however, only Reg Skrimshire of Wales could match the South Africans, whose passing and kicking skills had vastly improved even in the short space of four years.

In the first Test in Johannesburg, South Africa were captained by Alex Frew, who had played alongside Morrison for Scotland in their Triple Crown-winning year of 1901. The Lions had suffered several reverses and injuries in the provincial matches before that first Test, and would go on to win just 11 of their 22 matches on tour. Both the first and second Tests were draws, which set the scene for a tense closing encounter in Cape Town.

Digging out the green jerseys which they had worn in their first victory over the Lions back in 1899, the South Africans were well prepared, but became nervous when a downpour turned the pitch into a quagmire – conditions which were thought to favour the players of Britain and Ireland. Thousands of spectators watched from beneath umbrellas as South Africa persevered with their game plan, which involved their much better backs. Though the Lions had a try disallowed and there was yet more controversy over the winning try by South Africa, which came off a suspiciously forward pass, at the end most people agreed that the home side had thoroughly deserved their 8–0 victory.

The green jerseys were there to stay on South African torsos and the Lions had suffered their first-ever series loss. It was not to be the last, but at least they had a swift opportunity to wipe the slate clean as the very next year saw a tour to Australia and New Zealand. The 1904 squad was again captained by a Scot, the remarkable David 'Darkie' Bedell-Sivright, a veteran of the 1903 tour and the only man from that squad to play again for the Lions the following year.

Bedell-Sivright was a swarthy individual, a fearsome forward, and a real character on and off the field – he was alleged to have rugby tackled a cart horse. He once stated: 'When I go on to the rugby field I only see the ball, and should someone be in the road, that is his lookout.' He was very popular with the Australians and he loved them and their country, staying on for a year after the tour before returning home to study medicine. He was not enamoured of Australian referees, however. In the match against Northern Districts, Denys Dobson of Oxford University was sent off by the local referee, one Hugh Dolan. His offence was to say 'What the devil was that for?' – a near-blasphemy to Mr Dolan who ushered Dobson from the field, thus making him the first Lion ever to be sent off.

Bedell-Sivright intervened on behalf of his team member and the Lions left the field, returning after 20 minutes without Dobson but ready to thump the home side, which they did 17–3. In interviews after the match, the Lions captain explained his stance to reporters: 'He [Bedell-Sivright] regarded Mr Dolan as an incompetent referee. The team had borne with his incapacity so long as it merely affected them in their play, but when he chose to take up a position which reflected on their personal honour, they thought it time to show their resentment.'

An inquiry was held by the New South Wales Rugby Union and no action was taken against Dobson for his 'improper expression'. It was a whitewash by officialdom – and not the last time this would happen with the Lions.

Bedell-Sivright's side featured internationalists from all four home countries as well as two New Zealanders, medical students Pat McEvedy and Arthur O'Brien. Paddy Bush of Cardiff, a brilliant fly-half, marshalled the outstanding Welsh backs of the time. The Lions duly swept all before them in Australia, winning every one of their 14 matches, including the 3 Tests by a combined score of 50–3.

It was a different story entirely in New Zealand, where the Lions cause was not helped by Bedell-Sivright breaking his leg in the first match at Canterbury. The low point of the tour was the only Test against New Zealand, in which the Lions suffered their first defeat by the nation who would come to haunt them in the decades ahead. It was a case of dominant home forwards beating inventive Lions backs, which would also be a regular occurrence in the history of the tourists. Captain Bedell-Sivright remarked patronizingly that the colonials would not dare to come to Britain: 'you might succeed occasionally against local underdog teams … but would be out of your class against national combinations,' he is reported to have said.

How wrong could he have been. In retrospect, that 9–3 victory was the beginning of the rise of New Zealand rugby which would reach full glory the following year with the 1905 tour to the 'old countries' and the start of the All Blacks legend.

Both the principals in that notorious sending off, Dobson and Bedell-Sivright, would meet strange ends. The former was killed by a charging rhinoceros in Africa in 1916, while Bedell-Sivright died from an infected insect bite during the Dardanelles campaign in the Great War.

After tours in successive years, the next Lions did not leave home shores again until 1908, when Arthur F. 'Boxer' Harding, a 1904 tourist, captained the squad on its visit to Australia and New Zealand. In one way this was the least representative squad to tour in the 20th century, as only players from England and Wales featured. Scotland had fallen out with the RFU over the issue of New Zealand paying three shillings a day in expenses to its players on their 1905 tour to Europe.

'There can be no halfway house in rugby football', wrote J.A. Smith, the secretary of the SFU.

> *The daily allowance made to the players is directly antagonistic to the true spirit of amateur Rugby football. The payment means that, in addition to every possible expense, including uniforms, laundry, entertainments, gratuities and medical attendance, each player has received at least one pound and one shilling a week for himself, and my committee consider that this payment is tantamount to professionalism in a very insidious form.*

The Scots made it clear they would not play against New Zealand's 'professionals', and when England sided with the All Blacks, the SFU broke off relations with the RFU. Ireland also withdrew its cooperation on the same grounds.

The 1908 Lions therefore played in jerseys made up of hoops of white and red, the traditional English and Welsh colours, and that is one of the reasons many books and commentators refer to this as the Anglo-Welsh tour. But they were billed as the British touring party, and the invitation and organization were done in the now customary manner, so Lions they were, though by all accounts there was not the usual atmosphere of friendliness in the camp.

Selecting from just two nations and taking unproven players was to prove a pivotal point in the history of the British and Irish Lions. For after they returned a well-beaten side, the Welsh Rugby Union complained about the selection of players being for reasons of social class rather than distinction on the field. Two years later, that complaint would be formalized.

Whatever the reason for their failings, it certainly seems to be the case that the squad was weak when you consider the 1908 side's results. As well as two losses to provincial sides in Australia, they lost seven of their matches in New Zealand, including two of the three Tests against the All Blacks.

To be fair, in the middle Test of the three, the Lions were unlucky to get only a draw, but Harding's men apparently enjoyed too much of the lavish hospitality of their hosts and greatly underperformed in the final deciding Test, in which the All Blacks ran riot, scoring 9 tries and 29 points in all against none by the tourists.

The 1908 Lions did not even go down fighting, but then there had been a strange atmosphere in the party ever since they had lost one of their best players in the middle of the tour. In the biggest scandal to engulf the early Lions, Frederick Stanley Jackson, a Cornish giant who played for Leicester, was alleged to have been a professional rugby league player called John Jones from Swansea. Jackson was a star player, a lethal goal kicker who had helped Cornwall to the county championship, which in turn gave them entry to the 1908 Olympic Games where the men from the Duchy won the silver medal, losing to Australasia, i.e. Australia and New Zealand combined.

An Olympic medallist and one of the best-known players in the sport of rugby union involved in a murky business – not surprisingly, the newspapers had a field day, and the RFU had to act. A terse telegram was sent to tour manager George Harnett: 'Jackson is suspended. Return him forthwith.'

The player set off for Sydney, leaving his close friend and fellow Leicester player and Lion, John Jackett, in tears on the quayside. Jackett himself had a notorious past which was already well known – a muscular Adonis, he had posed as a nude model, strictly for art's sake of course.

But Jackson never made it home. Instead, he was greeted by pressmen at Sydney, and categorically denied any knowledge of the charges against him. He then disappeared, only to resurface in New Zealand after the Lions had finished their tour. Jackson had gone back to find a Maori woman that he had met during the tour, and it truly was a love match – they had four children, one of whom, Everard, would become an All Black prop before losing a leg fighting in the desert campaign in the Second World War.

Happy with his new wife in his new homeland, Frederick Jackson also played for New Zealand – funnily enough, at rugby league. He was capped for his new country in 1910 against the Northern Union, the then name of the British rugby league touring side, which beat New Zealand 52–20. Jackson lived until 1957, and despite research by his family, no one has ever been able to prove whether he was indeed either Jackson or Jones. The man himself never let on.

The Jackson scandal was just one of several problems for the 1908 Lions. This debacle of a tour was to prove a catalyst for the biggest change in the set-up of the Lions. Before the next tour to South Africa in 1910, and stung by the fact that the 'colonials' had become the masters of world rugby, the four home unions took a hand and decided that, from then on, the tourists would represent them as fully as any side which turned out in the white, blue, green or red jerseys of their home unions. Players selected for Tests would also be recognized – by some people at any rate – as full internationalists. The British and Irish Lions were formally born, though not yet called Lions.

CHAPTER TWO

THEN THEY
WERE LIONS
1910–1938

Right from the start of the 'official' touring party superintended by the joint Committee of the Four Home Unions, often known since then as the Lions Committee, there were arguments about selection. The Welsh Union, appalled at what had happened in 1908, called on their fellow unions to select the best available players 'irrespective of their social position'. The Welsh Union was correctly suspicious that the other unions, dominated by middle and upper-class interests, might prefer 'gentlemen players' rather than good honest stock from the Valleys. As a result, and with the Unions now fully behind the tourists, the first official British and Irish touring squad was as strong, if not stronger, than any of the parties who had gone south of the equator before them.

There was also recognition of the toll that injuries had taken on previous parties, as 4 replacements were later allowed to join the original 26 tourists. Of that 26, no fewer than 17 had already won caps for their country or would do so. The replacements were not too shabby either, as Eric

Milroy, Alfred 'Jim' Webb and Frank Handford all represented Scotland, Wales and England respectively. Milroy suffered blood poisoning on the tour, which severely debilitated him; Webb switched to rugby league but went back to the mines; Handford enjoyed his time in South Africa so much that he emigrated there, as did fellow 1910 tourists Phil Waller and Kenneth Wood, neither of whom even bothered to go home after the tour.

The much-travelled Tom Richards, who had been capped for Australia, was then working in South Africa, for whom he was nearly selected. On the basis that he had once played a season in England at Bristol, he joined the Lions. Photographs in a 'Pride of Lions' exhibition at Twickenham showed him in both Australian and Lions colours – nationality was apparently a moveable feast in those days. Richards would go on to play for Australia again and then win the Military Cross for his bravery in the First World War, but he died young from the long-term effects of mustard gas.

Also gassed and decorated for heroism during the war was Stanley Williams, the brilliant full-back of the 1910 party. He was another Lion to be caught up in a huge row between administrators, the Welsh union objecting when England selected Williams despite him having been born in Monmouthshire, then playing for Newport and having taken part in an international trial in Wales. Perhaps sickened by the whole affair, Williams played just one season for England before retiring at the age of 25.

The Lions had other stars, notably Charles Henry 'Cherry' Pillman of Blackheath and England who was reckoned to have single-handedly revolutionized wing forward play with his audacious and inventive skills. His new tactic of detaching from the scrum to challenge the fly-half changed the way the game was played.

The visitors were captained by Dr Tom Smythe of Malone and Ireland, already renowned as a fine leader of rugby men who had been captain for Ireland against Wales earlier in the year, and who had also been a locum doctor in Newport, where the local club was in its pomp and supplied no fewer than seven of the 1910 Lions.

These Lions were definitely an improvement on previous touring squads, but South African rugby had continued to develop, and in 1906 the original Springboks had toured Britain and Ireland, losing to Scotland but drawing with England and beating Wales and Ireland. Playing in their new colours of blue jerseys, white shorts and red socks, the Lions were unbeaten in five matches in Western Province but on moving north to Griqualand West, the Lions succumbed twice in a place where they had lost twice in 1903. And as on that previous tour, they also lost to Transvaal twice.

The first Test in Kimberley was played without the injured Pillman and was lost 14–10, the first try being scored by Alex Foster who would go on to captain Ireland. The adaptable Pillman returned for the second Test, playing at fly-half, and completely dominated play in an 8–3 victory in Port Elizabeth. The Springbok captain Bill Millar was later moved to write that 'if ever a man can have won an international match through his own inspired and lone-handed efforts, it can be said of the inspired black-haired Pillman'.

No one could know at that time that the deciding Test in Cape Town would be the last played by the British and Irish Lions for 14 years. It ended in an ignominious 21–5 defeat for the visitors, who were hampered by the loss of their full-back early in the match – there were no substitutions for the Lions in those days.

Cherry Pillman went on to inspire England to four successive international championships, which France had joined to make the Five Nations. All five of those nations would then be involved in the war that was supposed to end all wars. They would be augmented by many men from South Africa, Australia and New Zealand, including a sizeable number of rugby players. In total, some 125 rugby internationalists from the eight major playing nations would pay the ultimate price in service of their country. Among their number would be several British and Irish Lions, including 1904 captain Dr David Bedell-Sivright, Phil Waller, Eric Milroy and Blair Swannell, who was awarded a posthumous Military Cross for his gallantry at Gallipoli.

Yet perhaps the most extraordinary story of heroism by a Lion who toured in 1910 came some years after the war. Harry Jarman, a tough forward from Pontypool who played for Newport, sacrificed his own life to save a group of children at Talywain colliery in 1928. The children were playing on a colliery railway when Jarman, then working as a blacksmith at the pit, spotted some loose wagons heading for the youngsters. Without hesitation, he threw himself into the path of the wagons and derailed them, his consequent injuries proving fatal. Tackling a runaway train some 18 years after his tour, aged 45, and with nothing more than his own shoulders – in the long annals of their history, can there be any more outstanding example of the courage of a Lion?

When rugby returned to a sort of normality after the war, clamour grew for the British and Irish unions to send a touring party to the southern hemisphere again. The next tour would be to South Africa in 1924, and from then on the tourists would bear their immortal name, the Lions.

As with every other activity in the British Empire, after Armistice Day in 1918 the sport of rugby was determined to get back to its usual state as quickly as possible. In 1919, a team from the New Zealand forces triumphed against their opponents in Britain and stopped off to wallop several South African sides on the way home. The Springboks toured New Zealand and Australia in 1921, and the quality of their play was dazzling. But as in so many strands of life in Britain and Ireland, a return to prewar normality was just not possible for rugby in the home countries due to the colossal number of deaths and injuries sustained among a generation of young men.

The number of internationalists killed during the hostilities – 30 from Scotland and 27 from England alone – shows the scale of the losses. The worldwide influenza epidemic after the war also took its toll. It was going to take a good few years for a new generation to come through to replace those who had gone.

The political situation in Ireland also caused problems. The 1920 partition of Ireland into the 26 counties of the Free State, later the Republic of Ireland, and the six counties of Northern Ireland, had been mirrored by rugby much earlier. In 1874, the Irish Football Union had been formed from clubs in Leinster, Munster and parts of Ulster, while the Northern Football Union of Ireland, founded in the same year, was an association of clubs centred mainly on Belfast. With Ireland still a single political entity under the control of Westminster at that time, the two associations amalgamated to form the Irish Rugby Football Union in 1879. When partition took place, the IRFU Committee resisted attempts to politicize rugby and took the decision – unpopular in some areas, too – that it would continue to govern the sport in all 32 counties. By and large, and despite many problems down the years, the IRFU has remained united in the cause of rugby for all of the island of Ireland. It remains an intriguing question, given the strong feelings that partition and subsequent 'Troubles' have evoked, as to whether the British and Irish Lions would have continued to represent all five nations in these islands had not the IRFU taken that momentous decision to stay united. Certainly, there would have been a lot less fun without all the Irish tourists.

Arguably the greatest damage done to rugby union and to the Lions tours in the inter-war years came from the Great Depression. Money was scarce from the early 1920s onwards, and most players simply could not afford to take months off work, while employers became increasingly reluctant to give even unpaid leave of absence as this meant holding a job open for someone who might return from a tour with a serious injury, which was often the case in years to come. Other players took the money on offer from rugby league and switched codes rather than pursue caps and a tour with the Lions, which was really the only 'reward' that rugby union had to offer.

When the Great Depression arrived from 1929 onwards, the situation worsened considerably, and not even a sport that was so resolutely middle-class in most areas of these islands could escape the ravages of economic turmoil. Less damage was done in the southern hemisphere, though in Australia the economic situation probably helped the professional version of the oval ball game, rugby league, to achieve the dominance over union which it still enjoys.

Another problem was that the home unions still did not take the concept of a touring team entirely seriously. Their bread and butter was the international championship, which largely earned the money to bankroll the unions – there were no formal leagues in those days, and no television riches, and the Five Nations matches were for a long time the principal earners of cash. No one had any money left over to invest in a tour that was still seen as a luxury.

These problems meant that in the 21 years between the wars, just three Lions tours took place, compared to four in eight years between 1903 and 1910 inclusive. The first post-war tour to South Africa in 1924 may have been disappointing in terms of results – they were the first tourists to have a win record of less than 50 per cent – but at least they did return with a priceless asset.

No one seems entirely sure where the name 'Lions' came from. The official branding of the 1924 party and indeed subsequent parties was the British Isles Rugby Union Team, or BIRUT. The biruts? Fortunately, some ties made for the tourists had been embroidered with three lions – a heraldic device that bears a strong resemblance to the badge of the English football (soccer) team.

The lions did not appear on the blue jerseys worn by the players in matches, and photographs quite clearly show that, for the 1924 Tests at any rate, the jersey badge was, as now, made up of the insignia of the four unions quartered on a shield. But the lions on the ties made an impression, and perhaps it was some bright spark in the party, maybe even the captain Dr Ronald Cove-Smith himself, who first suggested that the tourists were all lions. Or perhaps it was some long-forgotten press correspondent who wrote of 'the lions', and the name stuck, not least because it was so much better journalistically than 'the biruts'.

Some officials in the various Celtic unions thought it was a bit presumptuous to use a symbol traditionally associated with England – Scotland's single lion is rampant, not couchant. Protests were made by administrators, but, for once, player power counted. The newly minted Lions were not unhappy with the nickname, even those from Ireland and Wales, whose emblems were a shamrock and a dragon respectively. By the time the 1930 tour came round, the nickname was so well established that the blue playing jersey was embroidered with three lions, just like the English football badge, and players were given a plentiful supply of lion brooches and pins to hand out to their hosts.

Dr Cove-Smith's Lions should have been the best ever to leave these islands. England had won the Grand Slam that year, their third in four seasons, and Scotland would do so the following year, and both those sides contained players who are now legends of the game. But in fact British and Irish rugby had fallen well behind the standards of the southern hemisphere teams, as would be proven when the All Blacks toured England, Wales, Ireland, France and Canada in late 1924 and early 1925, playing and winning four Tests and completing the 32-match tour unbeaten – hence their nickname of The Invincibles. The two tours overlapped slightly, but there was enough time between the final Test in South Africa and the Tests against the All Blacks for the Lions to arrive home and prepare themselves for another beating, this time in their own national colours rather than in the blue jersey of the British Isles Rugby Union Team.

On a tour that, at one point, saw the Lions go eight matches without a win, the South Africans were to hand out rugby lesson after rugby lesson.

The touring party was missing great players like Wavell Wakefield – later the first Baron Wakefield of Kendal, and the father of modern forward play as well as captain of England's Grand Slam winners – and G.P.S. 'Phil' Macpherson, who would skipper Scotland to their first Slam the following year. But that was no excuse, as the full squad of 30, which included two replacements, contained 24 past, current or future internationalists.

There were horrendous injury problems, however, many caused by the concrete-like surfaces of some of the South African pitches. Arthur Young, perhaps the finest scrum-half of the era and lynch-pin of England's Grand Slam side, missed three of the Tests, while W.S. Gainsford was injured in the opening training session and sat out the entire tour. Ian Smith, the Australian-born Scottish winger who set an international record of 24 tries that stood until David Campese beat it, played only two Tests. Some players, such as Roy Kinnear – later a Scotland international and Great Britain rugby league cap, and father of the late well-known comic actor of the same name – managed to play in all four Tests, as did fellow Scottish cap Neil McPherson.

McPherson's story is illuminating about the attitude of officialdom in those times. Though he was actually born in Wales, he qualified to play for Scotland because of his Scottish parentage, though this meant many long arduous trips north for the young man who played for Newport. He made the mistake, however, of accepting the gift of a watch worth 20 guineas to mark Newport's unbeaten season in 1922–23, and when the gift was made public, the supposedly whiter-than-white Scottish union banned him from the international side.

In that 1924 party, Dan Drysdale, Doug Davies, Robert Howie, Arthur Blakiston, and Cove-Smith himself were the only other ever-presents in the four Tests. The first three would all play a vital part in Scotland's 1925 Grand Slam, and Drysdale would later become president of the SRU, while Blakiston succeeded his baronet father and became Sir Arthur.

There was also no reliable goal kicker, and Scotland's full-back Drysdale had a miserable time missing what would now be considered certainties. In his defence, he had to play on while injured, the ball was much heavier in those days, and its flight high on the Veldt has baffled many more kickers than Drysdale. A forward, Tom Voyce of Gloucester and England, took over the kicking duties and fared little better. Voyce, who would become president of the RFU in later life, also had to play out of position in the backs, this happening several times as the Lions numbers were depleted. Willie Cunningham, an Irish international who had moved to live in Johannesburg, was called up as a replacement from 'civilian' life – as would happen to the accidental tourist, Andy Nicol, in Australia in 2001.

At one point in the match against the Border side in East London, the Lions were so desperate to make up numbers that a spectator called McTavish was pressed into action. Nothing more was known about him, and no more was ever heard about him, but there remains the intriguing possibility that out there somewhere are the descendants of an unacknowledged Lion.

Dr Cove-Smith admitted that the injuries had all but overwhelmed his squad. Later he wrote: 'Looking back, one cannot help but laugh at the subterfuges to which we were forced to resort to place 15 fit men on the field, and I have marvelled many times in retrospect that the fellows were able to put up such a good show in spite of all the handicaps.'

The Lions were also caught out by what some considered a piece of trickery by the Springboks. In order to combat the dynamic wing forward play of the Lions, South Africa's Test side lined up with a scrummage in a 3–4–1 formation, the wing forwards binding their support to props rather than the second row, as opposed to the traditional 3–2–3 system. The Lions refused to adopt the advantageous new formation and duly paid the price as the South African defence became even more formidable.

Forget these excuses, however. The fact is that the 1924 Lions were just not as good as their hosts, as the four Tests showed. The first Test at Durban saw the debut in the green jersey of the legendary fly-half Bennie Osler, one of the greatest of all Springboks. A prodigious kicker, Osler's clearances from defence and his probing kicks in attack rendered many of the Lions strategies redundant. His drop goal was the difference between the two sides in that first Test, won 7–3 by the Springboks. 'He kicked more than was warranted,' was Cove-Smith's later comment.

The second Test at Johannesburg was played in front of a crowd estimated at 25,000, of whom a large number had forced their way in after being locked out when the ground reached its supposed capacity of 15,000 – there was no longer any doubt about the popularity of matches against the Lions. It was no tense affair, however, South Africa recording their biggest ever win by 17–0.

Having lost so heavily to the Springboks and having failed to beat no fewer than eight provincial sides, the Lions at least salvaged a draw in the third Test in Port Elizabeth. The series was lost, and insult was added to injury when the Springboks snatched victory with a late try in the final Test in Cape Town.

The humiliation was complete, and the knives were out for the tourists back home – in the polite terms of the day, it was suggested by various complainers that the host unions' generous hospitality had helped the Lions rugby to reach a nadir. In other words, far too much drink had been taken.

W. Rowe Harding, the Welsh winger, later gave vent to his feelings about the tour and the Lions in general in his controversial book of 1929, *Rugby Reminiscences and Opinions*. 'Many unkind things were said about our wining and dining, but that was not the explanation of our failures,' he wrote, going on to blame instead the injuries, the long train journeys between venues and the hard grounds. But he then struck a more honest note.

It is not difficult to analyse the reason for our failure. Dissipation has nothing to do with it … the real reason for our failure was that we were not good enough to go abroad as the representatives of the playing strength of these islands.

It is not sufficient to send abroad some players who are of international standard and some who are second class. Every member of the team must be absolutely first class, or disaster is bound to overtake it.

Harding then slammed the home unions for not taking the tour or indeed the southern hemisphere nations seriously enough: 'There has always been too much condescension by the British rugby authorities about our attitudes both to our continental neighbours and the colonies.'

Having retired from rugby the previous year to pursue his career in law, Harding was free to castigate his targets in officialdom. It did his legal career no harm – he later became a judge – but the frosty atmosphere when he encountered the 'blazers' of the committee rooms can only be imagined. Harding, whose great-nephews Sam and Tom played top-class rugby in their native New Zealand and in England, was a man ahead of his time, and the next tour in 1930, a year after his words were published, would prove him all too correct.

One footnote from that tour emerged in 2005, when a blue 1924 Lions jersey came up for auction, apparently the one exchanged with Alf Walker of the Springboks after the final Test Match. It was said to be in the same condition as it had been at the end of the match, though presumably it had been washed. The collar of the jersey was torn off – proof that the Springboks have never given any quarter.

At the time that the 1930 tour was agreed, the finest side of that international era was Scotland, with rugby in the Borders enjoying a purple patch. The Four Home Unions Committee, which was responsible for selecting the touring party, apparently contacted 100 players about their availability for the trip Down Under, and a fair number of invitees were

Scottish. But it was a sign of the uncertain economic times that only one Scot, Willie Welsh of Hawick and Scotland, felt able to travel. The Committee's first choice as captain, England's Wavell Wakefield, was unable to tour, as was their second choice, Dr George Stephenson, then the most-capped player in the world, whose record of 14 tries for Ireland in home matches stood until a certain Brian O'Driscoll came along. Doug Prentice of Leicester and England eventually took up the captaincy, and clearly did a competent job of administration, as some years afterwards he became secretary of the RFU. He was not so successful as a player, and omitted himself from three Test teams.

The tour party still managed to comprise 29 players, of whom 11 were or would become England internationalists, with 6 Welsh caps, 5 Irish, plus Willie Welsh of Scotland. The star player was Welsh flanker Ivor Jones, who was nominated as 'The King' by the New Zealand press and public before Barry John was even born. Later president of the Welsh rugby union, Jones struck up a lifelong friendship with legendary opponent George Nepia.

Another Welshman who impressed his hosts was Jack Morley, who would return Down Under as a professional with the Great Britain rugby league tourists in 1936. Fly-half Roger Spong usually formed a great partnership for England with scrum-half Wilf Sobey, but the latter was badly injured in the first match of the tour and missed the remaining matches in which Spong nevertheless excelled.

Yet another of the touring internationalists was Carl D. Aarvold of Cambridge University and England, who later in life would be knighted and face opposition even tougher than the All Blacks – as Recorder of London he sat in judgement on the notorious gangster twins, the Krays. Other members of the party included Ireland's George Beamish, a Royal Air Force pilot who later became Air Marshal Sir George Beamish, KBE, CBE, and Brian Black, who also became an RAF pilot and was killed in action in 1940.

Alongside Aarvold at centre for all four Tests in the New Zealand leg of the tour was the then 23-year-old Harry Bowcott of Cambridge University and Wales, who would go on to be president of the WRU more than 40 years later. Thanks to his surviving to the great age of 97 – he died in 2004 – and his willingness to be interviewed by Lions historian Clem Thomas among others, Bowcott has provided us with real insight into what it meant to be a Lion in those days.

First of all, he was adamant that selection for the Lions was a great honour and hugely exciting for the young men of the day, as there were few opportunities to travel Down Under in 1930. Though they had a surprising amount of freedom – there was only one manager, no coaches and such training sessions as they did were taken by captain Prentice – the players were strictly controlled in one way, namely their finances. Each player was allowed to bring £80 spending money, which was handed over at the beginning of the tour to the formidable manager, James Baxter of the RFU. Players could draw their own money only by asking Baxter, who also doled out the daily allowance of three shillings per day – equivalent to 15p in modern money. Even that was paid in 'chits' of a shilling or sixpence at a time, as no money could be allowed to change hands for fear of breaching the professionalism laws. Meals and other costs were met from the tour budget, and of course, when they arrived at their destinations, the players rarely had to put their hands in their pockets – the hospitality of their hosts saw to that.

Players also had to bring a dinner jacket, as formal dress was compulsory for the nightly dinners on board the good ship *S.S. Rangitata*, which took five weeks to reach New Zealand, sailing westwards through the Panama Canal and across the vast Pacific Ocean. Some of the players had to rely on their clubs to provide them with their formal wear, as the tour party consisted of men from all social backgrounds, though all were apparently well mannered. Yet none of the tourists took the financial inducements they could have earned as Lions. Bowcott summed up their attitude years later, saying: 'I would have given up rather than play professional. I would never have taken the money.'

Team selection on that tour was by a committee of senior players with at least one representative from each of the home unions, though Bowcott admitted that Willie Welsh's strong Hawick accent meant no one could understand him – perhaps the reason why he played only one Test.

According to Thomas's account of Bowcott's memories while speaking in his eighties, there was one group of people who were not missed on the tour:

> There were, thank goodness, no pressmen, which was a wonderful thing, for we could do as we liked without looking over our shoulder.
>
> We were no better and no worse than the young men of today in our behaviour. We drank a bit and enjoyed female company, but we tended to carouse only after matches. Standards of behaviour were left to the individual. I will not say that the manager, Jim Baxter, could not care less, for he was a typical RFU man. It so happened they were all nice people.

Baxter was to play a crucial and highly controversial role on the tour. There had been reports filtering back to the home unions that New Zealand's approach to the laws had become lax, and confirmation came at half-time in the very first match against Wanganui, when the home side insisted on a break of ten minutes and a cup of tea.

Baxter was apoplectic. The agreement between the Home Unions Committee and the New Zealand Union was that matches would be played under IRB laws, which clearly stated that no one could leave the pitch without permission and only in special circumstances. The home union gave way on that point, but did not kowtow to Baxter on their interpretation of the scrummaging laws which saw the All Blacks pack down in a 2–3–2 formation with two hookers up front and a spare forward known as a 'rover' who was used to put the ball into the scrum and savage the opposition half-backs on their put-in. That the rover just happened to be the All Blacks' captain and best player, wing forward Cliff Porter of Wellington, who had also led the side on their 1925 'Invincibles' tour, gave the New Zealand officials added impetus to defend their stance.

To be fair, the laws at that time did not state how many players should make up a scrum, and the All Blacks continued to use the formation and the rover forward despite Baxter's accusations of cheating; accusations he extended to the New Zealand interpretation of the 'mark', which allowed the call to be made when both feet were off the ground. Baxter kept his most vehement condemnation for the appearance of All Blacks in advertisements, an early form of sponsorship that caused bitter arguments between the home unions and their southern counterparts for decades.

With a fine disregard for manners and convention, Baxter launched his onslaught at the post-match festivities after the first game against Wanganui. As Bowcott told Clem Thomas: 'He slaughtered them in one of his speeches after dinner and one sensed that they became afraid of him.'

They were right to be so afraid. On his return to England, Baxter single-handedly drove through a change to the laws so that in 1932 a three-man front row became compulsory, as is the case to this day. In a roundabout fashion, the British and Irish Lions had literally caused the laws of rugby to be altered. Some would say the change was not for the better, as the All Blacks reacted by creating a culture that was often too dependent on a rampaging pack as opposed to inventive backs. It worked pretty well for them though.

Off the field, apart from the rows over the rules, the touring party was hugely popular, and were much in demand at various official and unofficial luncheons and dinners. They made a particular hit when visiting a Maori meeting house in Rotorua, where some of the Lions were decked out in traditional Maori dress. A photograph of the occasion shows them looking mostly nonplussed at their apparel. As they made their way round the country, with journeys made mostly by train, crowds would turn out to see the Lions at every stop. There was simply no understating the demand for the Lions.

The 1930 Test series in New Zealand ended in massive disappointment after a cracking start for the Lions. Having lost only to the most powerful provinces of Wellington and Canterbury, the Lions arrived in Dunedin in fairly confident mood, and as always, raised their game for the full Test. A try in the final seconds gave the Lions victory by 6–3, and that after New Zealand's George Nepia had hit the post with his conversion attempt following the All Blacks' earlier try. It was the Lions' first victory over New Zealand in a Test Match, but in one way the 'All Blacks' could maintain they were unbeaten – the home team had played in white jerseys to avoid a colour clash with the blue of the Lions. It was this shirt clash in particular that in later years saw the Lions switch to their familiar bright red jerseys, sufficiently different – especially in the age of colour television – from the black, green and gold colours of their traditional opponents.

Despite a valiant effort after playing most of the match with 14 men, scrum-half Paul Murray having dislocated a shoulder, the Lions went down 10–13 in the second Test at Canterbury, Carl Aarvold's second try scored from 40 yards out being described as one of the best ever seen at that famous ground. With the series nicely poised at 1–1, the Lions gave the All Blacks a real fight in Auckland, going down by only 10–15, Harry Bowcott grabbing the opening try.

In Wellington, the fourth and final Test was watched by a record crowd for any match in New Zealand. Among the spectators was Lord Bledisloe, the Governor-General of New Zealand to whom the teams were introduced before the match. He clearly enjoyed his rugby, for the cup awarded in matches between Australia and New Zealand – which the good Lord presented the following year – bears his name.

The series could still be drawn, but at the end of a tiring match and exhausting tour the Lions wilted in the second half and the All Blacks ran in six tries in all, winning by 22–8. Despite their Test losses, the Lions left New Zealand with the praises of their hosts ringing in their ears, particularly for their sportsmanship and stylish play. Mr Baxter of the RFU was presumably not included in those plaudits.

The touring party then moved on to Australia and though they beat an 'Australian XV', the Lions lost the sole Test to the Wallabies in Sydney by the narrowest of margins, 5–6, and also lost to New South Wales. Such was their capacity for rugby, or maybe they just wanted a break on the way home, that the tourists played an unofficial match against Western Australia in Perth and ran up the cricket score of 71–3, a record points total that would not be exceeded for 44 years. As it was a 'scratch' match and did not figure in official records, Western Australia's blushes were spared. Unfortunately for them, the blushes really did arrive in 2001 when the part-timers of Western Australia went down by 116–10.

With the world's economies in meltdown, it would be eight years before the Lions toured again, though both the Springboks and New Zealand came north earlier in the decade and thumped their opponents. A party of prominent rugby players from the British Isles visited Argentina in 1936, as had also happened in 1927, but neither of these tours is classed as an official Lions venture. That may be due to long-running snobbery about Argentinean rugby in that era – Scotland, for instance, would not award caps for matches against the South American country until the 1990s. Alternatively, it may reflect the realization that Argentina was no match for the British and Irish players who visited: they won all 19 matches, including 5 'Tests', over both tours. With the giant steps forward taken in recent years by the Pumas, and with an under-strength Argentina having drawn with the Lions in a preparatory match for the 2005 tour, it's interesting to think what might happen should the Lions now visit that country. After all, Argentina beat England at Twickenham in 2006 and reached the semi-finals of the 2007 World Cup by beating France and Ireland in the group phase and Scotland in the quarter-final.

By popular demand in that country, South Africa was the venue for the 1938 tour, and the Lions went there despite the growing menace of Adolf Hitler's Germany, a country where rugby union had its own federation of clubs from 1900 and which had played many internationals, including winning two against France, before the Nazis effectively killed off the sport because of its 'Britishness'.

Captained by Sammy Walker, later a much-respected BBC commentator and then a robust prop forward for Ireland, the party was once again bedevilled by great players declaring themselves unavailable for the long tour south. The absentees included the Welsh wizard Cliff Jones, Scotland's Wilson Shaw and the mighty second row forward from England, Fred Huskisson. Injuries would also wreck many plans, with Haydn Tanner, Jimmy Giles and George Morgan all having to take a turn as a Test scrum-half, with Giles even turning out at centre.

The Springboks, by contrast, were at full strength and were coming off the back of a tour to Australia and New Zealand where they had beaten the former country twice and had won their first Test series in New Zealand by two victories to one. The Springbok side included the great forward Boy Louw and was captained by Danie Craven who was well on his way to becoming a legend of rugby. They were hailed as the champions of the world, and no one could disagree that their record made them so.

The Lions did have some very fine players, including Ireland's Harry McKibbin, who would later go on to be the president of the IRFU in its centenary seasons; the outstanding Welsh hooker Bill 'Bunny' Travers; the prodigious goal kicker Viv Jenkins, later to become a superb writer on rugby; and Gerald Thomas 'Beef' Dancer, a belligerent prop who was the find of the tour but never actually played for England, as the war intervened before he could break into the team. There were also three serving police officers in their ranks, Welshmen Eddie Morgan and Russell Taylor, and Bob Alexander of the Royal Ulster Constabulary. By coincidence, the 1989 Lions also contained three policemen, Dean Richards, Paul Ackford and Wade Dooley.

The early part of the tour was promising for the Lions, as they lost only to Transvaal and twice to Western Province. They arrived in Johannesburg for the first Test in confident mood, having gained revenge over Transvaal the week before. But with 14 of the Springboks who had bested New Zealand on tour, South Africa were ready to do battle to stay as unofficial world champions.

In what many who saw and reported on it claimed to be the best match ever in South Africa, the Springboks and the Lions played marvellous running and passing rugby, the home side finally triumphing despite the visitors taking the lead three times. Four tries to nil tells its own story: the Lions points all came from penalties in a 12–26 defeat.

The Springboks wrapped up the three-match series with a clinical 19–3 win in Port Elizabeth on a day when blazing sunshine sapped the Lions' strength. But there was still honour to play for in the third and final Test in Cape Town and no one should ever underestimate the pride of Lions.

In a thrilling match which went down to the final seconds when referee Nick Pretorius disallowed a Springbok 'try' for a forward pass, the Lions came from being 3–13 down at half-time to record a famous victory. The wind had been against them in the first half, but they took full advantage of the conditions in the second, and it probably helped that eight of the players were from Ireland and knew each other's game well. It should be recorded that the Springboks themselves notified the referee that Charlie Grieve's drop goal for four points had indeed crossed the bar. Bishop Carey's prayers almost 40 years earlier that the South Africans would always play like gentlemen were answered on that day.

The Lions had beaten the Springboks for the first time since 1910, and Sammy Walker was carried off the field in triumph after their 21–16 win. But there was no hiding from the fact that a Lions series had been lost again. There was little time for disappointment, however, as the players returned home to their own countries to await the visit of the Australian tourists in 1939.

The Wallabies had been in Britain for just one day when war was declared on 3 September. They had the consolation of a reception at Buckingham Palace by King George VI and Queen Elizabeth before they embarked on the long and now much more dangerous voyage home. Organized rugby effectively ceased for the duration of the war, though many scratch matches were organized, particularly within and between the various Services. Even the rules on professionalism were set aside and players from rugby union and rugby league played together and fraternized.

Almost all of that Lions party of 1938 saw their careers curtailed by the war. Bob Alexander and earlier Lions such as 1930 tourists Brian Black and Royal Tank Corps officer Henry Rew died as a result of wounds sustained in action, while Blair 'Paddy' Mayne, the fighting Irishman of the 1938 pack, won no less than four Distinguished Service Order medals, the Legion D'Honneur and Croix de Guerre. Amazingly, another Lions forward, Major General Sir Douglas Kendrew of the 1930s squad, equalled Mayne's feat of winning a DSO and three bars – only seven men in history have achieved that quadruple honour, and two of them were British and Irish Lions.

One of the most extraordinary of all the Lions, Blair 'Paddy' Mayne in particular would become a legend of military history as one of the original members of the SAS. He was named after his mother's cousin, Robert Blair, who also won the DSO before being killed in the First World War. Blair Mayne became a champion amateur heavyweight boxer and all-round sportsman, as well as a qualified solicitor, but it was rugby at which he excelled and he was soon selected for Ulster, Ireland and then the Lions.

A year after his return from South Africa, Mayne, who had been in the Territorial Army, joined the regular army on the outbreak of war. After volunteering for the commandos, he saw action in the Lebanon in 1941, where he allegedly had an altercation with a senior officer after calling him incompetent. Fortunately, SAS founder David Stirling stepped in and recruited Mayne for his new long-range fighting force in the North African desert. Mayne was eventually promoted to colonel and commanded the 1st SAS Regiment. It was while he was serving in Olden burg in Germany in the latter days of the war that Mayne single-handedly rescued a squadron of troops, for which he was recommended for a Victoria Cross. But his truculent attitude to authority probably cost him the highest medal of honour. Stirling said of Mayne: 'He was one of the best fighting machines I ever met in my life. He also had the quality to command men and make them feel his very own.'

After the war, and suffering from the effects of a back injury, Mayne returned to Northern Ireland but had difficulty coping with civilian life and volunteered for a polar expedition to the Antarctic. His health deteriorated however, and he came back to his home town of Newtonards to a job with the Law Society. His back pain got to the point where he could no longer even play rugby. Nothing, it seemed, could match up to the excitement of his playing days and war service, and he began to drink more; it is said he would challenge every man in a bar to a fight, and beat them all. One night after a drinking session, however, he was driving home when he crashed his Riley sports car and was killed at the age of just 40.

Mayne's life has been the subject of several books, and a film has long been planned about him. In 2005, MPs attempted to have his Victoria Cross finally and posthumously awarded, but the Government turned them down. He is commemorated in his home town by both a statue and a road named after him.

Mayne was by far the most famous of the 1938 Lions, but for all of them the world changed a year later with the start of the war. It would be 12 long years before the Lions would tour again. They would do so in a world transformed beyond recognition, where the concept of Empire would become outmoded and would be replaced by the gradual end of colonies and protectorate and the move to the Commonwealth. Nothing diminished in any way, however, the desire of the people of Australia, New Zealand and South Africa to have the British and Irish Lions visit their countries.

CHAPTER THREE

KARL MULLEN'S HAPPY BAND

Australia and New Zealand 1950

In the immediate post-war period, Great Britain, and to a lesser extent Ireland, had rather more to worry about than rugby. It was a time of strict austerity, and rationing still applied to many ordinary everyday items, including meat.

The tight rationing rules apparently did not apply to cigarettcs, as the 1950 tourists were given their supply free of charge for the entire duration of the six-month-long tour to Australia and New Zealand in which they played 30 matches, including six Tests. It was to be the last time the Lions travelled by sea to the southern hemisphere. They sailed out on the *SS Ceramic* via the Panama Canal, and came back also travelling westwards, so it could be said that they sailed around the world just to play rugby. On the way home though, they took a shortcut via the Suez Canal and Mediterranean Sea en route from Sri Lanka, where they had played an unofficial match against a team representing the former Ceylon, before stopping for dinner in Mumbai, then known as Bombay.

More than a few of the players had seen service during the war or had undergone their two years' mandatory national service in the forces, so they were used to being away from home for long periods. It was nevertheless particularly hard on newly married men or fathers with young children: 'I had to leave an infant son behind and when I came back he was just so much bigger,' as one 1950 Lion put it.

Two great characters of rugby and stars of that tour – both now in their late eighties – recently recalled what they were doing in the greatest skirmish of them all: the Second World War. It says a great deal about Dr Jack Matthews and Bleddyn Williams – and indeed all the rugby players who served in the war – that so many were anxious to get back to playing the game after what had been an 'interesting' time for them. Jack Matthews, who is now 88, managed to do both war service and national service, as he explained:

I was one of five children, with two sisters and two brothers, both of whom joined the army when war broke out. I was just starting to study medicine, but I wanted to join my brothers in action so I went off to Penarth without telling my parents and joined up as a fighter pilot.

I trained for five months of a six-month course and we were being taught to fly a new type of Spitfire, when my CO came up to me and said 'Matthews, you're out.' I said 'Beg your pardon, sir, what have I done wrong?' He explained that they had just heard from the Home Office that I was a medical student, and I was thrown out because it was an exempt profession.

I spent the war qualifying as a doctor in Cardiff, but before I could finish, I was called up for national service. I said 'Hang on, I've already done five months in the RAF, doesn't that count?' But Brigadier Hugh Llewellyn Glyn-Hughes, who was in charge of the Royal Army Medical Corps (RAMC) and also ran the Barbarians, persuaded me not to go back to the RAF but to join the RAMC. I was captain of Cardiff at the

time, and he was very persuasive in saying I could carry on playing at
Cardiff as long as I played for the RAMC in the inter-services Cup. I did,
and we won it.

I have a wonderful photograph of Field Marshal Montgomery
presenting me with the cup. Funnily enough, I don't think the RAMC
have won it since.

During the war, Matthews kept fit partly by boxing for his medical school
side, which travelled to St Athan to meet an RAF select in 1943. On that
occasion his opponent was an American 'guest' with a knockout reputation – none other than Rocky Marciano, who would later become the
only man ever to retire as undefeated heavyweight champion of the world.
Matthews managed to avoid being stopped by Marciano, something only
six of the great fighter's professional opponents achieved.

Matthews eventually went on to complete his service in medicine with
the RAF. His great friend Bleddyn Williams was also in the RAF, serving
as a pilot, and performed the unique feat of invading Germany and playing for Great Britain at rugby in the same week.

More than 63 years later, Williams tells the story of the last week in
March 1945 with relish:

After Arnhem there was a shortage of glider pilots so they were looking
for volunteers from among us surplus pilots for the big push over the
Rhine – it was 'you, you, and you', the usual way of volunteering, so I
became a glider pilot.

I had been picked for the Great Britain side which was due to play the
Dominions in one of the morale-boosting international matches that
were played occasionally during the war. The match was set for Leicester
on the Saturday after I was due to land in Germany, which we duly did
early that week in the massive push (Operation Varsity) to get our troops
across the Rhine.

On the Friday morning, the day before I was due to play for Great Britain, I was still in the camp in Germany, when my CO, Sir Hugh Bartlett, who later became captain of Sussex county cricket team, said to me 'Aren't you supposed to be playing at Leicester tomorrow?' I replied that indeed I was, but I had been sleeping in a slit trench all week and was looking rather unkempt by then. All he said was 'Pack your bags'. We were five miles inside Germany at this point, I should add.

I got a ride in a jeep to the Rhine, crossed over in a empty DUKW (amphibious vehicle) and there was another jeep waiting for me on the other side which took me to Eindhoven in Holland where I got a lift in a plane to Brize Norton in Oxfordshire. I was stationed in Essex at the time but waiting for me was the CO of the camp who grabbed a spare aircraft and flew me home.

I wasn't long married at the time and when I presented myself at the door of our digs my wife thought I was a ghostly apparition, because she had been told that there had been very few survivors of the attack.

I spent the night, went up by train to Leicester the following morning and I played for Great Britain and scored a try in our victory. War was incidental to rugby football, you see.

With two centres, one of whom had gone the distance with Rocky Marciano and the other who had invaded Germany, how could the 1950 Lions fail? Other former servicemen on the 1950 tour included Billy McKay, who had been a Commando and had served in the bloodiest conflicts in Burma, now Myanmar. Welsh scrum-half Rex Willis had served in the Royal Navy while Scottish captain Peter Kininmonth had seen action in Italy and as recently as 1947 had served on the North-west frontier in Afghanistan. Ken Jones served as a sergeant in India, and his victory in the All-India Games in 1945 kick-started a sprinting career that saw him run for Britain in the 1948 Olympics and win a silver medal in the sprint relay – almost sacrilegiously for a Lion, he perhaps unsurprisingly recalled the 1948 Olympics as the highlight of his sporting career rather than his touring experiences.

Of such tried and tested stuff were Lions made. The 1950 touring party was the first to be called the Lions by all and sundry, though they were still formally billed as the British Isles Rugby Union Team, and the initials BIRUT appeared on the tour blazer beneath the now accepted emblem of the four home unions' badges on a quartered shield. A more obvious change – as mentioned earlier – was the adoption of bright red jerseys, prompted by the previous blue colours clashing with the black jersey of New Zealand. The Lions in Red were here to stay.

The manager for the 1950 tour was a distinguished Royal Navy doctor, Surgeon-Captain L.B. 'Ginger' Osborne, then a selector for England and later a rear admiral. His good humour coupled with Mullen's inspirational captaincy made this one of the happiest of tours. Indeed, we know just how pleasant an experience it was from first-hand accounts in a DVD documentary of that 1950 tour called *The Singing Lions*. 'With all those Welshmen, what did you expect?' as Jack Matthews put it.

In the 1950 party, for the first time every player was an internationalist and all four home unions provided capped players. Although Wales's captain John Gwiliam could not tour, there were eventually no fewer than 14 players from Wales, Lewis Jones joining as a replacement for the latter part of the tour. Jones would become known as 'The Golden Boy' of Welsh rugby but, as we will see, he would become involved in a controversy that split his nation asunder.

The Welsh preponderance reflected the fact that the principality was enjoying one of its periods of domination over the other northern unions, having just achieved the Grand Slam. Great players like Williams and fellow centre Matthews – nicknamed 'Iron Man' by the New Zealanders 'because of my tackling, I think', he mused recently – and flying winger Ken Jones made the Welsh back line irresistible. 'I once beat Ken in a 100m sprint,' Matthews recalled, 'and when my time was beaten later on, I had to remind the new record holder he was running in spikes and we ran in flat shoes.'

Other Welsh Lions of 1950 included the Terrible Twins from Neath, lock forwards Roy John and Rees Stephens, as well as utility forward Don Hayward, prop John Robins and fly-half Billy Cleaver. Hooker Dai Davies and flanker Bob Evans became vital team members while the ever-cheerful Cliff Davies provided the baritone for the Lions choir.

Despite the tour having an English manager and selector, England had just three representatives, including captain Ivor Preece, which was not really surprising as English rugby was then in the doldrums, while Scotland had five and Ireland nine.

'The Welsh and Irish got on great,' said Williams, 'but really we all gelled right from the start, all the nationalities, and maybe it was because so many of us had been used to getting along with strangers during our time in the services.'

The best known Scottish player of the day, the great back row forward W.I.D. 'Doug' Elliott, was invited to be a Lion but could not make the tour as he was a farmer and would miss the harvest, as was also the case with another Scottish invitee, Hamish Kemp. Doug Elliot did ask if he could join the tour for part of the trip, but was refused. The Lions Committee wanted total commitment in those days, and he never did make a tour. He was 'a great character who was missed', in Jack Kyle's words. The leader of the Scottish contingent in 1950 was the barrel-chested flank forward Peter Kininmonth, while his fellow Scot, scrum-half Gus Black, was noted for his long and accurate passes which attracted the attention of an All Blacks team anxious to stop the Lions' backs from cutting loose. It says everything about his destructive opposite number, Pat Crowley, that Gus Black survived just two Tests before giving way for the third Test to Gordon Rimmer, who in turn was injured during the game and replaced by the Welsh utility back Billy Cleaver, before Rex Willis took over at No. 9 for the final Test – Crowley destroyed them all.

Both the team captain and its star player were Irish. A fine hooker, Dr Karl Mullen had been captain of Ireland's Triple Crown-winning sides of 1948 and 1949 and was first choice to captain the Lions. Firm and fair and with a surgeon's bedside manner about him, he would go on to become one of Ireland's leading gynaecologists, and with his wife Doreen would be at the heart of Irish society for many years. Doreen died in 2008 and Dr Mullen is now living quietly in Ireland.

Due to injury, Mullen missed a good number of matches but had a sound replacement as captain in Bleddyn Williams, while Dai Davies was such a success at hooker that Mullen stood aside for the team's benefit even after recovering. Incidentally, both Davies and the lightning-quick flank forward Bob Evans were policemen, the latter an inspector with Newport C.I.D. All those young doctors and policemen – yet it was somehow a trouble-free tour …

Bleddyn Williams would become one of the legendary figures of Welsh and Lions rugby, and at the age of 85 his memories of the tour and before are pin sharp. But he nearly didn't make the 1950 Lions tour at all.

As he recalled:

In the final Welsh trial before the Five Nations in the early part of January, Malcolm Thomas, who also came on the Lions tour, and I were in opposition. He tackled me and my leg was caught in such a position that I tore the ligaments in my knee. I was in plaster for some time, and though they picked me for the Lions, I still had to prove my fitness, which I managed to do in a match for Cardiff against Bath.

The great thing for me was that we went out by boat taking more than five weeks so that I was able to do all sorts of exercises with weights and by the time we reached New Zealand I was in pretty good shape. It also helped that we had so many doctors and trainee doctors around – Jack Matthews was a qualified GP, and Jack Kyle and Bill McKay qualified later, while Karl Mullen became a gynaecologist and Ginger Osborne was a dentist.

I got injured against Otago and missed the first Test, but it was only a pulled hamstring though I made it worse by playing on with the injury – there were no replacements then, of course, and you stayed on the field unless you had to be carried off.

That old law will mystify modern rugby fans used to the 'revolving door' replacements of modern matches, but Jack Matthews remembers that 'no substitute' rule ruefully: 'On the tour I think we finished with only 14 men on the pitch in about 20 to 30 per cent of the matches we played. You just had to carry on.'

Matthews himself was almost the victim of some skulduggery by an alleged Irish selector, who threatened him with expulsion from the Lions.

On the morning of our 1950 Triple Crown game against Ireland, I went to 'spend a penny', so to speak, and this fellow just said 'If you play well today you won't make the Lions tour, as I'm a selector and will see to it.' I ignored him and went out and played my usual game. We won 6–3, and I never heard another word.

One of the 'doctors in the making' on that tour was one of Ireland's all-time greats, fly-half J.W. 'Jack' Kyle, whose inventiveness sparked many a try-scoring move by the backs. Kyle and his fellow Irishmen proved a big hit off the field, and combined with the lads from the Valleys in many a singsong.

'We had won the Grand Slam in 1948,' recalled Kyle, 'and Wales had just won it, so naturally between the two countries we had the bulk of the party.'

Kyle's experiences of being selected were typical of the time. As a medical student at Queen's University in Belfast, he had already played for Ireland and was reckoned to be the outstanding fly-half of the day. He had hopes for receiving the selectors' call but in the end found out he had been chosen for the tour from a newspaper.

'My father, who was also John Wilson Kyle like me, was reading the *Belfast Telegraph* when he noticed a report saying 'the following have been selected …' and there was my name,' said Kyle. 'I know plenty of Lions who found out the same way.

> *In those days there was absolutely no question of any money or benefits accruing from playing rugby. My dad frequently said to me 'You're not going to earn your living from rugby, son, you had better pass your exams.*
>
> *When he read of my selection, fortunately I wasn't in the house. He read out the report and noted the fact that I would be away for six months and miss a full term, and then turned to my brother Eric and said 'Does that brother of yours ever intend to qualify?'*
>
> *I actually did take a few books and hoped to get advice from the other doctors on the tour like Karl Mullen, but I can't remember doing much reading and we only had one session where Karl tried to teach me a bit about midwifery and gynaecology.*

That may have been the only occasion when midwifery was learned on a rugby tour. As for gynaecology …

As a qualified GP, Jack Matthews' position was much worse – he had to pay a locum thousands of pounds to fill in for him while he was away so that he didn't lose his practice. Matthews said: 'My son was two at the time, and my wife said I could go on tour, but she wanted a maid to help out at home, so I had to pay for her, too. And all we got was seven shillings a day expenses and we even had to buy our own blazers.' The clothing allowance was also frugal – a Lions tie and two BIRUT badges which the players had to sow on themselves.

Jack Kyle did acquire something substantial from that tour – a brother-in-law, Noel Henderson, who was a student at Queen's alongside Kyle and Bill McKay. 'He was a very good centre who greatly strengthened our defence – he was always criticizing me for not getting up on my man, saying things like "Does the out half [fly-half] intend tackling his opposite number by tomorrow?"' Kyle had to forgive him later: 'After all, he married my sister and they had four daughters.'

Coming from lands beset by shortages and rationing, the Lions took full advantage of their hosts' generosity, and in turn they proved to be wonderful ambassadors for the sport in Britain and Ireland. The sparkling play by the backs in most matches and their sportsmanship in all of the games was rivalled only by their obvious enjoyment at the many receptions and outings laid on for them in New Zealand in particular.

'We had a wonderful time,' recalled Matthews. 'The people in New Zealand were often more British than the British, and were always asking us how things were "at home", even though they had never been there.'

The Lions played a full part in the social whirl that surrounded the tourists, as Matthews remembered:

> There were no pubs as such, and people just took us into their homes where we ate and drank merrily. Often they would take us out to hunt wild pigs – fortunately they also brought along professional hunters.
>
> I remember when we visited the Maori settlement at Rotorua and it was quite a sight to see our lads up there dancing with the Maori.

The pace was also leisurely largely because of the way the Lions got around: 'We would travel by bus or train, never by aeroplane,' recalled Bleddyn Williams, 'and would train on school grounds. We had no coaches so Karl would look after the forwards and I would take charge of the backs. Afterwards we would have to give a little talk or answer questions from the pupils.' Both he and Jack Matthews are adamant about the source of most of the questions – 'The girls, no doubt about it,' said Matthews. 'They really were very interested in all aspects of the game.' So there you have the true secret of the All Blacks' success – wives, mothers, grandmothers, sisters and daughters all keeping the men on their toes.

Jack Kyle recalled that the four national captains – Karl Mullen, Bled-dyn Williams, Peter Kininmonth, and Ivor Preece of England – did the selection chores: 'We went out without coaches and, to be frank, it was quite a leisurely affair at times.

'We had plenty of time to see the sights and scenery and at the age of just 24, being carefree and away with a crowd of chaps with nothing to do but play rugby and enjoy ourselves, it really was quite something, a tremendous experience.'

That 1950 visit is still called the 'Friendly Tour' in New Zealand, as much for the style of play exhibited by the Lions as by their undoubted social charms.

'It was all arranged beforehand,' revealed Bleddyn Williams some 58 years later. 'We threw the ball about because we all agreed that we wanted to entertain the people who came to see us, and we felt we did that.'

The appreciation of the backs in particular was shown by the fact that Kyle and Jones were named as two of the five players of the year by the *Rugby Almanack of New Zealand*. Due to injuries, other backs distin-guished themselves in unaccustomed roles, with Scottish fly-half or centre Ranald Macdonald making an impact as a winger.

Sadly, however, the results of the Test Matches against New Zealand brought only a small degree of contentment to the Lions. Having started off with three easy victories, the Lions were humbled in the first two difficult provincial games against Otago and Southland, before travel-ling to Dunedin for the first Test. The match against Otago in particular saw the Lions come up against that province's fierce rucking game that was to become such a feature of rugby in the land of the long white cloud.

A hard fought and highly creditable draw in Dunedin, where the Lions led until late in the game only for New Zealand captain Roy Elvidge to score a converted try, was followed by three defeats to give the All Blacks another series victory. The second Test was lost 0–8 in Christchurch, where the Lions were reduced to 14 men when flanker Billy McKay was forced off with a broken nose and concussion. McKay was obviously a forgiving sort – he liked New Zealand so much that he emigrated there after qualifying as a doctor.

Scores of 3–6 in Wellington and 8–11 in Auckland show just how close the Lions came to matching their opponents, especially in the latter Test. Bleddyn Williams still recalls the best try of the tour in that match.

> *We were 11–3 down and right on our goal line when I said to Jack Kyle, the finest fly-half I ever played with, to get the ball out quickly as we were going to run it. The ball went from Rex Willis to Kyle but it never reached me because behind me was Lewis Jones who nipped in and intercepted it, running up to their full-back and passing to Ken Jones and we scored at the other end of the field. Fred Allen, who later coached the All Blacks, says to this day that it's the best try they have ever seen at Auckland.*
>
> *From the kick-off I nearly scored a try but Peter Henderson, who was an Olympic runner like Ken Jones, caught me and pinned my arms in the tackle. He later told me it was the best tackle he had ever made.*

The All Blacks themselves had been whitewashed 3–0 by South Africa the previous year – so how good did that make the Springboks? The Lions would have to wait five years to find out.

By common consent, the problem for the 1950 Lions was that, apart from the first Test, their forwards could never quite match the All Blacks in gaining and keeping possession. Perhaps only Roy John of Neath, Ireland's Jimmy Nelson and Peter Kininmonth of Scotland were physically able to compete with the opposition in the Tests.

Some observers say that had the superb Lions backs been matched with New Zealand's forwards, it would have created a dream team the like of which had not been seen in world rugby. As it was, those peerless backs Kyle, Matthews, Williams and Jones had to make do with considerably less possession than their opposite numbers.

The results from that period in New Zealand show that when the Lions backs got plenty of possession against the lesser provincial sides, such as Wanganui and Taranaki, they scored a barrowload of points, winning 31–3 and 25–3 respectively against these two sides. Indeed, the Lions won every non-Test Match after their defeat by Southland. Against the mighty rucking pack of the All Blacks, however, they were forced into defensive duties in the main, and though they usually coped admirably, no side on the back foot can hope to keep out New Zealand permanently.

'We did play good rugby,' recalled Matthews. 'I was lucky enough and fit enough to play in all six Tests, and there were all these good players around me. We only just lost the series against the All Blacks by a few points over the course of the four games, and I've had many letters from New Zealand saying that our 1950 Lions were the best rugby-playing side that ever went there.'

Waving a fond farewell to their conquerors, the Lions moved on to Australia where again the hosts were magnificently hospitable and the rugby was rather less difficult. The backs feasted on much greater possession and ran in a total of 150 points in 6 matches.

The first Test in Brisbane was comfortably won by 19–6, with Lewis Jones scoring 16 points with a personal 'grand slam' – all the possible scores of a try, conversion, drop goal and penalty featured in his haul. The second Test in Sydney was even easier, with a scoreline of 24–3 in favour of the Lions.

Their Australian copybook was blotted, however, with a lacklustre performance in the final match against a New South Wales XV who surprisingly won 17–12. Perhaps all those long days of travelling, not to mention the hospitality Down Under, had taken its toll.

Despite the final setback and the losses in New Zealand, the tour was judged a massive success, not least because the Lions had boosted the public image of the sport.

Karl Mullen's words at the start of the tour summed up his squad's approach and resonate down to us today as embodying the proper creed of the Lions: 'We are not after records of matches played and won. We want to see the game played for the game's sake and to give you good football. We will be only too happy if you beat us in a good football match.' Sadly, not too many coaches and captains would dare to utter such sentiments in our winner-takes-all society of today.

Bleddyn Williams and many of his band of Welsh colleagues from that 1950 tour eventually did gain a measure of revenge over New Zealand, Wales beating the All Blacks during their tour of the northern hemisphere in 1953. Some 54 years later, he remains the last Welsh captain to have led his men to victory over the All Blacks. Williams would later become a company director and wrote on rugby for *The People* newspaper for 32 years as well as making countless broadcasts.

To their credit, both Williams and Matthews and their fellow Lions never turned their back on the Welsh Golden Boy, Lewis Jones, who committed the Great Sin of signing up as a professional less than two years after the Lions tour, joining Leeds for a then record fee of £6,000. Immediately ostracized by rugby union, Jones was was banned from having any contact with all clubs worldwide – he could not even buy a drink in a clubhouse for fear of 'tainting' a club. Many Welsh players and officials refused to speak to him, due more to fear of being expelled themselves rather than any personal animus against Jones.

His defection to rugby league at the age of 20 caused great controversy in Wales, particularly as he had been the Golden Boy of the sport. The headlines were blaring and most indicated that Jones's decision had been a betrayal, though many pundits pointed out that his move had been inevitable given the fantastic money on offer.

The hypocrisy of the rugby authorities concerning professionalism was exposed as well. In those days, the very mention of being involved with rugby league scouts could see you declared *persona non grata* in Union circles, as Bleddyn Williams recounts: 'It happened to George Parsons before the Victory International against France in 1947. He was kicked off the train while travelling to play for Wales because he was alleged to have been seen speaking to a rugby league scout. He eventually had to turn professional, and played almost 300 games for St Helen's.'

The charge of hypocrisy arose from the fact that everybody in rugby union knew that it happened. Two of the 1950 tourists – Bleddyn Williams and Jack Matthews – are happy to admit that they discussed terms with rugby league clubs, though they eventually rejected offers. Williams said:

> It happened during the war when I was about to go to America for pilot training, and in wartime there were fewer restrictions on mixing with league so I ended up at Salford and Wigan just trying to keep fit. My brother had played for Wigan before the war and the club manager obviously knew who I was. They offered me £3,000 on the spot to sign for them and I had to point out that I couldn't serve two bosses and was off to America in any case.
>
> When I came back they offered me £5,000 and then £6,000, and I gave them first refusal if I changed my mind, but in the end I just didn't want to do it.

Matthews was also 'tapped' by rugby league clubs: 'I had offers galore, but my parents wouldn't look at it. It wasn't for me but I didn't blame anyone who went "up north" to join rugby league as they didn't have any jobs, then. I wasn't against that at all, but league wasn't for me because they were two different games.'

Williams concurred: 'I am glad I didn't take the money and thus miss the 1950 tour, because I am very, very proud of being a Lion.'

As for the ostracization of Jones, both Williams and Matthews consider that it was shameful.

'It was ridiculous that he couldn't even go back and visit his old friends,' said Williams. 'Just ridiculous, but that was the way it was.'

Matthews agreed: 'We looked after any Cardiff player who went north and came back, even though they tried to bar them from the clubhouse. It was all a lot of rubbish.'

Lewis Jones lives in Leeds and has kept his ties to that city's club for which he starred for many years. The members of Gorseinon rugby club in his home village paid him the tribute of naming their new clubhouse after their local hero, and Jones himself came to open it in early 2008, making a welcome public appearance in Wales. More than 50 years on, all has long been forgiven and forgotten, but as we shall see in subsequent chapters, joining rugby league was still seen as treason for many years after the Golden Boy made his move north.

The Lions' attitude to those who left the union fold is proof that the companionship forged on those tours with their long sea voyages was unbreakable. Williams and Matthews, for example, have remained lifelong friends and both have been honoured by the Queen.

Jack Kyle has always been grateful for being a Lion, but points out the main difference between then and now was not just money but the players' attitude to the sport:

The fact that we had a career was more important than rugby. If you had a bad game and had an exam coming up afterwards, it soon got your mind off your game and onto the important stuff. In today's professional world there would be a video analyst and a coach discussing your game and where you went wrong. The most we ever got if we lost was 'Hard luck, chaps, you did your best.'

I have made and kept many friends through rugby and there's no doubt being a Lion enriched my life tremendously and opened doors for me. To give you an example – I worked in Indonesia as a surgeon from 1962 to 1964 and my wife and I went up to Hong Kong for a holiday and were staying at the Repulse Bay Hotel. We had just got in and were unpacking and the phone rang. It was a guy from the local rugby club inviting me along to their meeting that night.

I said 'How did anyone know I was in Hong Kong?' as I was pretty sure no one knew we were going there. He said 'The customs officer at the airport is a rugby man and spotted your name on your passport.' Those chaps were wonderful to us for the whole holiday, taking us for meals and arranging cars for us. That's the kind of thing that has happened to Lions over the years.

That 1950 band of happy Lions seems largely to have been blessed with success in later life. Ivor Preece enjoyed a long career with Coventry RFC, where he was both captain and president. He died in 1987.

Billy Cleaver rose through the mining industry to become deputy director of the National Coal Board in South Wales. Defying stereotypes about rugger lads, Cleaver had a lifelong interest in the arts and became vice-chairman of the Welsh Arts Council. He died in 2003.

Ken Jones lived until he was 84, having retired from rugby in 1957 when he was the record Welsh cap holder. The following year he had the honour of carrying the baton containing the Queen's Speech at the Commonwealth Games in Cardiff. 'What kept you?' said Prince Philip, after Jones took a wrong turning.

Peter Kininmonth returned from the Lions tour with a most spectacular find: his wife Priscilla, who was on board the ship which took them home. Kininmonth had a distinguished career in financial services before turning to a second career on his wife's farm where he became an award-winning master cheesemaker. He died aged 83 in 2007. Several of the 1950 Lions attended his funeral.

John Robins became a leading figure in physical education, and went on to coach the Lions in 1966 – more about that later. He ended his professional career as director of PE at the University of Wales in Cardiff. He died in 2007. Fellow Welsh cap Bob Evans achieved high rank in the police and was a stalwart for Newport all his life until his death in 2003.

Doug Smith would become one of the most successful managers in Lions history – again more about him later. Grahame Budge, who died in 1979, left a rugby legacy to his family which endures – his grand-daughter Alison Christie has been capped 61 times for Scotland.

The most extraordinary story of the 1950 Lions, one which they have kept to themselves assuming they know all about it, did not emerge until after the death of Don Hayward in 1999. No one should pretend that the Lions have been innocents on their tours, and there are countless tales of liaisons between tourists and women – some of them even of 'a certain age' – over the decades, though most are treated under the unbreakable code of rugby *omerta*, which states roughly that 'what goes on tour, stays on tour'. Not all such dalliances involved sweetness and romance, it must be said, but none had a happier ending than Hayward's tale.

The Welsh forward had loved his time Down Under in 1950 so much that he emigrated there, after meeting and marrying his wife Linda in 1952. He returned briefly to play rugby league for Wigan in the mid-1950s when his wife became ill. On returning to New Zealand, Hayward opened a butcher's shop in Wainuiomata, a suburb of Lower Hutt, though he later moved to Otaki. Linda sadly died, but Hayward remained in Otaki with his son Gareth.

One evening in October 1993 a knock came at the door of their house. On the doorstep stood 42-year-old Suzy Davis and her partner Tony Sims. They asked if he was Don Hayward, a member of the Lions tour party, and after being invited in, Sims blurted out: 'Suzy thinks you are her father.'

Indeed he was. Hayward had met Suzy's birth mother, Iona Potter, for just one night in Dunedin during the tour in 1950. He never knew that the then 29-year-old Potter had become pregnant and given birth to a daughter, who was named Elizabeth Victoria before being put up for adoption and acquiring the name Suzy Davis.

It wasn't until the age of 35 that Davis began the search for her real parents. Showing all the determination her father had displayed on the field, she spent years patiently combing through records until she found her mother, who had two other children from a subsequent marriage and who confirmed that her father had been a rugby player from Wales, though she could not remember his name.

Davis combed through rugby books and found pictures of the Welsh contingent in the 1950 Lions. Revealing her story in 1999, she told the *Evening Post* in Wellington: 'I remember looking and looking at the photo to work out which one it might be.'

Her birth mother was reluctant to say more about her illicit liaison in 1950, but after she contracted terminal cancer, Iona told Suzy that her only memory of the tall Welshman she had met in Dunedin was that he was a train driver from Pontypool. Armed with this information, Davis tracked down Hayward with the help of sportswriters.

His first reaction was: 'My God, I have always wanted a daughter.' A paternity test proved conclusively that he was indeed the father.

For the remaining five-and-a-quarter years of his life, Don Hayward cherished Suzy, and she grew close to the father she had never known. Ironically, for years she had passed his butcher's shop daily on her way to and from work as a teacher, and had never known that the man behind the counter was her dad. But then, they did things differently in the 1950s.

That tour to New Zealand and Australia would be the last time that the British and Irish Lions would be forced to spend many weeks on a ship travelling back and forth to the southern hemisphere. By the time of the next tour, the age of the passenger aircraft had been well and truly established.

The world was changing and modernizing, and so was the sport of rugby, albeit under much protest and at a snail's pace.

CHAPTER FOUR

ROBIN THOMPSON'S QUALITY STREET GANG

South Africa 1955

The 1955 tour to South Africa was the first to see the initial journey south undertaken by air, albeit in a propellor-driven aircraft rather than one of the new-fangled jets of the time. But the accolade of being the first Lion to fly south had gone five years earlier to Lewis Jones, the Welsh full-back who made the then long and hazardous journey to New Zealand to replace George Norton who was injured early in the 1950 tour.

Now known universally as the Lions, the tourists were eagerly awaited in South Africa. Having whitewashed the All Blacks in a four Test series in 1949, and having toured Britain, Ireland and France in 1951–52, completing the Grand Slam against the Five Nations and the Barbarians – Scotland in particular were humiliated 44–0 – and losing only one of 31 matches, the Springboks rightly considered themselves to be the champions of the world. Their devoted fans wanted them to prove it against the Lions, while the whole rugby-mad country was simply brimming over with excitement at the arrival of the tourists for the first time in 17 years.

It was also the first tour to be heavily covered by the press, a few of whose representatives, most notably former Lion and all round-sports-man Viv Jenkins, travelled constantly with the party – Jenkins eventually wrote a book about the tour. The first newsreel films of matches were shown in British cinemas, helping to build public awareness of the Lions, while from the likes of Jenkins, Clem Thomas and Cliff Morgan we have been handed down highly readable accounts of the tour. In short, the 1955 tour is the first where most of the action on and off the pitch was well documented.

The captain for the tour was again an Irishman, Robin Thompson of Instonians and Ireland, and though his playing ability was criticized, most notably by Clem Thomas, his quiet assuredness and capacity for hard work were undoubted, while he was desperately unlucky to be injured in the second Test. The vice-captain was the Scottish full-back Angus Cameron, but a knee injury curtailed his contribution. The manager was a large Belfast man, Jack Siggins, who had no hesitation in laying down the law to what was deliberately a young party. Siggins felt that only athletic youthful types would be able to cope with the conditions in South Africa, and discouraged the selectors from picking anyone over the age of 30 – he originally wanted 27 as the cut-off age – with only Trevor Lloyd of Maesteg and Wales being past his 30th birthday.

Bryn Meredith of Newport was the first-choice hooker in the squad. He recalled:

There were great players like Jack Kyle, Jack Matthews and Bleddyn Williams who could have played, but the manager didn't want anyone over the age of 30. He made his decision and that was the end of that. But we still had a team of great quality.

Personally, I was surprised to be chosen. When you start off you never think you're good enough for your village side, then you never think *you're good enough for your country and who was I to think I was good enough for the Lions?*

I was a schoolmaster at the time and how else was I ever going to go abroad to play rugby? So when I heard I was selected I was always going to go and that was that, even though I was just married at the time, and my wife Betty had to go and live with her parents while I was away. It can't have been too bad for her – we're still together all these years later.

The result of the age limit was that young stars emerged and made themselves famous on that tour, with the two best known being Cliff Morgan of Wales and Tony O'Reilly of Ireland. The former would become a much-loved broadcaster and senior figure in the BBC, while the latter, who celebrated his 19th birthday on the tour, became a very wealthy businessman and owner of newspapers, who organized, and paid for, reunions of the Lions from his era. The exploits of the handsome and witty O'Reilly as a Lion and afterwards in business could fill a book by themselves, and Bryn Meredith credits the Irishman with helping to maintain the strong squad atmosphere that persists among the surviving 1955 Lions: 'He is the one that has kept us together, organizing the reunions and taking us to see the 2007 World Cup Final. I don't think the modern professionals will be doing that sort of thing in years to come – these days they want paid for crossing the road.'

O'Reilly may have been the individual star, but on that 1955 tour the dominant figure was Cliff Morgan, who led by example and brought his keen intelligence to bear on tactics. Dickie Jeeps, one of the great characters of rugby union for nearly 60 years, recalled that he got his place in the Test team, despite being second or third choice scrum-half, because Morgan wanted him alongside:

I hadn't even played for England by then, but Cliff was a great player and fortunately for me he liked the way I played, passing the ball to the front of him so he could run on to it.

It meant that Trevor Lloyd rarely got a game, and I was so concerned for him that I went to see Jack Siggins to ask that Trevor should play. He just growled 'I manage this team, not you,' so it was hard for Trevor as he only played in about five games.

Morgan, the excellent English centre Jeff Butterfield, and O'Reilly were the fulcrum of a superb set of backs whose dashing play impressed their hosts throughout the almost four-month-long tour. Morgan repeatedly gave committed displays of controlling rugby in the No. 10 jersey, while O'Reilly dazzled on the wing or at centre, where he played in the final Test, with the flying Welsh sprinter Gareth Griffiths – a replacement for the injured Arthur Smith – and Cecil Pedlow sharing the wing duties as necessary.

Butterfield had an important role to play on the tour. Jeeps recalled:

Danny Davies from Cardiff was the assistant manager, but he was a quiet man, shall we say. Jeff Butterfield was a fitness fanatic, and he used to take the training and I can tell you, we trained harder on that tour than any other.

We were pretty fit anyway, though I remember my father, who had fought in the First World War and been wounded, telling me when I was first selected for England that he was still faster than me. So we had a race – and he won!

The forwards were more than useful, and for all four Tests the Lions had the same men in jersey numbers 1 to 3, with Bryn Meredith flanked by Swansea's Billy Williams and Neath's Courtenay Meredith making up an all-Welsh front row – the only tour since the war where one country has supplied the hooker and both props for all the Tests. Fellow Welsh-man Rhys Williams and captain Thompson usually provided the boiler room, with Scotland's Jim Greenwood the only ever-present flanker in the Tests.

Hugh McLeod was a tough prop forward from the Borders who might well have made the Test team and indeed would do so in 1959, but he lost out in 1955.

'I had no difficulty accepting the manager's decision to select the Welsh guys in front of me,' said McLeod.

> *I had just completed my national service – indeed I got away five weeks early so I could join the tour – and in the army you learn that orders is orders, and there was no arguing once the decision had been made.*
>
> *The fact is that I felt lucky to be on the tour at all. If it had not been for my mother and my future wife I wouldn't have been able to go on the tour because it was a rule that you had to have £40 in your wallet and that was a lot of money in those days. You also had to supply all your own gear except for a tie, and it was thanks to them that I was able to go.*

McLeod did acquire something on tour – a nickname: 'That fellow O'Reilly was awful quick with the gab, and the first time he saw me I was wearing my tracksuit with the legs rolled up about my knees. "Look," O'Reilly said, "it's an abbot", and the name stuck from then on.'

There were plenty of colourful figures on the tour, not the least of whom was an ordained army chaplain, the Rev. Robin Roe of Lans-downe, London Irish and Ireland, who would go on to win the Military Cross for his bravery while serving with the Lancashire Regiment in Aden in 1967, when he rescued soldiers from a blazing lorry under heavy gunfire. The medal citation read: 'His courage and example in the face of danger has been outstanding and his infectious enthusiasm and confidence under all conditions has been an inspiration to the whole Battalion.' A Lion even when he was wearing a dog collar – what manner of men were these?

Of them all, the Rev. Roe had perhaps the most misgivings about touring a land already disfigured by the apartheid policy of the ruling National Party with its Afrikaaner majority. Most of the Lions were not in the slightest politically minded, but a few such as Roe were troubled by what they were going to encounter. Yet he and the others decided to go, if only to see for themselves what the morally repugnant system was like.

Meredith said:

We didn't know what apartheid meant, but you soon realized that it meant that blacks went one way and whites another, and that there was demarcation everywhere. It didn't affect us much because we only met the people that wanted to meet us anyway, but it was certainly an eye-opener when sometimes a black man would come up and start talking to you for two minutes and then he would say 'I had better go now because someone might think I'm accosting you.'

I remember a boxer coming to talk with us and he said 'I'd better go now in case I get accused', and off he went.

Apartheid was one reason why the tour got off to a surprising start for the participants. They had gathered at Eastbourne College for pre-tour training and a get-together when a Foreign Office mandarin gave them a strong lecture on the ban on associating with non-whites. In particular, he stressed that on no account was there to be any sex with black or mixed-race people as that was a criminal offence punishable by imprisonment. It was a rude awakening about the realities of apartheid.

One of the perhaps forgotten men of that tour was Scottish lock forward Ernest Michie, who has rarely given interviews about his days as a Lion, but was happy to speak for this book. He said: 'I missed out

on the Foreign Office speech because I was a couple of days late in joining the party due to having to sit my final exams at Aberdeen University.
But I remember the message loud and clear – don't talk about politics
and be pretty circumspect about who you speak to.'

Michie is disarmingly modest about his achievement in being selected:

I had played for Scotland but I was very surprised to be chosen. The
University side was on a tour to London, going by bus which took about
20 hours because there was no motorway in those days.

We stopped every so often for a cup of tea, and at Watford or
somewhere I was dozing on the bus when one of the chaps, Doug
Robbie, who is now a doctor, came back from his cuppa and said 'Your
name's in the list of British Lions.' I said to him. 'Don't be daft,' and I
really didn't believe it until we met up with the London Scottish boys
who included Dr Doug Smith, who had been a Lion in 1950 and would
manage the 1971 Lions. He assured me it was true, so I began to believe
it then.

Michie really began to believe it when he made his first-ever flight on an
aeroplane, from Dyce Airport near Aberdeen to London to join the squad.
At Eastbourne, the squad not only got their instructions from the Foreign
Office but manager Siggins also handed out strict instructions on behav-
ioural standards and gave out the rules on cash – they would be allowed
just five shillings (25p) per day pocket money. In the event, some of the
Lions augmented their income by selling their complimentary match tickets, and such was the demand for Test tickets in particular that some
went for £50 each. That was strictly against the rules on amateurism,
but either a blind eye was turned or Siggins knew perfectly well what
was happening and ignored it.

Dickie Jeeps said: 'There was indeed a black market in tickets, especially for the Tests where they could have sold the tickets ten times over.

But by the time the first Test came around you would have made some friends, and that's where most of the tickets went, though there was undoubtedly a sale of tickets which nobody admitted to.'

The Lions themselves came up with the most famous code of tour etiquette, which has been known to touring Lions ever since as Lloyd's Law. During a team meeting with Siggins, Welsh scrum-half Trevor Lloyd suggested that if a player was lucky enough to get himself a girlfriend, no other player should attempt to muscle in, and all of them agreed to it. Some would suggest that Lloyd's Law did not prove to be binding on subsequent tour parties.

The Lockheed Constellation aircraft which was to be their 'safe' conveyance to South Africa played its part in the early adventures of the tourists. The Lions had to board and disembark a couple of times before taking off from Heathrow, and for those who had never flown before, such as Welsh back row forward Russell Robins, already jangled nerves were stretched taut. More than 50 years later he recalled: 'I'd never been on a plane before in my life and was beginning to feel nervous about it.'

The journey via Switzerland, Italy, Egypt, Sudan, Kenya, and Uganda took 36 hours, but the Lions were at least able to stretch their legs while the Lockheed was refilled with fuel and that most important of cargoes: booze.

On the flight between Khartoum and Nairobi, the captain encountered difficulties with the aircraft, which was being dragged down at the tail and veering in flight. Leaving the cockpit, he went to the rear where he found 20 sizeable young men crammed into a space designed for half-a-dozen people. The Lions were having a party, and how were they to know about such things as 'trim' and weight distribution? Ernest Michie confirmed:

There was nobody else left on the plane but us by that time. We were all moving about chatting to each other and having a drink and I don't think

the captain could work out what was going on as the plane became a bit
unstable with the surge of bodies to and fro and back and forward. He
came back to see what was happening, and found that hardly anybody
was sitting in their own seats. He politely asked that, if it wasn't too
much trouble, could we sit in our seats now and again?

On arrival at Johannesburg in the middle of the night, the Lions were amazed to find a huge crowd waiting to greet them. 'I honestly think there were 10,000 people there to greet us,' said Jeeps. 'It was packed, and was the first time we realized what we were getting into.'

Cliff Morgan had anticipated a welcoming party, though not a crowd of that size, and had appointed himself choirmaster, helped by Tom Reid of Ireland. Under Morgan's tutelage, the Lions had learned the old Afrikaaner folk song 'Sarie Marais' with its jaunty chorus that translates into English as 'O take me back to the old Transvaal, where my Sarie lives, Down among the maize fields near the green thorn tree, there lives my Sarie Marais'. The Lions gave voice in Afrikaans and were an instant hit.

Meredith said: 'The people took us to their hearts, and decided we were the best ever touring side even before we played a game.'

As always, getting the men of five different nations to gel together was a crucial part of the tour. 'If truth were to be told,' said Ernest Michie, 'the Irish and the Scots seemed to get on very well, but there was a preponderance of Welsh players in the squad and they tended to keep to themselves a little bit.' Farmer Jeeps has a more pithy description: 'The Welsh stuck together like shit to a blanket, as we said plenty of times on that tour.'

Yet gel they did, helped by Siggins' decision to rotate room-mates every few weeks. In order to help that bonding process, the 1955 Lions also set out on their first public duty the day after they arrived – a supposedly leisurely round of golf. Once again, thousands of South Africans turned out to welcome the Lions, though what it did for their nerves on the first tee can only be guessed at.

The Lions soon found out just how different rugby was in South Africa. The forwards were dragged into the sort of physical encounters they had never experienced before, but usually won sufficient ball for the Lions' superior backs to show their paces. The sheer quality of the Lions' play entranced their South African hosts, who nevertheless did not stand back in admiration.

Hugh McLeod said: 'I loved the hard ground, but a lot of the guys didn't. There was no such thing as an easy game in South Africa, no matter who you were playing. They were big guys and always at you. But the harder the game, the more I liked it.'

On a tour again beset with injuries, Clem Thomas developed appendicitis, had the necessary operation, and was back playing within five weeks. Arthur Smith, the flying Scottish winger, was not so lucky, playing in only four matches after breaking a bone in his wrist – his turn would come seven years later.

Like Smith, the walking wounded were plentiful. The Rev. Robin Roe played matches at hooker with two cracked ribs. Reg Higgins tore ligaments in the first Test and missed half the tour, while Rhys Williams had two front teeth knocked out against the Orange Free State but played on as his incensed colleagues took their opponents apart with the best form of revenge, winning 31–3.

It was after that match that the Lions also took measures to protect themselves against 'cheap shots', as Thomas described them. 'It became necessary to have a fixer to stop such unprovoked attacks', wrote Thomas in the *History*. 'I was made the avenging angel. Tony O'Reilly would come up to me and say "number four" or whatever, and I was supposed to go in and mete out punishment at the next opportunity, preferably at a nice loose maul. I don't know how I got such a difficult job!'

The Lions were learning fast about the South African approach to rugby, and it soon became clear that, in the Tests, if the forwards could raise their game to match the Springbok pack, the backs could finish the job. South African rugby might well be of a different order to the home-grown variety, but it did not make it necessarily better.

The clash of cultures off the field was just as pronounced. Clem Thomas recalled being presented with the skin of a freshly shot leopard, and later on in the tour a farmer presented him with a lion cub. 'Siggins insisted on me donating it to a local zoo, which I did with some relief', wrote Thomas.

As Bryn Meredith put it, 'there's no point in going 7,000 miles and not seeing some of the country' and by the time they had finished the tour, the Lions had covered more than 10,000 miles within southern Africa, including Rhodesia. All are agreed that a two-day visit to Kruger Park, the national wildlife reserve and safari centre, was the highlight: 'Travel was a bit primitive, but Kruger Park was a wonderful experience – I've been back three times since,' said Dickie Jeeps.

It was early on in the tour that a certain player did a disappearing act, having fallen in love with a local girl. His name has never been revealed and, true to their ties of brotherhood, even 50-odd years later his identity is still kept a secret. Apparently he really was injured, but not as badly as was made out and the only disease he was suffering from was lovesickness. The Romeo went off with his Juliet and missed several games as a consequence. He did eventually return to the party, and the cover story of his 'injury' held not only then but still does. 'What went on tour stayed on tour, even though he went off tour,' as one 1955 Lion put it. 'Anyway, the rest of us were just jealous.'

Dickie Jeeps had not long been married to his first wife, Jean, but does not blame his touring for the fact that they eventually split up:

It wasn't the tour or anything that happened on it; it was me. I did meet a girl after the first Test in 1955 and it was all perfectly innocent. She liked dancing and I liked dancing, but nothing else happened. And would you believe it – the first time I went into the Mayfair Hotel in London after being selected for England, there she was, working as a receptionist.

The Lions lost their opening match to Western Transvaal 6–9, before a run of ten victories and another loss to Eastern Province took them to the first Test in Johannesburg. Ernest Michie recalls that the Test side was decided pretty much in advance, but there was competition to be named as a reserve.

'In those days you would be named as a reserve but would only play if a member of the Test team dropped out before the match, as there were still no substitutes or replacements allowed during the match,' said Michie.

There were four second row forwards in the squad and one of them was the tour captain, so that meant there were three of us going for one place. I was named as first reserve but never got to play, and it was the closest I ever came to making the Test team.

In any case, I got to 'play' in one sense, because I had taken my bagpipes with me on the tour and I played the team onto the pitch for that first Test.

The match has gone down in history as one of the greatest internationals ever played. The Lions won 23–22 in front of a world-record crowd of 95,000, plus at least another 10,000 who got in by dubious means. Dickie Jeeps recalled how one stand was given over to black South Africans, and they roared their support for the men in red rather than green.

Jeeps explained: 'Many of them had got in over some scaffolding and it was absolutely packed. I was told many years later that Nelson Mandela had been in among them. It was good to have their support.'

The manner of the victory was very pleasing, the Lions playing running rugby and coming from behind, while also playing the second half of the match with 14 men after Higgins retired injured. A brilliant try under the posts by Cliff Morgan saw the Lions forge ahead and further second-half tries by Jim Greenwood and O'Reilly put them 23–11 up, only for South Africa to draw within a point with a late try.

The Springboks goal kicker Jack van der Schyff stepped up to take the conversion which would decide the outcome: 'I remember we were all standing under the posts,' said Dickie Jeeps, 'just watching and waiting, while Billy Williams stood there with his hands together saying, "the Lord will keep this out, the Lord will keep this out"'.

Divine judgement or not, the conversion was missed, and the Lions had won a Test in South Africa for only the third time in the 20th century.

Danie Craven was the dictatorial coach of the Springboks and his reaction was one of fury at his side's complacency. He dropped five of the team including goal kicker Jack van der Schyff who had missed the late conversion – he never played for South Africa again. The Boks went all out for revenge and got it in some style, outclassing the Lions 25–9 in the second Test.

The third Test proved crucial to the success of the tour. Angus Cameron's injured knee caused him to be left out and replaced by Doug Baker, while Clem Thomas came in for his Lions Test debut. Captain Robin Thompson also missed the match through injury. His place was taken by Irish giant Tom Reid, who formed a partnership with Rhys Williams that proved crucial on the day.

In his *History*, Thomas related a bizarre event in training before the vital Test: 'Danie Craven, obsessed by the idea that the British press were spying on him, took his players off the field and, when they had gone, took them back again for a session under bright moonlight.' The press dubbed it 'the moonlight sonata'.

It did the Springboks no good. Inspired by new captain Morgan, in the heat of Pretoria, the Lions took on the South Africans up front and won the toughest exchanges of the tour. Rhys Williams and Reid dominated the line-out, and even though badly injured, Courtenay Meredith stayed on the field and contributed to the forwards' dominance. Meredith's tongue had been almost severed, but despite being in agony, he insisted on being stitched up to play on, and was later re-stitched in order to play in the final Test as well.

Bryn Meredith said: 'The Springboks are always big and physical, but we decided to take them on up front that day. It was one of the hardest matches I've ever played, but we had a good pack and good backs and we were determined to win.'

Jeeps commented: 'You had to put up with the hard tackles and the bad ones, but that was part of the game, and anyway, we were as hard as they were.'

The Lions had also decided to change tactics behind the scrum, kicking rather than running the ball, and as a result there were no fewer than 63 line-outs in the match. The switch worked, and though the victory was narrow at 9–6, it was nevertheless deserved, not least because Butterfield had scored the only try of the game. With Morgan in control of the match, even Danie Craven had to admit that his beloved Springboks had been second best on the day. According to Meredith there was 'one hell of a party' that night.

No matter what happened, the Lions could not lose the four-match series, but by then they were exhausted and injury-ridden. Cliff Morgan had picked up an ankle knock but such was his importance that he would have been selected with any injury short of an amputation. The position of the captain was less clear. Robin Thompson's fitness after injury was under considerable debate, but the man himself maintained he was fit enough to play, and later described it as 'just another Lions myth' that he had forced his way back into the team.

Shortly before his death in 2003, Thompson nailed the 'myth', saying:

> Before the final Test the selection team of manager Jack Siggins, vice-captain Angus Cameron, Cliff Morgan and myself sat down. I said that I was fit and would like to be included. There were no qualms, no raised eyebrows; the trio were in full agreement.
>
> But after the game I got some very bad press. They said I had forced my way onto the team even though I was still carrying an injury. Where all that came from I just do not know.

It was no surprise when a fired-up South Africa hit the tired Lions with everything plus the kitchen sink in that final Test in Port Elizabeth. Tony O'Reilly broke his shoulder scoring the second of the Lions' two tries – it was his 16th of the tour, a new Lions record – but these achievements were scant consolation as the Springboks ran in five tries of their own for a 22–9 victory that squared the series.

Only now has Ernest Michie revealed the 'hex' which may have afflicted the Lions that day:

> Cliff Morgan was very superstitious, and with us having won the first Test after I'd piped them on, he didn't want us to take the field without me playing the pipes. But I was rooming with Johnny Williams who was a bit of a prankster, and who couldn't resist trying to have a go at playing my pipes, which were all set up and ready to go. Unfortunately he knocked the reed out of the chanter so I couldn't play them and couldn't lead out the team in the last Test. I remember Cliff Morgan moaning 'we'll lose, we'll lose'.

The series may have ended in a draw, but it was a victory for the quality of the Lions in one respect. One South African commentator wrote that his country owed 'a manifold debt to the British Isles rugby touring team. They have rescued our rugby from becoming a matter merely of boot and brawn.'

As they had done on arrival, the Lions serenaded the large crowd that turned out to witness their departure. They left for home as one of the most popular touring parties ever to visit South Africa, their stylish play having entertained more than 750,000 spectators at their 25 games. To their amazement, on arriving in London after stopping off to play and beat an East African XV in Nairobi, the Lions were given a heroes' welcome. The players did not know that, back home, the press coverage had been devoured by the rugby community in Britain and Ireland, and that newsreels of their matches had been popular in the cinemas.

The 1955 Lions enjoyed varying degrees of success in their lives after the tour. Dickie Jeeps went on to make two more tours with the Lions and later became chairman of the Sports Council – as we will see in chapter ten.

Ernest Michie's international career was cut short by the diktat of the Scottish Rugby Union. He returned from the tour to National Service and then got a job with the Forestry Commission in Nottingham. While there, Michie turned out for Leicester, but the SRU had taken drastic action to counteract Scotland's poor form in the early 1950s and had insisted that only 'home-based' players or those playing for London Scottish would be considered for selection. Michie was summarily dropped – even selection for the Lions was no guarantee of success against the short-sightedness of the blazerati of those days. Michie went on to enjoy a long career in the Forestry Commission and he and his wife Sybil, a nurse he met before the 1955 tour and who waited patiently for him to return, now live in Inverness.

Rhys Williams beat Michie to that second row place in the 1955 Test side. He would tour again in 1959, and go on to become one of the most respected figures in the administration of Welsh rugby, as well as a top official in the principality's educational sector. But his connection to South Africa, minted in 1955, cost him dear. He would have become president of the WRU had he not visited South Africa as part of its board's centenary celebration in 1989. Instead, after controversy broke out about the visit, Williams resigned his national position. He died in 1993.

Tom Elliot and Hugh McLeod, of those great Borders rivals Gala and Hawick respectively, became lifelong friends. McLeod said 'He was a great guy, even if he was a pailmerk' (an affectionate derogatory name for a resident of Galashiels). They never made the Lions Test team together but starred for Scotland for several years, becoming famous for their pre-match wrestling 'warm up' routine. Elliot became one of Scotland's most respected farmers, and was awarded an MBE for his services to the industry. He died in 1998, while Hugh McLeod still lives in Hawick and is a stalwart of the town's club, where he was once president and for which he famously absented himself from his honeymoon to play for.

The Lions of 1955 have had diverse careers. Jim Greenwood captained Scotland to a revival in the late 1950s before becoming one of the most respected coaches in the northern hemisphere and passing on his expertise to several future Lions while working as a lecturer at Loughborough College. Frank Sykes, the England winger, emigrated to the USA where he had a long and distinguished career as a teacher, latterly at Cate School in California where he even managed to encourage pupils into the delights of rugby. He now lives in Washington State.

One Lion who caused great controversy was none other than the captain. Robin Thompson provoked anger and fierce debate when he signed in early 1956 for Warrington, where his brother was a doctor. As had happened with Lewis Jones in 1950, once again a Lion was ostracized from rugby union. Sadly for Thompson, his playing career was cut short by a bone disease at the age of just 25, and he also endured a heart attack in his early forties, followed by several more after that. Thompson nevertheless became a respected rugby pundit and was inducted into the Rugby Writers' Hall of Fame shortly before he died in 2003.

Other 1955 Lions have had to endure dire ill-health in later life. Cliff Morgan enjoyed a stellar career in broadcasting and became one of the best-known voices on television and radio, most memorably being the commentator for the legendary Barbarians versus All Blacks match in Cardiff in 1973. Behind the scenes, Morgan became head of sport at the BBC, while his vocal talents were always in demand on radio. Most cruelly, when he was afflicted with cancer some years ago, his treatment required the removal of his larynx, and that wonderful voice has been silenced. Yet he still maintains his interest in sport and his former colleagues from his home on the Isle of Wight.

'What has happened to Cliff has been terrible, simply awful, especially when you consider that speaking was his way of life,' said Dickie Jeeps. 'But he is still in touch with letters and cards, and they are always so well written.'

It is always tragic when a physically fit person succumbs to dementia, and that is what happened when Alzheimer's Disease afflicted one of the most popular of the 1955 Lions. Former England scrum-half John Williams was diagnosed with the disease at the age of 68, and his family have suffered a nightmare ever since.

His wife Mary went public with the details in a very moving 'first person' article in the *Daily Mail* in an attempt to show how victims of Alzheimer's are often misunderstood and mistreated. Mrs Williams, who herself has survived a double mastectomy for breast cancer, told how the man the 1955 Lions knew as fun-loving Johnny the prankster had become a violent, forgetful, moody individual who had regressed to childhood. He would hit her, and seconds later act as if nothing had happened. When her son from her first marriage, Jonathan, was killed in a motorcycle accident at the age of 41, Williams would try to understand but seemed incapable of sympathizing – a classic symptom of the disease. Eventually Mary could no longer care for him at home and he had to be hospitalized. She wrote:

> It's almost impossible to equate the ruggedly handsome, energetic sporting hero I fell in love with and the broken man who cannot even remember his own name. This kind, generous and good man is now held for his own safety in the secure unit of a hospital specializing in patients with mental illnesses.
>
> My husband, who is now 76, is incontinent and unable to feed or wash himself. The dementia has made him so aggressive towards me and others that for months he was detained under Section 3 of the Mental Health Act – an extreme law giving doctors the authority to hold and treat a patient.

The Williams family also faced a long and heartbreaking fight to get his care paid for, as was his right under the National Health Service rules. The Lions Trust stepped in with a £10,000 donation to help pay for his care, but Mrs Williams faced losing her home until legal pressure and the *Daily Mail* article helped force a change of heart on the part of officialdom.

John and Mary's son James Williams, who visits his father very regularly, confirmed the heartbreaking nature of the disease that has robbed the Lion of his mind:

> His mental health deteriorated much, much quicker than his physical health, though he has gone downhill physically in the last few months because he isn't getting enough exercise. I try and get him out and about, but it's difficult for the hospital as there's only so much time each patient can be allocated.

The whole thing has been very hard to bear, especially for my mother, and in truth it has been a nightmare for all of us. Not only have we had to deal with the emotional side of what has happened to my father, but we have also had a long fight with the bureaucracy, ever since he was sectioned in early 2007, over which part of the NHS was responsible for his care. It has been a strain financially and emotionally, but we did get help from the Lions Trust, which was very kind of them.

People like Dickie Jeeps and Tony O'Reilly have also been very helpful – the Lions look after their own, we've found.

Life goes on for the Williams family and for those Lions who have survived from 1955, many of them in quite remarkable shape considering they are now in their seventies and eighties. Yet as is evidenced by the tragic ill-health that has afflicted Cliff Morgan and John Williams, in the end even Lions are only human. But then, so are we all.

CHAPTER FIVE

RONNIE DAWSON'S PROUD SQUAD

Australia, New Zealand and Canada 1959

The 1959 tour Down Under is generally seen as one of the less success-ful Lions tours, but the margin between success and apparent failure was tiny, and the British and Irish players who took part in it, while acknowledging the Test series defeat in New Zealand, pointed out that the quality of their rugby was very high at times.

Not for the first or last time, a tour by the British and Irish Lions provoked heated controversy. Later tours would see the subject of profes-sionalism, player misbehaviour and, above all, apartheid cause the Lions great turmoil, but in 1959, the trouble was caused purely by rugby matters on the field.

The main problem arose in the first Test against New Zealand in Dunedin, halfway through the 35-match tour. Don Clarke, the almost metronomic goal kicker for the All Blacks, put the home side 6–0 up with two penalties in the opening quarter. Back came the Lions with a penalty of their own plus two unconverted tries. Leading 9–6 at half-time, the Lions notched two more tries, the second of which was converted.

Wingers Tony O'Reilly and Peter 'Nijinsky' Jackson of Coventry and England had scored a try each, while another two went to outside centre Malcolm Price of Wales, showing how superior the Lions were in the backs. Price's brace, incidentally, was only the second time a Lion had scored two tries in a match against New Zealand, following Carl Aarvold's double at Christchurch in 1930. More importantly, the 1959 Lions were 17–9 up, and heading for a famous victory.

Clarke proved their nemesis, however, banging over three more penalties, the clinching score coming just two minutes from full-time. According to Test scrum-half Dickie Jeeps, one of those three crucial penalty goals should never have been given: 'I used to stand just to the outside of the posts to watch the ball going over, and that kick wasn't just wide of the post, it was outside of me!' To be fair, Ken Scotland, who was at full-back for the Lions that day, said that Jeeps had 'exaggerated slightly', maintaining that he saw the kick actually go right over the top of the post – still not a score, however, as the law states that the ball must travel between the posts, though it remains a grey area to this day.

'Unless the television cameras are there or there's a fourth official with a video replay, the ones on top of posts tend to be given as the kicker gets the benefit of the doubt,' said an international referee, consulted on the issue especially for this book. 'Back then, however, with home referees and touch judges, anything going directly over a post would almost always be given.'

Ken Scotland said: 'It's splitting hairs whether it was a score or not, but by the time we neared the end, the crowd were shouting "Reds, Reds" because of the way we played. But they kicked their goals and we didn't. I will always remember the scene of desolation in the dressing room afterwards. We were all devastated.'

Bev Risman, fly-half for the Lions in that match, said:

You hate to say it but that referee was determined that we were not going to win. He became totally one-eyed, and we were shattered because if we had won, it would have meant that the outcome of the series would not have been decided until the last Test. It really did start a whole debate about neutral referees.

The Lions had 'won' by four tries to nil, yet the scoreline was 18–17 in favour of the All Blacks, thanks to Clarke's world-record six penalties. The headline in a New Zealand newspaper said 'LIONS 17, CLARKE 18', and there is no doubt that Big Don's kicking performance that day was sensational, especially with a heavy ball in soft conditions. The issues of 'homer' refereeing and unfair points' allocation for scores were duly emblazoned over the back pages of newspapers in every rugby-playing country in the world.

The performance of referee A.L. Fleury of Otago province caused a great deal of anger. He appeared overly sympathetic to his countrymen, and he was quietly dropped from the roster of international referees, never being given charge of another Test.

Syd Millar, the man from Ballymena who became a true legend of rugby with his involvement in nine Lions tours and his successful chairman-ship of the IRB, is in no doubt the referee cost the Lions that first Test:

I will remember him forever. When I was in Auckland for the Commonwealth Games in 1990, I went to an event in a bookshop where a large crowd had gathered because the man with the microphone was asking questions and if you answered one correctly you got a book. He asked difficult questions about rugby and cricket and other sports and eventually he asked 'Who was the referee when Don Clarke kicked six penalties and beat the Lions 18–17?' I shouted immediately 'Fleury!' He said, 'How the hell did you know that?' as he gave me a book about rugby. I declined to tell him why I will never forget the name of Mr Fleury.

For the first time, Dickie Jeeps has revealed that the 1959 tourists were so concerned about the refereeing on the tour that they introduced their own form of video review: 'If there was a doubt about something, we used to go to the pictures and watch the newsreels. But what happened with the Don Clarke penalty, the one that missed, was incredible – we went to the pictures to see the newsreel, but of all the kicks, they had edited that one out. I wonder why?'

For the first time in any serious way, discussions began about the introduction of neutral referees for internationals, but that revolutionary concept was still too far off and seemed ungentlemanly. Indeed, it would be almost 20 years before they were introduced, and the issue of neutrality still rears its head today – the Lions demand for neutral umpires in the provincial matches for the 2009 tour caused a row in late 2008.

What was definitely up for debate, however, was the fact that a team could score four tries yet lose a match to six penalties. It had been just 11 years since the value of a drop goal had been lowered from four points to three after a similar argument about the unfairness of kicked goals being given more weight than tries. Now the controversy began all over again, with the penalty as the focus.

The most famous writer on All Black rugby at that time, or indeed any time, was T.P. McLean, later knighted for his services to journalism. Sir Terry, as he would become, thundered that the Test had been 'a day of shame' for New Zealand rugby – a pronouncement that really kicked off the arguments: should a penalty be worth the same as a try? As Bev Risman remembered: 'Everybody wanted to have their say, and clearly even the New Zealand people felt it was unfair.' The debate would rage on throughout the 1960s, with that first Test always cited as a prime example of the injustice caused by the scoring system. Only in 1971 were the laws altered to make a try worth four points, increased again in 1992 to five points.

It was of no avail to the bitterly disappointed Lions as they trooped off that pitch in Dunedin. But the sporting manner in which they accepted defeat, as well as the excellent play of their back line in particular, had won them many friends in New Zealand and elsewhere.

The 1959 Lions included one man who had toured New Zealand nine years earlier, Malcolm Thomas, and six survivors of the 1955 tour to South Africa, namely Jeff Butterfield, Dickie Jeeps, Hugh McLeod, Bryn Meredith, Tony O'Reilly and Rhys Williams.

The manager was Alf Wilson, described by Hugh McLeod as 'a cantankerous old bugger' but by the more diplomatic Ken Scotland as 'a gruff military type'. Scotland added: 'I thought he and assistant manager Ossie Glasgow did a good job, especially with all the many duties they had.'

The Lions Committee's choice of captain was perhaps unfortunate in one respect. No one doubted Ronnie Dawson's playing ability or the Irishman's leadership qualities, which had been amply demonstrated for Ireland earlier that year, but, as a hooker, Dawson faced competition for his place from Bryn Meredith, then probably the best hooker in the world. That Meredith would be omitted from all the Tests came to be a considerable bone of contention, especially among Welsh Lions fans, and would eerily presage a similar argument 24 years later when Ireland's skipper Ciaran Fitzgerald was Lions captain and was played in preference to the outstanding Scottish hooker Colin Deans.

A devastating player in the loose, Meredith had scored six tries on the 1955 tour and was known for his ability to hook against the head and steal the opposition ball on their put-in: 'But that doesn't happen nowadays as they just chuck the ball straight to the back row anyway.' He may be less than enamoured of the modern game, but holds no grudges against Ronnie Dawson or the management on that tour:

I was one of the few players who didn't get to play in a Test on that tour, but I kept trying to compete for the place and having a go, and I think that's what you have to do in those situations. He was captain, and I said to myself if I was skipper, what would I do, and I know I would have done as he did.

As well as I played, I was virtually an also-ran, but you have to make the best of things and some of the midweek games I played in were some of the toughest matches on the tour, because the big games on the Saturdays always had a bit of form to them whereas the midweek matches was a bit like playing a side from the Valleys – always bloody hard work. They kept it tight and it wasn't orthodox football, I can tell you.

Meredith was also injured early in the tour, but whether or not he should have been the Test No. 2, Ronnie Dawson showed many remarkable abilities as captain, not least his devotion to improving the quality of training and coaching, about which we will learn more in chapter eight.

Ken Scotland said:

I thought Ronnie Dawson was absolutely outstanding in his leadership, and the training every day meant that we were all fit; as a result, I think I played the best rugby of my life. I also thought that senior players like Bryn Meredith, Malcolm Thomas and Jeff Butterfield, who had been a star in 1955 but suffered from injuries, all showed a tremendous example, because even though they didn't feature in the Tests as they would have wanted, they never complained and all mucked in.

Dawson was the fourth Irish captain of the Lions in a row, and he, Wilson and the senior players decided to go for a style of rugby that would make them hugely popular wherever they went – attack, attack, and attack. It proved to be exciting stuff, highly popular with the spectators, and led to a tour where all sorts of scoring records would be broken, with the Lions amassing 842 points in all, including a remarkable 165 tries scored. O'Reilly would help himself to 22 of those 3-pointers, while the brilliant Peter Jackson of Coventry and England scored 19 – the two wingers were the undoubted scoring stars of the tour, which speaks volumes for the attacking nature of the Lions' play. Jackson in particular is still remembered for his mazy, jinking runs. Scoring against Hawke's Bay, he beat so many men and covered so much of the pitch that reports tell of him beating at least one opponent twice on his way to scoring.

The 1959 tour was the highlight of the brief international rugby union career of fly-half Augustus Beverley Walter Risman, universally known as Bev. A geology student at Manchester University – 'I had to delay my finals for a year to go on the tour,' he said – Risman was the son of Gus, a legendary figure in rugby league and a proud Welshman. Bev recalled:

I had the choice to play for Wales or England, and it was difficult as my father was very much Welsh and I was Lancastrian born and bred. There was plenty of resentment in Wales when I made my decision – you could tell that by the way they said I was useless. The cartoons in the Welsh press were all about 'black sheep' and things like that. It all blew over eventually, though.

In Australia Risman suffered an early disappointment that again showed the crass snobbishness of rugby union when dealing with rugby league. He was invited by a rugby league club in Sydney to be guest of honour at a dinner celebrating the great career of his father, Gus, who was as much a hero to the Australians as to the British. Bev recalled:

Alf Wilson asserted his authority and said it would not be appropriate for me to attend a rugby league function. It was a big let-down, as my father had friends all over Australia who remembered him from his tour there in 1946 and who were in attendance.

It didn't stop me meeting my father's friends, however, and so many of them came to see me that Tony O'Reilly gave me the nickname Bev 'friends of my dad' Risman.

One of the most entertaining players on the tour was full-back 'Scotland of Scotland' as Ken Scotland was known, then a Cambridge University blue and later a stalwart of Heriot's FP. Scotland is often credited with revolutionizing full-back play by coming into the attacking line frequently but he remains as modest and unassuming as he was in 1959:

Most of my early career was at stand-off [fly-half] and I really came to full-back slightly by accident. I played three seasons at full-back at Cambridge and students had more time than anybody to experiment, so we developed the style of full-backs joining in attacks whereas previously they had usually been restricted to counter-attacking. It was novel at the time, but whether it was totally novel I can't say.

The timing of the tour was important for me. Had it been a year earlier I would not have gone as I wasn't in the Scottish team, and a year later it would have been very difficult as I would have been sitting my finals at Cambridge, so a lot of it was luck that the timing was right for me.

Finance also wasn't a problem for me because I was then a student and on tour we got ten shillings a day expenses, so I probably had more money on tour than I normally had. It was a terrific experience for me to play with all those great players, and I got to know them all well because we rotated rooms every time we moved and over the length of the tour, you more or less roomed with everybody in turn.

One man who did not change room-mates was Hugh 'The Abbot' McLeod, who had struck up a friendship with Rod Evans, the Welsh lock forward who suffered from a prevailing disease on those long tours – homesickness, which also afflicted Ray Prosser. 'It was a lot more common than you might think and Rod had not long been married and was missing home dreadfully,' said McLeod, who was noted for his impeccable behaviour on tour. 'He was so bad with it that I thought he was going to bale out, so the manager made sure we just stuck together and I think it helped.'

Others who would become great men of rugby were members of that Lions party. Syd Millar of Ballymena and Ireland, who would go on to play three tours in all as well as coach the Lions in 1974 and manage them in 1980, was one of the props. Millar is of course best known for his chairmanship of the International Rugby Board, from which he stood down when his term expired after the 2007 World Cup. Remarkably, one of the other 1955 Lions, Ken Smith of Kelso and Scotland, also went on to achieve high office, chairing the IRB.

Millar said:

My memories of the 1959 tour are that we played good rugby and we had a terrific team spirit. You have to remember in these days when 20,000 people can follow the team to Australia and New Zealand, and when they're talking about 50,000 going to South Africa, that we were very much on our own, and it was definitely an 'us against them' mentality which drew us all very close, no matter where in these islands we came from.

With ten men from Ireland, nine from both England and Wales, and five from Scotland, the 1959 Lions were also a good mix of youth and experience, with Bill Patterson, who was called up as a replacement, the only uncapped player, though he later did play for England. Gordon Waddell of Cambridge University and Scotland was on the tour to notch up a notable double, his father Herber having been a Lion in South Africa 25 years previously.

The first leg of the tour took the Lions to Australia. At the end of the exhausting four-day journey they made landfall in Darwin. The Harlequins and England lock forward David Marques stunned everyone on his arrival in Australia by disembarking from the aircraft in full city-gent morning suit, including rolled-up umbrella and bowler hat. One can only wonder if the Aussies got the joke.

On the pitch at last, the Lions lost to New South Wales – no disgrace as that state team contained many internationalists – but won their other two matches against Victoria and Queensland before Brisbane became the setting for the first of six Tests on the tour. The Lions comfortably beat Australia by 17–6, and added a 24–3 victory in the second Test, O'Reilly scoring tries in both matches.

The move to New Zealand saw the Lions lose just 2 provincial matches, to Otago and Canterbury, while they won the other 19. At Wanganui, Bev Risman was involved in an amazing incident that gave him the unwanted distinction of being the first player in international rugby to have his score chopped off by police intervention. Risman said:

I was lining up to kick at goal, but the touch judge 60 yards away had his flag up to indicate something. A police constable walked onto the pitch, but the referee told me to ignore him and take the kick, from which I scored. Only then did the referee decide that he had better speak to the constable, who pointed out to him that the touch judge had been standing for five minutes with his flag up. The ref then duly walked over and spoke to the touch judge – the two of them from New Zealand, of course – and the next thing was that the referee had disallowed the goal and was marching us 60 yards back to where the touch judge was standing. Fortunately we still managed to win 9–6.

The Tests proved a different story. As we have seen, the first Test was lost by the narrowest of margins, thanks to Don Clarke's boot, and in the second Test, which featured the first appearance against the Lions of the legendary Colin Meads, it was Clarke who again did the fatal damage to the Lions' hopes of a series win. With just a minute to go and the Lions leading 8–6, Clarke scored a try and converted it to give the All Blacks victory by 11–8.

Injuries were by now taking their toll – 'it was so bad they had to play me at hooker,' said McLeod, whose previous experience in the position was in the Hawick Sevens team. Bev Risman was also out with a broken ankle, his absence arguably being the worst loss to the Lions. 'I thought I would be on the plane home, but fortunately it was diagnosed as a chipped bone and I was able to stay.'

Big Don Clarke was at it again in the third Test, banging over a drop goal with his left foot at a crucial point in the match. Inspired by Meads, the All Blacks inched ahead before half-time before two late tries made the scoreline 22–8 for New Zealand.

The series was lost, but the Lions were proud men and in the fourth and final Test they threw everything at the All Blacks and tries by Jackson and O'Reilly put the Lions ahead. Bev Risman's return from injury was inspirational and he scored a superb solo effort, though he has now revealed the real reason for that piece of brilliance: fear.

'I saw this mass of All Blacks and I thought, "I'm not going into there", so I ran round the blindside and put my head back and just belted for the line,' said Risman. Two penalties by Clarke brought the score back to 9–6, a lead which the Lions held until late in the game. With victory in sight, the Lions conceded a penalty that was well within the range of their previous nemesis Clarke, scorer of 39 points against the Lions in the Tests to that point. But somehow Clarke's accuracy deserted him, and the Lions had won a Test in New Zealand for the first time since 1930.

I think it was probably the greatest example of team spirit I was ever involved in,' said Scotland.

It was wet and not the sort of day that suited us. Everybody was tired, we had lost the series, but we still managed to get it together to win the Test, and again it was by scoring tries to none.

They were proud and determined men, those guys, and it was all about being able to leave with our heads held high. Very few people beat the All Blacks in New Zealand and I still regard it as one of life's great triumphs.

For once, even the All Blacks were happy to concede defeat, so popular had the touring party become. No wonder, for they had played thrilling running and passing rugby throughout the long tour, scoring an average of 25 points per game.

There had also been a terrific social scene surrounding the Lions, with Tony O'Reilly always to the fore in the fun and games, along with fellow Irishman Andy Mulligan. 'They were both talented mimics,' recalled Ken Scotland, 'and they were very good at taking the mickey out of everybody. They would frequently get hold of the public address systems and keep everyone entertained with their impersonations.'

But in a disturbing omen that in years to come was to be realized, one newspaper reported on the merrily drunken activities of some Lions after a reception in New Zealand. It was case of 'tut tut, aren't they naughty' rather than a serious attempt to damage the tourists' reputation, and – unlike in later days of tabloid pack hunts – the rest of the press decided the matter was not worth probing, so the issue died. The players were, after all, amateurs who were not being paid for their efforts. 'They have earned the right to let their hair down', was how one commentator put it.

About the worst thing anyone could remember – or was willing to mention – was Dickie Jeeps being a bit boisterous in his cups. 'He flung a few oyster shells at the top table and I think he hit one of the presidents,' said Hugh McLeod. 'But it was all right, the shells were empty.' McLeod added: 'The hospitality was fabulous but the boys didn't go over the score. They were model tourists.'

'We didn't suffer from coverage of almost anything other than rugby,' said Ken Scotland. He and Syd Millar pointed out that the half-dozen journalists covering the tour would eat with the players and sit with them on buses: 'Now you need a fleet of buses to carry the media,' said Millar.

In keeping with the former missionary activities of the Lions, the 1959 party stopped off in Canada on the way home, being given a fright by British Columbia before winning 16–11 and then running riot against Eastern Canada, the 70–6 victory being the last and biggest of the tour.

It is worth pointing out that while the players and their fans were disappointed to lose the series in New Zealand, the close nature of the Tests against the All Blacks and the victories over Australia, as well as the generally outgoing conduct of all the players and the happy atmosphere within the party, led to the official report to the Lions Committee declaring that the 1959 tour was a success.

Looking back almost 50 years on, Dickie Jeeps is sanguine in his views: 'A lot of our players did not perform to their full strengths, in my opinion. We played some good rugby, but compared to the 1955 side, where we had such a good back line, I think we didn't have enough skills in all the positions. Were we robbed though of greater success by the refereeing? Yes, is my answer to that.'

Ken Scotland would have been an automatic choice for the 1962 tour, but work commitments meant he could not go. He latterly worked in Scottish heritage and conservation but is now retired and lives in Edinburgh with his wife Doreen, and occasionally plays a round of golf with Bev Risman. Scotland was reported on the deceased list by the *Daily Telegraph* in December 2008, but he quipped: 'Reports of my demise made interesting reading, especially to me.'

Risman played for England several times more before following his father into rugby league. To show the contrary nature of union's approach to league, Bev Risman received a 'good luck' letter from the then president of the RFU, who emphasized that he would always be welcome at Twickenham. 'But when I tried to go and visit pals at some clubs, the alickadoos would be over right away, telling me I wasn't welcome. It didn't stop me seeing my friends, though, and I made a point of deliberately being seen on both sides of the league–union divide.'

Risman was the first Englishman to be a Lion in both union and league – Jason Robinson was the second – and captained Great Britain in the 1968 Rugby League World Cup. A geology and PE teacher by profession, he also lectured at various universities and went on to become heavily involved in developing rugby league and then tennis in the south of England where his wife Ann, a school principal, chaired Berkshire County Council and was honoured by the Queen with an OBE.

Risman returned to New Zealand for the first time a few years ago and was 'nabbed' at customs for having an orange in his pocket. 'One of the customs officers spotted my passport and said "Risman, Lions, 1959? Remember that first Test when we beat you 18–0?" I said "It was 18–17 and we scored four tries and you got none." He looked at me and said "Right, pay your fine and get on." Memory can play tricks, can't it?'

Peter Jackson had a successful career in business and went on to serve his beloved Coventry in a variety of roles, eventually becoming club president and also secretary of the National Clubs Association. He died in 2004. That same year saw the death of Jeff Butterfield, the former teacher who went into business before opening the Rugby Club in Hallam Street, London, which he ran for 25 years.

No doubt the issues of that 1959 tour will be discussed at length over a small sherry or two if the surviving players meet up for a 'Golden Anniversary' during 2009. Ken Scotland said: 'I'm hoping that there will be a reunion of us all 50 years on, though I haven't heard anything official. We all got on remarkably well, and still do.'

Perhaps the 1959 example shows that not all Lions tours should be judged on the outcome of one Test series alone, especially one in which the tourists were essentially robbed of victory. The Lions did trounce Australia over two Tests and if a try had been worth four points instead of three, the Lions and the All Blacks would have squared the series. As it was, in two of the Tests the Lions were just one score behind the All Blacks. In the next tour, in terms of points the margin of loss in the series would be even smaller, but it did presage a decade of disappointment for the British and Irish Lions.

CHAPTER SIX

ARTHUR SMITH'S BIG BOYS DIDN'T CRY

South Africa 1962

Possibly because the 1950s had promised much, the 1960s were to be years of disappointment for the Lions, especially in New Zealand and South Africa. The 1962 tour to the latter country started a run of three successive tours without a victory against either the All Blacks or Springboks.

In that summer of 1962, no one could ignore the political situation in South Africa, which had just become a fully-fledged Republic with a constitution based on the apartheid system. There had been calls for the Lions not to tour, based, it should be said, on concerns for the players' safety in a country where revolution seemed imminent after the African National Congress, continuing its long campaign for freedom, had gone underground. Indeed, it was on the day after the third Test on 4 August that Nelson Mandela was arrested and charged with incitement to strike and with illegally leaving South Africa.

The Lions were thus deprived of a fan. It is often thought that Mandela developed his interest in rugby only after he became President, but no one could have used the sport's popularity in South Africa as assiduously as the great man did without knowing a little about the game. As we learned in chapter four, Mandela stood cheering on the Lions when they won the first Test in Johannesburg in 1955.

That support from black and coloured people was one reason why the 1962 tourists could not ignore what was going on around them, but, as in 1955, they had been well warned to keep their views to themselves. The efficient management of naval officer Brian Vaughan and the captaincy of a quiet and dignified Scotsman, Arthur Smith, helped keep the Lions out of the political news.

Though he had missed out on the 1959 tour, Smith of Edinburgh Wanderers and Scotland had been hailed as a potential star for the Lions after his terrific performances in the dark blue of Scotland while still a student. In his very first match against Wales in 1955, which was Scotland's first victory in 17 internationals, he scored a try so memorable that the game was referred to afterwards as 'Arthur Smith's match'. The son of a Galloway farmer, Smith went on to play a total of 33 consecutive games for Scotland, making the No. 14 jersey his own.

A true all-rounder, Smith was a champion sprinter and long jumper as well as academically brilliant – he gained a First in mathematics at Glasgow University before adding a PhD at Cambridge. Picked for the Lions in 1955, his broken wrist meant he played just four matches on the tour, the last of them in the 'homeward' match against an East African select in Nairobi. He spent his convalescence practising his place-kicking and in that final match in Kenya he ran in five tries.

After missing out on the 1959 tour, Smith led Scotland in the first major overseas tour by a home union when they visited South Africa the following year. Having been trounced 44–0 by the Springboks just a few years previously, the Scots did much better in the only Test, losing 10–18, with Smith scoring 8 of the Scottish points. Modest and unassuming, but with a rare intelligence, Smith was a popular choice as captain of the Lions, and made it clear that he would bow out of international rugby after the tour as he had secured what he considered to be the ultimate honour in the sport.

The problem for the Flying Scotsman was that the Lions' selection committee, not for the first or last time, had saddled the captain and manager with players who would play a completely different sort of game to the running one that Smith and the Lions normally favoured. In short, he was going to be lucky to see the ball in the Tests, because the selectors had picked a huge pack whose mobility would obviously be limited. The selectors' decision was understandable, because South Africa had toured to the northern hemisphere in 1961 with giants in their pack and had won every match except the final game against the Barbarians. In that match, the Baa-Baas set aside their normal free-flowing style and took on the Springboks up front in a forward battle which, to most people's surprise, South Africa lost. It was easy to see why the selectors were influenced to go for bulk and brawn.

Tour manager Vaughan would come in for criticism for the 'un-Lionish' tactics, even though these were forced upon him by the selection. In every other way he was much respected by the Lions and their opponents. Vaughan was joined on the tour by an assistant manager, Harry McKibbin, the Irish internationalist who had toured with the Lions in South Africa in 1938.

Among the players were several men who would become legends in rugby, most notably Willie John McBride, then just 22. He would go on to play on five Lions tours and set a record of 17 appearances in Tests, before returning to manage the Lions in 1983. His *annus mirabilis* was 1974, and we learn much more about this great man and the historic tour of that year in chapter ten.

It says everything about McBride that he defied a recently broken leg and medical advice to make his first tour in 1962. Playing against France on 14 April, he had been kicked by prop forward Amedee Domenech but, unwilling to leave Ireland with 14 men, he played on despite being in excruciating agony. It was only after the match that McBride discovered he had played nearly 30 minutes with a badly broken leg. He was in a plaster cast when told he had been selected for the Lions who were leaving for South Africa in a little over a month's time. McBride recalls:

> Most people told me I wouldn't be able to go, but I was determined. We all had to produce a medical form signed by a doctor to say we were fit to travel. I went down to see my GP and told him 'Doc, you have to sign this.' He did so, and the last thing I said to him was 'I won't let you down.'
>
> They took the plaster off four days before we were due to meet up in Eastbourne, and it had wasted away to skin and bone, but I knew we had a few weeks before we had to play and I was sure I could build it up.

Welsh hooker Bryn Meredith remembered his first meeting with Willie John McBride:

> He was on his first tour and we were down to share a room in Eastbourne where we all gathered before leaving for South Africa. I was in the bedroom when in came this chap on crutches. He was a big raw-boned youngster that I'd never met before so I said to him 'they must think a lot of you if they picked you with a broken ankle or leg', and do you know, they were right!

A fellow Ballymena player, Syd Millar, was in the Lions party again, and this time at least he would not lose out financially:

> In 1959 I got half-pay but by '62 I had changed jobs and was with Shell who gave me full pay while I was on tour both in '62 and '68, and I was very grateful to them for that. In those days people had jobs and you

*maybe trained two or three times a week at most, and to be able to tour
and get full-time training and work at the game for months was a huge
bonus.*

*I was also just thankful to have the chance to tour with the best
players and to play against the best in South Africa, who at that time
were the best in the world. Many of us had played against them when
they toured in 1961, and we had made contacts, so that while the games
were tough, very tough, we were happy to mix and mingle with them
afterwards.*

Bryn Meredith was making his third tour with the Lions, and Welsh tight-
head Kingsley Jones made up a formidable front row alongside him and
Millar. That Jones was in South Africa at all was testament to his courage,
as the player had suffered a serious spinal injury the previous year and
had only recovered in time to make the Welsh side against France in the
1962 Five Nations.

Behind them in the Test side at first were Keith Rowlands and Bill Mulcahy, with McBride coming in for the final two Tests after his outstanding play in a midweek match made him a player the selectors could not
ignore, even with his relative inexperience. Meredith played all four Tests,
though modestly he pointed out that the best other candidate for the position, England's Stan Hodgson, broke his leg in the first match of the tour.
It was a double break, tibia and fibula, and Hodgson's Lions career was
over. Showing great sympathy, the South African union offered Hodgson the opportunity to stay and convalesce. Knowing, however, that a
replacement could only come out to South Africa if he went home, the
Durham player insisted on being repatriated to allow Bert Godwin to take
his place.

H.O. Godwin therefore joined the party, having declined his original
selection because he could not afford the time off work. His initials are
an interesting story in themselves. Welsh-born Herbert was a down-to-

earth working man, a toolmaker and later a foreman at the Massey-Ferguson factory in Coventry for whose city club he was playing when he was selected for the first of his 11 caps for England. Observing that every other player in the English team had at least two initials whereas he, having no middle name, was listed as just H. Godwin, his fellow Coventry players suggested adding a second initial, and they plumped for an imaginary 'O'. Too late Godwin realized what his new initials spelled, and he remained H.O. Godwin for the rest of his international career.

Rugby nicknames tend to stick to you forever. Derek Prior Rogers, always known as Budge, was another player like Sid Millar who would make his name as an internationalist and administrator – he was honoured by the Queen with an OBE for his services to rugby.

Keith Rowlands of Cardiff and Wales was the most mobile of the Lions pack and he, too, went on to be a leading figure in the sport, appointed in 1987 as the first permanent secretary of the International Rugby Board. He and McBride clashed on that tour, largely because the young Irishman had no hesitation in telling Rowlands that he was out to get his Test place. 'That's what I was like back then,' said McBride.

Another Lions legend making his debut in 1962 was the great Irish fullback Tom Kiernan, about whom we will learn more in chapter eight.

The pack included a giant of a man, army captain Mike Campbell-Lamerton. At nearly 6ft 5in and weighing 17st 8lb in his socks, the Scottish internationalist was selected as a lock forward but was transformed on the tour into a more than useful No. 8. His son, Jeremy, would follow him into a Scotland shirt in 1986. Campbell-Lamerton would return as captain for the 1966 tour, but for Welsh flanker Haydn Morgan, who would later go on to coach London Welsh, the 1962 tour was his second and final Lions outing.

Another serviceman on the tour was Royal Marine Commando Richard Sharp, a brilliantly dashing fly-half who was expected to be the lynchpin of the Lions attacks. His main rival for the No. 10 shirt was

Gordon Waddell, who completed a then unique father–son double by following in his father Herbert's footsteps, both playing as Lions in South Africa. Waddell often played at centre on the tour alongside another fly-half turned centre, Mike Weston. Both were strong kickers, and that was to be another crucial element of the Lions' tactics in 1962.

Dickie Jeeps was making his third tour, and is candid in his view that the 1962 squad was simply not as good as the 1955 contingent, but is also adamant that the Lions' management was woefully under-prepared:

> It happened on all three tours but particularly in 1962 when no one appeared to have done any research on the opposition. People thought they knew about the Springboks because of their tour the previous year, but we didn't really know that much about them or any of the provincial sides at all. We hadn't sent anybody out to check out Rhodesia or the Transvaal, and there were certain games which were a lot easier than we thought they would be, and a lot which turned out to be much harder. If somebody had done any research it would have been so much better for us.

Injuries would once again take their toll. Apart from Hodgson's leg-break, several key players were injured early, most notably Dewi Bebb, the winger of Swansea and Wales who had been timed at 9.9 seconds for the 100 yards and was expected to flourish on the hard South Africa ground. Another Welshman, David Nash, contracted a blood infection and also had to return home. Ireland's David Hewitt pulled a hamstring, which took weeks to mend.

Nevertheless, the Lions were able to play to their more traditional running style in the provincial matches, and indeed opened the tour with a 38–9 victory over Rhodesia. They would lose just two of the non-international matches, against Northern Transvaal and Eastern Transvaal.

In the Tests, however, the Lions' forwards packed down to grind out a war of attrition against their Springbok opponents. It was not pretty, but it almost worked, especially in the first Test in Johannesburg – a drab affair that ended in a 3–3 draw and was enlightened only by two fine tries, the Lions' equalizer coming from Ken Jones's 60-yard dash. Arthur Smith's conversion attempt failed, but at least the Lions were not behind in the four-match series.

After the second Test in Durban they were indeed behind, but in a highly controversial manner. Another dire forward battle saw no scoring until five minutes from time when the Springboks went 3–0 up thanks to a penalty by Keith Oxlee. As the Lions threw everything at the Springboks, they won a scrum in the final minute right on the South African try line. In a rehearsed move, Bill Mulcahy called for the Lions to wheel the scrum and Keith Rowlands dived to claim the 'try'. But the South African referee, Ken Carlson, did not award the score, saying he was unsighted. For once, the Lions complained long and loud about the refereeing, as they had been robbed of at least a draw.

'We should have won that Test,' said Syd Millar. 'I have no doubt that we scored that pushover try and in the end that was the difference. It was very controversial at the time, and it stuck in my memory. I was able to do something about it though in 1974 when I coached the Lions in South Africa.' As we shall see …

It was the second major controversy of the tour, the first coming after Springbok back François du Toit 'Mannetjies' Roux had inflicted a fractured cheekbone on Richard Sharp with a high tackle in the loss against Northern Transvaal. The victim himself may not have complained but the Lions' management and the press, including the South African newspapers, had been withering in their criticism of Roux and it was expected in some quarters that he would be left out of the Test side as a punishment. The selectors, however, ignored the calls, and it was Roux who started the move that gave the Springboks their try.

Dickie Jeeps said: 'There were a lot of incidents like that in South Africa, but that was the worst. We showed, though, that we were prepared to stand up for ourselves and fight fire with fire when necessary.'

Perhaps the most extraordinary example of bravery in the face of physical intimidation came from flanker Glyn Davidge of Newport and Wales who had joined the tour as a replacement when many felt he should have been a first choice. Playing against the tough men of the Orange Free State, Davidge was stretchered off three times with a recurring back injury, but each time the former star of the British Army team insisted on returning to the field and saw out the match despite being in great pain.

The clamour to see the third Test in Cape Town saw an estimated 5,000 people locked out of the Newlands ground into which a record 55,000 crowd had crammed. It was Willie John McBride's Test debut and his main recollection is of how nervous he was before the start. He also had an amusing encounter with giant Springbok prop Mof Myburgh. McBride tried to strike up a conversation about the lack of grass on the pitch. 'I didn't come here to * * * *ing graze' was Myburgh's focused reply.

In what was becoming a familiar routine, both packs hammered away at each other, and while the Lions unusually dominated the set play, the Springboks were superior in the loose. Sharp was back from his injury and scored the opener with a drop goal, but South Africa soon equalized with a penalty by Oxlee. Eight minutes from time, the Lions won a scrum against the head deep in their own territory, and Sharp took the risk of running the ball. The brave attempt failed, however, and when the ball went loose, Oxlee pounced for a try, which he converted himself to put South Africa 8–3 up. The Springboks had won the match and the series with those late scores that also brought up their first 1,000-point mark in Test rugby.

The fourth Test in Bloemfontein was an anti-climax, the Lions going down fighting but ultimately well beaten by 34–14. For men like McBride, Millar, Kiernan, Welsh flyers Dewi Bebb and Ken Jones, Mike Weston, flank forward Alun Pask, and Campbell-Lamerton, that 1962 tour had been painful but was also a learning experience which they would find useful on future Lions tours.

Syd Millar's verdict on the 1962 tour is that the injuries to key backs like Richard Sharp did the most damage:

In 1959 the difference between the Lions and the All Blacks had been Don Clarke's boot. In 1962, it was also a very close series; we had good forwards but we lost Sharp and others in the backs and that determined the way we played afterwards. It was not to our advantage, I would say. The Springbok backs turned out to be more adventurous than ours, and that was not what you would have expected.

Meredith summed up his judgement of his third tour:

I don't think the 1962 side was particularly good, and certainly not as good as the 1955 team. We had some good forwards and a couple of good backs, but it wasn't a side that stamped its authority at all. You have got to have a couple of really hard forwards who take some responsibility when they go on the field, and we didn't have that in 1962.

For Meredith, his time with the Lions was over, but Millar would make a surprise return in the next-but-one tour before switching to coaching and achieving his greatest feats in 1974.

Their front row partner Kingsley Jones returned home to play for Cardiff and Wales but his career was cut short at the age of 29, just when most props reach their peak, after being seriously injured against the All Blacks. Jones took over the family fruit-wholesaling business and died in 2003.

Others from that tour did not enjoy longevity, either in rugby or life itself. The captain, Arthur Smith, stuck to his word and retired from international rugby at the summit of his career. He died tragically early of cancer in 1975 at the age of just 42. Scottish rugby, the Lions and their fans, and many people in South Africa all mourned his loss.

Gordon Waddell did not play in another international. On that tour to South Africa, he met his future wife, Mary Oppenheimer, daughter of mining magnate Harry, one of the country's richest men and a critic of the apartheid system. Waddell went on to a long and distinguished career in business and also served as a Progressive Party MP in the South African Parliament. He remarried after divorce and now divides his time between homes in the Scottish borders and London.

Bryn Meredith had a varied career after his playing days. After teaching and a spell as a sales rep, latterly he did some after-dinner speaking, but now lives quietly in retirement in Usk.

'I still go to the internationals,' he said, 'but the team I watch most nowadays is my village club because they play for the sheer joy of playing, just as we did back in the 1950s and 1960s.'

His life could have been entirely different, for Meredith was also approached to sign up for rugby league:

I was offered terms to go north, around £2,500 at first, and though it doesn't compare to the sums the players get nowadays, it was enough to buy a house in those days. But I turned it down – I must have been a bloody fool!

The fact is that switching to rugby league just didn't appeal to me. It's a good game to watch, but back then I always thought it was sort of dirty, though I know now it was as clean as rugby union. I just thought that if you were playing for money, then sport would go out of the window. I also knew I would be losing a lot of friends, because even if you spoke to a rugby league scout back then you were kicked out of union, so I've no regrets about my decision.

Being a Lion did not make Meredith a celebrity:

> *The big difference between then and now is television. We could stay*
> *pretty anonymous, but these days everything is captured on camera and*
> *in close-up and everyone sees it right away, whereas even when the*
> *cameras started covering our games they were a hundred yards away and*
> *people only saw them in newsreels.*
>
> *Nobody recognized you, and when I became a sales rep it didn't make*
> *the slightest bit of difference – unless I met a rugby fan, I was just*
> *another guy.*

Times would change for the Lions, as we shall see.

Both Stan Hodgson and Mike Weston are well and living in Durham. The former still runs miles every week, while the latter, like so many rugby players in old age, has had replacement joints fitted.

Bert Godwin retired from playing in 1968 after making 250 appearances for Coventry. He later ran a guest house in Teignmouth, Devon. He died, aged 70, in 2006. Glyn Davidge, the iron man who refused to leave the field despite being in agony, also passed away that year at the age of 72.

The assistant manager on that 1962 tour, Harry McKibbin, a solicitor who reached the rank of major in the wartime Royal Artillery after playing for the 1938 Lions, became president of the IRFU – as did his brother and fellow Irish internationalist Des, to make a unique double. Harry McKibbin also became chairman of the IRB, on whose committee he served for 20 years, while two of his sons, Harry Jr and Alistair, were capped for Ireland. Honoured by the Queen with a CBE for services to rugby union, Harry McKibbin died in 2001.

None of these Lions will ever be forgotten, but perhaps the strangest sort of immortality ever to befall a Lion came to Richard Sharp, who now lives in Cornwall. In 1980, a writer with a similar name to the county,

Bernard Cornwell, was looking to name a character he had created for a novel – a handsome swashbuckling soldier. 'I wasted hours trying to find my hero's name,' Cornwell once told the Sharpe Appreciation Society.

> *I wanted a name as dramatic as Horatio Hornblower, but I couldn't think of one (Trumpetwhistler? Cornetpuffer?) so eventually I decided to give him a temporary name and, once I had found his real name, I would simply go back and change it. So I named him after Richard Sharp, the great rugby player, and of course the name stuck. I added an 'e', that was all.*

Cornwell also knew everything about his rugby hero and how he had been injured by Mannetjies Roux. In one of his novels about Richard Sharpe's adventures fighting the French in the Napoleonic Wars, one of Sharpe's more unpleasant opponents meets a particularly nasty demise. The name of the dastard done most cruelly to death is Colonel Leroux.

Not many Lions get revenge taken in their name by a fine writer such as Cornwell. Mostly they have to do their retaliation on the field, but in the 1960s the Lions had yet to realize that the most effective form of 'retaliation' is the type you get in first. Hard lessons remained to be learned.

CHAPTER SEVEN

MIKE CAMPBELL-LAMERTON AND HOW THE LIONS WERE MAULED

Australia, New Zealand and Canada 1966

The refereeing controversy that had marred the second Test in South Africa in 1962 came down to the question of whether 'home' referees could be trusted to be neutral in their judgements. On the Lions next tour four years later, at least in the New Zealand leg, questions were again raised about referees but much, much more so against the actions of the home players themselves. The All Blacks largely played within the laws, but the provincial players took tough tactics to the limit, and some would say they went well beyond legality, judging by the type of injuries sustained by the tourists – broken noses and fingers, bruises from punches, stitches to heads and bodies from stamping in rucks.

The word 'legend' is used about quite a few of the people in this book, but in the case of Jim Telfer, captain and coach of Scotland and his beloved Melrose, there is no other description. He is in no doubt that provincial sides were sent out with one mission in mind: 'To soften up the Lions.' Telfer said: 'When you got to play against the All Blacks, they were quite clean matches, but all the district teams just wanted to try and prove we were a bunch of softies. It was very intimidating stuff.'

Even before the tour started, there was a serious row over the selection of the captain. Mike Campbell-Lamerton was indeed a captain, having served in that rank in the army with distinction on active service in Korea, Kenya and elsewhere. No one could doubt his bravery and durability – he once stepped on a land-mine and, realizing just in time what he had done, stayed motionless until a bomb disposal expert defused it. On another occasion he fell 60ft from a helicopter and sustained injuries that would have ended the sporting career of many a man, only to return to play for Scotland and the Lions again.

Campbell-Lamerton had been one of the few successes in the forwards in the 1962 tour to South Africa, where his sheer bulk and courage under fire, plus his height in the line-out, made him a valuable asset in matches where the Springbok heavy guns were brought to bear. Starting off in the second row, the selectors had moved him to No. 8, and he had grown into the role by the time the tour was over. Yet Campbell-Lamerton himself knew that he was limited in his rugby skills – and his lack of speed, particularly at the vital breakdown, was a sore point. He was also at the veteran stage, celebrating his 33rd birthday on tour. Furthermore, although he was a fine military officer, he was a likeable and decent man who lacked authority in rugby terms.

'He was a nice man, and I think he was chosen because officers were supposed to be born leaders,' said Telfer.

But that isn't always the case. In fact he was no longer even captain of Scotland at that point, Stewart Wilson having taken on the job. There were doubts about his tactical nous and his ability to even get into the team, as Mike was not the best in his position in the squad. I was asked to give my view at a selection committee and I said 'Mike, I think you will have to drop yourself', which allowed Willie John McBride and Delwe Thomas to play together in the second Test in New Zealand, and they did very well.

Campbell-Lamerton was often on his own, too. 'In those days, the tourists' captain did not get the full panoply of support that they get nowadays,' said Campbell-Lamerton's son Jeremy, who was to play for Scotland three times himself.

As well as all the political bit, meeting and greeting, and the speech-making, the captain had to be the leader on the field, as well as play his own game, and in my father's case, do some of the coaching as well. With a team of only three of them to manage a tour that lasted all of five months, it is a wonder that he coped at all.

Alun Pask, by contrast to Campbell-Lamerton, was a dynamic flanker who had just captained Wales to the Triple Crown and Five Nations Championship. He had a habit – annoying to the purists but endearing him to the fans – of running with the ball clasped in one massive hand, using the other great paw to break tackles or push away opponents. He scored more than his fair share of tries, too, often with a swan-diving flourish. On one occasion with Wales, when full-back John Dawes went off the field for attention to injury, Pask took over the role and did so with aplomb, so comprehensive were his rugby skills.

'Alun Pask should have got the job,' said Colin McFadyean of Moseley and England, who made his single Lions tour in 1966. 'They had picked 12 Welshmen, however, and perhaps they were afraid of overwhelming domination by the men from Wales.'

The selectors had gone with the Scot, but Pask was effectively a vice-captain, and he was vocal in his support for Campbell-Lamerton. The captain would need it, as he became the target for a particularly vicious whispering campaign which the New Zealand press both fed off and encouraged.

Manager Des O'Brien, who had somehow managed to play rugby for Ireland and hockey for Wales, tried his best to keep a lid on things, but the odds were against him, for he, too, was basically a man who didn't appreciate that a manager has to be ruthless and hard. He had also been given an assistant, John Robins, who was charged with coaching the squad – the first official coach to be appointed by the Lions.

The problem for Robins was that proper demarcation lines had not been laid down, and neither he nor Campbell-Lamerton nor O'Brien could agree on who was to do what. No one really knows what happened between the three men, and not even Campbell-Lamerton's son Jeremy, has a clue: 'My father really was an old-fashioned honourable gent, and he would never complain about anything like that, especially not to his children. Even if wronged, he would never complain, and I think that is the mark of the man.'

For his part, Robins would always tell one of his close friends, 'I'll tell you some day', but that friend swears he never did. But the fall-out affected relationships on the tour, and Robins eventually played a secondary part, largely because he sustained a serious injury early in the New Zealand leg of the tour, as Jim Telfer recalled: 'He was refereeing a bounce game when he damaged his Achilles' tendon quite badly. It was a pity, as he was a good coach and the players then had to take over the coaching.' Colin McFadyean, of Moseley and England, also remembered the occasion:

It was a light-hearted game in which the manager Des O'Brien took part. I remember John [Robbins], to whom I was close because I was a student at Loughborough where he taught, getting injured and having to go off to hospital. I also remember it because at half-time the locals whipped on a former All Black full-back, Bob Scott, and he gave an exhibition of goal

kicking, banging those old heavy leather balls over from halfway –
nothing special, you might say, except that he was barefoot!

Des O'Brien's personal tale of woe, related to the authors at various times in later life, is highly illuminating about the pressures the men behind the scenes suffer on Lions tours.

'I felt under pressure almost from the start,' said O'Brien some years ago.

It was fine in Australia when we were winning, but as the tour progressed, things began to go wrong and we were losing matches, so consequently the criticism piled up, and while I could handle that, it was just the relentless nature of things which upset me. I really wasn't my normal self.

It was a great honour to be asked to manage the Lions, but I rather let things get to me and at one point I actually feared for my sanity and wondered if my wife would recognize me as the same person when I got home – that's if I got home.

He need not have worried on his wife's score, as Ann O'Brien, in her own words, 'just got on with things'. As a young mother of four children – a fifth arrived later – on a smallholding near Oxford, she was kept 'very, very busy' but always took an interest in her husband's rugby career. She remains a bright and vivacious lady and backs up her husband's account of those difficult days more than 40 years ago, as well as giving shrewd assessments of players past and present: 'Jonny Wilkinson seems too intense, you know,' she opined.

O'Brien recalled:

A stroll in the park? Led by Dr Ronald Cove-Smith, the 1924 Lions are piped onto the field in Johannesburg for the second Test against South Africa. They lost 17–0.

The 1924 Lions lost 16–9 in the final Test in Cape Town.

The 1930 Lions line up for the third Test against New Zealand in Auckland. The All Blacks won 15–10.

BRITISH ISLES RUGBY UNION TOUR 1950

Frank Thompson, Crown Studios, Wellington, Photo copyright.

Back Row—
G. M. Budge J. D. Robins R. Macdonald J. S. McCarthy M. F. Lane D. M. Davies V. G. Roberts M. C. Thomas T. Clifford
Second Row—
D. W. C. Smith G. W. Norton J. E. Nelson D. J. Hayward J. R. G. Stevens E. R. John R. T. Evans J. W. McKay N. J. Henderson K. J. Jones
Sitting—
W. B. Cleaver P. W. Kininmonth B. L. Williams (vice-captain) Surgeon Captain (D) L. B. Osborne, R.N. (hon. manager).
K. D. Mullen (captain) E. L. Savage (secretary) I. Preece C. Davies J. Matthews
In Front— A. W. Black J. W. Kyle W. R. Willis G. Rimmer

ATHLETIC PARK, WELLINGTON

The 1950 Lions pictured in a souvenir programme for the third Test in Wellington on 1 July. The Lions lost the match 6–3.

The 1959 Lions on the charge, led by Ken Scotland.

1959 Lions tour third Test programme.

THIRD TEST

BRITISH ISLES

NEW ZEALAND

LANCASTER PARK, SATURDAY AUGUST 29, 1959
OFFICIAL PROGRAMME   ONE SHILLING

Top left. The 1959 pack in the line-out against the All Blacks, featuring Hugh McLeod (left) and Rhys Williams.

Top right. Lion Alun Pask scores against Western Provinces during the 1962 tour.

Above. Des O'Brien, manager of the 1966 tour. He wrote the most damning tour report of all, which was suppressed.

Right. Barry John in action in 1971 against the All Blacks.

The great Gareth Edwards in training for the 1971 tour.

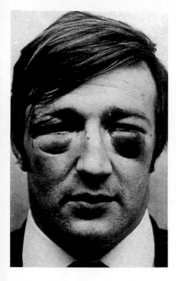

Wounded Lion. Sandy Carmichael's injuries after the Battle of Canterbury in 1971.

Former Prime Minister and leader of the Conservative Party, Ted Heath, came to meet the 1974 Lions. Gordon Brown, Willie John McBride, a real live lion cub and a stuffed Springbok get in on the act.

They said he couldn't kick. J.P.R. Williams, the legendary Welsh full-back, in clearance action during the 1974 tour of South Africa.

Fergus Slattery relaxes in 1974. He wasn't relaxed for long when Willie John McBride discovered his pipe was missing.

The magnificent Lions pack of 1974.

Mike Gibson of the British Lions is tackled during a tour match against the Maoris in Auckland in 1977.

Andy Irvine chased by the All Blacks in the second Test in 1977.

One of the most famous rugby pictures of them all – Fran Cotton gains immortality in the mud during the Lions' match against the Junior All Blacks in Wellington in 1977. The Lions won 19–9. The kit-man wept.

Bill Beaumont on the charge for the 1977 Lions.

Springbokke
British Lions
TWEEDE TOETS   SECOND TEST
Stadion/Stadium, Bloemfontein   14/6/80

The programme cover
for the second Test in
1980, featuring captains
Bill Beaumont and Morne
du Plessis. South Africa
won 26–19.

Reading all about it. J.J. Williams and Steve Fenwick on
the morning after the 13–9 defeat by the All Blacks in the
second Test of 1977.

*Eventually in the middle of the New Zealand part of the tour, I just had
to get away, and as I had been asked by the Home Unions Committee to
check out the state of the game elsewhere in the Pacific, the New Zealand
Union arranged for me to visit Fiji. I was away for over a week, and in all
honesty, it was the best thing I could have done because I don't know if I
could have carried on.*

Ann heard of her husband's misgivings at the time:

*He did enjoy himself at times but often found it very trying. It was the
last long tour by the Lions, and he was away for almost six months in all.
If they had stopped after the Australian part of the tour it would have
been fine, but when they got to New Zealand and all these injuries started
to happen, he really felt hard pressed. Our plan had been to telephone
each other once a month – it seems laughable now with mobile
telephones – but we ended up speaking once a week as the problems
began.*

O'Brien did have experience of being in charge on tour, having skippered
Ireland in Argentina some 14 years previously: 'They arrived there on
the day that Eva Peron died, so they all had to wear black armbands and
then they were sent off to Chile until after the funeral,' said Ann.

O'Brien did not appreciate the pettifogging officialdom he encountered when he came up against the home union officials, who were hide-
bound by tradition and their sacred oath of amateurism – 'I practically
had to beg the Committee to sanction an extra pair of grey flannels for
the players,' he once said, 'and even then they had to hand them back at
the end of the tour.'

Over the course of the tour, no one could deny O'Brien or Campbell-
Lamerton's appetite for work, however. The task of liaising with the media
and making pre- and post-match speeches as well as speaking at the

myriad functions organized by the hosts and the Lions management nearly always falls to the captain or manager, and requires people who are prepared to communicate on behalf of the squad. Campbell-Lamerton calculated that by the end of the tour he had made more than 250 speeches and given more than 100 interviews to television and radio alone, on top of his daily and sometimes hourly contact with the press pack: 'My father was not the type to shirk responsibilities, and he took on all the sorts of tasks that an entire PR team would do nowadays,' said Jeremy Campbell-Lamerton. Jim Telfer agreed: 'He took his job so seriously and worried about things so much that he lost two or three stones in weight. The media coverage was as bad then in some ways as it is now, always in your face, and if you are not brought up in that kind of pressure situation it hits you hard.'

For his part, even O'Brien's renowned sense of humour was stretched: 'I remember having to make nine different speeches in one day. I confess I used the same jokes over and over again. I did enjoy our school visits, though, and the youngsters were very keen to ask questions.'

Events on the pitch, however, overshadowed everything and at least a few of the Lions were prepared to learn from the All Black masters. As well as the returning McBride, the new Lions for 1966 included several men who would become major figures both for the Lions and their own countries, such as Jim Telfer. Ray McLoughlin of Gosforth and Ireland would become a highly influential figure as a forward, while his fellow countryman Mike Gibson is revered as one of the greatest backs ever to grace the sport of rugby union. He was also flexible, playing at centre alongside McFadyean in all four Tests against the All Blacks despite normally being a fly-half for Ireland. Another Irishman, hooker Ken Kennedy, is remembered as a quintessential tourist, always full of humour and enthusiasm. Noel Murphy had toured in 1959 but missed the 1962 tour with a broken collar bone. Now he returned as part of a fine back row, which featured either Pask or Jim Telfer of Melrose at No. 8 with

Murphy's fellow Irishman Ronnie Lamont the fourth member of the quartet that between them shared back row duties in all six Tests. Some, such as Willie John McBride, say Lamont was the forward of the tour, and he certainly did not lack courage or aggression, laying out cold one of the All Blacks during a match. A woman spectator promptly smacked Lamont with an umbrella, before McBride defended his friend by snapping the offending 'weapon' in two.

Another Scot, Sandy Hinshelwood, would lighten up many a dark day at Murrayfield with his lightning bursts up the wing. In 1966, he contested the No. 14 jersey with Stuart Watkins of Wales, each playing three Tests. The Scottish hooker Frank Laidlaw would win a record number of caps in that position for his country and played two Tests in 1966, while Stewart Wilson, who had replaced Ken Scotland as full-back for Scotland, took over at No.15 after England's Don Rutherford broke his arm in the first Test in Australia. Terry Price of Llanelli and Wales came out as a replacement, but this fine player was clearly unfit when he arrived – another example of bad planning at home.

Delme Thomas played for the Lions in a Test before he was capped for Wales, eventually appearing 25 times for the principality. In front of him, alongside Kennedy and McLoughlin, was Denzil Williams who went on to become one of Wales's greatest prop forwards, though he began his career as a lock.

At fly-half, Mike Gibson having moved to accommodate him, was David 'Dai' Watkins, who took over as captain after Campbell-Lamerton dropped himself. He would become a star in both union and league, and played all six Tests, while Ireland's Roger Young and Alan Lewis of Wales divided the Test No. 9 jerseys equally.

The party was light on English players, rugby in that country going through an extended fallow period, but Colin McFadyean would later captain England in his brief international career. He was a popular tourist, not least because he came up with a rallying cry to respond to the Haka, and he was the only England player to feature in all four Tests against the All Blacks. There was only one English forward, David Powell of Northampton, who never made the Test side.

McFadyean could have played for Scotland as his father, Captain Angus John McFadyean, who was killed in action at Anzio when Colin was just a year old, was Scottish. 'I had the choice, and was invited to a sort of trial match for the Scots, but an England selector told me not to play or I would never be picked for England. I had to choose, and after all, I had been born and raised in England.' He blamed his decision to snub the Scottish trial for the fact that the Scottish-dominated Barbarians Committee never once invited this Lion and England captain to play for them.

McFadyean is no doubt that the 1966 tour was the 'best experience of my life' not least because as a young man there were plenty of attractions in Australia and New Zealand – girls, mostly.

'I had played for England three times, and I had a good game up at Murrayfield even though we lost 6–3,' said McFadyean.

On the way home, somebody came on the coach and said 'they've picked the Lions' but I never thought I would be selected, and I didn't believe it at first. I was brought up on stories of the '55 and '59 tours and to be a Lion at 22 was absolutely unbelievable.

I had qualified as a PE teacher and was teaching at Central Boys Grammar School in Birmingham. They were good to me and when I came back I had four months' salary in the bank – I went out and bought a brand-new Mini for £650.

We also had free cigarettes and free Guinness on the tour plus ten shillings a day expenses – you needed the money in Australia but once we got to New Zealand they wouldn't let you pay for a thing, even letting us into the cinemas for free.

As for the girls, well I was a free agent at the time, and everywhere you went in New Zealand the banks in town would have the pictures of the

Lions in the windows and the local girls, whose dream was to capture an All Black but who would take a Lion as second best, would sort out who they wanted to meet and would come and proposition you to some extent – I may be gilding the lily after 40-odd years, but that's how it seemed at the time.

I do know one player just disappeared for ten days – no names, of course, even after all this time. I asked where he was and was told 'Keep it quiet, he's off with his woman.' He came back and played as if nothing had happened and nobody said a word. Those were the days …

The tour began with the controversy over the captaincy and almost ended with the row over the allegations of dirty play by provinces and cheating by the All Blacks. In between, the Lions played a lot of good rugby in what was a punishingly long tour, with 35 matches played over the space of five months in Australia, New Zealand and Canada.

The best performances came in Australia, where the national side, like England's, was in the doldrums. For the first time since 1904, the Lions emerged unbeaten at the end of a stay in Australia, although they did draw one match against New South Wales. The surprise was the easiness of the second Test victory in Brisbane. Having had to come from behind to win a tight first Test in Sydney 11–8, nobody could have foreseen what happened in the second Test. Everything clicked for the Lions in the second half on that balmy day in late May. Leading 3–0 at half-time, the Lions ran rampant in the second half, the tight five winning everything and the back row of Telfer, Noel Murphy and Pask at No. 8 setting up position after position which the backs exploited to the full. They scored five tries in all, each of them converted by full-back Wilson, as the Lions romped to a 31–0 victory.

Six weeks later, it was to be an entirely different story in New Zealand against the All Blacks. By then, the tourists had already lost three non-Test encounters against provincial sides, and their electric form of Brisbane had shorted out. There had already been several warnings that the home teams were going to indulge in a frequently violent approach to play, and as the tour neared its climactic weeks, the Lions found themselves on the receiving end of brutality.

Nor was the Lions' preparation ideal. They turned up at Queenstown airport to do some training, only to find that the grass they had been allocated was part of the airstrip, meaning they had to scatter for the hangars every time an aircraft wanted to take off or land. Again, a sheer lack of planning.

In that first Test in Dunedin, the All Blacks unleashed a devastating new weapon – perfectly legal, too – in which the centres would deliberately set up rucks to enable their colleagues to win what became known as 'second-phase' ball, the forerunner of the 'phase' style of play which is now so common in rugby. Facing the likes of Colin Meads in his pomp alongside All Black greats such as Ken Gray and Brian Lochore, the Lions pack struggled to compete and the backs had little ball to work with. When they did get it, they found the All Blacks in their faces. The final score of 3–20 in New Zealand's favour did not exaggerate their superiority.

The Lions had three weeks to put things right, but instead found themselves embroiled in a massive row which at one point threatened the continuation of the tour itself. At Lancaster Park in Christchurch, captain for the day Jim Telfer was appalled at the foul play of Canterbury province – from the first scrum to the last, punches were thrown.

Willie John McBride was an early target, at one point being smothered by a mass of kicking and punching opponents who threatened to tear him apart because he wouldn't release the ball: 'I looked up and my team mates were nowhere to be seen, and I knew then we had no hope of winning against the All Blacks.'

Colin McFadyean had his nose broken not once but twice in that match: 'My opposite number hit me with his elbow while I wasn't looking and broke my nose. Our hooker Ken Kennedy, who was a doctor, immediately straightened it. Then, when I was lying on the ground later on, Fergie McCormick accidentally kicked my nose and broke it again. This time I had to go to hospital to get my nose straightened.'

In his after-match speech, captain-for-the-day Telfer let rip: 'I would not describe today's game as dirty because all our games in New Zealand have been dirty.' It was not as if the locals could accuse Telfer of being a whinger – the big Borderer had toughed it out probably better than any Lion. He was just incensed that dirty play had forced the sort of battle he did not consider to be in the spirit of rugby.

His words caused a colossal row, with the media calling for his head. The press in New Zealand and at home were full of claims and counter-claims that had simmered behind the scenes for weeks before exploding from an unrepentant Telfer – and he is only slightly less so more than four decades on.

'It seems to me looking back now that players then were not supposed to say anything,' said Telfer.

> I was promised by the press that I would be sent home and would never play again, but that was just upper-class snobbishness and it wasn't even discussed. I was maybe wrong in saying what I said, but it was the truth as I saw it and I have no regrets about speaking out. Perhaps it should have been the captain or the manager who should have said it, but it fell to me on that day.

Des O'Brien backed Telfer with a few choice words of his own on the subject. Telfer's speech and O'Brien's reaction had finally brought the home sides' tactics out in the open, and it was not appreciated by the New Zealand union, the press or the Lions Committee. It cost Telfer the honour of ever captaining the Lions again, both in New Zealand and later.

A week later, in the match against Auckland, the home side kicked off what Telfer would later call 'a game of absolute thuggery'. Far from toning things down, the provincial side were not going to be intimidated into backing off. Neither were the Lions. The result was a bloodbath and, almost incidentally, a 12–6 win for the Lions.

'The difference was that they were very professional about the way they did things, but we were amateurs,' said Colin McFadyean. 'We were completely naive at times.'

Jim Telfer points to another reason for thuggery:

> *There was no television covering every match in those days, so they knew they would get away with it; nobody would know about it unless they had been at the game or heard a radio broadcast or read things in the newspapers. They had looked on us as a soft touch and were out to prove they were harder men than us.*

The headlines were of the 'disgrace to the nation' variety and serious commentators predicted that players might die unless something was done. There were suggestions, obviously fanciful, that the tour might be called off, and in the end the Governor-General of New Zealand personally intervened before the second Test, holding meetings with the chairman of the NZRU and the two captains. The jaw-jaw seemed to stop the war-war, and from then on, though matches remained tough and hard, there were many fewer instances of dubious play.

The social side of the tour remained great fun, and a highlight was a reception for the Lions at the British High Commission. One of the journalists covering the tour, Tremayne Rodd, who had been capped 14 times for Scotland and would later become the 3rd Lord Rennell, appeared in almost casual clothing compared to the ties and tails of everyone else. Des O'Brien remonstrated with him only to hear Rodd's reply: 'Oh it's all right, I'm staying here.' Rodd would later figure in an important case to decide whether writing about the sport as a journalist disqualified you from playing it. The IRB decided that it did, proof that in 1970 there were still plenty of idiots running the sport.

The New Zealand press carried 'hints' about drinking to excess by several Lions and officials, and there was no doubt that Willie John McBride and the Welsh contingent in particular enjoyed a libation. Telfer said: 'But that was only to be expected, because rugby is a working man's game in Wales and they liked to go to the pub after a match – and you couldn't keep that wild fellow Willie John shut away for long.'

Indeed not! McBride himself described how he and Ronnie Lamont trashed the New Albion hotel in Greymouth after the two of them were installed in the lesser Old Albion. 'Ronnie rode a horse and I rode in on a bicycle,' recalled McBride. 'The locals blamed "bandits" for wrecking the place, and we never let on, though we were sore laughing.'

Colin McFadyean remembered how people would come to the Lions hotels and take them on outings on jet boats and even aeroplanes:

One chap invited me up in his aircraft, which had dual controls, and we were flying over Milford Sound when he said, 'Would you like to try flying?' – and I said yes and grabbed the controls. After a while he said, 'Well done, you've been flying us for the last five minutes', and that's when things went a bit wobbly …

Defeat in the first Test was not fatal; the Lions could still get back to level things. It was at this point that Mike Campbell-Lamerton showed sense as well as courage. Realizing he was badly out of form, he dropped himself for the second Test in Wellington, his place going to the uncapped Delme Thomas. Five other changes were made, but to no avail. Despite a gallant attempt on a rainswept day, the Lions were no match for the blistering All Blacks pack and though they led 9–8 at half-time, there was an inevitability about the way New Zealand turned the screw in the second half, eventually winning 16–12.

The third Test, on a cold day in Christchurch, was all too predictable. Though at one point early in the match things did not look too comfortable for the home side, the Lions struggled with injured players while the All Blacks just seemed to grow stronger, taking advantage of mistakes by the Lions to wrap up the match 19–6, thus winning the series.

New Zealand had history in their grasp, as they had never whitewashed a touring side before. In front of a record crowd at Eden Park in Auckland, the All Blacks' forwards bested their opposite numbers in most departments, but especially in the loose play where their unsurpassed rucking game put the Lions on the back foot throughout. Victory was achieved by 24–11, after the Lions had been just 8–10 down at half-time. Colin Meads 'sorted out' David Watkins during that match: 'He hit me first' was his claim to the referee. Watkins had already had experience of local referees – in one match at a scrum he asked the referee which side had the put-in. 'Don't be bloody silly, son,' he was told; 'it's our ball.'

In that last Test McFadyean scored a try which he only finally got the chance to watch in 2008: 'I was presented with a DVD that had the pictures of all four Tests. There I could see myself for the first time scoring that try – it was a bloody brilliant try, I can tell you.'

In retrospect, the Lions were not at their best in New Zealand, but they also had the misfortune to come up against one of the finest All Black sides of all time. The 'blackwash' was humiliating to many in northern hemisphere rugby who did not understand that this New Zealand side was of a different breed entirely.

On the way home, Campbell-Lamerton's men stopped off to do some more missionary work in Canada, and were duly given a lesson by a British Columbia side who did not take kindly to being told they had no chance against the mighty Lions. A 3–8 defeat was followed by a final match

against Canada, which the Lions won 19–8 to earn at least some satisfaction from what had ultimately been a pretty disastrous tour.

More than 40 years on, Telfer still has vivid memories of those crucial
days in New Zealand, which he admits did so much to form his own
uncompromising rugby creed:

> *The '66 tour was where I formed my own rugby philosophy and began my*
> *admiration for the All Blacks. I took a lot from that tour, and also took a*
> *lot from learning about the people of other countries, the English, the Irish*
> *and Welsh. I learned who I would like to work with, and who I would like*
> *to have alongside me in a war. It was a character-building exercise.*

After returning home, Des O'Brien made his vital contribution to the
British and Irish Lions, one that very few people – even those on the
tour – ever knew about. Only much later in life did O'Brien admit to the
authors of this book that his end-of-tour report to the Lions Committee contained some of the most trenchant criticisms ever penned about
the whole way in which the Lions operated. The man himself described
the contents of the 12-page report as 'incendiary' not least because he
questioned the commitment of the home unions, the abilities of the selectors, the lack of financial support, the paucity of coaching, the length of
tours, the need for neutral referees and even the very future of the Lions
should the Test team keep being defeated. He concluded by laying out
a large number of sensible recommendations for future tours, such as:
early selection of coaches and managers; instigating proper lines of managerial authority; a better-thought-out and much shorter itinerary; neutral
referees for (at least) Tests; and proper research and planning, not least
about the teams and difficulties the Lions would face. Above all, while
accepting that there had been individual failings on the tour, he laid the
blame fair and square on the system and those in charge – in other words,
the Lions Committee itself.

'I didn't miss them and hit the wall,' is how O'Brien put it. The report was never published and is believed to have been circulated only to a few people within the home unions, so powerful and condemnatory were its contents. In the long run, almost all of O'Brien's recommendations were implemented, even though it took years. The Committee at first made only a few adjustments to the way things worked, such as shortening the tours, and O'Brien regretfully concluded that he had been 'over the top' in what he had written. Mrs Ann O'Brien recently confirmed that the report had been 'blistering, saying "never again should a team go out so unprepared"', Jim Telfer confirming that this sounded exactly like the kind of thing O'Brien would write.

'I did not know he had written these things,' said Telfer, 'but Des was an honest and highly intelligent man who had been highly successful in business, so he would have made the correct conclusions.'

Des O'Brien remained an energetic gregarious type with a thirst for learning until almost the end. He did not hold any grudge against New Zealand and he and Ann visited the country several times, making many friends. O'Brien made his home in Midlothian after being posted to Scotland by his employers Guinness and was a popular character at many rugby events and especially Ireland matches at Murrayfield. After he retired he went back to university to study Scottish history, among other things. His wife Ann recalls him studying French until a few weeks before he died peacefully, surrounded by his children and grandchildren, at the age of 86 on Boxing Day 2005.

Sadly, two of the 1966 Lions suffered early deaths in tragic circumstances. Terry Price was killed in a car accident in 1993, aged 47, while two years later, Alun Pask was killed in a fire at his home. He left a wife and three children.

Other Lions enjoyed success. David Watkins went off to rugby league and was duly ostracized from union as tradition demanded, but he became a Lion under the professional code and later a renowned broadcaster.

He remains friends with Colin McFadyean and they still play golf occasionally.

McFadyean was a victim of England's panicky selectors in the late 1960s. They made him captain in 1968 because he had the most caps – 'just nine' he said, 'but it was still the most, because the whole team had 41 caps among them. Then they dropped me just as quick.' McFadyean then enjoyed a long career in education and sports administration, both in Britain and as far away as Hong Kong. He once coached Bristol RFC and still does supply teaching in the Gloucester area.

Jim Telfer and Willie John McBride continued their learning curve in South Africa just two years later. The Swinging Sixties it may have been, but the Lions were set to be hung out to dry again.

CHAPTER EIGHT

TOM KIERNAN'S FROLICSOME BRIGADE

South Africa 1968

With Des O'Brien's stinging report on the table, the calamitous tour of 1966 provoked something of a secret debate within the home unions committee. Lessons needed to be learned quickly from the debacle in New Zealand, for the next Lions party was due to leave these shores less than two years later, destination South Africa. While failing to act immediately on most of O'Brien's recommendations, the committee saw the sense of bringing forward the appointment of a tour manager, and did so a whole year in advance.

Given the weight of problems that had caused Des O'Brien so much personal trauma, they decided to go for a man who simply did not let a crisis get to him: the unflappable David Brooks, who had just returned from a tour of South Africa by his beloved Harlequins. A useful loose forward in his day, Brooks was a successful businessman who had already earned a reputation as a sound administrator with genuine enthusiasm for his job and for rugby in general. He was to become that rare beast, a popular Lions manager, and in time he would serve as president of the

RFU in 1981–82, showing far-sightedness in his support for such controversial ideas as sponsorship and a club championship.

In 1968, Brooks would need every ounce of his equanimity, not least because by then the political situation around the world was vastly different from previous eras. Depending on one's point of view, there was either a wholesale youth revolution or a summer of love under way, and sometimes both. Alongside anti-Vietnam demonstrations and student riots in Paris, there was still plenty of anger left over to be directed at the supposedly wilful ignorance of those rugby unions that wanted to maintain links with sport in an apartheid-ridden South Africa. We will deal with this issue in a later chapter. Suffice it to say for now that the Lions tours to the land of the Springboks in the 60s, 70s and particularly in 1980 led to massive upheavals in rugby and sport in general.

In 1968, the issue of South African apartheid and race in general was high on the agenda, but not because of the Lions. In April, just 16 days after Martin Luther King had been shot by a white supremacist, Enoch Powell had given his infamously racist 'rivers of blood' speech. Shortly afterwards, opinion polls found the white population of Britain was split three-to-one in favour of the MP's anti-immigrant stance. With public attention focused on racial issues, apartheid in South Africa was inevitably going to be discussed.

Though rugby held its collective breath and waited for the Lions to become a political football, in the end it was cricket that endured months of turmoil over the eventual inclusion of Basil D'Oliveira in the England side due to tour South Africa some months after the Lions. The story simmered all summer, but exploded just a few weeks after the Lions came home. What would have happened to the Lions had 'Dolly', as he was affectionately known, been selected for the South African tour before they left we'll never know. As it was, he initially only made the substitutes list, as the MCC bowed to the pressure of South African Prime Minister John Vorster and did not select D'Oliveira, a naturalized British citizen who had been born in Cape Town and was officially classed in that country as 'coloured', meaning that he could not play in any formal sport with 'whites'. Would the sight of a coloured man playing on an equal basis with whites really have caused revolution in South Africa? Vorster's Government wasn't prepared to find out.

After weeks of massive media coverage, when D'Oliveira was finally called up as a replacement for an injured player, the South African Government – after a muddling attempt to bribe the player to withdraw – insisted that their national side would not play against any team with D'Oliveira in it. The MCC finally found its spine and the England cricket tour was cancelled, amid huge controversy that included parliamentary debates, with members of Harold Wilson's Labour Government strongly making the case that South Africa should suffer a sporting boycott.

To be fair, most British and Irish people at that time had no idea about apartheid and its workings, but the D'Oliveira case and its long-felt ramifications changed not only entire sports but also public and political attitudes to sporting links with South Africa. The British and Irish Lions, as well as the Springboks themselves, would become the focus of considerable attention after D'Oliveira.

The man himself had a simple statement to make – he just wanted to play with the best. By and large, that was the attitude of most of the Lions at that time. The Springboks were still considered the world's best side and the Lions wanted to prove themselves against them. But then none of the Lions was coloured.

Tom Kiernan, Ireland's star full-back from Cork who had first been selected for Ireland in 1960 and had toured to South Africa with the Lions in 1962, was a popular choice as captain. He had missed out on the 1966 tour for the understandable reason that he was getting married, though modestly he said that the full-backs who did tour – Don Rutherford, Stewart Wilson and Terry Price – would all have been picked ahead of him anyway.

With his experience of the 1962 tour, he was well aware from the outset that apartheid could be a major issue for the tourists. Yet pre-D'Oliveira, the publicity about rugby and apartheid was, at least compared to following tours, relatively mild. As Kiernan put it:

There wasn't any great pressure on us going out. There were some interviews and the question was raised with me about how I felt. I would say it had raised its head 100 per cent more than in 1962, but it wasn't as big an issue as it became in 1969 when South Africa toured Britain and Ireland.

Jim Telfer agreed:

The atmosphere around the tour was very unhealthy because of the apartheid issue, but there weren't quite the political problems we might have expected. The following year the Springboks came to us and that was when it all kicked off; it was a bit of a disaster really. The pressure on rugby didn't really build until 1974, in my opinion.

In retrospect, the 1968 tour should have been a triumphal procession by a team of stars, a blend of hardened experience alongside thrilling young talents. In the later category were Gareth Edwards, Barry John and Gerald Davies of Wales, who would become three of the greatest players of their era, indeed of all time. They would be part of a back line featuring Mike Gibson and Kiernan himself. It should have been magical, but it never happened.

As Kiernan pointed out:

We had Gareth, Barry, Gerald and Mike, yet they did not ever play together in a Test Match on the tour. Mike Gibson was injured in the first match, Barry John in the first Test, Gerald Davies had hamstring trouble, as did Gareth Edwards – that they couldn't play together was one of the most disappointing things in the tour. I would also say we were not as strong as South Africa in the pack, so we needed all guns blazing in the backs and that never happened.

Gerald Davies – the flying winger of Wales, twice a Lion as a player and due to manage the 2009 Lions – was honoured to be selected for the 1968 tour. He vividly recalls what inspired him to reach the pinnacle in rugby – those black-and-white newsreels from 1955 which inspired a whole generation of rugby players and fans to follow the exploits of the Lions.

It was in 1955 that I first learned the value of the Lions. I remember clearly going to the Regal Cinema in Llanelli and seeing the Pathé newsreel with its famous cockerel symbol. That was the only place you could go to see the Lions, and it was most probably a week to 10 days after the match had taken place. I was growing up in Llanelli and going to Stradey Park to see the Scarlets play, usually on a bleak wintry day with grey clouds; and then, to see these men playing in the South African sunshine on the yellow grass with palm trees in the background, well, I thought, there is a different kind of rugby somewhere down the line, and I want some of that. That 1955 tour, which was full of great players and ended with the Test series drawn, has always been something of an inspiration to me.

By 1968, the boost to the Lions' image from favourable press coverage and the popularity of the newsreel coverage in both 1955 and 1959 had long since disappeared. The failures of 1962 and 1966 had damaged the Lions' reputation, but conversely, thanks largely to television, more than ever before the Lions were now public property, which in turn made them fair game for the press and broadcasting media.

They were definitely 'in the know', those press chaps in the Sixties. Like so many Lions before him, Gerald Davies found out that he had been selected to tour from a journalist.

I was working as a teacher in Cardiff when I got a message in the classroom to go and answer a telephone call. I put the prefect of that class in charge and went to the secretary's room to take the call. It was from Brian Hoey, a journalist with BBC Wales, who said 'Gerald, what do you think? You've been selected to go to South Africa with the Lions.' That was it. Nothing official, just that call from Brian, but of course, I was highly delighted.

The political strife over apartheid may not have stopped the tour but it cost Gerald Davies a packet: 'Different education authorities had different attitudes to giving people time off for sporting contests involving South Africa. I worked for a Labour authority, and though I did manage to get time off, it was without pay.'

The forwards had old hands like Syd Millar, McBride and Telfer, as well as Scotland's giant Peter Stagg, all 6ft 8in of him, and the brilliant English hooker John Pullin. Amazingly, the man who was reckoned by many to be one of the great successes of the tour, Scottish flanker Rodger Arneil, only made the party as a late replacement.

Pullin, the West Country farmer who played for Bristol and England, has long concealed a secret which, had it emerged at the time, would have seen him stay at home in 1968 and might well have ended his international career.

'Playing for England in the match against Ireland, I remember getting an injury to my back and playing on,' said Pullin.

I played with it until the end of the season and it did get a bit better. It turned out I had fractured a vertebra, and it continued to bother me for years afterwards.

But there was no way I was going to miss the chance of going to South Africa with the Lions. I knew it would be a great experience and might only happen for me once in my career, so once I was selected I decided not to mention my bad back and kept it a secret from everyone. It had eased a bit by the time we got to South Africa but I still felt the pain.

Thanks to the relatively new phenomenon of reporters chronicling the social side of a Lions tour, we know that the 1968 tourists had a whale of a time. In fact, if you read South African press accounts alone, you'd think the Lions were merely partygoers intent on having a good time, with David Brooks the leader of the gang.

Undoubtedly the tourists enjoyed a swell time, encouraged by 'Brooksy' who was the life and soul of the party. He had a trick of knocking the bottom off wine glasses, leaving Lions and others nonplussed. He also introduced the after-match 'happy hour', which became an instant Lions tradition, although, as Willie John McBride said: 'The trouble is the "hour" went on for hours and hours.'

After one party in a Cape Town hotel, Brooks was handed an invoice for £900 for 'damage' to the hotel. 'It couldn't have been a very good party,' quipped the tour manager.

There was no shortage of players ready to join in the fun, including great life-enhancing characters such as Ireland's Mick Doyle and Welshman John O'Shea, the latter being appointed 'judge' of the players' court, always a feature of rugby tours. O'Shea found the quiet man of the tour, Maurice Richards, guilty of 'doing nothing out of place' and sentenced his fellow Welshman, who was a religious man, to throw a glass against a wall. Amazingly, the glass bounced off unbroken – divine influence, said some.

A few of the Lions decided to play up to their reputation and formed the Loyal Order of Wreckers, as opposed to the 'kippers', who enjoyed a quieter life. Another group called themselves the Burners and took to setting fire to shirts and ladies underwear – after their female owners had divested themselves of their garments, you will understand.

On one train journey, the Lions had two carriages to themselves, and such was the riotous nature of their party – with no little damage done to the fittings – that the railway company detached the carriages and left them in a siding until the Lions had cooled off.

Nevertheless, Kiernan felt that the partying and Brooks's role in it were greatly exaggerated:

The South African press were very guilty of that, I must say. I actually have great memories of David Brooks because he was an all-round man. He was a jovial character but he was also very sensible and knew his rugby. He had to give speeches on every occasion and did them well.

He had his priorities right and made sure the work was done first, but he knew how to enjoy himself and how to get others to enjoy themselves. Yes, he liked a party, but that is part of rugby and touring; even nowadays, if you don't enjoy a party then you might as well pack it in.

Gerald Davies has promised to ensure that the 2009 tour has some fun on it, because he sees it as part of the team-building process:

The camaraderie among the players back then was simply fantastic and that is what you try to re-create all the time on a Lions tour. It was about people getting on with each other and playing with each other, and wanting to play for each other. In both the tours that I was on as a player the spirit was terrific. There was always, of course, that delicate moment when the Test team was announced, and that was when the real character of a squad showed itself. As far as I was aware, there were no problems with the selection on both those tours, which shows you the togetherness of the squads.

As in previous tours, all who took part in that 1968 tour cited the four-day visit to Kruger Park as the highlight of the off-pitch activities. Kiernan said:

We were in the back of wagons watching all the amazing wildlife – unforgettable. I also enjoyed our visit to Namibia and all the isolated places we visited. The fact that I had been in South Africa previously meant that I knew people there, which was helpful; I'm still in touch with them today.

All good fun, then, but events on the pitch were deadly serious. As Kiernan put it:

There are no easy games in South Africa, because all their teams are physical. I don't mean physical in the 'dirty play' sense, but because of the sheer strength and pace of the South Africans. The matches were usually played on hard grounds with a bouncing ball, which also made for a physical game.

By all accounts Dawson, who had been the Lions tour captain back in 1959, kept the players on their toes and as fit and well coached as possible. No less a personage than Dr Danie Craven thought the 1968 Lions a good team, saying 'they gave us grey hairs', and he was a pretty good judge.

Syd Millar goes further in explaining how Dawson led a revolution in coaching in Britain and Ireland:

*In 1959 when I had toured with the Lions to Australia and New
Zealand, the All Blacks couldn't understand why we didn't have a coach.
By the time we came to South Africa in 1968, we had learned the hard
lessons, but in terms of coaching in these islands we were still feeling our
way and writing our own coaching manuals, and we were still behind in
terms of analysing the opposition, for example.*

*Ronnie Dawson has never received the credit for what he achieved.
With all due respect to John Robins, who had his problems in 1966, it
was Ronnie who was really the first Lions coach and he set the pattern
for those who followed.*

Kiernan agreed: 'Since he had retired from playing and even before,
Ronnie Dawson was passionate about the necessity for coaching in Britain
and Ireland. He was very much in charge and it was well organized.'

All the more reason why the outcome of the Test series was hugely
disappointing, though in fairness they were up against a superb side
containing Springbok greats like lock forward Frik Du Preez, hooker Gys
Pitzer, winger Sid Nomis and a back row trio of Thys Lourens, Tom
Bedford and Jan Ellis, all under the captaincy of Dawie de Villiers. The
Lions won all but one of the non-Test Matches, and came out ahead in
some tough and very close tussles, such as the 9–3 defeat of Orange Free
State and the 22–19 victory over Northern Transvaal. These results were
also achieved against a backdrop of a horrendous injury list, especially
to the star players.

Gerald Davies recalled:

*I suffered from injuries throughout the tour. I had a bad ankle injury
early on, and it took some time to recover from that. Then I dislocated
my elbow after a late tackle in the match against the Orange Free State,
so by the end of the tour, I had not fulfilled my ambitions in the Lions
jersey.*

Jim Telfer felt much the same:

*I had been injured the year before playing for Melrose and I had only
come back and played one game for Scotland before the touring team
was selected. To be honest, I had slowed down a bit and I was really past
my best by that time. I also picked up injuries and at one point they had
to leave me behind in Cape Town for treatment.*

One of the injuries that most influenced the outcome of the series was
the broken collar bone sustained by Barry John after a 'spear' tackle in
the first Test in Pretoria. The Springboks narrowly though deservedly
won that Test by 25–20. As proof of the injury jinx, the man who was
brought out as a replacement for John, Ireland's Ken Goodall – who had
originally been selected to tour but had stayed at home to complete his
exams – promptly broke his hand in his first match and had to return
home again.

In the second Test in Port Elizabeth, local referee J.P. Schoeman's interpretation of the scrum law was basically that South Africa should win
every one, and he gave penalty after penalty against the Lions. Brooks
issued as strong a condemnation as had ever been given by a tour manager,
and there were talks to ensure such a biased view of the laws did not
recur – the case for neutral referees had once again been advanced,
however.

John Pullin commented:

*Really we needed to have 15 points on the board before we got on the
pitch – the referees were that bad. I don't think we stood much chance of
winning any of the Tests. Danie Craven had them all in his pocket
anyhow, because he picked the Test referees. Any referee in a provincial
match who looked like being half fair didn't get a look-in for the Test
Matches.*

Even more serious was the so-called Battle of Springs, when Eastern Transvaal came out in full fighting, scratching and kicking mode. At least some lessons had been learned from 1966, and the Lions gave as good as they got. The referee eventually issued a general warning to both sides, and as luck would have it, the next person to throw a punch was John O'Shea, who thus became the first Lion to be sent off for foul play – David Dobson's dismissal in 1904 had been for a supposedly blasphemous uttering.

As O'Shea left the field, he was punched in the face by a spectator, which caused a near riot involving Lions players and reserves against just about everybody else in the ground. People used to seeing the handbag-waving that typically passes for a rugby fight nowadays would not believe the Battle of Springs, and they would certainly admire the punch by which Willie John McBride laid out O'Shea's assailant.

Violence was a feature of quite a few matches. John Pullin recalled that in one Test Match he was knocked out cold by his opposite number Gys Pitzer:

He was the best hooker I ever played against, but unfortunately for me, he was also a heavyweight boxer. I can't even remember the circumstances that led up to the fight – well you couldn't even call it a fight really, because the only thing I remember is his fist about an inch away from me before I went out like a light.

Pullin was also on the receiving end of 'treatment' from the great Frik du Preez: 'He came round the front of a line-out, heading for the try line, and I should have stopped him scoring. He just swatted me away like a fly.'

With referee Schoeman ensuring that the Lions were held to a 6–6 draw in the second Test, going into the third the tourists still had a chance of winning the series, but in that match, as in the others, their only real weapon was Tom Kiernan's boot. South Africa scored the sole try of the match and again won a tight game by 11–6.

The final Test in Johannesburg was a 'dead' rubber as far as the series went, but the Springboks always play for pride and the Lions were exhausted from travelling, partying and, above all, injuries – third-choice scrum-half Gordon Connell came in as Gareth Edwards and Roger Young were both injured. Though the forwards excelled themselves, South Africa's backs were superior on the day and the Test ended 19–6 in favour of the Springboks. The last score was a penalty by Tom Kiernan, which gave him a new points' record for a Lion on a tour. Of the 38 points amassed by the Lions in the Tests, he had – almost unbelievably – scored 35 of them.

Kiernan said: 'We only scored one try, and even that came off a kick, Willie John following up and gathering a rebound. We just didn't have the firepower.'

As in most Lions' Test series, it was the inequality between the packs that made the difference. John Pullin was succinct in his summing up: 'They were bigger than us, more powerful and faster, and they had a real win-at-all costs mentality.' Willie John McBride was even shorter in his judgement: 'We (the forwards) weren't good enough.'

For Jim Telfer, the main highlight was achieving his ambition of captaining the Lions, albeit in midweek matches:

Despite the supposed 'ban' I had received in New Zealand after my speech following the Canterbury match, I actually did captain the team three or four times, and I was looked on as Tom Kiernan's vice-captain. I enjoyed the responsibility, but was injured too often to enjoy the whole tour.

Gareth Edwards, for one, felt that the tour was important for the legacy it left:

> *Ronnie Dawson the coach (though he was still called assistant manager)
> was excellent in his preparation of a talented group of players in 1968,
> and they developed a spirit that acted as a catalyst for later tours. A
> number of players on that tour would stay together in the 1970s and they
> developed a bond which they carried on into future tours.*
>
> *We may have lost the series but we won every provincial match except
> for a rather controversial loss against Transvaal, and that takes some
> doing in South Africa.*
>
> *It was a fun tour, and though we took the playing very seriously and
> had some excellent players, we just weren't good enough in the Tests. It is
> still a big part of our lives. We had a 40th anniversary reunion of the
> 1968 tour recently and you could still feel the warmth of the
> comradeship.*

Tom Kiernan went on to become Ireland's most-capped player, amassing 54 appearances in the green jersey in 14 seasons. He switched to coaching, and was in charge of the Munster side that famously beat the All Blacks in 1978. He then coached Ireland to their great successes in the early 1980s. An accountant by profession, he moved into the administrative side of the game, and at first was against professionalism, but he realized after the inaugural World Cup that television money pouring into the sport would make the payment of players inevitable. Kiernan backed Vernon Pugh, the chairman of the IRB, whose hard work and diplomacy was in no small way responsible for the transition to professionalism. When the Heineken European Cup came into being in the 1995–96 season, Kiernan was made first chairman of the organizing company and was chief among the promoters in making the tournament such a success. He was also instrumental with some far-sighted colleagues in ensuring that Ireland went down the route of putting its resources into the provinces, and that judgement has been proven overwhelmingly correct, Ulster and Munster in particular proving as good as any side in Europe.

On his return home in 1968, David Brooks submitted a report to the Home Unions Committee which was just as hard-hitting as Des O'Brien's had been two years previously. This time, the committee listened and began to address issues such as proper preparation for tours. Brooks would later become life president of his beloved Harlequins to whom he was devoted until his death at the age of 77 in 2002.

As Edwards said, many of the 1968 Lions would tour again in 1971, and most would enjoy success in later life, though some had to battle great adversity. Mick Doyle became a vet in his native Kerry and coached Ireland in the mid-1980s, winning the Triple Crown in 1985. His attacking philosophy was summed up in his famous quote 'give it a lash'.

His later life is one of the great stories of a Lion refusing to be beaten by circumstances. Doyle suffered a heart attack at the opening dinner of the inaugural World Cup in 1987, but within four days he was back in a tracksuit on the sidelines. The man known as the Doyler battled back bravely and become a noted commentator on the game.

Doyle proved to have true Lion's courage when he suffered a massive brain haemorrhage in 1996. After four weeks in a coma, he was forced to learn to speak and walk again, but – as he pointed out himself – he had been very lucky: only 0.16 per cent of people suffering such a haemorrhage survive it. He not only got back to full health but wrote a moving account of his illness called *Zero Point One Six – Living In Extra Time*, adding to an earlier well-received autobiography. Doyle also got involved with the charity Headway Ireland, which works for people with brain injuries. He was killed in a road accident in 2004, aged 63. No less a person than Bertie Ahern, the Taoiseach (Ireland's prime minister) paid tribute to Doyle: 'He lived life to the full and is associated with some of the finest moments in Irish rugby. In private he also successfully fought very serious illnesses. I know that his tenacity and courage gave heart to many others.'

Another member of the 1968 Lions also suffered a brain haemorrhage and stroke, though at a much younger age. Keith Jarrett was beloved of Welshmen everywhere for the feat of scoring 19 points on his international debut against England. After the 1968 tour, he moved to rugby league to play for Barrow, where he suffered his brain injury and was finished with rugby at the age of just 25. There followed a long and undignified battle over insurance compensation for Jarrett. He, too, battled back and hopes to publish his life story in 2009.

Roger Young became a dentist and enjoyed his time in South Africa so much that he emigrated to Cape Town where he still lives. Sandy Hinshelwood of Scotland, a qualified pharmacist, emigrated to Australia where his son Ben was born. The latter chose to play for his father's country, winning nine caps, and also captained Worcester in the Guinness Premiership before injury enforced his retirement in 2005.

A year after the tour, Maurice Richards of Wales followed the well-worn path north to enjoy a career in rugby league with Salford. So, too, did Mick Coulman of England, who later coached the Lancashire club. Ken Goodall also switched codes but injuries curtailed his career at Workington Town. He went back to teaching and lived long enough to be reinstated by the IRFU after the arrival of professionalism. He died in 2006, aged 59.

Another teacher by profession, Jeff Young of Wales, left education to join the RAF and rose to the rank of Wing Commander. Latterly he became the first technical director of the Welsh Rugby Union, and was awarded the OBE for his services to the RAF and rugby. Sadly, he developed Alzheimer's disease and died in 2005 at the age of 62.

Bob Taylor, arguably the outstanding back row forward of the tour, captained Northampton and England. He taught PE and maths, served as a magistrate in Northampton and became president of the RFU in 2007. John O'Shea emigrated to Australia and worked in the drinks trade. He married the Australian Olympic sprinter Marlene Matthews, who was double sprint champion in the Commonwealth Games at Cardiff in 1958 – 'It's very embarrassing to be married to a woman who once ran faster at Cardiff Arms Park than me,' he once remarked.

The last word should go to captain Kiernan: 'We had a reunion recently and as many as 23 or 24 of the 1968 Lions managed to make it to the House of Lords in London – that proved we weren't wreckers! It was great to see all the old faces and we had a wonderful time together recalling the stories.'

Happy memories for the participants, then, yet the 1968 tour must be deemed a failure in terms of the Test results, though the drawn match had at least prevented a whitewash. The Lions were in the doldrums, but little did anybody know that the new decade would bring a whole new glamour to rugby, and greatly enhance the lustrous name of the British and Irish Lions.

CHAPTER NINE

JOHN DAWES AND THE GREAT REVIVAL

New Zealand and Australia 1971

Mistakes had been made. Lessons had been learned. If the 1960s was the nadir of Lions rugby, then the early 1970s was undoubtedly the zenith for the tourists. It all came down, as it usually does in sport, to a happy coincidence in which fine players came together with great coaches and managers, all imbued with an attitude that they had learned from the past and now would not be beaten.

By 1971, in order to counteract what was going on in South Africa and New Zealand, where the game was all but professionalized, the home unions and many top clubs had completely overhauled their approach to coaching. The emphasis all round was on much greater fitness and far more dedication to training, especially for those players who wanted to be internationalists. It was a painful exercise for unions to whom the amateur approach was still their creed.

By that time, the idea that individual countries could tour southern hemisphere countries was also well established. Indeed Wales had toured

New Zealand in 1969, losing both Tests, though some of the home refereeing was highly dubious.

While they could see some All Blacks benefiting from playing – via commercial activities off the field – the Lions were still very much amateurs who were paid peanuts. They got just 75p per day (15 shillings in old money) for 'expenses' in 1971. That the home unions were willing to embrace something as alien as a professional approach to coaching and preparation is proof of how desperate the situation had become. Had they not done so, the likelihood is that the Lions might well have died of neglect.

Instead, in one glorious tour, the British and Irish Lions restored and enhanced the honour of rugby in the home countries. The year 1971 was indeed an *annus mirabilis* for the Lions, yet the omens were not good for the team which set out for New Zealand via Australia in the early days of May. The All Blacks still had many of the team that had so decisively defeated the Lions just five years previously and that had toured Britain and Ireland losing only one match in 1967. Legendary players like Sid Going, Alex Wylie, Laurie Mains, Colin Meads and Ian Kirkpatrick had created a juggernaut that was expected to sweep aside the Lions. The received wisdom was that for all the genius the Lions undoubtedly possessed in their stellar back line, the forwards just would not be able to compete against their illustrious opponents. Meads, Kirkpatrick and Co. would win all the ball and be key to the series, went the theory, but theory was to be proved quite wrong.

The Lions had men of world-class quality, especially in the backs. The peerless Gareth Edwards at scrum-half could look along his line and see next to him Barry John, the fly-half whose performances on the tour would earn him the nickname 'The King'. Mike Gibson was still supreme in the centre alongside another great Welshman, John Dawes, who was seen as the perfect choice to captain the side after leading Wales to the Grand Slam of 1971. On the wings were two players already on their way to legendary status, Gerald Davies of Wales and England's David Duckham, he of the long legs and flowing motion. Behind them at full-back was another man destined to be a legend, J.P.R. Williams. That septet of stars would stay together for the final three Tests in New Zealand, Duckham replacing John Bevan after the first Test, the Welshman having lost form after an astonishing start to the tour in which he scored 11 tries in his first 5 matches.

Many people at the time considered that it was the backs who won the series with their attacks, but the Lions' eventual triumph would not have been possible without the staggering defence provided by all the players and the contribution made by a pack of forwards who were not prepared to lie down to their opposite numbers. The Test pack had six ever-presents, Ian 'Mighty Mouse' McLauchlan of Scotland, John Pullin of England and Sean Lynch of Ireland in the front row; Willie John McBride at lock; John Taylor of Wales at flanker; and Welsh star Mervyn Davies at No. 8.

Davies opined that the Lions pack never got sufficient credit for their defensive qualities. He said:

I can't say that over the course of the Test Matches we were better than them up front, but there were some periods where we were definitely on top and were able to get some very good ball for the backs which they were able to put to good use. In reality, we were nearly always on the back foot, however, and it was the way we defended that enabled us to win.

Tour captain John Dawes agreed:

You win Test Matches by having a good defence and taking your chances when they come. It was a case of every man defending, because, in the Test Matches at least, they had so much more of the ball. But we tackled and tackled, got up again and tackled some more – that was the story of the series.

The back-to-the-wall performances were inspired by Dawes, Gibson and J.P.R. Williams in the backs and up front by pack leader Willie John McBride, though there was nearly no McBride in 1971. The big man had come home very disillusioned from the 1968 tour and told the selectors to their faces – there is no other way with Willie John – that despite being an automatic choice, he was not inclined to lose again: 'They told me that this time they were going to pick the players to do the job, and that changed my mind.' Had he not done so, the next tour to South Africa would have been closed to him and his personal history would have been so very different. And lest it be forgotten, by 1971 Ireland was deep in the midst of 'The Troubles', but you can search every utterance of anyone from that island involved in the tour and you will find no significant reference to those hellish events. The six men of Ireland, north and south, on the 1971 tour were determined to let nothing come between them, or between them and their fellow tourists, and nothing did.

There is no doubt that, in 1971, consistency of selection enabled the Test XV to gel together, and when the two forwards who stepped up from the midweek side, Derek Quinnell of Wales and Scotland's Gordon Brown – big Broon from Troon – did so with efficiency, it was largely because every player on the tour was working to the master plan prepared by the coach, Carwyn James.

The genius of James was to prepare his teams to face everything that would be thrown at them, though in truth he would have had to be Angelo Dundee, the trainer of Muhammad Ali, to ready his men to face some of the brutality that came their way. A Welsh nationalist, poet and wine-drinking intellectual – he refused to touch New Zealand wine, which he rated as inferior, and always ordered Châteauneuf du Pape – James had understood the harsh reality of the physical challenge facing the Lions.

He is credited with coining the famous phrase 'get your retaliation in first' – a lesson that it took the Lions some time to learn.

He was strong in getting his own way about things, as was the case with his views on New Zealand referees. Just one referee, the highly respected and scrupulously fair bank manager John Pring, was put in charge of all four Tests at the specific request of the Lions management, i.e. James. Another referee had been put forward by the NZRFU, but James rejected him on the understandable grounds that when he had refereed a match during the Welsh tour of New Zealand in 1969, the said gentleman was seen actually jumping for joy when the All Blacks scored.

James was technically the assistant manager, supporting former Lion, Doug Smith, who had toured Down Under in 1950 and also won eight caps for Scotland. A doctor from Aberdeen, Smith was a big man in physique and personality, hard but fair, and enjoyed the respect of all the players. 'He was the best manager I knew,' said Willie John McBride.

Smith acted as the perfect counterfoil to James, allowing the coach to do what he did best while taking on himself all the many other tasks that managers were increasingly asked to fulfil as Lions tours became ever more public property. He did so with humour and honesty, and also took charge of all medical matters with the tourists. Smith was also not afraid to take on board the views of the senior players, forming what he called a 'brains trust' with the likes of McBride and Gibson.

He and James also worked closely and well with John Dawes, who is still the only Lions captain to win a Test series in New Zealand. Even though he had just captained Wales to the Grand Slam, the man himself did not think he was a certainty for the job:

Doug and Carwyn played their cards close to their chests, and I suppose they had to do that. Doug had told me that he would call me when a decision was made, and I remember that on the Sunday when the selection committee met, I had to wait about 12 hours and take hundreds of calls asking me if I had been given the captaincy. I had to answer every one because I thought it might be Doug, and eventually, about half-past-midnight, it was finally him to tell me I had been appointed.

I was greatly honoured; it was the pinnacle of my rugby life, but I knew the enormity of the task that faced us if we were to go to New Zealand and win, simply by the fact that no Lions team had ever done it before.

Dawes was teaching at a grammar school in Hounslow in Middlesex at the time, and, fortunately for him, the headmaster was Gordon Lister, a Geordie who loved his rugby: 'I had roped him into supporting London Welsh where I was playing at the time and he was a big ally in getting me paid time off for the tour.'

Smith, James and Dawes immediately bonded, and the manager could even tolerate his captain's quips that he only liked the job 'because as a good Scot, he knew the manager wouldn't have to buy any drinks!' In retaliation, Smith instructed Dawes to ensure that no matter where they went on tour his favourite tipple of Campari would be available: 'I had to carry the remnants of his Campari in my bag in case there wasn't any at the next stop.'

According to Dawes, Smith was firm with the players and with the New Zealanders, but was a natural manager and ambassador: 'It seems incredible but after every match, and don't forget we played 26 of them, in his speeches he told a different story, was always funny, and never repeated himself – a fantastic feat.'

The Lions gathered in London before setting off to their usual pre-tour camp at Eastbourne. 'The training there was a bit of a joke, really,' said Dawes, 'as everyone was reluctant to train hard in case they got injured. But we did some of the necessary "bonding" things, like appointing a choirmaster – a very important role on tour.'

The choirmaster job went to John Taylor, the Welsh flanker. He knew more about pop music than most and soon introduced the Lions to the Beach Boys' hit 'The Sloop John B'. This being a tour full of overgrown boys, as all rugby players are, some of the Lions decided they didn't need words and just sang 'boo-boom, boo-boom'. The clever tactic of Taylor was to put the singers and the 'boo-boomers' together and a memorable tour song was created.

The early coaching sessions were a real eye-opener for those who had not experienced the unique style of Carwyn James. Instead of a hectoring, they were treated to a man talking sense about rugby, always quietly but effectively.

Gerald Davies was happy to lead the Lions' unanimous chorus of praise for Carwyn James:

He was terrific because, by and large, he was different to any other coach at that time. Many people felt that coaches should be dictators, and be sergeant-majorish all the time, shouting to get their way. But Carwyn was not like that. He was a teacher and lecturer, and the quality of a great teacher is not to tell a pupil the answer but to get the pupil to find out for himself. Carwyn had that quality of drawing out the best talents from a player, and he did so almost in a philosophical way. The best coaches are those who bring out the best in players, and Carwyn James certainly did that.

John Dawes agreed: 'He was an understanding coach who had no favourites. Some of his best coaching sessions were held at the dining table, where he would do more listening than talking.'

If ever a Lions tour could be said to revolve around one player, that man was Barry John in 1971. With his elusive running, devastating side-step and magical boot, the fly-half was already worshipped like a prince in Wales, but on this tour he became The King, the nickname that has stuck for nearly four decades. John Pullin observed of him:

> *Barry didn't like the rough stuff, and he didn't make that many breaks, but he could kick the ball beautifully. People always said he was lucky because the ball would roll into touch, but he did it so many times it was nothing to do with luck. It was fantastic to have him playing behind you as he could always turn the All Blacks and keep us going forward.*

Sandy Carmichael said much the same: 'Barry John and Gareth Edwards could run and win a game for you. There's no one like that around now. Mind you, Barry had to play it his way because he hated going into a ruck – told me he didn't know how to spell the word.'

The man himself is very self-deprecating. 'Ruck? Tackle?' he said. 'I'm still trying to find the bastards that pushed me into them because if I got involved in a tackle somebody had to have pushed me.'

John had a three-year-old reason to show his best in 1971: 'I had toured in 1968, of course, but my tour ended when I broke my collarbone in the first Test. We'll never know what might have happened, but the Springboks were a very good side. By the time we came to New Zealand, Wales had just won the Grand Slam. I was ready for it.'

The extraordinary thing is that John and coach James, contrary to some accounts, did not spend hours plotting the All Blacks' downfall: 'He hardly talked to me,' said John.

> *I can't honestly remember him ever sitting down with me and saying 'Look at the game like this or do this or that.' By and large he left me alone. He knew that he didn't have to tell me when to drop somebody short or when to open up, he just backed his playmakers and let us get on with it.*

Barry John and Carwyn James deservedly get much of the credit for the Lions' success, but the veneration accorded to James over the decades is perhaps misplaced. According to John Pullin and others, Carwyn James was not omniscient and forward play was definitely not his forte: 'He said he didn't have a clue about front row play and didn't know much about the forwards generally, so he left us to work things out for ourselves, led by Willie John McBride and Ray McLoughlin.'

Ian 'Mighty Mouse' McLauchlan confirmed this view:

Carwyn wasn't particularly interested in tight forward play, but he and Doug Smith were perfect psychologists and they led people and got the best out of them, which is 50 per cent of the job. You don't have to know everything about being a prop forward; you need to be able to pick the right people, which they did, and then get leadership on the field, which they did, and then you have to instil the belief that you can win. The results showed their success.

Willie John McBride, however, was adamant: 'Carwyn James is the greatest Lions coach I ever worked with.' There is no higher praise.

In many respects, Ray McLoughlin of Ireland was the unsung backroom hero of the tour. He had toured with the Lions in 1966 and would win 40 caps in all for Ireland. Though he had to leave the tour through injury, before his departure McLoughlin exerted a powerful influence on the tight play of the Lions' forwards. 'Carwyn wanted to get inside the mind of a forward,' said Dawes, 'and he turned to Ray for that as he was probably the nearest in intellect to him. He was a very valuable man for Carwyn.'

McLoughlin worked closely with Willie John McBride, the latter providing the necessary leadership to the pack: 'It worked well, with Ray providing the brains and Willie John the leadership,' said Dawes. With loose forwards of the belligerent quality of Mervyn Davies and John

Taylor, the battles up front would be much more equal than anyone outside of the Lions foresaw.

There were some players who knew they were travelling as understudies. John Spencer of Headingley and England was then a trainee solicitor and needed dispensation from the Law Society to make the trip. He said: 'I knew that with John Dawes as captain I might not make the Test side, but I still wanted to go because to be a Lion is the icing on the cake, the ultimate experience in any player's career.'

Ray Hopkins of Maesteg and Wales, who is always known as Chico, was the seemingly permanent understudy to Gareth Edwards in the Welsh side. He was working as a fitter and turner with the Coal Board when the call came to his home in Maesteg to say he had been selected:

My father Dick took the call at the telephone box across the road from our house, and he was nearly knocked down rushing across the road, he was so excited. He was a huge rugby man and was responsible for everything I did in rugby. It was a huge honour, and as a player from a small club I was just delighted to even have been considered.

Though the tour was to New Zealand, the cash-strapped Australian RFU begged the Lions to stop off in Australia for what were seen as a couple of warm-up matches. With every man jack of them jet-lagged, the tour got off to a bad start with an 11–15 loss against Queensland, whose coach Des O'Connor described them as 'the worst Lions ever'. The Lions were dismayed that the mascot they carried, which by tradition was given to the first team to beat them, was handed over straightaway.

When they squeaked a narrow 14–12 victory in the second match, against New South Wales, it began to look as thought the doomsday merchants might be right about the tourists' chances in New Zealand.

In the first press conference after their arrival, Doug Smith made an astonishing prediction, that the Lions would win the series 2–1, which was all the more unlikely because it meant that one of the four matches would have to be a draw. 'We all looked away at that point,' said Dawes. 'Nobody wanted to associate themselves with that sort of statement.'

The Lions in 1971 had a different approach to the problem of playing the best side on a Saturday and the lesser lights on a Tuesday or Wednesday. Carwyn James did not believe in such a division, as John Pullin remembered:

> There never were two distinct teams as such, and apart from a few players, maybe only Barry John and Gareth Edwards, no one was guaranteed a place in the Test side. The midweek games were being won well, some by very good scores, and you knew you were not an automatic selection, not by a long way.

John Spencer agreed: 'A lot of us played equal amounts of midweek matches and Saturday games. There was no definite Test side and since there were only 30 players on tour, there was always a chance of an injury and you would have to be ready to play.'

John Dawes explained why:

> The selection was done by Doug, Carwyn and me, and in our first meeting in New Zealand we decided to write off what had happened in Australia and pick the teams for the first six matches to ensure first of all that everyone got a game, and to avoid the situation where there would be separate midweek and Saturday sides. It worked quite well until the week before the first Test when, after the midweek team and Test team were announced, Bob 'Boss' Hiller, who was captain of England and was chosen to captain the midweek side, said he wanted all his XV to go for a drink and the Saturday side wasn't invited, thereby undoing all our good work! But there was no rancour – everyone understood what was going on.

Gerald Davies has fond memories of Hiller:

On a Lions tour you need great characters, and in 1971 there were two who stick out in my mind, Bob Hiller of Harlequins and Chico Hopkins from Maesteg. They were from different countries and different parts of the social spectrum but they were great pals, very funny together like Laurel and Hardy.

Bob was unlucky because J.P.R. Williams was in his pomp, or else he would have gained a Test place, and he certainly kicked a lot of goals for the midweek side. He was always very quick-witted, and ready with a remark, even on the pitch. Those were the days when kickers didn't have tees and had to make their own hole in the ground, which was the case with Bob who was an old-fashioned 'toe end' kicker. In one of the games against one of the country teams, he was preparing his mark when someone in the crowd shouted 'Hey Hiller, do you want a shovel?' and quick as a flash, Bob shouted back, 'No, mate, just lend me your mouth; it's big enough.'

Hiller, who had started off as a teacher but was then working for the 3M company, had no regrets about taking time off to tour, even though he knew he didn't have much chance to make the Test team:

We had a fantastic time and I have nothing but happy memories of both my tours. I played in the midweek side in 1971 when at the time I had already been captain of England, but the fact is that JPR was the best full-back I have ever seen in a Lions jersey, and if I was picking an all-time Lions XV, he would be the first name in the team sheet. Mind you, I was a better kicker than him!

Hiller really could kick goals – his record of 44 conversions in all matches on a tour stands to this day, and with the truncated tours of modern times, it will probably be his for ever. Other fine players who did not make the Test side included Ireland's Fergus Slattery, whose time would come in 1974, Scottish back Chris Rea and England's great Cornish prop, Brian 'Stack' Stevens.

With talent abounding no matter what day they played, the Lions duly went on a run of eight games without defeat, including victories over the New Zealand Maoris, whose scrum-half was the great All Black and one-time Mormon missionary, Sid Going, who scored the first try. Sid's brother Ken played at centre for the Maoris, as his opposite number John Spencer recalled with feeling.

On a tour, if they see you can't handle the physical stuff, the word soon gets round and every team tries it on. I stood up to him, even after he straight-armed me and I had to go off and get 12 stitches while the referee warned Ken. I came back on and ran at him with a stiff arm and flattened him, and then I got the referee's warning that Ken had received a couple of minutes earlier. Things calmed down after that. Doug Smith also gave me a warning but the rest of the players thought I had done the right thing.

The tough stuff stayed on the pitch, and the social side of the tour was very happy, as John Pullin remembered: 'It was a marvellous tour with plenty of fun and games – that's what we went on tour for! The New Zealanders were fantastic hosts and couldn't do enough for you.' John Spencer agreed: 'If you were wearing your Lions jersey or blazer, everything was free. I even went to the post office for stamps and they wouldn't let me pay. Personally I liked the Sunday School – a lunchtime session each Sunday that most of us took part in.' And no, it wasn't a school for studying scripture …

Chico Hopkins recalled that the players used to visit schools and give a talk, each player taking it in turn to speak at a different school:

And it was just my luck that I was picked to speak at the biggest school of all, with 3,000 mainly Maori kids crammed into the assembly hall. My dad had written the speech for me and it was full of things like 'Maesteg is a veritable paradise', but did I not go and knock the lectern off the stage, and nearly kill four of the kids! They had to send for the medics. I dried up at that point, but fortunately some of the lads had come with me and got up to speak in my place.

By the end of the first month in New Zealand, the tourists were playing top-drawer rugby and the home fans were delighted to see the skills displayed by Edwards, John and crew. The few unpleasant incidents in the early provincial matches, due largely to overenthusiastic play by the hosts, were no indication as to what was going to happen when the tourists fetched up in Lancaster Park, now the AMI Stadium, in Christchurch. Those Lions with memories of 1966 could have told them that the Canterbury side took no prisoners, and Willie John and others did say that. But bad as 1966 had been, the 1971 Battle of Canterbury was much worse.

After the match, the Canterbury apologists said the Lions had brought things on themselves by 'killing' the ball. In that case, why was most of the damage inflicted illegally by fists? No New Zealander has ever satisfactorily answered that question.

By the end of the match, Sandy Carmichael, one of the toughest props in rugby, had been punched clean out of the tour, sustaining a quintuple fracture of the cheekbone during the match – amazingly, he played on to the final whistle. So bad were his injuries that at first the surgeons thought he had fractured his skull. Had the assault been conducted anywhere but on a rugby pitch, his assailant would have gone to jail. To this day

Carmichael has refused to name the culprit, but other Lions are convinced it was All Black prop Alister Hopkinson.

'It was a sneaky backhander at a line-out,' said Carmichael. 'I know who the guilty party is, but I have never told. The only other person who knew was Doug Smith and Doug's sadly no longer with us.'

Carmichael added: 'Put it this way, it just stays hanging over Canterbury if I don't tell, and it keeps getting brought up every 25 years or so …'

Fergus Slattery was laid out by a punch that almost cost him two teeth, while both John Pullin and Gareth Edwards were flattened by punches from behind. Pullin said: 'It happened to me after I went through the line-out – I wasn't daft enough to do that again! It was definitely Hopkinson who did the damage. At least this time I wasn't knocked out cold as happened to me with Gys Pitzer in 1968.'

Mervyn Davies, out with a nagging groin strain, watched from the stands: 'I had been injured and let's just say I wasn't too unhappy to not be on the field in the Battle of Canterbury. It was an unfortunate episode in New Zealand's rugby history; the attacks were vicious, and we lost key players out of the tour completely. Is it significant that the Canterbury match was arranged for the Saturday before the first Test?'

Ireland's Mike Hipwell was also invalided out with a cartilage injury, but one of the worst injuries was self-inflicted. Ray McLoughlin was one of the Lions who tried to 'get his retaliation in first', and he broke his thumb in doing so. He joined Carmichael on the plane home. Or did he?

John Spencer said:

We called Ray 'Sir John Wilder' after the entrepreneur character in the Power Game *television series of the time. When he wasn't playing or training, he was away doing deals of some sort or going in disguise to spy on the All Blacks. After he was supposed to have left, he kept emerging in different parts of the country and borrowing rooms and building up telephone bills. I don't think he left until days after we had supposedly said goodbye to him.*

After the 'Battle', the Lions reacted with muted concern, but with no regard for diplomacy, New Zealand's coach Ivan Vodanovich poured oil on the flames with his statement that the first Test would resemble 'Passchendaele' if the Lions were to lie on the ball. Doug Smith went quietly to work, and the New Zealand rugby authorities eventually had to issue a statement saying there would be no such 'battle' in the first Test.

'The fact that we won at Christchurch and the way that Doug handled things was a sort of a turning point in the tour,' said John Dawes. 'Across New Zealand, they all thought we were going to lose the Tests, but after that Canterbury match I think they suddenly realized "Hang on, this isn't a bad team and they could be in with a shout", and we definitely gained a measure of respect.'

That respect showed itself in a surprising quarter: the usually hostile New Zealand press, who were unanimous in condemning the Canterbury tactics. T.P. McLean, doyen of the nation's sports journalists, recognized a kindred spirit in Carwyn James. 'They had a very friendly relationship,' said Dawes, 'and the rest of the press seemed to follow Terry McLean's lead so we had a relatively smooth time from them.'

It was still a hotly contested match at Carisbrook in Dunedin. Ian McLauchlan and Sean Lynch came in for Sandy Carmichael and Ray McLoughlin. Still combative all these years later, the Mighty Mouse didn't think it was a foregone conclusion that Carmichael and McLoughlin would have been the Test props: 'It's been perpetuated over the years that they were the first choice, but I would point out that I had been selected against Otago, and I would have backed myself and Sean Lynch against anybody. In any case, Sandy didn't follow my advice – stand up and kick him in the face first!'

Lynch was a very strong man, as John Dawes recalled:

After one session during which he had a few drinks, we had to tie him to his bed to get him under control, but the funny thing was that he was scared of flying. The next morning we were due to travel and Carwyn had actually arranged for him to make the trip by car, only for Sean to say that he wanted to die with the rest of us.

John Pullin, for one, had to adjust his game considerably to accommodate Lynch and McLauchlan: 'Ian was small for a prop, and I was quite big for a hooker. Ian was a great player, but I thought Sean Lynch was just as good and never got the credit he deserved.' Both men rose to the occasion magnificently. For Mighty Mouse especially, it was the start of a run of eight successive Test matches in the Lions front row.

Behind their props, the rest of the forwards battled ferociously, and they were helped by the inexperience of the New Zealand side, which had six new caps that day. In truth the Lions were also fortunate, especially when a poor clearance kick by flanker Alan Sutherland inside his own 25 (as it was then) was charged down by McLauchlan who duly scored the first try.

In 2009, McLauchlan joked: 'Lucky? A run-in from 64 yards? As the years go on, the yards go on ...'

By that time in international rugby, replacements were allowed for injured players and understudy Hopkins got his chance when Gareth Edwards went off injured just as, for the first time, the Lions got close to the All Blacks line.

Hopkins said:

I never felt inferior to Gareth, and always thought I was closer to him in terms of skill etc. than was made out by the press. His big advantage was that he was based in Cardiff and the Western Mail supported him, and everybody knew that Cardiff and the Western Mail *ran Welsh rugby in those days.*

Hopkins filled in admirably, but it was Barry John who saved the day, kicking the ball with such accuracy to either corner that All Black full-back Fergie McCormick was soon chasing shadows. Even though they were often camped in the Lions half, John would simply clear the ball for miles downfield, forcing the All Black pack to chunter back. And it was John who sealed the 9–3 victory with two penalties.

The key to the kicking tactics had been planned the previous week at the Battle of Canterbury, and involved just a single word exchanged between coach James and Barry John:

At half-time in that match Carwyn called me to one side and said just one word. We both spoke Welsh and what he said was 'diddorol' which is Welsh for 'interesting'. That was all he had to say, because between us it meant that I should be watching their full-back Fergie McCormick, so for the rest of the match I just watched Fergie and his positioning, getting an insight into his play. So the next week in the first Test I knew his game plan and that's why I kicked the way I did and it worked for us. I'm happy to say, because he was a good player, that he was dropped after that match and never played for the All Blacks again.

Mervyn Davies had definite views on that win:

We expected another battle in that first Test. I don't think we saw the ball at all and we just defended, defended and defended and somehow managed to win. The first Test is always vital because, if you win, the outcome of the series will go all the way to the fourth Test. We were the first Lions to win their first Test in New Zealand and that's why I think it was the most significant match on the tour.

John Pullin agreed: 'It came to me during one period in that Test that we had no chance against them. They were so superior at times that we couldn't believe we won. We were very lucky that day, but we won and that was all that counted.'

Ian McLauchlan felt the All Blacks made the mistake of believing their own publicity: 'They thought they were invincible, the press thought they were invincible, but a lot of guys in our camp said "they're just 15 men against 15 of us, so let's go", and by the final whistle we knew, and they knew, that they weren't invincible any more.'

Barry John concluded:

I thought we were in trouble after the first 20 minutes because I had hardly touched the ball. They had so much possession I thought they had brought their own ball onto the pitch and were never going to part with it. How we got to 9–3, I will never know. But it was our defence that won it. In his book on the tour, John Reason summed it up perfectly saying 'The All Blacks were like a river flooding towards its banks, but the banks never broke.'

It was a different story in the second Test in Christchurch, the All Blacks running out comfortable winners by 20–12, with Sid Going playing particularly well. The All Blacks showed their intentions from the start. Peter Dixon, the England flanker, caught the ball from the kick-off and was promptly flattened by the All Black pack. He had to go off and have his head wound stitched, but returned to the fray.

Ian McLauchlan said: 'I thought we played better in the second Test but the breaks didn't go for us and the crucial score was when we were in their half and suddenly Ian Kirkpatrick broke and ran all the way. We came back at them after that but it wasn't enough.'

Barry John said: 'We had lost, but we had chances and were not helped by the penalty try against Gerald Davies at a vital time, but, coming off, we felt we could take them and win the series. Strange, but in defeat we actually felt more confident.'

The Lions needed to regroup, and were not helped by another vicious match against Hawke's Bay where John Pullin was knocked out by a punch. He recalled:

> That was a sore one in the eye. It was one of their forwards who hadn't ever made it into the All Black team. He was a nasty piece of work and way over the hill, and we were giving him a roasting so he resorted to that punch. Can't even remember his name now, because the punch was the only impression he made on me.
>
> It was a dirty game, that one. I remember things got so out of hand that a woman in the crowd chased Gareth Edwards to hit him with her umbrella – quite heated, you might say.

Showing his disgust at the home side's antics, Barry John cheekily invited his opponents to 'come and get me' with the ultimate insult: he sat on the ball. John said:

> Well, if you've got the ball all the time, you can sit on it, can't you? Nothing wrong with that. Mind you it was still in play. The crowd were shouting 'Kill, kill', and it was only then I noticed that I was sitting two yards outside the 25. Their pack came charging at me like a herd of wildebeest, but I had enough time and belted the ball downfield. Ever seen a herd of wildebeest turn in mid-air? They were screaming, and I was shouting 'get back to where you came from' – great fun. Of course, a couple of the papers did have a go at me, saying my halo was dropping, but I just said 'Bollocks to the halo, they were kicking shit out of our boys.'

In those days of few televisions, John was still not a household face. Chico Hopkins told the story of being frequently mistaken for The King by autograph hunters: 'Eventually I just said to them, "No, I don't feel like signing today as I am thinking about the tries and goals I'm going to score on Saturday." Barry used to go off his head: "Don't tell them things like that" he would say.'

New Zealand recalled their former captain Brian Lochore for the third Test, in which Broon frae Troon and Derek Quinnell made their Test debuts. Quinnell had not yet been capped by Wales but his performances on the tour had earned him the right to face the All Blacks. It was an opportunity he seized with aplomb.

It would be a game the Lions would never forget, as they ripped into the All Blacks from the start, scoring two tries, two conversions and a drop goal in the first quarter – all the points bar Gerald Davies' try scored by Barry John – for a 13–0 lead, which they held till half-time. Try as they might, the All Blacks could only muster one try by Mains and the match was won 13–3.

John Pullin delivered the following verdict:

We hammered them that day. We had seen it coming about eight weeks previously when we thrashed Wellington on the same pitch 47–9, and now it had all come together for us. From having thought of them as invincible, I suddenly realized that their pack just was not as good as the forwards we had faced in South Africa in 1968. The Springboks were a lot harder, and while I had a great deal of respect for the likes of Colin Meads, he was only a shadow of his former self. Some of them were past it, to be honest.

By that time, a Sunday newspaper in Wales had referred to Barry John as 'the King' of fly-halves, and he certainly ruled the roost that day. John said:

We came out of the blocks, got the points early and Derek Quinnell did a great job in shackling Sid Going. When you see Sid having to stop and change direction, it's a big psychological plus. We could feel the confidence growing, and Mike Gibson and John Dawes were tackling everything to a standstill.

No matter what happened, the Lions could not lose the series, and they marched on, undefeated in three more matches, to Auckland for the fourth and final Test. For sheer excitement, there has probably never been a Lions match like it. It was a gritty encounter, largely bereft of running rugby, and once again the forward duel ended in honours even.

The All Blacks opened the scoring after just four minutes with a try by Wayne Cottrell, converted by Laurie Mains. A penalty by Mains put New Zealand further ahead, but these Lions were not going to accept defeat. A penalty by Barry John and his conversion of Peter Dixon's try made it 8–8 at half-time, and after John goaled another penalty, flanker Tom Lister, who had replaced Alan McNaughton in the New Zealand back row, scored an unconverted try. With the scores at 11–11, enter J.P.R. Williams to make his bit of history. Calling for the ball just inside the All Blacks' half, he fired over an outrageous drop goal to put the Lions in front where they stayed until the 72nd minute when Laurie Mains equalized with a penalty. Sensing history was theirs, the Lions' defence held and they had earned a 14–14 draw and the first and only series victory by the Lions in New Zealand – exactly as Doug Smith had predicted, 2–1, with one drawn.

Ian McLauchlan commented: 'I don't think we played particularly well, but maybe there was an element in some minds that we were at the end of a long tour and they were just ready to go home. Anyway, we had won the series, and that was all that mattered.'

John Pullin agreed:

We played reasonably well but nowhere near as well as the third Test. You could argue that we were a bit lucky because I don't think even JPR thought he was going to score with that kick. If it hadn't been so crucial with so much at stake, we would probably have played much better, but the result was everything. It was a draw that felt like a victory.

John Dawes said:

When that drop goal went over, none of us could believe it, because the chances of him scoring were so remote. But if you look at the film of it, JPR just turns to the stand and gives a salute. Apparently he had told a few people that he felt like dropping a goal in the match – if he had told the rest of us we would have just laughed. I don't think he ever dropped a goal in his career again.

For Gerald Davies, it was one of the most sublime moments of his life: 'To beat New Zealand on their own patch wearing that famous red jersey was nothing less than the fulfilment of a dream.'

Barry John, the great flair player, admitted that he deliberately chose caution over attack in the last quarter of that final Test:

We didn't do ourselves justice, and in that last 20 minutes there were a couple of occasions when I deliberately chose the option of kicking to the corner and keeping the pressure on rather than throw the ball out to Mike Gibson. We could have scored at least one try, but I chose the percentage option. But then we were only minutes away from achieving everything we had worked for over four months of the tour. Yes it was the safety factor that was in my mind, but we got the job done.

At the final whistle there was just relief. We had made history. But believe it or not, there was then a feeling of emptiness about it all, because we had achieved the Everest of challenges in our rugby lives.

Gareth Edwards summed up his view of the tour:

Ronnie Dawson had helped lay the foundation in 1968, but in 1971 we still had a mountain to climb. People forget in this age of professionalism how new the concept of coaching was in those days, and Carwyn James was the man who took coaching to new levels. You also had the coming together of a rather talented group of players who had the benefit of that coaching.

Nowadays, thanks to television, we are all aware of the strength of provincial rugby in New Zealand, but back then I don't think people really appreciated what a feat that was to go through the tour unbeaten by any of the provincial sides.

The manner in which we won the series captured the imagination of the public, and as is their wont, it raised the public's expectations of us.

The public reaction to their series triumph surprised the players, who returned home hailed as the heroes of the hour.

John Dawes said:

We weren't aware of what had been happening back home with the media building us up as we kept winning. As we were flying into Heathrow, the captain of the plane had a quiet word with Doug Smith and told him that there was a massive crowd at the airport. Doug passed on the message, and there was a lovely spontaneous reaction from us all. We were all in casual travelling gear, but before we landed we all put on our Number Ones, our tour blazers, flannels and shirts and ties. Doug didn't ask us to do it; we just felt it was the right thing to do, and a kind of tribute to him. Doug watched us coming off the plane and he was as proud as ten peacocks. It was a very emotional occasion.

John Spencer was amazed at the reception:

The airport was full. It was just incredible, a bit like the England World Cup team's return in 2003. People were cheering and shouting, and it seemed like everyone in the whole place was there just to see us. We had no idea that the enthusiasm at home was so great, because when you are living out of a suitcase in hotels for months, you don't really know what's going on at home.

Ian McLauchlan said: 'There were just thousands and thousands of people and they were all euphoric. I had never considered that so many people followed rugby closely, never mind bothering to come out to Heathrow to see the team coming home – it was a tremendous feeling.'

The 1971 Lions got together again just a few months afterwards, meeting up for the BBC Sports Personality of the Year broadcast on which they won the Team of the Year award and memorably sang the tour song 'Sloop John B', which promptly became a favourite of rugby clubs everywhere. Her Royal Highness The Princess Royal, then just Princess Anne, won the main award that year, and chatted to the players. Perhaps meeting such Scottish charmers as Broon from Troon influenced her decision to become patron of the SRU.

Carwyn James later upset the All Blacks again, coaching Llanelli to their famous victory over the touring side in 1972. He had already stood as a parliamentary candidate for the Plaid Cymru party even before the Lions tour, and John Dawes felt his nationalist politics ruffled too many feathers at the Welsh Rugby Union: 'That was his undoing. It wasn't seen as the done thing.'

John Spencer was upset after the end of the tour when James refused to accept an honour from the Queen, believed to have been an MBE.

Although I knew he was a devout Welsh nationalist, I felt he could have accepted the honour for the benefit of all the boys. Some of the English lads felt it was a bit of an insult that he wouldn't accept it. I discussed it with him and he told me he understood my point of view but he had made his decision. I had great respect for him, but I did have a tinge of disappointment about that.

James never coached Wales, but it was probably his insistence on picking not only the team but even the selectors which meant he never got the job he wanted. He continued to coach at home and abroad, and loved to travel – he went to South Africa for the Lions tour in 1980. His sudden death in Amsterdam in January 1983, at the age of 52, stunned Wales and the Lions.

Dr Doug Smith did accept the OBE he was offered. He stayed in general practice in Essex until retirement and maintained his interest in rugby, joining the SRU committee. He died in September 1998.

Remarkably, at the time of writing in early 2009, only one of the players from the 1971 Lions has died, though most are now in their mid-to-late 60s. We will read about the late, great Gordon Brown in the next chapter.

John Spencer is still in full-time practice as a solicitor in Yorkshire. He stayed in rugby on the administrative side, was chairman of Club England and now represents the RFU on the new Professional Game Board. By contrast, John Pullin takes little interest in rugby nowadays, saying it is a 'different game' to that which he played. He is still a farmer in the West Country, though he confessed that he would have loved to have had the chance to play rugby union professionally – he was approached to play rugby league but he was a union man who preferred his farming life to life up north.

Peter Dixon is well and living in Durham. Just like Mighty Mouse, the distance from which he scored his famous try in the last Test has now grown from a few yards to, oh, at least 80, as he joked in a recent interview. John Bevan switched to rugby league, playing 332 times for Warrington and scoring 201 tries in 13 seasons, being capped for Wales and Great Britain – another 'Double Lion'. He moved into sports teaching after he retired from playing.

Chico Hopkins said that he felt 'a different player' when he returned from the tour. Carwyn James asked him to join Llanelli, where he and Phil Bennett formed a formidable partnership, one which was regularly compared to Edwards and John. Both men starred in that memorable Llanelli victory over the All Blacks in which their captain was their fellow 1971 Lion, Delme Thomas.

Chico's story is yet another example of a Lion overcoming great adversity in his later life. While at Llanelli, his father Dick dropped dead while watching his son play in a match against Crosskeys. 'That knocked the stuffing out of me for a long time,' said Hopkins. Shortly afterwards, the then 25-year-old Hopkins turned professional with Swinton for a record fee for a scrum-half of £10,000. He said:

> But I had never really come to terms with the death of my father, and I also went away from Maesteg too quickly afterwards. I would come home, still thinking he was there, and of course he wasn't.
>
> I missed him so much and I was under a lot of pressure, so eventually I had a breakdown.

In turn that would lead to nightmarish years for Hopkins as he battled frequent bouts of depression:

> You don't know what brings them on, do you? It lasted for more than eight years and I don't think I am right yet.
>
> The funny thing was that I always used to be a quiet guy but now I go all hyper and can't stop talking. People that used to know me say, 'You've

become a right gobby bastard.' Funnily enough I have a mate who's also been ill and from being an extrovert he's now an introvert. You just don't know how things will affect you.

I also suffered from alopecia, which was really devastating as I used to have lovely black curly hair. So I didn't like going out to dinners and it was only when I went to a Lions 'do' a few years back that I found the courage to go out again.

Hopkins' health has improved and he still forms a double act with his old chum Bob Hiller, who quipped:

He's always calling up for a chat and telling me I'm tight because I never call him! He's a great character, but so are they all. When we had our 25th anniversary reunion at Celtic Manor in 1996, obviously I had kept in touch and seen a lot of the guys since 1971, but even those I hadn't seen since then – well, it was like starting again where we had left off.

Hiller went back to teaching in 1976, and retired in 2002, the year that he became president of Harlequins, a position he still holds.

Not very far from his old colleague's club in the west of greater London, John Dawes is president of London Welsh. His place in Welsh rugby lore is secure, because after retiring as a player, he coached the national side to two Grand Slams. He has since worked extensively in the media and written several books. Another one of the '71 Lions who made a career in the media was Chris Rea, who became a very fine writer and radio commentator and is now the IRB's controller of broadcasting. Stack Stevens, capped 25 times for England and selected 83 times for Cornwall, has recently campaigned to have his home county admitted to the Commonwealth Games in its own right.

Barry John may just have been the single most talented rugby player these islands have ever produced, and it was no surprise that he later formed a firm friendship with the late, great George Best, most people's idea of the greatest soccer talent in British and Irish history. 'The King' and 'The Best' enjoyed almost mythical status in their respective sports, both young and handsome, both retired early, and both enjoyed each other's company while also liking a drink – which is a bit like saying the All Blacks can play a bit.

John stunned the sporting world the year after the Lions victory. At the age of just 27, acclaimed as the best player in the world, he turned his back on rugby and retired after Wales's Five Nations match against France. Though he understands the problem of sportsmen who achieve great feats and lose their motivation to carry on reaching the heights, he is adamant the pressures of celebrity rather than any lack of motivation were the reasons for his retirement.

'I was an amateur player but had to live like a professional,' said John, who returned from the tour to go back to work for the Forward Trust, part of the Midland Bank. 'It was claustrophobic for me in Wales at that time, and I remember one day crossing Queen Street in Cardiff and the traffic stopped. The whole lot of them. There were horns hooting, and people calling out – it was like New York, and all I had done was cross the road.'

On another occasion, a young girl attending the opening of a bank extension curtsied to 'The King' – at that point he knew things had gone too far. He walked away from the stage he had graced so vividly.

Apart from his relationship with Best, who died of liver failure in 2005 after years of chronic alcohol abuse, John never enjoyed the trappings of fame such as wealth. He later owned a restaurant in Cardiff, and in recent years has been a media pundit with an often trenchant column in *Wales on Sunday*. He regularly meets up with John Dawes, Mervyn Davies and his many old friends from the great days of Welsh rugby in the 1970s.

His two convictions on drink-driving charges, for the latter of which he was ordered to attend alcohol counselling, fuelled rumours that The

King was heading the way of The Best, but interviewed in early 2009, just a few days after his 64th birthday, his mind was as sharp as a tack and he seemed in good physical health for a man just a year away from collecting his state pension. He was about to carry out one of the many kindnesses he is known for, delivering a specially requested picture to an old friend celebrating his 80th birthday – a signed photo of The Best and The King.

'I have never worried about what people say about me,' said John. 'I know who I am and what I can do, and how I go about my life. I am very happy. I have four great children and nine lovely grandchildren scattered around the world.'

He laughed: 'People who know me know that it's a case of "long live the King" and bring on whatever's next.'

As for that nickname … 'I have signed thousands of autographs and there is one thing I have never done. People have asked me can you sign it Barry "King" John, but I have always said no way, not a chance, because the moment I do that will be the moment I start believing it and that will be the finish.' With a cackle he added: 'And I've become a bit of a philosopher, too.'

Barry John doesn't live in the past, but what a past it was. With him at the helm, the 1971 Lions pulled off the impossible and won in New Zealand. Would their successors achieve the improbable and beat the Springboks in their own menacing backyard? First of all the Lions had to get to South Africa, and in the 1970s, that was no certainty.

CHAPTER TEN

WILLIE JOHN McBRIDE'S LEGENDS

South Africa 1974

The 1974 Lions tour to South Africa put rugby where it didn't want to be – on the front pages of every newspaper in the land. Controversy abounded from long before the start of the tour, and continued throughout it, with events on the field eventually overshadowing even the massive political row that the tour caused.

Protests against apartheid in South Africa had been growing over the years. The Springboks' tour in 1969 and South Africa's cricket tour to Britain in 1979 had been disrupted by mass protests led by Peter Hain – later a Labour Cabinet Minister – and his Stop the Tour organization. But that was nothing compared to what occurred in Australia in 1971. The presence of the South African team led to massive and sometimes violent protests in every town and city they visited. The Premier of Queensland even declared a state of emergency at the time of their visit.

That same year Sir Donald Bradman, the great 'Don' himself, was in charge of Australian cricket. He flew to South Africa and confronted Prime Minister Vorster before returning home and banning the South

African cricketers 'until they choose a team on a non-racist basis'. Bradman's action showed that the worldwide anti-apartheid movement was winning its case, and for the first time the Lions came under serious pressure to boycott South Africa.

In the early 1970s, Britain's Conservative Government had an ambivalent attitude to links with the apartheid regime in South Africa, but on coming to power in February 1974, the new Labour Government wrote to the Home Unions Committee asking that the Lions tour to South Africa should not proceed. The hypocrisy of a government which still allowed all sorts of trading links with South Africa while asking a rugby team to stay at home caused many people in the rugby community to side with the 'blazerati', who wanted the tour to go ahead regardless.

Many leading figures in the home unions took the position that rugby, and indeed sport in general, should stand apart from politics. They argued correctly that no formal boycott had been declared by the Government, and that it was up to each individual to decide whether or not they should tour.

Some administrators and players, however, had come to the realization that apartheid was intrinsically evil, and two of the most high-profile individuals to take a stand were none other than those stars of the 1971 Lions tour, John Taylor and Gerald Davies of Wales. Both men declared themselves unavailable to tour, Taylor making his abhorrence of apartheid clear, while Davies was less vocal. Both men would receive considerable opprobrium for their actions, but they also garnered a great deal of support.

Interviewed for this book, Davies, who of course will manage the 2009 tour to South Africa, explained:

I had a coloured friend at Loughborough training college, the University as it is now, who had come from Cape Town on a scholarship. That was around 1963 to 1966. I got to know him very well as he was interested in rugby and was away from home, and we became friends. When I was out in South Africa on the 1968 tour he phoned me up and we arranged to meet, but he told me he couldn't come to our hotel, so I had to go out to meet him. Of course, we had already seen those divisions everywhere.

That was my personal experience of apartheid, and it was a very unpleasant moment. We had spent a lot of time together in Loughborough and gone to pubs and not even had to think about anything like that; then suddenly you realize that it wasn't so easy to do that in South Africa. It was very poignant for me, I have to say, and so when I came to my decision not to go on the 1974 tour it was something I remembered. At that stage I didn't make any political statement; it was just between me and my moral conscience.

Those who did go on tour were subject to a barrage of criticism from one side, and also direct political pressure – Labour MPs wrote to Lions individually asking them not to go. With the Labour Party's opposition to the tour now confirmed, many local authorities in England, Scotland and Wales decided to stop their employees from taking part or at least to not pay their wages.

Ian McGeechan recalled that it was touch and go whether he could tour:

The first time I had an inkling that I might be selected was on the plane back from Dublin after we had played Ireland, and the Sunday Times *had printed a list of players which they thought might be selected. My name was on it, and that was honestly the first time I had given the matter any thought. Then one morning a letter arrived with the Lions badge marked on it, and that is how I found out I had been selected.*

I had some difficulty getting time off. Leeds was a Labour Council, and they opposed contacts with South Africa, but I had a great headmaster who knew the chief education officer, who in turn was able

177

to get a quorum for a meeting of the committee. The headmaster came into my class and told me I was to take the rest of the afternoon off and go down to the council offices. He told me I was to go in to the meeting and tell them that I had been picked for South Africa and wanted permission to go. The issue was raised at the full council meeting, but by then it was too late and I had my permission. I had a lot of people very supportive of me and that's why I was able to go.

Also a PE teacher, Ian McLauchlan then worked for Edinburgh Corporation. He said: 'I didn't care about what the Government or the Corporation said, I was going and that was that.' When his Welsh employers opposed him going, the flying winger J.J. Williams, then a teacher, changed his career and moved into marketing. It seemed that the majority of the players, while uneasy about the apartheid system, felt that rugby and politics should not mix.

Though he too was a PE teacher, Roger Uttley, by contrast, was given paid time off by his education authority in Northumberland, although he met with some criticism in the staffroom:

It was water off a duck's back to me as I was just pleased to be going. I genuinely thought at the time that it was better to go and find out what was happening, because you have to remember that few people really knew what was going on in South Africa at that time.

McGeechan said: 'I was aware of the apartheid issue, but perhaps naively I thought politics should not be part of anything to do with sport, and I still feel that way.'

The South African Government did make concessions that were seen as vital to the cause of black and coloured rugby in South Africa. In certain games, there was to be no segregation in the crowd, a major change of policy.

Each of the communities had its own governing body, and for the first time it was agreed that the Lions could play matches against teams chosen from those 'other' unions, and whether that was patronizing or not, the two matches against the 'coloured' South African Republic Federation XV and the 'black' or 'Bantu' South African Rugby Association Leopards proved very popular and undoubtedly helped to bring forward the cause of non-white rugby.

Sandy Carmichael recalled: 'I was in the stands that day when the Lions played the Leopards, sitting beside the wife of the captain of the black team. She was a lovely lady, and it struck me that had it not been for the Lions, I probably would never have met her.'

Tour coach Syd Millar said:

> I still don't know if we were right or wrong to go, but we did feel that if we went we could get certain changes made. I did feel it was disingenuous of the Government to use sport as a soft option, because I remember a report in the paper that UK trade with South Africa had increased by so many per cent – so what the hell were they doing complaining about us?
>
> The Labour government disowned us and tried to remove passports, and then banned the British diplomats and Embassy staff in South Africa from attending the matches, though they were there, I can tell you.

Andy Irvine of Heriot's FP and Scotland said: 'I think that the fact that we played black and coloured teams with no segregation in the stands was a real breakthrough in South African history because, until then, that simply would not have been allowed to happen under the apartheid system.'

Some Lions were indeed naive, because a few of them were genuinely taken aback when the hotel in which they had gathered in London was besieged by protesters, several of whom were arrested.

Sandy Carmichael recalled:

I was one of those who genuinely believed sport and politics shouldn't mix, but if I ever meet that Peter Hain, I'll thank him, because after the protests in London the possibility that we would be besieged at our training camp at Eastbourne meant we were able to go out a week earlier and train in the sun and at altitude. It was a big help to us all.

So much for the politics – what about the playing side? If the Lions of 1971 were the best that had left these shores in decades, then those who toured in 1974 could claim to be equally as good as their glorious predecessors.

Gareth Edwards felt the success in 1971 caused undue expectations for the successor tourists:

In 1974, it was as if the public were saying you've beaten New Zealand so of course you're going to beat South Africa. It did put a huge amount of pressure on us, but I don't think the public appreciated the challenges of playing against these big physical players and also playing at altitude.

What that 1974 side had was not just players of quality, but proven and experienced players who had the confidence of knowing that they had beaten New Zealand. There was also a physical hardness, gained from experience, in the spine of the team. But there was a slight trepidation on our part, because we felt a sense of responsibility to the public back home and to rugby in Britain and Ireland. It made things more difficult for us.

Without a doubt, the 1974 squad contained the best pack of forwards ever to tour with the British and Irish Lions, and the backs included several of the men who, playing as the Barbarians, had put the All Blacks to the sword in that memorable match in Cardiff in 1973.

Including replacements, the squad had nine players each from Wales and England, eight from Ireland, and six from Scotland, one of them that giant of physique and personality, Gordon Brown. It is often thought that big Broon frae Troon persuaded the party to adopt 'Flower of Scotland', a comparatively new composition by the Scottish folk duo The Corries, as the tour song. In fact the credit should go to Billy Steele, who had a fine voice and, as choirmaster, introduced the song to the Lions. He thus helped start a process that resulted in 'Flower of Scotland' becoming the official pre-match anthem of the Scottish Rugby Union.

One of the youngest players was Roger Uttley, then 22 and playing with Gosforth RFC, now the Newcastle Falcons. Said Uttley:

> *I had just completed my first season as an England international, and while I wasn't exactly in awe of the players I met as we got ready to travel, nevertheless I was just pleased to be in the same squad as the likes of Gareth Edwards, Ian McLauchlan and Willie John McBride who I had seen playing for the Lions on television – in black and white, of course. Willie John was coming up for 34 at the time, in fact he had his 34th birthday in South Africa – it was like going on tour with your father.*

With all the political hoopla, the job of leading the Lions in 1974 was always going to be difficult. Alun Thomas had toured with the Lions in 1955 and was a popular choice as manager, while Syd Millar of Ballymena and Ireland, who had toured three times as a player, was hugely respected as a coach, particularly of forwards: 'One of the two best coaches I ever worked with and a master tactician,' said Ian 'Mighty Mouse' McLauchlan.

Millar said that he took 'a simplistic view' of what was needed to win in South Africa:

> *Rugby in that country is about the scrum and the maul because of the nature of the ground and the size of the players, so in 1974 I wanted a team that I thought would compete up front. We spent a lot of time on*

the scrum and defence, and a lot of time on simple back play, because we
had some very good backs and they knew what to do.

Millar drilled the scrum relentlessly:

I knew the scrum was the key to the South African game – it was their
forte and the rock on which they built their rugby, and they usually had
the best scrum in the world – so we reckoned if we beat them there that
would be a huge psychological blow to them and they would have to
change the pattern of their play, which is what happened. When we
added a fourth man at the line-out we completely dominated the
set pieces.

Sandy Carmichael recalled that the scrummage practices became so
intense that he and Fran Cotton, who had taken the Test place that might
well have been Carmichael's, ended up in a fight:

I had swapped to loose head and Fran was at tight, so he was out of his
normal position. I couldn't help myself and lifted him out of the scrum,
but as soon as he was back down, Fran slammed me one. Right in front
of the watching press. Oh, dear.
    The following morning at 7am Syd Millar was banging on my door
saying 'Carmichael, get out here, you have to come and kiss Fran.' So there
we were at seven in the morning posing for photographers and hugging
each other and saying how everything was okay. Aye, that'll be right …

Roger Uttley enlarged on Millar's methods: 'Syd drove us very hard and
he had us scrummaging like demons. It was all "live" scrummaging and
we had some monster sessions. I particularly remember one in Cape Town
that went on for hours. But he had the wisdom of experience and knew
what was needed.'

The third and most important member of the triumvirate was Willie John McBride, who was to prove the most successful captain in Lions history and who was making his fifth tour as a player, a record he would share with Mike Gibson, originally unavailable for the tour but called in as a replacement. The pivotal relationship among the tourists was between McBride and Millar, the two men of Ballymena sharing the same uncompromising philosophy.

For this book, Millar has given an insight into the way a Lions coach and captain work:

> I did the planning each night for the next day's session or match, with a lot depending on who we were playing next. I left the motivation on the day to Willie John, and Alun Thomas left us alone to get on with the rugby while he dealt with his responsibilities.
>
> I had gathered a lot of information about rugby in South Africa, seeking out ex-pats in particular, so I knew a lot about the provincial sides and which players were likely to make the Springbok Test side – whose back row was quick, whose defence wasn't good, that sort of thing.

Millar revealed some behind-the-scenes psychology on referees that had a major effect on the tour's outcome:

> We also did analysis of the referees, and I spoke to Dr Danie Craven and made sure we got the referees we wanted for the first three Tests. In two instances, the referees were men who had not done a good job in the provincial matches and who had apologized to me, and all I said was 'what we want is a referee that's fair'. In the Tests, they duly were fair.

Manager Thomas was also a fair man, but was noted for his careful approach to money, as the amateur rules were still very much in force. The players' daily permitted expenses had shot up to a whole £1.50, but they wanted for nothing in bed, board and 'ancillaries', as Roger Uttley recalled: 'Our South African hosts were incredibly generous everywhere we went. Wherever we stopped off at a new place we would each get 250 Rothmans, a pack of Castle lager and a bag of oranges.'

Clothing was a different issue, as Sandy Carmichael remembered:

In 1971, it was decided we would all wear red tracksuits, but it took the committee three months to decide that we wouldn't have to pay for them. By 1974, they had agreed we could take two pairs of boots, one of them free, one of which you had to pay for yourself, and they also gave us Adidas training shoes, but they made us pay 10p or something so that we wouldn't be breaking the rules.

It could be argued that the Lions' management extended cost consciousness even to medical matters, because Millar made sure that Irish hooker Ken Kennedy, a qualified doctor, travelled as a player. Millar said:

I chose Ken not just for his skill on the field but because of his medical expertise. He developed exercises for helping breathing at altitude on the High Veldt and also to build upper body strength. He really kept a lot of the guys going, and, of course, he later became a specialist in sports medicine.

Thomas was involved in one amusing incident with Bobby Windsor. The manager's hotel bill had been charged with £87 worth of calls, but Thomas had checked the numbers rung and found they had been made to someone in Newport, where Windsor lived. The manager looked accusingly at the prop, but quick as a flash Windsor replied: 'Which one of you bastards has been phoning my wife?'

The traditional visit to Kruger Park was the highlight of Roger Uttley's tour of a country that was in some ways still undiscovered:

To me it was still the Dark Continent, vast and unknown. It was also old-fashioned. We would travel in ancient Dakotas. If you wanted to phone home you had to book a call two days in advance, and I've still got the Air Mail letters that my wife Kristine and I exchanged.

The hotel we stayed in at our Stilfontein training camp was one of those old-time spa hotels and there were three or four of us to a room, four big lads in our single beds, and no en-suite facilities.

When we went to Kruger Park, which was fantastic, we had guys chasing game in the back of open pick-up trucks – players just wouldn't get away with that these days.

It was while they were relaxing at Kruger Park that some of the most amusing incidents of the tour occurred. 'It was a tour full of characters,' said Uttley. 'In fact, I'd say every one of the Lions of 1974 was a character in one way or another, and they did get up to some fun.'

Bobby Windsor was a regular prankster but was on the receiving end himself on a safari visit to Kruger Park. The tough-as-teak steelworker was genuinely frightened by the animal noises there, and his colleagues wound him up with stories of cheetahs able to leap the 16-foot high fence around the compound: 'He hated creepy crawlies,' said Ian McLauchlan.

Tom Grace and I got a branch and waited until he got into bed and poked it through the window to tickle his head. He got up to see what it was, and then stood on the tail of the Lions mascot which had been put in his room. He jumped up and then kicked the poor lion mascot across the room. We couldn't contain ourselves and burst out laughing, then took off before he could catch us.

A window featured in another incident, this time at the Carlton Hotel in Port Elizabeth, as Roger Uttley recalled:

*We played hard on and off the field, and on this occasion a few drinks
had been taken and a bed ended up going out of an upstairs window.
Fortunately the hotel had an awning all round it and the bed never
actually reached the ground or it might have killed some poor innocent
bystander, though it was very late at night.*

The players let their hair down in the usual fashion – drinking. The Sunday
School was reconvened, but Ian McLauchlan is adamant that the tour
was relatively dry:

*The coaches had stated that they didn't want anyone drinking midweek
and I would say that was observed 95 per cent of the time because the
players knew they had a job to do. There were occasions when players
maybe got homesick and needed a splash-out, but the coaches
understood and there were no repercussions and reprimands. It was self-
discipline by the players and coaches rather than the manager.*

Some players did enjoy the odd serious session. Carmichael recalled that
when the series was won, he and Stewart McKinney went on a bender:
'We started at six o'clock on the Saturday night and finished at ten to
one on the Monday morning – and we still made training at nine that
morning.'

The main player to incur the wrath of manager Thomas, though not
of Millar or McBride, was Andy Ripley. The unconventional Ripley went
off to see African townships for himself, but that was not the reason for
his trouble. His dress was always casual, and he was told by Thomas
that he had to smarten up for a function by wearing his blazer, grey slacks
and tie – which is exactly what he wore, nothing else. Thomas kicked
Ripley out, but the big fellow just laughed.

All the 1974 Lions pay tribute to the leadership of Willie John McBride.
For McBride, victory was everything, and that meant the opposition's

attempts to physically intimidate the Lions had to be resisted with all force, and not always entirely legally – which brings us to the major rugby controversy of the tour, the infamous 99 call.

When you write about the Lions and start to look at the stories behind the tales, you often find that matters are somewhat different after decades of, shall we say, verbal nourishment. So it is with the 99 call. To read some accounts, you would think that in just about every match they played, the 1974 Lions smashed into their opponents after a piece of dirty play against a man in a red jersey. It has become almost axiomatic that the 99 call rang out across the playing fields of South Africa, and this 'truth' is repeated endlessly. As the editor character said at the end of the film *The Man Who Shot Liberty Valance*, 'when the legend becomes the fact, print the legend'.

The trouble is that the 99 legend is more like a myth. According to several Lions, the maximum number of actual 99 calls during the whole tour was two. The real truth is that on most occasions when the Lions retaliated *en masse* against rough stuff, the call was unnecessary as the players had already begun smacking their opponents.

The tactic existed, without a doubt. There is absolutely no question that in full consultation with Syd Millar and those Lions who had survived from the 1968 and 1971 tours, Willie John McBride and the players – 'it came from them,' said Syd Millar – instituted a deliberate practice of mass battering to start whenever the South African players began their rough stuff.

Derived from Carwyn James's belief in 'getting your retaliation in first', McBride decreed that if any of the opponents carried out any dirty play, all the Lions were to respond by bashing the nearest member of the opposition. The captain's reasoning was that while a referee might send off an individual spotted punching an opponent, he would not dismiss a full team. McBride has always claimed that the original call was to be the emergency services 999 number, but it was too long and he cut it to 99. In fact, said several Lions, he never got to the first nine most of the time.

In his memoirs, McBride mentions making the 99 call just once, and that was against Northern Transvaal. He told the writer David Walmsley in *Lions of Ireland* that 'the whole thing (the 99 call) has been overplayed. I would say there were possibly four incidents in all the games and that was about it'.

Syd Millar agreed: 'A lot has been made out of something that was quite simple. It was just a way of saying to referees we are not going to let any of our guys be picked on. It happened infrequently, and an awful lot has been made of it since.'

Ian McLauchlan said:

As far as I'm concerned it never existed. It grew out of after-dinner speeches by Willie John and Gordon Brown and others who greatly exaggerated things.

Some of the guys were just not the type to punch somebody, and others couldn't do it because they just didn't know how to. Those of us that could took care of things.

Andy Irvine stated:

It has been overdone. There were three or four scuffles, as we saw it. The fact is, that Lions pack was dirtier than the Springboks or any of the teams we played, and guys like Ian McLauchlan and Bobby Windsor didn't muck about – if anything, we probably intimidated them as much as we were intimidated ourselves.

In his autobiography, *Ripley's World*, Andy Ripley pointed out that it did not feature in the midweek matches at all and added: 'The 99 call has been embellished down the years. It might have happened once or twice, but to hear some of the stories now you'd think we were shouting 99 when we came down to breakfast and ran out of orange juice.'

Roger Uttley expanded further:

At the outset, Willie and Syd sat everybody down and said 'For a lot of you, who haven't been down to the southern hemisphere before, they rely on physical intimidation. We have always had the players to cause them a bit of damage but in the end we have always been beaten up. So on this trip there will be no backward step at any stage of the proceedings. We go forward at every opportunity. If any one of our guys is picked off, then everybody has got to respond and step in, and wipe out the nearest green shirt or whatever.' It was all done on the premise that they might send off one man but not the whole team. It was all for one and one for all, quite simple.

There was talk of 'how will we know' and that was when the 99 was mentioned. But when something kicks off, there isn't any chance to shout, you just respond.

In those days you didn't have neutral referees, touch judges had no influence on the game, and from a player's point of view you had what might be construed as an advantage in that the television cameras were so far away they were useless at identifying what went on.

It was a question of everybody having to stand up and be counted, and for someone like me that was a big step. Before I went away, the people at Gosforth had one perception of me, but that was altered when I came back.

In my first training game I flattened one of our props and the coach Nick Mahoney blew the whistle and said 'Hey, what's happened to you, you can't hit people like that', but I just told him it was what I'd been doing on tour. I grew up a lot out there.

Sandy Carmichael said that his unwillingness to take out an opponent without being directly provoked himself may have contributed to him being left out of the Test team:

I got concussed in an early match and Fran Cotton took my place. Shortly after that, Syd Millar told me that I didn't have enough 'knuckle', while Fran certainly did. In other words, I wasn't prepared to start flinging the punches. I accepted that fact and in some way I was quite proud of it.

What appears to have happened is that the '99 call' became an easy short-hand for the numerous fights that happen in a lot of rugby matches, and which certainly took place on the tour. McBride's concept, and the admittedly enthusiastic manner in which some Lions embraced it, did prove very successful in stopping the Springboks from waging their usual campaigns of physical intimidation, but it also gave the 1974 Lions an unsavoury reputation which rather besmirched the excellence of their achievements. But that's what happens when legends become facts.

What was undeniable in 1974 was that the Lions were much fitter than previous tourists, the results of the now compulsory long sessions of fitness training by internationalists. As had happened in 1971, the Lions used just 17 players in the four Tests, Irvine coming in for compatriot Steele after two of them, with the injured Gordon Brown being replaced for the final Test by Chris Ralston. 'The lack of serious injuries was a big factor in our success,' said Millar.

In retrospect, South African rugby was not at its best in 1974. As with the All Blacks in 1971, there was no settled team and many new caps were blooded against the Lions. In the non-Test Matches, the Lions' pack gained an overwhelming share of possession, which allowed the supremely talented back line to cut loose. Men who would become legends, such as J.J. Williams, Ian McGeechan and Andy Irvine, joined Edwards and Bennett, Dick Milliken and Billy Steele, plus Gibson and the incomparable J.P.R. Williams in feasting on a plentiful supply of the ball.

The pack was anchored by front row greats Bobby Windsor, Fran Cotton and Mighty Mouse McLauchlan, with McBride and Brown in the boilerhouse, and Fergus Slattery, Roger Uttley and Mervyn Davies in their pomp in the back row.

That pack was formidable in many respects, as Andy Irvine pointed out: 'Six of them captained their country at one point or another, but mind you, there were five captains of their countries in the backs. There was a massive amount of expertise.'

That quality was soon brought to bear as the Lions strolled through the provincial matches, running up several cricket scores. The tour opened with a 59–13 victory over Western Transvaal, and reached a peak with an extraordinary 97–0 win over South Western Districts. Even though a try was now worth four points, to get so close to the magic 'ton' was a stunning display by the Lions and featured a record-equalling six tries by J.J. Williams.

The Lions had also set out their stall in regard to South African intimidation. They went three matches without major incident, but in the fourth match, against Eastern Province, Syd Millar's intelligence-gathering paid off. 'We knew they were planning something, we knew they had been asked to test us out,' he revealed.

Captain for the day Gareth Edwards politely asked the home captain to cut out the rough stuff. When no agreement was forthcoming, and Edwards himself was the target of a sneaky rabbit punch, the Lions simultaneously launched themselves at their opponents, several of whom were knocked to the ground. More furious punch-ups ensued, but at an early stage in the tour a point had been made – these Lions would not take any nonsense.

'That was the day it started,' said Sandy Carmichael, who was a spectator along with Willie John McBride. 'I remember Gordon Brown got felled at a line-out and Stewart McKinney dropped the guy who did it with a punch that travelled just a few inches. The freakish thing for me was that they were playing in the same colours as Canterbury in 1971.'

Mervyn Davies said: 'The Springboks and the provincial sides always relied on physicality, if that's what you call it, but in 1974, we were able to match that physicality and beat it.'

The provincial games included the matches against the 'coloured' South African Republic Federation XV and the 'black' South African Rugby Association Leopards. The coloured team and their supporters did not like being beaten at all, but the Leopards and their supporters loved the Lions, especially when, after thumping more than 50 points onto the board, the Lions' defence 'accidentally' gave way to allow a try to be scored.

Against the Leopards and other sides, Bobby Windsor used to act as cheerleader for the black sections in the crowd, while the long-haired unconventional Andy Ripley became a cult figure, as Roger Uttley recalled: 'He became a major hero to the blacks because he would prance about in a pair of sandals cut from tyres, just like them. He was very popular.'

The first Test in Cape Town could not come quickly enough. Newlands was wet and windy, and, as usually happens in such conditions, free-flowing rugby was not an option, meaning it was the pack that did all the hard work for victory.

'It was mud up to our ankles in places,' said Mervyn Davies, 'and that suited us just fine. We annihilated them up front and they were screaming and hollering in the scrums. It was a significant moment as we knew we could dominate possession in the Tests from then on.'

South Africa played with the wind at their backs in the first half but the Lions held them to 3–3 at half-time. In the second half, with their scrummage entirely dominant, the Lions ground down their opponents, and two penalties by Bennett and a drop goal by Edwards gave them victory by 12–3. It had not been pretty, but it was rugby adapted to the conditions and the win was thoroughly deserved.

The scrum was the key to victory in the second Test, this time played at the Loftus Versefeld in Pretoria. The Springboks selectors had been panicked into making a whole raft of changes, and the Lions' forwards consequently blew away their disjointed unrehearsed opponents. Playing on hard ground, the backs were able to get involved, and Bennett in particular was magnificent, scoring one try of such quality that even the partisan home fans gave him a standing ovation. Despite a couple of close things, the Lions restricted the Springboks to just nine points from the boot of Gerald Bosch, while at the other end the South African defence was pierced time and time again. The final margin of victory was five tries to nil, the scoreline reading 28–9. It was the Lions' biggest ever victory over South Africa and, at the time, the record loss by the Springboks.

After a couple of unconvincing performances, the Lions warmed up for the third Test by beating that year's Currie Cup holders Northern Transvaal. It was a hard encounter, but nowhere near as brutal as what would come in Port Elizabeth.

The third Test is known now as the Battle of Boet Erasmus stadium, and the venerable old ground had never seen anything like it. To put matters in context, there had been an undercurrent of bad feeling between the two teams after the first two Tests, the South Africans going to the press and accusing the Lions – very untypically, it must be said – of being unsociable. That was not actually the case, but with constant press attention and even harassment, the Lions were careful not to be seen drinking too much at high-profile events.

Springboks' coach Johann Claassen hyped up his players by forbidding them to read newspaper accounts of the Lions' activities, then holding closed-door training sessions and delivering team talks in Afrikaans, intent on creating a siege mentality. McBride concentrated on readying his men for what he knew would come.

Sure enough, the Springboks emerged late to play the match, their eyes glazed with a win-at-all-costs attitude. The Lions knew exactly what to do, however, and when – after a couple of niggles and with the score level at 3–3 just before half-time – the Springboks raked a red jersey in a ruck, the Lions were transformed into tigerish fighters: 99 wasn't necessary.

Andy Irvine said: 'They had brought in a real heavy hitter, a hard man more than a rugby player called Moaner Van Heerden. So we knew from his selection what to expect. Our guys did not take one step back.'

Even in the midst of the mêlée there was humour. Ian McLauchlan said: 'I remember Geech (Ian McGeechan) chasing up the middle after Moaner and I said to him "What are you doing?" because Geech wasn't the type. He said "I'm going to get him to chase me and bring him back to you."'

Order was eventually restored, and the Lions had won the fight. They rubbed salt in the Springboks' wounds by scoring a try, Gordon Brown stealing line-out ball for the score that put the Lions 7–3 up.

In the second half, with the wind behind him, Andy Irvine scored a penalty from inside his own half. When Bobby Windsor retaliated to some rough stuff, it was the signal for all hell to break loose. The fight lasted for minutes, players squaring up to each other or diving on opponents, and in the process try-scorer Brown broke his hand belting a hard Springbok head – in the video of the match he can clearly be seen doing so, as well as taking a retaliatory thump that knocks him off his feet.

Carmichael said:

JPR was the real problem because the fights would all be more or less sorted and he would arrive on the scene having run from full-back and swing a punch and it would all start up again. But the Springboks by then had realized they would have to play rugby, and we were better at rugby than them.

Two further tries by J.J. Williams, one of them converted by Irvine, and two drop goals by Bennett gave the Lions victory in the match by 26–9. They had won the series, the first to do so in South Africa since 1896.

The fighting did stop long enough for both sets of players to help Springbok forward Johannes De Bruyn, who was blind in one eye, search for his glass eye. Gordon Brown loved to tell the story of how 'Cyclops' as he called him, stuck the eye back in its socket with grass hanging out – as always with Gordon, the tale was perhaps a trifle exaggerated, and the story grew in the telling.

The battle had been won and the war was almost over. The Lions continued unbeaten, their wins including a 34–6 victory over Natal that featured an 11-minute stoppage and police on the pitch after the crowd threw fruit and beer cans at the visitors following JPR Williams' blatant assault on the opposition captain Tommy Bedford.

Having gone unbeaten throughout the tour, the midweek dirt-trackers came to the last provincial match in Springs against Eastern Transvaal on the Wednesday before the final Test. Sandy Carmichael said:

The Lions had come a cropper there before. That match was our test, we knew we couldn't let anyone down, and were determined to win and show what we could do. The side that played that day would have graced any international XV. We played them off the park and beat them 33–10.

In the final Test, the last match of the tour, the Lions finally conceded a try to the Springboks, but were holding them 13–13 and looked set to win in the final seconds when Fergus Slattery, who had been one of the great tour successes, plunged over for a try, which press photographs showed was touched down correctly. Mystifyingly, referee Max Baise disallowed it, and the Lions were robbed of a 100 per cent win record with almost the last act of the tour.

'The referee did his bit for his country,' said Ian McLauchlan, though Mervyn Davies is more magnanimous: 'I think they just about deserved the draw and it was good for South African rugby that they weren't whitewashed.'

Gareth Edwards said:

A lot of us didn't fully appreciate our success at the time. You tend not to when you are in the trenches with your head down and just keeping on going. After we drew the fourth Test, which meant we had won the series and were unbeaten, I remember sitting in the dressing room where we were all knackered, and looking at Gerald Davies and saying 'We won the series', and then we both said at the same time 'So what?' We just didn't know what we had done. But when we got home and there were all these people waiting for us at the airport, then it began to sink in.

I've since met plenty of South Africans in recent years and when you tell them we went unbeaten against the provincial sides they don't believe you, because to them that is nearly as big an achievement as winning a Test series.

The Lions returned to Britain and Ireland to the proverbial heroes' welcome. As Syd Millar recalled: 'There were thousands there to greet us, and after all they had done to stop us going, after our unbeaten tour, there at the airport was the Labour Government's Sports Minister.'

Television coverage in colour had massively boosted the team's public profile, and it was no surprise when, like their predecessors in 1971, they were named the team of the year at the BBC Sports Personality of the Year Awards. Once more 'Flower of Scotland' rang out.

The sheer physical cost to the players was high. Roger Uttley said:

For me, on that tour in 1974 everything that could have gone well went well. I started out as the fourth choice second row man, but because I could play anywhere in the back five, if I wasn't first choice I was on the bench, so I ended up on the pitch in 16 of the 22 matches.

Up until the tour I had been very fortunate in my career, but afterwards, possibly due to some of the battering that I took in South Africa, I had injury problems to contend with.

Indeed he did. His back plagued him for many years and meant that he missed out on the 1977 tour, but as we shall see, he returned to Lions duty as a coach in 1989.

Sandy Carmichael enjoyed success in the plant hire business, and indeed did some work for his French-owned company while in South Africa, but suffered a terrible legacy of his years of toil in the front row. He has had no fewer than five hip-replacement operations, had a double hernia operation in 2004, and also has a metal plate in his leg after breaking his femur in a fall down stairs. Troubled by arterial fibrillation, arthritis and diabetes, Carmichael in his 60s is father to two young children from his second marriage, adding to his two elder children. 'You just have to keep going,' he said, 'and look after other people.' Referring to his years of medical problems, he said simply: 'Even though I know what all those years of playing led to, I would not change a single thing.'

Gareth Edwards went on to play for Wales in two further Grand Slams, retiring in 1978. He became a team captain on *A Question of Sport*, following in Cliff Morgan's footsteps, and went on to be a successful media pundit. He was voted the Greatest Ever Player in a poll in 2003, made a CBE by the Queen in 2007 and is now a director of Cardiff Blues. A statue of Edwards was erected in the St David's Shopping Centre in Cardiff.

Ian McLauchlan retired from rugby in 1980, the year he left teaching to form the highly successful corporate hospitality, conference and event management and marketing company which bears his name.

Andy Ripley became a highly successful executive in the financial services industry as well as a television celebrity by winning *Superstars*. He set world records and became world champion at indoor rowing. At the age of 57 in 2005, he was diagnosed with prostate cancer after suffering a pulmonary embolism. He has battled the disease ever since as well as writing a book and publicizing the condition.

Mervyn Davies, 'Merv the Swerve', was voted Wales's Greatest Ever Captain and the Greatest Ever No. 8. These accolades came long after Davies' career finished instantly when he suffered a brain haemorrhage while playing for Swansea against Pontypool in the Welsh Cup semi-final in March 1976. Davies had already suffered a scare, having been diagnosed with meningism in 1972, but played on and was set to captain the Lions in 1977 when his near-fatal brain attack occurred. 'It felt like the All Blacks were doing the haka inside my skull,' is how he described the pain.

His life was saved by prompt medical attention, but Davies slipped into a coma, in which state he lay for many weeks. He emerged to find himself partially paralysed and underwent years of rehabilitation; he still suffers problems with his balance, for instance. He described his battle to regain health, and his problems with alcohol, in his moving autobiography *In Strength and Shadow*.

'One minute you are a strong 29-year-old playing rugby and the next you are lying in hospital with a brain haemorrhage,' said Davies. 'You have to be physically fit to survive it, and I suppose the mental toughness from my years of playing helped me. But I don't think you ever fully recover from something like that.'

Davies received lots of help and support from his fellow Lions, whom he jokingly refers to as 'the biggest freemasonry in the world'. 'It was like having an extended family to call on,' he said. 'But that is what the Lions are – a family.'

It could not be foreseen in 1974, but that family had just achieved its ultimate triumph. The arguments continue as to whether the 1971 or 1974 Lions were the greatest touring party to leave these islands, but in terms of results there is no doubt that Willie John McBride's Lions set an unbeaten record in South Africa; one that has not been bettered since.

CHAPTER ELEVEN

PHIL BENNETT'S BAD NEWS BOYS

New Zealand and Fiji 1977

The problem for the 1977 British and Irish Lions was that their record was always going to be compared to what had been achieved in 1971 and 1974. In short, the 1977 tourists were on a hiding to nothing. They did not take a hiding, not by a long chalk, but still came away with nothing.

It was a depressing tour, not least because the weather in New Zealand was seriously wintry throughout the three months the Lions were there. It seemed that wherever they went, the wind and the rain followed them, and, for once, New Zealand became the Land of the Long Black Cloud.

The captain of the tour was Welsh fly-half Phil Bennett, the pride of Llanelli, and one of the scourges of South Africa in 1974. He recalled the tour as one of the worst experiences of his life:

I had so enjoyed the tour in 1974, and it put British and Irish rugby on a huge high. But in that year my wife Pat and I lost our baby and it took all the gloss off of the tour.

I had been away touring the world since I was 17 or 18 and it was fantastic, but by 1977 I had responsibilities and I was hugely in two minds as to whether I should go on the tour at all. We had been fortunate to have a son almost immediately after losing the baby – the surgeon said he was a one in a million chance – and I had these thoughts about whether I should go away again for that length of time after losing one child and also miss a summer of watching our new young son grow up.

I think I was persuaded by the thought that it would be 'one last tour' and because I was given the captaincy, but it all weighed heavily on my mind from the start. Even as we were leaving London, I was thinking, am I making the right decision?

Possibly it affected me off the field, but I know it affected me on it at times, because if you go on the field and you are not 100 per cent focused, it does show.

It did not help Bennett's cause that his great Welsh colleagues Gareth Edwards, Gerald Davies and J.P.R. Williams declared themselves unavailable for the tour, and they were sorely missed, because it was in the back line that the Test series was lost.

Bennett said:

The loss of key players from 1974 really hurt us. Not only were Gareth, Gerald and JPR not able to go but we had lost Mervyn Davies, and another big loss was Roger Uttley, who pulled out late with a back injury. If we had been able to persuade Gareth in particular to come it would have suited him because of the amount of kicking that was needed at half-back. At the time he had perhaps lost half-a-yard of pace, but there was no better scrum-half at kicking to put the ball in front of forwards.

Fran Cotton is adamant: 'If Gareth had played, we would have won the series. No disrespect to the scrum-halves on the tour, but he would have made the difference.'

The man himself is still racked with doubts about his decision to stay at home. Edwards said:

Looking back, I do wonder if I should have gone on that 1977 tour. I deliberated long and hard about it, and I lost several sleepless nights worrying about what to do. I was torn between wanting to be with the boys and be loyal to the team again, to go into battle with my friends, because that is how you felt as a Lion, but I had other responsibilities. What we tend to forget is that we were all amateurs back then, and we had bills to pay and had to earn the money to pay them. The reasons I did not go on the tour were that I had a young family and I did not feel that I could go and ask my boss for more time off, as he had already been very good to me. To be fair, neither my wife nor my boss said no to me, because I didn't give them the chance. It was all my decision not to go.

It was not an easy decision, because playing for the Lions is something very special and you do not want to give it up lightly. In 1968, I was a student and I didn't have any responsibilities, and I wasn't married so I could afford to take three or four months away on the tour. In 1971, if it wasn't for the support of the engineering company that I then worked for, I could not have afforded to go on the tour, and it was the same in 1974 where the benevolence of my boss enabled me to go, but by 1977, I was married with two young boys and there were constant demands on me to play rugby for Wales or the Barbarians or whatever.

You can talk about my profile as a player being good for the company but I just thought, well, I've had a good career and been able to juggle things but do I want to leave my family and go and ask the boss for yet more time off? I have no doubt that he would have said 'Gareth it is up to you', because he always supported me. But eventually I looked at my two

youngsters and I thought 'you've been there and done it in New Zealand'
so I made the toughest decision of my career and didn't go.

Every now and again when the boys talk about the tour and you know
that they came within a whisker of being successful, you wonder 'should
I have gone?' But then I remember what my dear old friend Gordon
Brown said, 'Gareth, there were only five days on which it didn't rain', so
maybe I did make the right decision.

Gerald Davies' pace would also have made a huge difference. He said: 'I
did have a chance to go to New Zealand in 1977, but I knew then that
my career was coming to a close, and I felt that three months on tour
was not something that a 32-year-old could cope with.'

Edwards was replaced as first-choice scrum-half, not by Dougie
Morgan of Scotland as expected, but by Edwards' understudy Brynmor
Williams, who would not get his first Welsh cap until the following year,
after Edwards finally retired. Up against the great Sid Going in three
matches, he did well in the circumstances.

The tourists did include Andy Irvine, star of the tour at full-back, as
well as a new centre pairing of Ian McGeechan and Steve Fenwick, even
though they had Mike Gibson in their number, the latter equalling Willie
John McBride's record of five tours as a playing Lion. Playing mostly in
midweek games, the great Gibson never complained about his loss of
status, and, just as in 1974, despite not playing in the Tests, he was once
more a leading figure on the tour.

McGeechan was delighted to be back again, after three seasons in
which his career with Headingley and Scotland had thrived on the back
of his Lions' appearances. He said:

The Lions meant more to me then, and still do, because I never expected
to be part of it. They were always up there, something to aspire to, and
frankly, I just couldn't believe I was there. Then to play eight Test Matches

*over the two tours was something I had never thought I could achieve, so
it had a huge impact on me. In terms of my confidence and how I viewed
the game, being chosen for the Lions definitely changed me for the better.*

When Nigel Horton, of Moseley and England, was also injured on the
tour, the selectors called for a replacement in the formidable shape of
Bill Beaumont, who would go on to become a Grand Slam captain of
England and one of the most famous rugby people of all time.

Beaumont said:

*You get told some time before the tour that you are a reserve and should
keep yourself free. I got a phone call one morning to say that Nigel
Horton had broken his hand and they needed a replacement and would I
go. I said 'Of course' and within 48 hours I was on a flight to New
Zealand. Fortunately I worked for the family textile business at the time
and my dad and uncle gave me the time off.*

*I went out with the feeling that everyone had, that you always wanted
to be a Lion because it was the ultimate accolade for any player, and here
was I getting the opportunity. I knew I was effectively the sixth choice in
my position, but I hoped I could make it into the Test team.*

*I knew a few of the players from internationals and Barbarians matches,
and I knew Gordon Brown because my club Fylde used to play West of
Scotland regularly, but I hardly knew any of the Welsh players. But the lads
were great and welcomed me and I soon got on well with everyone.*

Beaumont gave an interesting insight into his motivation on tour:

*I wanted to prove to people that I could play rugby, and I especially
wanted to prove it to the coach and manager who hadn't picked me. That
was what drove me all the time, I wanted to show these guys that after
playing for England I was good enough to play for the Lions.*

The squad eventually consisted of eighteen Welshmen, six English players, five from Scotland and four Irishmen, Wales still being top dogs at the time. The journalist Frank Keating took a note in 1977 of the jobs which all these amateur players did at home. Thanks to him we know that the tour party consisted of eleven teachers, three company directors, four salesmen, two electricians, a National Coal Board official, a solicitor, a chartered surveyor, a scrap-metal merchant, a plasterer, a chiropodist, a Post Office lineman, a building society rep, a sports-shop manager and an articled clerk. Leaving aside the number of teachers, it was a fair cross-section of society in Britain and Ireland, and Keating's list is a reminder that these men and their employers all made sacrifices for the cause of the Lions.

The manager of the party was George 'Dod' Burrell of Gala RFC, a former international who would go on to become president of the Scottish Rugby Union. The assistant manager and coach was John Dawes, who had already served a term as the coach of Wales and would do so again after the 1977 tour.

There were tensions between some players and the three selectors – Bennett, Dawes and Burrell. Bennett explained:

I have been on tours with Wales and the Lions where everything was rosy but there were still undercurrents behind the facade, because players felt they should be selected but weren't, and there were similar frustrations on that tour.

But there were many other things that made it an unhappy tour, and one of them was the atrocious weather. If you can't get out in the sunshine and perhaps play a game of golf or something, as happened in South Africa, and if the wind is blowing and it's raining like you've never seen before and you are stuck in a hotel day after day ... well, it didn't help.

Both Burrell and Dawes would come in for heavy criticism for their part in the tour's public relations exercises, or rather, the lack of them. The New Zealand press seemed to consider themselves a cross between a 16th man and cheerleaders for the All Blacks, if you judge by the hostile headlines dished out to the visitors. The Lions themselves say they were not affected too much, but Burrell, Dawes and Bennett certainly were.

Every move of the Lions was being scrutinized, exaggerated and downright lied about. Bennett said: 'Every little thing was picked on. If somebody spilled a pint in a pub it was practically front page news.'

Andy Irvine agreed: 'The New Zealand media had a real go at Phil as captain, possibly because there was a huge rivalry between Wales and New Zealand at the time – Wales then were the blue-eyed boys.'

From start to finish, the New Zealand media hammered at the Lions, accusing them of being everything from drunks to lousy lovers. There was slight credence to the former accusation, as players were pictured in hotels and pubs, but the payment of women for stories about sexual activity incensed everyone connected with the Lions. A tabloid weekly called *Truth* paid one woman to say she had bedded four of the Lions: 'I found them boring, self-centred, ruthless, always on the make and anything but exciting bedmates. Give me the down-to-earth Kiwi male any day.'

Truth thundered in an editorial: 'The Lions make a great pack – of animals. The touring rugby side is a disgrace to its members and their homeland. Only one word to describe their behaviour – disgusting.' The front page headline screamed 'Lions are Louts and Animals.'

The breathless accounts by 'Wanda from Wanganui' about what she did with the Lions transfixed the nation. Clem Thomas, who covered the tour, called it 'the worst and most despicable press coverage I have heard of'.

Phil Bennett said: 'The worst thing was that there were reports with no names, so that wasn't very nice for guys with wives and families back home. The phone calls were soon going back and forth.' Since a 90-second phone call used up a Lion's daily expenses of £3, you can guess how badly the players were affected.

Fran Cotton was given 'the treatment' by one paper:

Just before the third Test, one paper printed that famous photograph of me covered all over in mud with the headline 'The villain'. For some reason I was singled out and I still don't know why.

Personally I think a lot of it was due to that fact that we had won the previous two series, and because in 1976 New Zealand had lost a Test series 3–1 to the Springboks in South Africa. That was the first series to be shown on television over there and it had been quite violent, so I think a feeling had grown that the All Blacks had to win the series against us at all costs. It wasn't just their team, it was the whole population, and the abuse we got in the press and from the public at games was terrible – at times you had to pinch yourself that here you were as an amateur player taking all this stuff from spectators who'd come in their thousands to see you play.

Phil Bennett confirmed that the treatment of his players by members of the public became almost animalistic:

I had such respect for the New Zealand rugby people ever since I toured there with Wales in 1969 when I was 18, but from the first couple of days there was this atmosphere of 'we have got to win at all costs' and it got out of hand.

At one big provincial match, which we won, the public got right around us – there were no police cordons in those days – and threw beer on us while a few were even spitting on us. It wasn't typical, but I wondered what had happened to the New Zealand I had admired and respected.

206

A lot of it was whipped up by the press. I have worked for the press for many years and I know that you can't beat them. If we had contested things, it would have just prolonged it, so we decided to say nothing.

The tour management put up the shutters and tried to discourage any press activity at all, which dismayed those rugby correspondents who were there simply to report straightforwardly on matches and surrounding events. Even former Lions like Clem Thomas were shunned in a remarkably myopic manner.

The management, and by extension the entire touring party, let the negative image get to them, and just when they needed to be entirely positive, the psychological damage done to players, as well as managers, began to show itself as tempers frayed.

One player was undoubtedly hurt mentally. Bobby Windsor, the hooker from McBride's Invincibles of 1974, was not a comfortable flyer, and when a pilot on one of the internal flights decided to show off his aerobatic skills, the Welshman was petrified. It may have been coincidence, but Windsor's form deserted him and he lost his place to Peter Wheeler.

There were problems even with the food. Bennett said:

We had moved to a hotel in a small town to get ready for a midweek match. The players said to look at the menu. It was soup or melon and chicken or fish for the main course – again, as it had happened before. I said 'Hang on, we were playing in front of 60,000 people last Saturday; shouldn't we at least have an à la carte menu?' 'You have got to go to the New Zealanders,' I told Dod Burrell, 'and say we have had enough of this shit. We have been getting booed everywhere, so we need some good food and some good quality time by ourselves.' Dod had a terrible time persuading them to put steak on the menu, and it was little things like that which blew up into bigger ones.

Yet Lions being Lions, they still managed to find time for the occasional enjoyment. As Fran Cotton said:

> *There were some great characters on the tour and the two I always remember were Willie Duggan and Moss Keane from Ireland. They were immense fun, and I remember on the night before the first Test they couldn't sleep and sent down to room service and ordered a crate of Guinness, which they polished off before they eventually got some sleep. That summed them up for me.*

Coupled with poor morale, there was also the realization that the All Blacks had improved since losing the 1971 series. Giants like Meads and Lochore were long gone, but Ian Kirkpatrick and captain and hooker Tane Norton were still forces, while new star players like Frank Oliver, Lawrie Knight, Andy Haden and Graeme Mourie all boosted the pack.

Behind the scrum was a plethora of talent. Sid Going, Doug Bruce, Bryan Williams and Grant Batty would surely have figured in any All Black 'best of' selection, and it was the New Zealand backs, rather than their forwards, who inflicted the most pain on the Lions. In a reversal of the historic trend, the Lions won the battle up front against the All Blacks, but lost the clash of back lines.

The first part of the tour gave little indication of the trouble to come, at least on the field. The Lions won all of their first eight matches, including victories over the dangerous provincial sides of Hawke's Bay and Otago. But in the match immediately before the first Test, against the New Zealand Universities' combined XV, the midweek men, the dirt-trackers, lost by 21–9. It was an unhappy portent of events to come.

The first Test saw the All Blacks go 10–9 up, but Phil Bennett kicked his fourth penalty to make it 12–9 for the Lions. With the Lions' forwards in the ascendancy, the backs mounted an attack. Bennett can recall the moment: 'I have been fortunate to have my share of luck in the game but on that occasion, though there were four of us breaking and only one All Black in our way, Grant Batty just managed to intercept a pass and ran away to score. Things like that turn a game.'

Even with the wind at their backs, the All Blacks could not add to the score, and though they tried valiantly, the Lions were unable to gain any more points. The 12–16 scoreline was devastating to the Lions confidence, and unlike the previous two tours, the axe was wielded on the Test XV. Out went six players and in came the fit-again Gordon Brown and newly arrived Beaumont, whose second row partnership would remain for the final three Tests.

Beaumont recalled: 'I had only played in three provincial games, but in one of them I was alongside Gordon Brown and he said to me "If we play well we'll get into the Test team." I said "Don't be stupid", but he was right and we played in the winning side and kept our places.'

With Dawes not versed in the ways of tight play, the players, led by Terry Cobner, imposed their own will on coaching the pack, and the result was a performance in which the forwards took the second Test by the scruff of the neck. In yet more rain-sodden conditions, the Lions' forwards dominated all facets of the play and gave as good as they got in a massive brawl following a late challenge on captain Bennett. As in 1974, these Lions would stand for no nonsense.

They were 10–0 up within 20 minutes, Bennett's two penalties adding to J.J. Williams's terrific try. Bennett added another penalty in the second half, while Bryan Williams kicked three in total to make the final score 13–9 for the Lions, who had to withstand a typical late onslaught from the All Blacks.

'We absolutely murdered them up front,' said Andy Irvine. 'I felt we had been unlucky in the first Test but it all went right for us in the second.'

The third Test in Dunedin saw yet another quagmire of a pitch, and going into the match in such conditions, the Lions were actually favourites to win, not least because the previous match had seen them thump Auckland 34–15, while it had been the turn of the All Blacks to ring the changes with six switches of personnel, including the major shock of Sid Going being replaced by Lyn Davis. It was the end of Going's international career and he retired as the most-capped scrum-half in All Black history.

For once, the bookies got it wrong. New Zealand came out of the traps like greyhounds and were 6–0 up in 60 seconds, Ian Kirkpatrick pouncing on a Lions defensive error for a try that Bevan Wilson converted. Willie Duggan and Andy Haden then exchanged tries and the hectic start saw the All Blacks lead 10–4 after 11 minutes.

Both J.J. Williams and Brynmor Williams damaged hamstrings, and were replaced by Ian McGeechan and Doug Morgan respectively. Phil Bennett's goal kicking went awry and contributed to the Lions missing six out of seven attempts at goal. Bevan Wilson had his kicking boots on, however, and slotted two more penalties which, added to a Bruce Robertson drop goal against a sole Andy Irvine penalty, meant a final scoreline of 19–9 in favour of the All Blacks.

They could not now win the series, but the fourth and final Test gave the Lions the chance to square it. They would come so dreadfully close to doing so, not least because at Eden Park the Lions' pack gave an outstanding exhibition of forward play. At one point the All Blacks were reduced to putting just three men in the scrum, because their opponents were almost guaranteed to win the ball.

Fran Cotton said:

I had never seen it before in a game of top-class rugby. They were under so much pressure in the scrum that they couldn't cope and went to three-man scrums. It was a perfectly legal thing to do at the time, and very smart as it enabled them to clear the ball quickly away from the Lions' strength, which was in the forwards. People now just remember that it was a huge embarrassment for the All Black forwards, but it worked for them.

Yet even with territory and possession to spare, the Lions somehow contrived to lose the match, thanks largely to the backs making heavy weather of it. The Lions were 9–3 up at half-time, thanks to a brilliant Morgan try, and were in cruise control until Bevan Wilson kicked a second penalty. In the dying minutes, however, Lawrie Knight snatched the try that gave New Zealand the lead by 10–9.

Bennett recalls:

Knowing we were just minutes from winning the match, when I got the ball just inside the 22 instead of looking for someone to pass to or kicking the ball to touch, I took the safe percentage option and cleared it downfield. They returned it with an up and under, a couple of our players misjudged it and Lawrie Knight grabbed it and scored. That score summed up the series for me.

Even then the Lions had one last chance to win. Fran Cotton said: 'We had a scrum on their five-yard line in the last minute, and if we had kept cool heads we could have done something and won, but they managed to clear it. That was the end and I can tell you it was the worst feeling I have ever had after a game.'

The All Blacks had clinched the Test series 3–1. The bad news didn't end there. In a forgettable first, on the way home, the Lions stopped off in Fiji to play their national XV and were promptly beaten 25–21.

The players' verdicts on the tour share a common thread – disappointment at the results but also a feeling that it was not as black as it has been painted.

Bennett said:

The four Test Matches were what really mattered, and in all honesty you could say we should have at least drawn the series or even won it 3–1. We had a great pack but behind it there were players such as myself who didn't perform. We also made some tactical errors.

But with all due respect to New Zealand who had some great players, it was one of those tours where you have to say 'we blew it', and it was a case of us losing, rather than them winning it. I can take losing, but to lose like that ... well, it took me a long time to get over it.

Fran Cotton observed:

It became known as the 'bad news' tour but I never understood that, because a lot of the players really enjoyed the tour, and I for one loved New Zealand and loved playing there. Certainly, losing the last Test 10–9 when we could have squared the series was probably the most disappointing moment in my entire rugby career. We were certainly very competitive, but I just think the three-quarter play lost confidence as the tour went on and a lot of that was due to the weather – the rain and mud was no problem to us up front, but it did affect them.

Andy Irvine is convinced that the 'bad news boys' got an undeserved reputation.

That tour was nowhere near as bad as the press comments at the time and subsequent books made out. The difference between being a hero and a being a monkey is absolutely marginal, and in our case in 1977 it was one point, thanks to the 9–10 score in the final Test. Had we won that last Test and come back with a 2–2 draw in the series, things would have been so different.

In a postscript to the tour, the Lions got together shortly after their return to play a special match against the Barbarians to mark the Silver Jubilee anniversary of Queen Elizabeth's ascension to the throne. In an entertaining game played at Twickenham, the Lions won 23–14 – 'It was a great fun game,' said Irvine.

The victory salvaged something from a tour that had promised so much but delivered a lot less. It will always be judged a failure because it followed the successes of 1971 and '74, but while the '77 Lions undoubtedly did not come up to previous standards, at a distance of three decades their record in the face of considerable adversity – all bar one provincial match was won, don't forget – does not seem too bad at all.

Phil Bennett retired from international rugby in 1978, and for many years has been a respected commentator on the game as well as an entertaining after-dinner speaker. On Millennium night in 2000, he and his wife Pat miraculously survived a horrific car crash in which their BMW overturned, the only injury being a head knock for Phil. Despite the disgraceful treatment he received in New Zealand he has been back there several times and says he has long since regained his respect for the country and its fanatical rugby community.

Mike Gibson ended his Lions career having played on five tours, the same as his fellow Irish legend Willie John McBride. Given the shortness of careers in the professional era, and the fact that there is now a standard four-year period between each tour, their joint record will never be beaten. Gibson now works as a solicitor in Belfast.

After his troubles in flight, Bobby Windsor vowed never to fly again after retiring from international rugby in 1979, until he was cured of prostate cancer in 2005. Cancer having killed his first wife and other members of his family, Windsor realized that a fear of flying was nothing at all, and has vowed to fly to South Africa for the 2009 Lions tour.

Sadly, two of the 1977 Lions did not manage to beat cancer and died at a comparatively young age. Welsh fly-half John David Bevan – not to be confused with 1971 tourist John Charles Bevan – was a schoolteacher who played three times for Wales and later coached the national side. He died of cancer in 1986 at the age of just 38.

Cancer also took Gordon Brown – Broon frae Troon or Broony to his friends – who fought a long and brave battle against the illness, which was diagnosed in 1999. From a famous sporting family – his father Jock played for Scotland at soccer, his mother was a hockey internationalist and elder brother Peter captained Scotland at rugby – Brown was such a character that it would take a book to tell of his exploits. He would take almost an hour to walk from the Murrayfield car park to his seat in the stand or press box, as he would talk to everyone who greeted him – they all knew him, and he truly was rugby royalty in Scotland.

His form of cancer was non-Hodgkin lymphoma and at first it responded to chemotherapy and other treatment. A brilliant raconteur and after-dinner speaker, Brown carried on as long as he could, raising thousands for cancer charities, always supported by his fellow Lions.

You will remember how Brown helped a South African player find his glass eye during the third Test in 1974. In the midst of Broony losing his battle against cancer, Johannes De Bruyn came to Britain to greet his old opponent at a dinner. He not only confirmed the story, but presented Brown with the glass eye mounted on a carved wooden rugby ball.

Broony attended a fund-raising dinner in his honour just three weeks before he died. When his death was announced on 19 March 2001, several Lions and journalists seized on the words that Broon frae Troon had helped to make famous with his renditions of 'Flower of Scotland'. 'When will we see your like again?' from the chorus was transformed by Mervyn Davies and others to 'We shall not see his like again'. His funeral in Troon, attended by many Lions, was both a sad and funny occasion, a true celebration of the man.

Both authors of this book knew the big man, and Martin Hannan worked closely with him on the ill-fated *Sunday Scot* newspaper. We can both tell you from the heart that we really never will see the likes of Broony again.

CHAPTER TWELVE

BILL BEAUMONT AND THE BAD LUCK TOUR
South Africa 1980

Ever since President Nelson Mandela attended the World Cup final in 1995 while wearing a green Springbok jersey, there has been some rewriting of rugby history. With the spirit of reconciliation abounding after Mandela and Springbok captain François Pienaar's love-in, more than a few people would like to forget the fact that rugby often played a morally dubious role when many people were trying to force South Africa to give up its apartheid system.

As we saw in 1974, governments seemed happy enough to carry on trading with South Africa for fear of damaging their own economies. At least when Margaret Thatcher came to power in 1979, she had the courage of her convictions and stated that economic sanctions would not work, yet the British Government still argued that a sporting and cultural boycott of South Africa should go ahead. Failure to call for such boycotts would have damaged Britain's relations with Commonwealth countries such as Australia and the black African nations who had already boycotted one event, the 1976 Olympic Games, because of rugby. The

All Blacks had toured South Africa that year, egged on by their own Prime Minister Robert Muldoon, who was firmly in the 'sport and politics shouldn't mix' camp. The black African nations retaliated by refusing to compete at Montreal.

Long since removed from the Commonwealth, by 1980 South Africa had become a pariah nation. The South Africans could just about live with their expulsion from international athletics and world soccer, especially since the latter sport was very much seen as the pastime of the black community, but being deprived of international cricket and rugby really hurt them.

Meeting at the Gleneagles Hotel in Scotland in 1977, the leaders of the Commonwealth developed an eponymous agreement which effectively called for a ban on sporting contact with South Africa – governments were to take 'every practical step to discourage contact', in the words of the Gleneagles Agreement. Some countries went further, passing laws to ban any such contacts with South Africa, and since Australia was one of the first to do so, that very much reduced the number of countries against which South Africa played rugby. It wasn't just the Commonwealth countries – France would not issue visas to South Africa's rugby players, who were denied the chance to tour there.

Throughout the late 1970s, pressure grew on the home unions to stop their ongoing contacts with South Africa. A year after the Gleneagles Agreement, the International Rugby Board went to South Africa and investigated the effect the apartheid system was having on rugby in that country. They demanded change as the price for maintaining links with South Africa.

In what was seen by hard-liners in that country as a step too far, the South African Rugby Board promised that from April 1979, rugby in South Africa would be 'non-racial' and that the national team would be based on merit rather than colour. It was too good to be true, and most anti-apartheid campaigners pointed out that the brave new world just would not happen as long as the hateful system was still in place as part of the Republic's constitution.

As a result of these concessions, the South African Barbarians were allowed to tour Britain in 1979, though without British Government approval. The Irish Government in fact forced the withdrawal of its union's invitation to the touring team, even though it featured non-white players. That tour, and the protests it engendered, only served to heighten the concerns that many people felt about the proposed British and Irish Lions tour to South Africa in 1980.

The pressure on the Tours Committee of the home unions grew apace. The Sports Council, chaired by former British Lion Dickie Jeeps, and also the Sports Minister Hector Monro, a former president of the Scottish Rugby Union, allegedly both sought a cancellation in keeping with the Gleneagles Agreement. Jeeps was most reluctant to do so, and only now, nearly 30 years later, has he broken his silence on what really happened.

> It wasn't the easiest job being chairman of the Sports Council, and at no time did I ever tell them [the Lions committee] that they shouldn't go. The Government were dead against it, but no one ever put me on the spot and asked me what I really thought. If they had, I would have said 'Why shouldn't they go?' but no one ever asked me. They probably knew what the reply would be, so I was never asked outright.
>
> I did feel it was a good thing that the Lions had insisted on playing coloured and black teams. I think that helped to break down barriers.

It was not seen that way by anti-apartheid organizations and groups such as Halt All Racist Tours (HART) and the South African Non-Racial Olympic Committee (Sanroc), who all promised demonstrations if the tour went ahead. The same African nations that had boycotted the 1976 Olympics said they would stay away from the 1980 Games in Moscow should the tour proceed.

The players themselves were rarely consulted. Most said they were happy to let the decision be made by the committee and their own unions. Not surprisingly, citing the 'changes' within South African rugby brought about by the IRB's pressure, the committee, after consulting the four unions, decided to go ahead with the tour.

In doing so they received help of sorts from an unexpected quarter – the Soviet Union. The full-scale invasion of Afghanistan in December 1979 and the months of military incursions deep into that country by the Red Army made the Lions tour somewhat secondary news, especially when President Jimmy Carter instituted moves for the USA to lead a boycott of that summer's Olympics by all the non-communist nations. Though people like Bishop Desmond Tutu continued to rail against the Lions tour, the Olympics were a much bigger story.

The British Government also made a rod for its own back, refusing to order the British Olympic Association to pull out of the Moscow games. The Westminster Government merely 'asked' them to do so, and then said that it was up to individual competitors to decide whether they wanted to go to Russia or not. Having taken that stance with the BOA, the Government could no longer bully the home unions into boycotting South Africa. Individual freedom to choose was what mattered.

'If it hadn't been for the Olympics,' said Andy Irvine, 'and the fact that they went ahead, I don't think the tour would have happened.'

Tour captain Bill Beaumont agreed:

We melted into the background when the Olympic issue was raised. We also didn't have any grand farewells, and just slipped away quietly from Heathrow one Saturday night.

As a sportsman you tend to cocoon yourself, which you don't do later. In later life, you look at things and say 'Was that the right thing to do?' especially when you consider the difference between that country now and back then. As a player you wanted to go and test yourself against the best, but that didn't mean you supported a regime – far from it, as we knew it was abhorrent. But you are in a cocoon, and I still ask myself were we being selfish in doing what we did?

For good or ill, the tour was on, albeit in a truncated fashion as it was agreed that the entire tour would last just 10 weeks and involve only 18 matches. Some players found excuses not to go, some of them for economic reasons at a time when jobs were often hard to keep, but most who were asked if they were available for selection indicated their acceptance.

Some were put under considerable pressure. John Beattie, now a respected commentator and programme host with BBC Scotland, was a 22-year-old civil engineering student at Glasgow University at the time, and delayed his final exams so he could tour. He said:

There was pressure on me not to go. For example, I got letters from MPs and various organizations. I'll admit I was young and didn't really realize the ramifications of what I was doing, but in blissful ignorance I was told that everyone else was going, so I thought I would, too.

Beattie was amazed by what he found in South Africa:

I saw the whites-only bus stops and the blacks-only bus stops, of course, and all the rest of the segregation, but the thing I remember is being taken to visit a farm where the black workers were in low-grade housing which had a four-inch mains pipe alongside, pumping out a type of maize beer. The workers had free access to this beer and I suppose that was to keep them docile and under control. It was all very surreal and I found the ideology very strange.

We also got taken down the gold mines, where all the workers were black. It was truly astonishing to see these guys working in horrendous, very hot conditions. We got to hold a hot gold ingot and then were allowed to buy cut-price diamonds, which were guaranteed to double their value when you got home – I think the whole team became diamond smugglers.

Beattie found other aspects of touring strange, especially the £14 per week expenses and the 'benefits' of sponsorship which the rugby authorities had reluctantly embraced: 'We all got taken to the Adidas factory in Northampton and were allowed to pick some gear. Most of us took a couple of pairs of boots with the effect being that when we got out there and started wearing them, we all came down with blisters and couldn't play.'

The choice of captain and manager was going to be crucial, and there was no debate about who would fill either post. The committee asked Syd Millar to be manager, and the tough Ballymena man steeped in Lions lore proved to be the perfect choice on a tour that would require discipline above all. He asked fellow Irish internationalist and double Lions tourist Noel Murphy to be assistant manager, and the two men from north and south of the border and from different religious backgrounds formed a terrific partnership.

Millar explained why that fifth tour was important to him:

The Lions are unique, particularly now as there are no touring sides – the various nations go north or south, play internationals only and come away. In 1959 we Lions were away for nearly five months, and in 1980 it was still two-and-a-half months, and when I tell that to modern players they look at you in disbelief that you played 20-odd games.

Having played in three tours and coached the 1974 tour, in 1980 I wanted to use the experience I had gained. So, for instance, we had players appointed to do various jobs as in 1974 and the same in 1980 – I wanted to make it a tour where players did more than just play.

The choice of captain was equally easy. Bill Beaumont had led England to the Grand Slam and had beaten the All Blacks as captain of the North of England. He was head and shoulders above every other candidate. Beaumont's Lions would prove to be unsuccessful as far as the Test series went, but thanks in great part to their likeable captain, they were hugely popular off the field, with Beaumont finding a like-minded spirit in Syd Millar. Said Beaumont:

> I thought in 1977 that we weren't the greatest tourists, that we had become an insular group, and that was part of the trouble with the tour, so when I was appointed captain for 1980 I was determined to make sure we enjoyed ourselves on and off the pitch. It was a very happy trip and we enjoyed everything except the Test results.
>
> Syd and I became great friends and later would be on the IRB together, but back then I was struck by just how much he knew about South African rugby – he knew more than they did.

Perhaps tellingly, the horde of press people who had followed the tour looking for juicy stories about drinking sessions or worse found themselves filing copy about inconsequential matters such as visits to safari parks. In 1980, the Lions were just not the big story, for debauchery was at a minimum. One player, John Beattie, was involved in a foretaste of greater troubles to come. He had been asked to write a column for his local paper, the Glasgow *Evening Times*, and would phone his copy to a ghost writer on the paper. 'But the tour management found out I was doing it and, even though I wasn't getting paid for it, I was forced to stop,' said Beattie. Later tour managers would wish they had the same power.

The tourists have gone down in Lions history as the unluckiest set of players ever. From start to finish the squad was beset with injuries and illness, with the backs suffering more than the forwards. Replacements were sent out from Britain and Ireland almost on a weekly basis so that the original 30-strong squad of players was augmented to 38 in all.

'We had eight different half-backs in the first eight games,' said Bill Beaumont, 'and the rate of injuries was just frightening. We lost Andy Irvine before we even got on the plane.'

Irvine recalled what happened:

I was selected and went down to London to meet up with the lads, but I had pulled a hamstring in the Hong Kong Sevens and while I thought it was repaired sufficiently they gave me quite a testing medical on the morning we were due to fly out and it wasn't 100 per cent right. They weren't prepared to take me unless I could play from day one, so I had to drop out at the last minute.

A few weeks later I was sitting at home listening to the first Test on the radio because there was no live television coverage at that time. Somebody got injured and half-an-hour after the match finished I got a call from Syd Millar asking if I could fly out the following day, though I was actually replacing Mike Slemen, whose wife had taken ill. I ended up playing in three Tests and almost every Saturday game, though my hamstring still wasn't right, and the rest of the time I was getting physiotherapy. I never really felt comfortable or confident, which was a shame because I was at my peak at the time.

In the very first minute of the first match against Eastern Province, Stuart Lane, one of six Cardiff players in the Lions, damaged knee ligaments and had to retire, not only from the match but from the tour and international rugby. His 55 seconds on the pitch is the record for the shortest match time in a Lions jersey. It was a cruel blow for the Lions as Lane was expected to be a major contributor at flank forward, but obviously it turned out to be much worse for the player himself.

The same fate of ending his career because of an on-field injury struck Irish full-back Rodney O'Donnell. John Beattie took up the story:

I roomed with him and he was a great guy but very superstitious. I couldn't get to sleep at night because he would only get into bed without touching the top and bottom sheets at the same time – it used to take him about 14 attempts to do so. He wouldn't walk on lines in the pavement and he had a real fear of the number 13. On Friday, June 13, he wouldn't come out of his room all day. Then in the match where he got injured, against the Junior Springboks, he fractured his sixth and seventh vertebrae tackling Danie Gerber, who was wearing the No. 13 shirt. 'I fecking told ye so,' he kept saying.

Fran Cotton's heart troubles led to an encounter with a rather famous surgeon:

I had been feeling rather poorly because of an infected leg, and should never have played with it, but I decided to play in the match before the first Test against the Federation XV because I was so desperate to stay in the team and be considered for the Test side – in those situations, rational decisions go out the window.

About 20 minutes into the game I had these terrible pains in my chest and became disorientated. The game was stopped and I got whisked away to the local hospital in Stellenbosch. I explained my symptoms, they did some tests and the doctor came back to me and said 'I'm sorry to tell you Mr Cotton, but you've had a heart attack.' I was just totally devastated.

I was sedated and the following morning I was transferred to the Groot Schuur hospital in Cape Town which was famous because that was where Christiaan Barnard performed the world's first heart transplant. I was actually being wheeled along the corridor on the first floor still wearing my Lions tracksuit when Barnard came walking the other way. He spotted the tracksuit and came over and said 'What's the problem?' and I said 'They tell me I've had a heart attack.' He said 'Well, if you need a new one just pop upstairs and we'll fix you up.' You can bet that made me feel a lot better ...

Bill Beaumont and Peter Wheeler also ran into Barnard when they went to visit their stricken colleague:

It was frightening at the time because we were told it was a heart attack. We got to the hospital and met Christiaan Barnard, and Peter immediately cracked 'Have you got a big enough heart for him?' But fortunately it wasn't needed.

Cotton was eventually flown home, where he was diagnosed not with a heart attack but with a condition called viral pericarditis, an infection of the sac around the heart.

I had to rest for two months, but I got fit and came back and played for England against Wales, though psychologically I had perhaps lost some of my passion for the game. But with all that fitness work, here was I, a prop forward, pulling a hamstring after half-an-hour. I came off and never played rugby again because I realized my body was telling me enough was enough. In some ways I'm glad I retired because I had lost some of the edge in my game, and anyway, I was 34 and had had the bulk of my career and enjoyed every minute of it before that match in South Africa.

Apart from Cotton, Lane, O'Donnell and Slemen, Welsh scrum-half Terry Holmes and his compatriots Gareth Davies and David Richards plus England's Phil Blakeway were all badly injured. Beaumont said: 'We really had the most terrible injury problems. It's not an excuse, it's just what happened.'

The irony is that, for the first time, the Lions were accompanied by their own doctor, none other than 1950 Lions tourist Dr Jack Matthews. And after all the problems caused in international rugby by suspiciously homeward-leaning referees, the Lions having suffered more than most, the International Board had finally seen sense and brought in neutral referees for Test Matches. Francis Palmade of France, who is still active as a match commissioner and assessor, thus became the first neutral to officiate at a Lions Test, with his compatriot Jean-Pierre Bonnet taking over for the final two Tests.

The Lions were able to socialize, as Beaumont and Millar had wanted, but not everyone enjoyed himself on that tour. John Beattie, honest as always, broke the normal ranks to say he did not savour the experience.

My whole memory of the tour is coloured by the fact that we lost the series and I was not selected for any of the Tests. Therefore I did not enjoy the tour and, as a 22-year-old, I didn't really enjoy being part of this group of 36 men, almost all of them appreciably older than me.

I enjoyed playing at altitude, I was faster than most and thought I had played well, but it was weird to me to see older guys who hadn't done so well being selected ahead of me. But that remark doesn't apply to the likes of Bill Beaumont, Jeff Squire and Graham Price, who were very good and had been on Lions tours before. Bill Beaumont was the brute force in the pack – you didn't want to run into him.

I was very disappointed at being a dirt-tracker. To me it was a waste of time. I didn't learn anything from the coaches – nothing at all. We just played and there was no structure to it whatsoever. I remember coming back and thinking I have not learned anything.

Eventually Beattie's disenchantment boiled over and he is the first Lion openly to confess to having left a tour without permission:

> It all just got to me and I had had enough of the tour, so I went AWOL. I was so fed up I just walked out and went away on my own for three days.
>   We were on a break and there was not going to be any training so I just left. I disappeared, I'm not saying where, and I don't think anyone even knew I was gone because nobody said a thing to me when I came back.

Beattie is correct about that. Informed in early 2009 that he had 'lost' a tourist in 1980, Bill Beaumont said: 'He did what? I never even noticed.' But there were some amusing times, as Beattie recalled:

> John O'Driscoll was one of those mad Irishmen they always seem to have on Lions' tours. I met his nephew [Ireland and 2005 Lions captain] Brian recently and told him that I once had a plate fight with his uncle in a corridor in a South African hotel. It was John's party trick. He would take a whole stack of plates up to a corridor and start throwing them. The funny thing is that he was a respectable doctor who sounded like an English high court judge, but inside there was this bit of Irish lunacy.

From the first provincial match against Eastern Province on 10 May to the last non-Test game against Griqualand West on 8 July, the Lions never lost a match against any of the eight provinces and the six invitation and select sides they played. Normally, such a record would have seen them acclaimed as highly successful, but sadly for Beaumont and his men, the Test series was a different matter.

They were up against a pack which could at best be described as average for the Springboks, with only captain Morne du Plessis, who would later manage the South African side which won the 1995 World Cup, and loose forward Rob Louw as truly excellent players. 'We were miles better up front than them,' said Beaumont.

In the backs, however, South Africa had discovered a diamond in the shape of Henrik Egnatius Botha, known to the rugby world as Naas. Just 22, this prodigious kicker with fast hands would form a useful partnership with scrum-half Divan Serfontein. It was Naas Botha who largely put the Lions to the sword with his kicking for goal and from hand, and he built himself a stellar reputation which, even in the long years of South Africa's exile, he never lost.

The Springboks also had an adventurous full-back in Z.M.J. 'Gysie' Pienaar, and two solid centres, Willie du Plessis and the Zimbabwean D.J. Smith, with his fellow Zimbabwean Rob Mordt on one wing and Gerrie Germishuys on the other. The seven backs would play together throughout the four Tests, which gave them a considerable advantage over an injury-disjointed Lions back line.

The first Test in Cape Town was a close affair, with Tony Ward, the mercurial Irish fly-half, almost winning the match with his prodigious kicking, scoring a Lions' record in South Africa of 18 points with five penalties and a drop goal. But the try count in South Africa's favour was 5–1, the sole Lions four-pointer coming from Graham Price, while Botha kicked three conversions, the final score being 26–22 in favour of the Springboks.

It was another psychologically damaging loss, not least because the Lions' pack had outplayed their opposite numbers. In all four Tests, Beaumont and fellow English lock Maurice Colclough packed down behind a formidable front row in Clive Williams of Swansea and Wales, England's Peter Wheeler and Pontypool legend Graham Price. The back row of John O'Driscoll, Jeff Squire and Derek Quinnell were supreme competitors, as was Colm Tucker who replaced Quinnell for the final two Tests. All in all, a formidable line-up that more than matched the Springboks.

They certainly did so in the second Test in Bloemfontein, but with the back line radically altered by injury or loss of form – Andy Irvine, Bruce Hay, Clive Woodward, Ray Gravell and Gareth Davies replaced O'Donnell, Slemen, Jim Renwick, Dave Richards and Ward respectively – there was no continuity and little evidence of rehearsal by the backs. Gysie Pienaar had a field day with misdirected Lions' kicks and though the tourists had by far the better of the attacking play, a couple of tries and the boot of Botha saw South Africa lead 16–9 at half-time. With Davies off injured and replaced by Ollie Campbell, who was on his way to becoming such an influential figure in Irish rugby, the Lions pulled things back to 15–16. But tries by Germishuys and Pienaar against a try by Gravell allowed the Springboks to coast home by 26–19.

The third Test in Port Elizabeth was now crucial for the Lions' hopes. The forwards were dominant throughout yet the backs failed to capitalize on the copious amount of ball supplied to them. The Lions led by just 10–6 at half-time, Bruce Hay having scored the only try and Ollie Campbell having notched two penalties, Naas Botha replying with a penalty and a drop goal.

For all their pressure, the Lions knew they were only a single score ahead, and Germishuys duly scored against the run of play, Botha converting for a 12–10 victory. Again it was a match the Lions should have won, and the forwards were not slow in saying so.

With the series lost, the fourth and final Test in front of 68,000 people in Pretoria was simply a matter of pride for the Lions, who were desperate to avoid a whitewash. Botha had an off day, and tries from Clive Williams, Irvine and O'Driscoll against one from Willie du Plessis won the match.

Even while the tourists had journeyed round South Africa, the apartheid system came under pressure. There had been bombings and shootings, with police cracking down on student protests – the South African Government even banned Pink Floyd's record *Another Brick in the Wall* after schoolchildren and students sang it at demonstrations. There was even a Parliamentary debate in Westminster on why the Lions were still touring.

After the Lions returned home, it was predicted by several pundits – including some who had been with the tour and seen apartheid for themselves – that the 1980 tour would be the last to South Africa for some considerable time. The following year, with the blessing of Prime Minister Muldoon who saw it as a vote winner, the Springboks were allowed to tour New Zealand amidst wholesale protest riots and civil disorder, which included anti-apartheid demonstrators using a light plane to attack one Test with flour bombs. In Britain and Ireland, the pressure on the home unions to break off relationships with South Africa finally told, not least because a new generation of officials and administrators was coming into the sport who objected to apartheid.

Bill Beaumont has been back to South Africa several times and rejoices in the changes in that country. He was also a guest when the Springboks held a reunion and was able to meet former opponents, such as Botha and Du Plessis, and reminisce about the 1980 tour.

Sadly, Beaumont has also had to attend the funerals of fellow Lions from 1980. Bruce Hay of Boroughmuir and Scotland had a long and brave battle against cancer before dying of the disease at the age of 57 in 2007.

That same year saw the death of Ray Gravell of Llanelli and Wales. Gravell was one of those Lions who became much more famous after his playing career was over, becoming a noted broadcaster and actor on small and big screen. He contracted diabetes and had a leg amputated, but remained upbeat and active before dying suddenly of a heart attack, aged 56.

Though no one could know it at the time, the unlucky 1980 tourists would be the last Lions to visit South Africa until 1997. In the intervening 17 years, that country was transformed, while the Lions went elsewhere.

CHAPTER THIRTEEN

CIARAN FITZGERALD'S MEN CUT DOWN
New Zealand 1983

When Australian media mogul and well-known gambler Kerry Packer set up his rebel cricket circus in 1977, no one could have foreseen that his activities would have a direct impact on the British Lions tour to New Zealand six years later. By bringing large amounts of money into the sport, Packer changed the loyalties of many of the men who made their living from cricket. Within rugby union, a great many people wondered if the same thing would happen to their sport.

Packer's fellow Australian entrepreneur David Lord set out to see if avowedly amateur rugby players could be tempted by the prospect of making their living playing the game they loved. Previously, any rugby union player wanting to earn money from sport had to join rugby league, or cheat through things like boot endorsements. Having talked to many players, particularly in the southern hemisphere, Lord seemed fairly confident that he could set up a Packer-like circus involving top players in televised matches.

In 1983, Lord went public with his idea for 'World Championship Rugby', and caused a sensation throughout the rugby world. While many people dismissed the sports promoter's plan as pure fantasy, within the hallowed halls of the various rugby unions the threat from Lord was taken very seriously indeed. But perversely, there was a bigger threat around – the proposal for a Rugby World Cup.

In 1968, the International Rugby Board had forbidden any of its member countries from trying to host a World Cup, but throughout the 1970s and again in the early 1980s, the idea of such a championship was hotly debated. There was a clear split between the four original home unions and the rest of the world. The British and Irish unions were convinced that a World Cup would lead directly to professionalism. The problem for them, however, was that players across the world really wanted to see such a tournament, as did more than a few officials and administrators, and both the Australian and New Zealand unions had pledged to work for a World Cup.

The fate of the British Lions was also an issue under consideration at the time. The trend for more and more individual countries to go on tours had chipped away at the unique nature of the Lions. Such tours also made players think seriously about how long they could give almost total commitment to a sport that did not recompense them with anything other than the dubious rewards of fleeting fame. Would the Lions – only a touring party, albeit the best – survive as an entity if the World Cup, or David Lord's World Championship Rugby, came to fruition? Such questions were certainly being asked, not least because even though the 1981 tour was cut back to ten weeks, the demands of relatively new domestic leagues, cups and other competitions were taking their toll on players.

We cannot be sure how many Lions Lord spoke to, or whether any of them gave his ideas any sort of serious consideration, as total secrecy surrounded the project – and still does. 'It was talked about,' said one

Lion, 'but nobody admitted anything, and anyone who did would have been on the first plane back home. That much was clear to us.'

David Lord would eventually announce that he had signed up more than 200 players on a provisional basis for the professional tournaments he had planned. He even stated that it would begin operations in 1984, so it is no wonder that the Lions tour to New Zealand took place under the microscope of the media, which was reporting almost daily on these developments throughout 1983.

Since it seemed that the vast majority of the players signed by Lord were from the southern hemisphere, the home unions were less worried about Lord than they were about the World Cup. It seems crazy now, after six successful tournaments, that anyone opposed the idea, but when the vote was eventually taken in 1984 to set up the Cup, the four home unions were united in opposition, and it took South Africa, who knew they wouldn't even be able to compete because of the various boycotts against them, to swing the vote in favour.

In hindsight, of course, the vast sums of money generated by the World Cup, as well as the new funds that were already pouring in from television rights, made professionalism inevitable, though it took until 1995 and Rupert Murdoch's massive deal with the New Zealand, Australian and South African unions to bring things to a head. But even in 1983, individual players were beginning to question why the various unions could pocket hundreds of thousands of pounds from matches involving them, yet they would be banned from playing if they accepted any payment other than the laughable 'expenses' which the unions paid them.

Peter Winterbottom said:

It was the last of the really long tours, and I had to give up working in farming to go on the tour. We never got paid anything other than £20 expenses. I remember Roy Laidlaw, who I believe was a truck driver at

*the time, telling me that he wasn't getting paid while he was away and the
local butcher had given free meat to his wife and kids to support him.*

*Then when we got there, we played 18 games in front of average
crowds of 26,000. Somebody was making money, but it wasn't us. It
seems staggering, even peculiar, that people had to sacrifice so much to go
on the tour, but that was just the way it was.*

It can be seen in hindsight that the four home unions were fighting a losing
battle against progress by the time the Lions toured in 1983. The New
Zealand media, as ever, were intent on portraying the 1983 Lions as bad
boys, but the main concern of the British press seemed to be speculating
on which of the Lions might defect to any new professional game. As in
1980, the Lions would need to be disciplined and focused on the job in
hand and maintain high standards of behaviour off the field. Once again
there would also need to be firm managers in charge of the party, so the
selectors turned to two great Lions, Willie John McBride and Jim Telfer,
to lead the squad.

McBride had originally wanted to be coach, but when asked to manage
the side he went along with the idea, only to regret it later. Telfer and he
were two strong and abrasive characters that did not always mix well.
as both subsequently acknowledged in their memoirs.

Interviewed for this book, Telfer said:

*The sad thing for me was that I genuinely thought that I was ready to be
the coach of the Lions. I had been coach for Scotland for a couple of
years, and the B team before that, so I was fairly experienced and also
had been on Lions tours, while my rugby philosophy had been formed on
the tour to New Zealand in 1966.*

*I felt ready for the job, but the problem was that I was on my own,
there was only one coach and I had to do everything myself. At Scotland I
had Colin Telfer as my assistant, but in New Zealand in 1983 I had to do*

everything, and there were 30 players to be coached. I had also never
really coached backs before, as that was Colin's job.

In a move which seemed perfectly sensible given that Ireland had won
the Five Nations championship in the two previous seasons, Ciaran
Fitzgerald translated his captaincy of his country to taking charge of the
Lions. His selection as captain initially caused little comment, and indeed
there was much more concern about the number of players selected who
seemed to be out of form or possibly prone to injury. Not the least of the
problems was that the Five Nations championship of 1983 had been
of poor quality, with England and Wales in a trough and Scotland not
much better.

As is always the case when selectors have to make choices, people
scratched their heads at the omission of their favourite players, but eventually it would be the selection of Fitzgerald as captain which would cause
the greatest controversy, not least because many people in English rugby
considered that an excellent Lion, Peter Wheeler, lost out on a place on
the tour as a result of Fitzgerald's captaincy. Paul Dodge was another
strangely absent player.

The main reason, however, was that while the Irish Army officer was
a fine and dignified leader off the pitch, and hard worker and sometimes
inspirational on it, he was clearly the second-best hooker in the squad.
Colin Deans of Scotland had just enjoyed a marvellous Five Nations
season and was at the peak of his considerable powers. In training and
in the midweek dirt-tracker matches, Deans was clearly superior to
Fitzgerald, and as the Tests approached it was openly stated that he might
be preferred to the squad captain. A few All Blacks mischievously stated
their belief that Deans was the better man, which was not calculated to
make Fitzgerald feel good about himself. The press also wrote incessantly
of Fitzgerald's failure to throw in properly at the line-out, and Willie John
McBride was convinced that referees read these reports and took an

unduly harsh view of any wavering off a straight line by the captain. So much so that McBride asked the press to lay off Fitzgerald.

'There were many people who didn't think that, judged purely in playing terms, he warranted his place on the tour,' said Peter Winterbottom, 'but he was chosen as captain and that should have been that. Instead, there were all these problems over selection, and yes, it had an effect, though I was one of the youngsters and didn't really understand what was going on.'

It is fair to suggest that Fitzgerald should have done a Campbell-Lamerton and dropped himself, especially after the first Test. But in the Lions' set-up at that time, the matter of selection was down to the captain, coach and manager. Telfer admits he voted for Deans, who was upset that he did not get selected, but McBride sided with his captain, who felt he had a duty to lead and kept himself in the Test side.

Telfer said:

I had two disadvantages from the start. Willie John was a great manager but he was also in effect the chairman of selectors. Ciaran Fitzgerald was a fine man, but I didn't think he was a good enough player to be in the team. Willie John chose him to play, and I had to go along with that.

Apart from Fitzgerald, McBride and coach Telfer had other and perhaps more pressing problems to contend with. McBride got involved in confrontations with a hostile press, while Telfer met player resistance to his faith in a long intensive preparatory period leading up to the Tests. He had little success in persuading some players to adapt to his style, unashamedly based on the All Blacks' rucking game. Telfer's attempts to fit the men to the pattern, rather than the other way round, led to the big secret of the tour – how close the players came to open rebellion.

John Beattie said that Telfer was undermined by grumbling among the players and by the difference between Telfer's commitment to a rucking game and the mauling style preferred by England and, to a lesser extent, Wales:

> *Jim Telfer was doing all the right stuff in my opinion, and what he was saying was absolutely right, but there were meetings behind his back by a cabal of mainly English players who decided they didn't want to play the way he was coaching.*
>
> *It wasn't an open rebellion, thought it was close; it was just lack of willingness to go along with what he was asking. They had their own style of playing and wanted to adhere to it, and he gave them too much respect. That led to some very confused messages on the field.*

It was a pity, because the pack should have been a match for anybody. It contained forwards of the calibre of Graham Price, who was making his third tour and became the Lions' most capped prop ever. Price was already a rugby immortal because he formed one third of the famous Pontypool front row with Bobby Windsor and Charlie Faulkner – it is a popular misconception that all three were 'capped' by the Lions, for though they toured together in 1977, they never played together in a Test, and Faulkner never made it into a Test side. Yet Price was no certainty for a Test place because Scotland's Iain 'The Bear' Milne was pushing him hard all the way.

Peter Winterbottom was by common consent the best performer among the Lions, but acknowledged that he had to be at his best to stay in the Test side:

> *I had serious competition in the person of Jim Calder, who was a great player. I was lucky enough to get the nod in the first Test, because I have spoken to Willie John McBride since and he told me it was bloody close between us. I was fit and managed to stay uninjured and kept my place, but I was delighted for Jim when he came into the back row alongside Iain Paxton for the third Test.*

Ian Stephens, Maurice Colclough, John O'Driscoll, Steve Bainbridge, Bob Norster and Jeff Squire were all quality players but some found it difficult to adapt, while Stephens and Squire were injured after the first Test and flown home.

The Scots–English divide allegedly caused Colclough to become a mortal enemy of John Beattie, who himself had suffered a serious injury to his knee the year before. Said Beattie, however:

> *Me and Maurice at each other's throats? A complete myth, all stemming from the fact that I'm supposed to have singled him out and punched him during a Calcutta Cup match. I actually liked him. He was a great guy who smoked cigarettes and drank red wine by the barrel and the only thing I would say is that he wasn't fit enough in 1983, but he was a very good player in his time.*

Another soon on the plane home was Terry Holmes, the superb Welsh scrum-half, who suffered a horrendous knee ligament injury. His loss was a devastating blow to Telfer's plans, given Holmes's defensive as well as quick passing qualities. But many other players never reached the heights they were capable of, despite remaining uninjured.

With the new punishing schedule of 6 games in just 17 days before the first Test, and then Test Matches every fortnight thereafter – 'It should never have been agreed to,' said McBride – there simply was not time for Telfer to get his men playing the way he wanted.

'I originally thought that the players of Britain and Ireland would have improved enough to take on the All Blacks, but I was wrong,' said Telfer. 'There were some players who could step up, but a few who chose not to.'

Peter Winterbottom described the situation:

I was 22 at the time and in fact I had my 23rd birthday on tour. I was training like mad and with Jim Telfer we trained every day without fail. I got myself as fit as I have ever been, but the older guys were all breaking down – they were knackered.

There was no backing off, and it was a case of the harder the better as far as Jim was concerned. Everything had to be 100 per cent and I think he drilled people too hard at times. For instance we went on what was supposed to be a holiday up at the Bay of Islands and everybody thought we would get a couple of days off but Jim had us training every day, and it was tough training, too.

A few guys were pissed off and felt he was over the top, but as far as I was concerned I didn't know any different and just got on with it. We might have been better thinking about the game, instead of being drilled all the time.

Willie John McBride said he confronted Telfer with his concerns over the amount of work the players were doing, but in the end he had to let the coach do as he wished, and at first things did not go too badly.

The only loss in the initial six games was 12–13 to Auckland, where the first real signs of possible line-out problems emerged, those great All Black locks Andy Haden and Gary Whetton dominating as they would do for most of the Tests. Against Manawatu at Palmerston North one week before the first Test, the match descended into a brutal affair, and both Fitzgerald and Paxton picked up head wounds while other players were festooned with bruises and stud marks. Once again the Lions had their own tour doctor, Donald McLeod, and he was kept busy patching up the injured.

The first Test at Christchurch was a tight affair, the loss of Holmes with ruptured ligaments proving disastrous in the long term, though Roy Laidlaw did well in his place. With players of the calibre of Haden, Whetton, Murray Mexted, Jock Hobbs and Andy Dalton in their pack, and with

Dave Loveridge behind the scrum keeping the likes of Stu Wilson and Bernie Fraser supplied with ball, the All Blacks did not lack for quality, and it was something of a surprise when the Lions led 9–6 at half-time. But a try by Mark 'Cowboy' Shaw proved decisive in turning the game in the All Blacks' favour and a stunning drop goal from distance by full-back Alan Hewson clinched it 16–12 for New Zealand.

If the first Test was disappointing, the second was a hammer blow. Having gone on a run of three straight wins since Christchurch, scoring 150 points for the loss of 29, the Lions were confident of success at Wellington's Athletic Park, especially when the All Blacks began by playing with the ferocious wind at their backs and were only 9–0 ahead at half-time. The Lions felt they simply had to attack to win, yet the All Blacks put up the shutters and the Lions could not penetrate, both sides failing to score in the half. In the Lions' history book, the match was notable only for a family double, as Michael Kiernan gained his cap, following in the footsteps of his uncle Tom.

In the meantime, the social side of the tour was proving that there were considerable differences between New Zealand and 'Blighty', as ex-pats called home. Peter Winterbottom explained:

We were in Wairarapa having a meal with the local dignitaries and it was two Lions to a table. I was with Jim Calder and thinking to myself 'What are we doing here?' but we had to make conversation and a couple of the older New Zealanders seemed keen to ask questions about Britain. I don't know what they thought of us, but they started pointing to the vegetables in turn and saying 'Do you have those in your country?' It was like 'These are mushrooms, do you have those in your country?' No wonder we still felt in those days that we really were on the other side of the world.

Apart from that, the telephones didn't work, air mail took a week and the hotels were primitive at times.

John Beattie couldn't understand the difference in the approach to rugby:

> *Just as in South Africa, there was a terrible drinking culture among the Lions. We were going out to play the toughest team in the world, so I thought we would be going out to play hard, live like monks, and we wouldn't be allowed to smoke or drink, but instead the self-destruct button was pushed and everybody went on a bender at times.*
>
> *It was accepted that if you were in the dirt-trackers then you could go and get drunk, while the Test team got drunk at the weekend. It was just madness, complete madness, and I am convinced looking back that in South Africa in '80 and New Zealand in '83, the Lions could have won both series if the players had behaved.*

The New Zealand press did their best to play up the rowdiness, as Beattie recalled: 'They planted a woman to try and sleep with some of the boys to get stories of guys being unfaithful, and one small incident in a pub was blown out of all proportion, but we were our own worst enemies at times.'

The worst incident was when Eddie Butler, who had picked up a skin rash in a game – a common problem for forwards, and often known as scrum pox – was reported to have the sexually transmitted disease herpes. Willie John McBride told the reporter the truth but the herpes story was printed anyway – 'Just another of the tricks the locals got up to,' said McBride.

Needing to win the third Test to save the series, the Lions opted for an attacking strategy, even though the chill wind and muddy surface militated against them. The two Scots drafted into the team, John Rutherford – playing at centre instead of his usual fly-half to accommodate Ollie Campbell – and Jim Calder, twin brother of Finlay, both showed up well, the former scoring the Lions' second try after their fellow Scot Roger

Baird had gone over for a try early in the match. It left Baird with an unusual record. In all his 27 'cap' internationals he never scored a try for Scotland, yet managed one in his four Lions' Tests and six on the tour in all.

The series was lost and for once the heart went out of the Lions. Though they won their remaining three non-Test Matches, by the time they got to the fourth Test at Auckland the All Blacks were brimming with confidence while the Lions had somewhat lost the plot and went down in abject fashion as the mighty All Black pack turned on the power and blew their opponents off the field. Ollie Campbell and Gwyn Evans' penalties were the Lions only reply to three tries by Stu Wilson and one each from Haden, Hobbs and Hewson, who also struck four conversions and two penalties for a personal haul of 18 points in a 38–6 slaughter.

'More than a few players were already on the plane back home mentally,' said John Beattie, 'but the truth is that over the series, the All Blacks were a very good side, one of their best ever teams, while the 1983 Lions were not a very good vintage.'

Peter Winterbottom added: 'We contested three Tests very well and were poor in the fourth. Personally, I thought we were unlucky not to win at least one Test, but you have to look at the quality of the All Blacks in 1983 and conclude they were just the better side.'

The fourth Test had been the Lions' record defeat, though South Africa had scored seven tries against them in Cape Town in 1955. The 4–0 'all black wash' was also the Lions' worst performance since 1966, although that side at least won two Tests against Australia. A long period of introspection followed the Lions' return home, and Telfer and Fitzgerald took a lot of criticism, but even though they had had chances to win, in the final analysis the 1983 Lions were beaten over four Tests by a better team.

McBride went home and wrote a scathing report on the whole tour. According to the man himself, it was quietly binned by the Home Unions Committee. Telfer in particular was a disillusioned man, the last Test being what he called 'the worst experience of my rugby career', one that made him seriously question his future in the sport.

'I came back really sickened from New Zealand,' said Telfer.

The system we had in Britain and Ireland at the time was counties, provinces or districts, as we had in Scotland. They were just no match for what they had in New Zealand with its national championships and strong competition at all levels. They also had better players than us, though we did have some good individuals.

I would say I was very disillusioned with the concept of the Lions, because we were trying to put the men of four unions together and wield them into a Test side in the space of four or five weeks, which was very difficult.

Though they had had their differences, Willie John McBride, to be fair, told a press conference that he hoped Jim Telfer would get the chance to coach the Lions again because of the experience he had gained. Telfer replied: 'Is there life after death?'

Yet Melrose's finest got over his initial disappointment quickly and had also learned many lessons in New Zealand. The very next season, with the Scottish Lions Laidlaw, Rutherford, Jim Calder, Baird, Paxton, Deans, Iain 'the Bear' Milne (why he never played a Lions Test remains a mystery) and John Beattie at its core, he would weld together a Scottish side who would win the Grand Slam for only the second time in the country's history, ending a wait of 59 years.

'They were all very good players,' said Telfer, 'and full credit to them because they learned a lot in New Zealand on the Lions tour and brought the lessons home with them, and we went on to win the Grand Slam.'

The 1983 Lions went their separate ways, and many players were happy to see the back of the tour and still don't like to talk about it, at least on the record. John Beattie qualified as a chartered accountant and

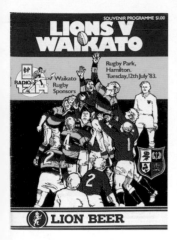

1983 Lions v Waikato programme.

Protecting the ball and each other – 1983 Lions (from left) Iain Paxton, Jeff Squire and Bob Norster shield Graham Price with the ball during the first Test in Christchurch which the Lions lost 16–12.

avid Campese hounded by the 1989 Lions.

1989 Lions v Australia
third Test programme.

Finlay Calder, the 1989 captain, going for the loose ball
during the first Test against Australia. The home side
won the match 30–12.

The Battle of Ballymore. The second Test in Brisbane, 1989.

1989 Lions: Rory Underwood, Dean Richards, Rob Andrew, Ieuan Evans and Brian Moore celebrate after the third Test.

The famous mascot. Gavin Hastings leads out the 1993 Lions, followed by Kenny Milne, for the match against North Harbour, which the Lions won 29–13.

The great John Kirwan evades the Lions' Jeremy Guscott, first Test, 1993.

Who said South Africa is always sunny? Scott Gibbs evades a tackle during the Border v British Lions match at Basil Kenyon Stadium, East London, 1997.

That drop goal – Jeremy Guscott fires the ball over to win the 1997 series against South Africa.

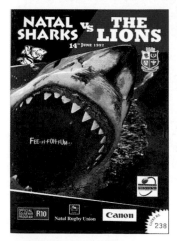

1997 Lions v Natal Sharks programme.

The 1997 Lions celebrate winning the series.

Putting your face where your heart is – the Barmy Army displays its support for the 1997 Lions.

eady for battle – the Lions pack of 2001 in the first Test at Brisbane.

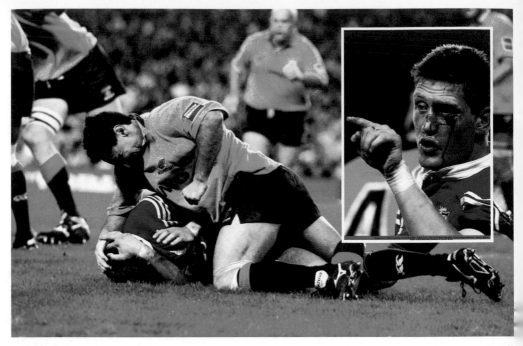

Before and afters. Duncan MacRae gets stuck into Ronan O'Gara during the match against New South Wales Waratahs in 2001; the damage is all too clear.

Jason Robinson shows the elation of scoring against Australia in the first Test of 2001.

Clash of giants. Martin Johnson and Justin Harrison during the third and final Test at Stadium Australia in Sydney on 14 July 2001. The hand belongs to referee Paddy O'Brien.

The courage of Broony. Gordon Brown (centre) with brothers John and Peter at a fund-raising benefit evening in his honour at London's Grosvenor House Hotel on 28 February 2001, just three weeks before he died.

Right Eminence Grise – spin doctor Alastair Campbell looks on at a Lions briefing before the 2005 tour.

Below The moments that change a series. Lions captain Brian O'Driscoll grimaces in agony seconds after his shoulder was dislocated in a spear tackle by Tana Umaga and Kevin Mealamu.

WANTED – the shirt that said it all. A British and Irish Lions fan wears a t-shirt with a photo of All Black Tana Umaga for the 2005 tour.

He couldn't lead Wales to a second successive Grand Slam in 2009, but could Ryan Jones lead the Lions to South Africa?

A proud tradition in very safe hands – chairman, coach and manager of the 2009 Lions; (from left) Ar Irvine, Ian McGeechan an Gerald Davies.

became a regular broadcaster on rugby and other sports for BBC Scotland as well as coach of West of Scotland RFC. He was in the commentary box when his son John got his first cap for Scotland against Romania in 2006.

Robert Ackerman turned professional and enjoyed success with several rugby league clubs. He then became a teacher.

Roger Baird became a successful grain merchant and has long been involved in the coaching side at his club Watsonians. Also on the coaching side at his old club is Dusty Hare at Leicester Tigers.

Ciaran Fitzgerald enjoyed a long career in the Irish Army and is now a rugby pundit for Setanta television. John Carleton moved from teaching into financial services, an industry which also features Graham Price, who also writes on rugby.

Terry Holmes's injury problems continued even after he joined rugby league side Bradford Northern for a reputed £80,000. He dislocated his shoulder in his first match and played only 40 games before retiring two years later. Reinstated to union, he had spells as coach of Cardiff and Caerphilly while simultaneously building a career in business.

Bob Norster is currently chief executive of Cardiff Blues. Trevor Ringland is a solicitor in Belfast. Steve Smith joined forces with Fran Cotton to found the highly successful Cotton Traders leisure clothing firm. David Irwin is now the medical coordinator for Ulster Rugby. His fellow Irish international Hugo MacNeill works in financial services in Dublin. Iain Paxton coached Boroughmuir rugby club to the Scottish championship and is still involved at the Edinburgh club. Eddie Butler became a journalist and broadcaster, and has covered a variety of sports for the BBC. Jim Calder scored the try that won the Grand Slam for Scotland against France in 1984 and now runs a successful executive recruitment firm.

Colin Deans coached at Northampton Saints and is involved with the successful Eden Park clothing company started by French internationalist Franck Mesnel. Ollie Campbell also moved into the clothing business in Dublin. Mike Kiernan is a financial advisor in Cork. Jeff Squire emigrated to South Africa and runs a travel company.

Roy Laidlaw and John Rutherford set a world record as half-back partners, playing 35 times for Scotland together. The former is an electrician, who went on to manage the Scotland Sevens side and is now director of rugby at Jed-Forest, while his colleague Rutherford is a coach at Selkirk.

Sadly, one of the 1983 Lions, Maurice Colclough, died at the age of just 52 in 2006. Like his fellow 1980 Lion, Bruce Hay, he succumbed to a brain tumour. He left a wife, Annie, and five children.

As for the All Blacks, it says everything about the relentless drive for rugby perfection in that country that of the team which thumped the Lions in the fourth Test, only Gary Whetton and Warwick Taylor survived to win the inaugural World Cup less than four years later.

By the time of that World Cup, the 1986 'window' for the British Lions to tour South Africa had come and gone. Sense prevailed and the four home unions could no longer withstand the pressure of the anti-apartheid lobby, which focused on freeing that one-time Lions fan, Nelson Mandela. As long as apartheid continued, South Africa would be exiled from just about every sport.

In what was clearly a poor substitute in playing terms, to celebrate the centenary of the International Board the British and Irish Lions played a one-off Test in Cardiff on 16 April 1986 against a select side drawn from the 'other unions' in the board – that team of stars was simply called 'the Rest'. Colin Deans not only finally got his Lions 'cap', but was also named captain of the side. He and indeed every player in the 21-strong party got a Lions blazer and tie, and it was certainly regarded as a full international match at the time, even if some records discount it. The side was managed by Clive Rowlands and coached by Mick Doyle.

Given the talent available to the 'the Rest', it is perhaps not surprising that the Lions struggled. Serge Blanco and Patrick Esteve of France joined the likes of Australians Nick Farr-Jones, Michael Lynagh and Simon

Poidevin plus All Blacks Murray Mexted, John Kirwan and Cowboy Shaw under the captaincy of Andrew Slack, who had skippered Australia to Grand Slam success against the four home unions in their 1984 tour to Britain and Ireland.

All the players certainly took the match as seriously as any other Lions game. A storm blew in just after kick-off but the poor weather conditions did not take the heat out of the challenges. Farr-Jones scored an early try, converted by Lynagh, which was followed by a Gavin Hastings penalty and John Beattie's try for the Lions, but John Rutherford had to go off with a broken nose and the Lions also lost their main source of line-out possession, Wade 'The Blackpool Tower' Dooley with a knee injury. Though the Lions led 7–6 at half-time, with the Rest's pack well in control, Lynagh put his side ahead with a penalty and Poidevin scored the clinching try eight minutes from time, Lynagh converting for a 15–7 victory to the Rest.

It was a useful exercise to keep the Lions name alive, but not what was wanted, i.e. success. That would come three years later in Australia. It would be a long wait, though a certain new competition called the Rugby World Cup proved an interesting diversion for many players.

CHAPTER FOURTEEN

FINLAY CALDER: NO COMPROMISE

Australia 1989

With South Africa out of the picture not only for Lions business but for all rugby contact, the Home Unions Committee accepted an invitation to conduct a party of Lions to Australia for a tour exclusively of that country for the first time since 1899. It would also be the first time in 23 years that the Lions had played Test Matches in Australia.

The World Cup of 1987 had proved to be a glittering success, with the final between New Zealand and France watched on television by tens of millions around the world. To reach that final, which they lost 29–9, France had beaten Australia in a pulsating semi-final. The Wallabies had at one stage been second favourites for a tournament partially staged in their country, and had beaten both England and Ireland as they progressed to the semi-final, so they felt very strongly that they could beat the Lions in a three-match Test series.

It was now 15 years since the Lions had won a Test series, and not a few pundits openly speculated that they might never do so again. Australia had suffered some years in the doldrums in the 1970s, but, under maverick coach Alan Jones, their brilliant success on the 1984 Grand Slam tour of the home unions and then the World Cup showed that there had been a resurgence of rugby union's fortunes in a country where rugby league was still king.

In 1988, England had also been beaten in both Tests played by them on their tour of Australia, so it was a question of whether the extra resources of the combined unions would be enough to topple the Wallabies. It would be a tall order, the Australian side including some of Australia's all-time greats such as the legendary winger David Campese; Michael Lynagh, a star at fly-half or centre; captain Nick Farr-Jones, then rated the world's best scrum-half; dynamic hooker Tom Lawton; locks Bill Campbell and Stephen Cutler; and a back row that featured the destructive Jeff Miller and Steve Tuynman. The Australians also had a new coach, Bob Dwyer, whose successful defensive tactics were revolutionary at the time.

The Lions party was managed by former Welsh scrum-half and captain Clive Rowlands, who had taken charge of the 1986 one-off team but was much more famous for coaching the renowned Welsh side of the 1970s. He will forever be remembered as one of the kickers in the infamous 1963 Scotland–Wales match, which produced 111 line-outs and led to a change in the rules prohibiting kicking to touch except from inside your own 22. Though many thought he would favour the men of his beloved Wales, Rowlands, known as 'Top Cat', would prove to be a diplomat and an excellent manager, passionate about his rugby, firm when required, but also an emollient force on the occasions when things began to get rough.

David 'Dai' Young recalled: 'Everywhere we went he had a smiling face and never had a bad word to say about anyone. He set the highest standards for us all, on and off the field, and in return we were never left short of anything. We weren't English, Welsh, Scottish or Irish; we were Lions.'

Scott Hastings of Scotland was making the first of his two tours and remembers that when he arrived at the hotel where the Lions gathered, unity didn't seem likely at first.

It was the Oatlands Park Hotel at Weighbridge in Surrey, and the Welsh were in one corner, the Irish in another, and the Scots and English at opposite sides of the room. How were we going to merge these four different groups with their different styles of play? The rivalries are undoubtedly part and parcel of a tour, but it's all about how people react with one another and it was amazing how quickly things changed – that's just one of the things which makes a Lions tour so special.

There was also rivalry among the Scots alone. Hastings said:

We were determined to be the fittest group on tour. After the nine of us were named, we all went into extra training, with the boys from the Borders all gathering for sessions at John Jeffrey's farm while those of us from Edinburgh would get together with Dougie Morgan. We found out they were doing extra sessions so we did extra sessions – but sadly for us, they had the benefit of JJ's breakfasts.

Much of the credit for melding the disparate groups into a formidable force went to the head coach, Ian McGeechan, a man who would become synonymous with Lions coaching. He said: 'I had been assistant coach with Scotland for three years and had only just taken over as national coach, and now Clive Rowlands wanted me to coach the Lions. Needless to say, I bit his hand off.'

The third member of the team, with specific responsibility for working with the pack, was Roger Uttley, the Harrow schoolmaster who was part of the successful English set-up under manager Geoff Cooke. Uttley and McGeechan were veterans of the 1974 'Invincibles' tour to South

Africa. He said: 'I think we both desperately wanted the Lions to recapture the glory of that era. That was definitely the way I thought, but we knew we faced a very tough task, as Australia had a great side.'

Coupled with the canny management of Rowlands, McGeechan and Uttley ensured that the Lions of 1989 were well prepared for the challenges they faced. The choice of captain was inspired, as the man himself was truly inspirational. His twin brother Jim had been a Lion in 1983, and Finlay was determined that his Lions would not suffer the fate of their predecessors. He imbued the Lions in Australia with the courageous spirit of William Wallace himself, and did that some six years before the film *Braveheart* hit the screens. Typically modest, he himself would rather pay tribute to the other players and to the triumvirate of Rowlands, McGeechan and Uttley, but there is no doubt that the qualities of leadership that he showed, and the determination and discipline he instilled in the tour party, were vital components in the overall success.

There was barely a weakness in what was probably the strongest group of Lions to travel south since 1974. The pack for the Tests was to prove the dominant department, with a supremely combative back row behind a tight five who laid the foundation for eventual victory by ensuring a solid platform, though they struggled in the first Test.

The front row of David Sole of Scotland, Brian Moore of England and Dai Young stayed together for all three Tests, while England's second row of Paul Ackford and Wade Dooley came together for the final two. The first choice back row of Calder alongside Englishmen Mike Teague and Dean Richards was interrupted only by injury to Teague, Derek White of Scotland coming in for the first Test.

That first Test came early in what was another truncated tour of just 12 matches. The opening week had seen the Lions recover from their travel and jet lag at a superb country club, the Burswood, near Perth. Roger Uttley had spotted the venue on a previous visit, and noticing that the Lions were set for a bog-standard hotel, he suggested the move to

Rowlands. 'Leave it to me,' said Top Cat, and that became his catch-phrase for the tour. McGeechan said: 'Clive told me "The players have got to feel important" and that week at the Burswood, more than anything, showed how they were looked upon. It set the tone for the whole tour and we never looked back.'

The first six games had seen the tourists in fine form overall, with the toughest matches, as ever, being against New South Wales and Queensland. The latter game saw some violent incidents, with Welsh centre Mike Hall being badly raked, which provoked retaliation from the Lions. Australian forwards Bill Campbell and Mark McBain claimed with some evidence that they had been punched. The Aussie press called it 'thugby' from the tourists, and the media atmosphere around the Lions grew noticeably chiller.

Off the pitch, the Lions were enjoying socializing and playing golf and other sports, much of it organized by the 'duty boys'. This concept of a 'duty roster' is one of the Lions' long-standing traditions. In 1989, for instance, Clive Rowlands appointed two players each day to be 'duty boys', their role being to make sure that players were on time for buses and training sessions, that bags were remembered, and that social activities were organized. The tradition may have fallen away on recent tours, but expect Gerald Davies to reinstate the roster in 2009.

One of the activities in Queensland in 1989 nearly turned to tragedy. A group of Lions had gone on a river-rafting trip near Cairns when their craft tipped over in the rapids, and Young, who was not a strong swimmer, got into difficulties and had to be hauled from the water. 'It was almost shades of R.L. Seddon in 1888,' said Scott Hastings. The incident was made light of at the time, but it was considerably more frightening than was portrayed.

In the modern game, playing matches of real intensity in the space of just three weeks inevitably leads to injury problems, and so it proved, almost certain starters for the first Test such as John Devereux and Mike

Teague having to be left out. Paul Dean, the Irish fly-half, had been injured in the very first game in Perth and Rob Andrew had flown out from England to take his place, but Craig Chalmers of Scotland was preferred at No. 10 for the first Test with Brendan Mullin of Ireland and Mike Hall in the centre, after Scott Hastings declared himself unfit with hamstring trouble. Rob Jones was peerless at scrum-half, with his fellow Welshman Ieuan Evans on one wing, England's flyer Rory Underwood on the other and Scotland's Gavin Hastings at full-back. All kept their places for the three Tests. Evans in particular had the unenviable task of dealing with the mercurial genius of David Campese, the most famous player in the world. It was to be a job well done by the Welshman.

Perhaps their triumphal progress to the first Test in Sydney had made the Lions complacent, or perhaps they simply underestimated the desire of the Australians to win, but the tourists were knocked sideways by a determined pack that seemed to gobble up ball and kept Farr-Jones and Lynagh in full flow throughout. The result was a four tries to nil 30–12 victory in which all of the Lions' points came from the boots of Gavin Hastings and Chalmers.

One Lion described it as 'a bolt out of the blue', while Scott Hastings said: 'The Wallabies showed their true class and ripped the Lions to pieces. Suddenly the pressure was on.'

Clive Rowlands mused: 'Was I simply a one-eyed Welshman who, even in defeat, believed we were always better? Perhaps we had been overconfident, but we certainly learned from the experience.'

Perhaps unfairly, the backs took most of the blame for the defeat, and Chalmers, Mullin and Hall were dropped for the second Test in Brisbane. But a much more serious change of personnel was considered. Finlay Calder felt he had not performed to the expected standard and offered to step aside for the team's sake. He said: 'The press were calling for heads to roll, my own included. I called a meeting of the management and offered to stand down for the second Test. "If you go, I must go also," was all Clive said. The matter was closed.'

At this point the phenomenon that was 'Donal's Doughnuts' came into play. Every touring party in recent decades has seen a clear split between the main Test squad and the midweek men, the 'dirt-trackers'. But, given the potential for injury, it has always been hugely important that the players in the midweek side should stay fit and focused, and ready to step up to the Test side. It has been absolutely crucial that the captain of the dirt-trackers keeps his men busy and inspired to perform to their best, and in 1989 that man, fortunately, was Donal Lenihan. A survivor of the 1983 tour who would go on to manage the Lions in 2001, Lenihan made the dirt-trackers his own pride and joy, and when Rob Andrew, Jeremy Guscott, Scott Hastings, Mike Teague and Wade Dooley were called up to the side for the second Test, they did so in fine fettle, having been part of the hard-working 'Doughnuts'.

In the match after the first Test – the midweek game against the Australian Capital Territory in Canberra – the Doughnuts produced a remarkable performance, as Scott Hastings recalled:

We were in trouble midway through the first half and indeed were still down at half-time, but in the second half we were superb and ended up winning 41–25. As we came off the pitch, all the boys who had played in the first Test stood and applauded us into the dressing room, showing the unity in the squad.

Rowlands described the match later as the 'turning point' of the tour.

Gavin Hastings would set all sorts of scoring records in his career. He was joined in the side for the second Test by his younger brother Scott, who would go on to become Scotland's most-capped player. Both played for Watsonians in Edinburgh and had made their debuts for Scotland in 1986 in the same match as David Sole gained his first cap. Now they would both appear for the British and Irish Lions in the same Test.

Scott Hastings remarked:

For me it was all about wearing the jersey that had been donned by fantastic players, people that I grew up watching in those many matches with Bill McLaren as the prince of commentators. People like Steve Fenwick, Barry John, Jim Renwick, J.P.R. Williams, Mike Gibson, J.J. Williams, Willie John McBride and all the others whose names just roll of the tongue even after all these decades.

To get the opportunity to travel to Australia and wear that pristine red jersey – it didn't have any logos in that day – with the badge of the four unions ... well it just doesn't get any better for a rugby player in these islands.

Clive Rowlands was a magnificent motivator and I remember how he would talk of having pride in the badge, and how the badge would get bigger as the tour went on. And it did.

That second Test has gone down in rugby history as the Battle of Bally-more. In retrospect, the events of the match in Brisbane on 8 July were predictable. Anger at losing the first Test and the sheer hype in the Australian media, including a distasteful amount of gloating, provoked a reaction in the Lions camp which basically came down to 'win at all costs'.

In the opening minutes, Rob Jones and Nick Farr-Jones, two scrum-halves of impeccable character, got into a little war of their own, after Jones stood on the Australian captain's foot. Reminiscent of the so-called '99' events 15 years earlier, this provided an excuse for the Lions' pack to charge into their opponents. Since three of that pack were police officers – Paul Ackford, Wade Dooley and Dean Richards – solicitor Brian Moore joked that it was 'the most legal fight in history'. French referee

René Horquet, it should be said, showed considerable bravery diving in to try and stop the fights.

Roger Uttley has confessed that he may well have started the Battle of Ballymore:

There was a bit of niggle in all the games on tour, to be honest, and Ballymore was hardly a battle in comparison to some I had seen on previous tours. We got trounced in the first Test and the Australians were a bit cocky and saying what they were going to do, but we knew there was going to be a French referee and that he would have more of a laissez-faire *approach.*

I had a word with Robert Jones and said 'If we are going to get into these guys, then we need to unsettle them and ruffle them, so just you get stuck into Nick Farr-Jones and be a bloody nuisance.' At the first scrum he stood on Farr-Jones's foot and he reacted badly. It all kicked off from there.

The rucks in particular were ferocious and some of the Lions' play was ruthless. There was not just one but several mêlées during a bad-tempered match in which punch-ups between individual players sparked bigger brawls – the worst being when David Young seemed to stand on Stephen Cutler and the whole Wallaby XV went ballistic. The wonder was that Horquet did not send anyone off, but in the days before the yellow card and sin bin, referees were often reluctant to dish out the ultimate punishment of dismissal.

With Calder driving them on, the Lions' forwards rucked and mauled for dear life and won the war of attrition, but did so only late on. In the closing minutes, Australia were ahead 12–9, thanks to Greg Martin's try and Lynagh's conversion and two penalties. But then the Hastings brothers intervened.

Scott Hastings recalls:

We were in a good position and I threw out a Barnes Wallis pass – you know, the bouncing bomb – to Gavin and fortunately he gathered it and went in and scored. The funny thing was that Gavin had just had a head knock and was seeing double – I'm just glad he picked up the right ball. He didn't even know the score at that point.

A further moment of individual brilliance by Jeremy Guscott, his try coming off his own precise chip kick, put the Lions in control, and Andrew's conversion of the try made the final scoreline 19–12. Many pundits felt that the introduction of Rob Andrew, Jeremy Guscott and Scott Hastings had been crucial in that Test, but the arrival of Mike Teague gave the pack a huge lift and his barnstorming displays in the second and third Tests won him the man of the series award.

The Lions soon had a swell party going but the Australian media howled their fury. Conveniently forgetting that it takes two to make a fight, television news and sports programmes and newspapers across the country highlighted the undoubted violence in the match, and the vast majority of the pundits blamed the Lions. Everybody had their say, including politicians, and Farr-Jones showed how much the Battle of Ballymore had got to him by predicting 'open warfare' in the third Test. The Australian RFU hardly helped the situation by calling for the IRB to look at using video evidence in disciplinary procedures and saying they were going to prepare a video of certain incidents and send it to the Committee of the Home Unions.

As so often happens in these situations, quiet men talked behind the scenes, and peace broke out. The third Test a week later in Sydney was anything but anodyne, both sets of forwards uncompromising in their play, but there was no illegality. Once again the Lions' forwards won the battle for domination, yet for all their titanic efforts, allowing Rob Jones and Rob Andrew to control things, the match would be remembered for one mistake by a Wallaby back – not just any old winger, but David Campese himself.

Before that, though, there was a curious incident during the match. Someone had smuggled a rabbit into the Sydney Football Stadium, and as Gavin Hastings made a break he looked up at the giant screen and saw the rabbit running beside him. 'It was the "bullet", a pre-planned move in which Gavin came like a bullet between us two centres,' said Scott Hastings. 'But the move evaporated and I turned to Gavin and said "Where are you?" He said "I tripped over the rabbit." I only found out later it was true. You just couldn't imagine it these days, but it happened.'

A converted try by Ian Williams and a Lynagh penalty against three penalties by Gavin Hastings meant a 9–9 scoreline at half-time. Lynagh put Australia ahead with another penalty, and though the Lions' forwards were turning the screw, there seemed to be no way through a tigerish Wallaby defence.

Almost in frustration Rob Andrew tried to drop a goal but his effort was well wide and fielded comfortably by Campese, who had seen little of the ball. As Ieuan Evans closed on him, as he had done throughout the Test series, Campese seemed to sense space that no else did and, even though he was behind his own try line, he threw a pass out to Greig Martin. But the full-back was taken unawares and the ball bounced off him and fell into the path of Evans, who merely had to flop down on the ball for one of the most crucial and bizarre tries in Test history.

With two more penalties by Hastings, the Lions were 19–12 up and looked to be certain to win, but Lynagh goaled two more penalties, and with the scoreline at 19–18 in favour of the tourists, a brave Australian side tried everything in their power to get the clinching score. The Lions held out, however, and indeed almost scored again in the dying seconds, to snatch a famous victory.

It was their first series win since 1974 and the first time since 1899, again in Australia, that the Lions had lost the initial Test yet come back to win the series. Manager Clive Rowlands openly wept tears of joy afterwards, but expressed his sympathy for Campese. 'He was crucified for his mistake, but how often has his playing genius created and rescued his teams from their dire plight?'

The Lions celebrated with the mother of all parties. Brian Moore ended up on the famous Sydney Harbour Bridge, running against the traffic and doing aeroplane impressions, and having to be rescued by two British journalists – 'I don't remember a thing,' he claimed.

The tour was not over however, and after a romp against New South Wales the Lions played what was effectively a fourth Test against an Anzac XV, which was actually much more Wallaby than All Black. A close and tough match – Ieuan Evans and Brendan Mullin both dislocated shoulders – ended 19–15 for the Lions. At the farewell dinner afterwards, the famous surgeon and war hero Sir Edward Dunlop, a former Wallaby, fell and broke his nose. Covered in blood, he called for two spoons and reset the nasal cartilage himself. It was just a fortnight after his 82nd birthday.

Back in Britain and Ireland, Calder and his men were given a muted welcome. The violence did cast a shadow over the tour, but most Lions fans were just glad to see the team successful again. Ian McGeechan's verdict is that it was a 'good tour' but not covered well by the media:

It almost happened undercover, as if we had woken up one morning and found we had won a Test series. We only lost one match on the tour, we had a great captain in Finlay, and Donal Lenihan's Doughnuts showed just how important it was that the midweek team worked well.

Roger Uttley said: 'We had a good squad but we didn't have the benefit of a long run-in to the first Test and it took time to get the selection and combinations right. But once we did, the rest followed on.'

Uttley has effectively retired as a teacher but still takes an active part in schoolboy rugby, though he has pledged to spend more time with his wife Kristine. Clive Rowlands went on to become President of the Welsh

RFU, but his term of office was marred by a row over links with South Africa. He and his wife Margaret have both since battled cancer and survived.

Some of the 1989 Lions have had interesting lives since then. Gareth Chilcott now runs the Gullivers Chilcott corporate hospitality organization, has written two books and at one point appeared on the professional stage in the rugby league play *Up 'n' Under*. Brendan Mullin went on to become chairman of London Irish in the professional era, and works in investment banking.

Mike Teague runs 'one of the best pubs in the world', said a fellow Lion, opposite Kingsholm, the ground of Gloucester RFC. Mike Hall became a television pundit and property developer, and in the latter role was involved in the disputed development of a new stadium for Cardiff City FC.

Except for Peter Dods, the entire nine-strong Scottish contingent of the 1989 Lions featured in Scotland's famous 1990 Grand Slam triumph over England. Fellow Lion Brian Moore still doesn't like being reminded of that day.

On a sad footnote, the Battle of Ballymore seems likely to have been the last Test played by the Lions at the famous old ground, which is now seriously dilapidated. The 2001 Lions did play Queensland at Ballymore – that match became a brawl, too – but the Brisbane Test was played at The Gabba cricket ground, and though there have been abortive plans to reconstruct Ballymore, it seems likely that the new Suncorp Stadium or The Gabba will host Tests in Brisbane from now on.

The final word on the 1989 tour goes to the captain: 'Two years later, with much the same team, Australia won the World Cup at Twickenham,' said Calder. 'They proved beyond doubt they were a very, very good side. But then, so were we.'

CHAPTER FIFTEEN

GAVIN HASTINGS AND THE TALE OF TWO TOURS

New Zealand 1993

Following the money-spinning multi-million pound success of the 1991 World Cup played in the four home countries and won by Australia, beating England at Twickenham, demands grew for rugby union to become fully professional or at least an open sport in which amateurs and professionals could mix. There was now simply too much money in rugby for something not to give, and the 1993 tour by the Lions to New Zealand was a case in point. The host union raked in huge sums of money both from the sale of match tickets and from the television rights. Yet the players earned nothing – that situation surely could not continue.

The major questions before the tour were, as usual, the selections and the captaincy. Will Carling had been unfortunate to miss the 1989 tour to Australia, and, apart from Scotland's Grand Slam success in 1990 and the loss to Australia in the 1991 World Cup Final, he had led England to a period of domination to rank with any they had enjoyed in the history of the sport. When England beat Scotland in the Calcutta Cup match at Twickenham, it seemed almost set in stone that Carling would be handed the job of leading the Lions that summer. But in the background there were more than a few officials within the RFU who did not actually like the English captain. The feelings were mutual, and led to Carling's remarks about the game being run by '57 old farts'.

Gavin Hastings, on the other hand, was a popular and charismatic Scot who was well liked within the other unions for his affable personality as well as his undoubted talents on the field which had seen him set all sorts of scoring records. He also had the experience of the previous Lions tour, and crucially, had been one of the stars with Scotland on their 1990 tour of New Zealand.

Gavin observed:

I can only imagine that from Will's point of view he was hugely disappointed not to be the captain, but having said that, I felt I was the better choice because Will had not played in New Zealand and I had been there three times and people knew who I was. I had also been with the Lions in 1989, so I thought I was the right man for the job.

The man chosen to coach the 1993 Lions was Ian McGeechan, earning himself the distinction of being the first man to be selected as coach for two tours. With Geoff Cooke – who had been in no small part responsible for the recent success of England – selected as manager of the tour, along with another English coach, Dick Best, as assistant to McGeechan, the selectors, who were chaired by Cooke, possibly saw the appointment of Hastings as necessary to counterbalance the preponderance of Englishmen in the tour party. As well as Cooke and Best, there would be no fewer than 17 players from England on the tour, that country's largest representation for decades and half of the total number of players who would eventually make up the party.

Ireland had just two forwards in the original party, Nick Popplewell and Mick Galwey, and none at all in the backs, although Vince Cunningham and Richard Wallace joined later as replacements. Since Ireland had beaten England in the last match of the Five Nations – a result that some people believe cost Carling the captaincy – the chorus of disapproval from the Emerald Isle was understandable.

A third international captain, Ieuan Evans of Wales, was included among a classy set of backs, while there were two sets of brothers in that year's Lions, Rory and Tony Underwood of Leicester and England joining the Hastings brothers. Kenny Milne of Heriot's and Scotland was selected to tour, ten years after his brother Iain had toured with the Lions to New Zealand. Wallace's arrival meant that the Lions' backs literally contained three 'flyers' – he and the Underwood brothers are now all qualified pilots.

England supplied both the fly-halves for the tour, Rob Andrew and Stuart Barnes. The all-English back row of Ben Clarke, Peter Winterbottom and Dean Richards was to prove a major success in the Test side, while English duo Martin Bayfield and a raw young lighthouse called Martin Johnson would be the second row for the final two Tests, the former player dominating the line-outs. This being New Zealand, two of the busiest men in the Lions backroom were the doctor, James Robson, and the indefatigable physiotherapist Kevin Murphy.

Making his second tour ten years after his first, Winterbottom expected a tough time:

> *I had missed out in 1989 for various reasons, including injury, but the truth was I had played too much rugby and had lost a bit of spark. I took the summer off and got back in to the England team, and by 1993 I was pretty fit and free of injury. I had played out in New Zealand the year before with Hawke's Bay and I knew just what a testing time we would face, but I was very keen to go. You always want to be a Lion and play against the best.*

At that time, the Lions' selectors were heavily criticized: by the Irish press for taking only two of their players, and by the English for not taking enough. Indeed, at one point in the process, it looked as though 23 of the 30-strong party would be from England. There has usually always been a strict code of silence about the selection process, but assistant coach Dick Best broke this in an interview some time after the tour, giving an illuminating insight into what really happened behind closed doors.

The selection meeting started at nine and didn't finish until 5.30pm and it was a fight. You saw the true meaning of this Lions thing. It wasn't about taking the best squad, it was just about getting your own boys on that tour. Geoff Cooke and I were fighting to get players like Jeff Probyn. But there was a strong anti-English lobby after that defeat to Ireland and we lost out in the vote. The trouble was, many of the guys the selectors insisted we take just weren't up to it, and that quickly became apparent.

Before the tour, much of the media chatter was about how many tries would be scored in the Tests. The IRB had boosted the value of a try to five points the previous year, with the conversion remaining at two points and the penalty and drop goals staying at three. Since 'under the post' scores were effectively worth seven points, it was presumed that both sides would be going all out for touchdowns, but in the end the boots of Gavin Hastings and Grant Fox were often the deciding factors.

Conforming to the by-now standard format of 13 matches, the playing part of the tour lasted just six weeks from 22 May to 3 July. Again, with such a high-intensity programme, there were injuries galore, none worse than the horrendous damage sustained by Scott Hastings in the 24–37 loss to Otago, the first of no less than four non-Test Matches – out of ten – which the Lions would lose. Hastings had come on as a replacement for Carling, who was himself injured, when he went into a tackle on Josh Kronfeld with his head inexplicably on the 'wrong' unprotected side, and emerged with his face swelling up like a balloon. His tour was over, and he required four hours of surgery to repair the damage.

'I just mistimed the tackle and went in with my head first instead of my arm,' said Hastings. 'I knew it was curtains for my tour right away and it turned out I had a double fracture of the jaw and a fractured cheekbone.'

In the first Test a week later at Lancaster Park in Christchurch, the England captain Will Carling – perhaps affected by his leg injury – was a shadow of his usual self. His loss of form was so dramatic that he was not picked again for the Test side.

Gavin Hastings is adamant that Carling was dropped purely on his poor form on tour and that all selectorial decisions should be taken on that basis:

A Lions tour for me is all about the players and how they perform on the tour. It's not about what people have achieved for their countries. When you look back at the 2001 and 2005 tours, you can see there were some players who were never going to make the Test side, as the people in charge had decided to pick a team based on past form. I just don't subscribe to that point of view. If two players are both playing well, and one has more experience, then you might go for him, but when one player is clearly playing better than the other then you have to go for him. If Scott Gibbs had been fit, for instance, Will would not have made the team for the first Test.

Winterbottom agreed with Hastings:

Will was not playing well and Scott Gibbs was, and most people said that Will had lost his form and was going to have to go. Yes, he was a bit put out, but fair do's to him, he always tried his hardest on the pitch and didn't back out, though he did moan a bit about it.

The row over whether Carling acted like a spoilt brat rumbled on for years. The player had not enjoyed aspects of the tour, such as having to share a room when as captain of England he had always had the privilege of a room to himself. He claimed that losing the captaincy was no big deal, but being relegated to the dirt-trackers was undoubtedly painful.

'There was an undercurrent of tension simmering away,' said Scott Hastings, 'and I just think Carling lost his way.'

Carling himself revealed his attitude in a later interview:

> For the first time in my life I had been left out of a team on form and it hurt like hell. I lost focus on the Lions tour and my performances nosedived. My depression became so bad that, 10 days into the trip, I asked Geoff Cooke if anyone had ever voluntarily left a Lions tour.

It is well known that Dick Best and Carling later fell out over the former's removal from his coaching job at Harlequins at the behest of Carling and other players. In 2005, Best still had not forgiven Carling and revealed his thoughts on the 1993 controversy:

> He [Carling] went into a sulk, refusing to speak to anybody. He went to see Geoff Cooke and asked if he could go home. Cooke told him that if he did, he was finished as an international rugby player. But he was a very unhappy bunny and that attitude spread like a cancer through the squad.

Carling was not the only man at Lancaster Park to have an off day in that first Test. Referee Brian Kinsey of Australia committed three major gaffes, at least two of which were blatant errors that cost the Lions the match. The first mistake was right at the start when Grant Fox hoisted a high one, which was caught by Ieuan Evans on the Lions try line. Frank Bunce was up to challenge and wrestled with Evans for the ball, both men going down in the 'in goal' area. From a distance, Kinsey gave the try, but television replays showed conclusively that Evans had never released his grip on the ball. But there was no video evidence or technical official in those days, and the try stood, much to the chagrin of the Lions.

The second decision concerned the Lions' first penalty goal. Jeremy Guscott looked set to put Will Carling in for a certain try under the posts but Michael Jones blatantly held the England captain. Instead of a penalty try, to which nobody could have objected, Kinsey awarded a penalty, so a sure six points became only three.

The last Kinsey decision really did hurt the Lions. Leading 18–17 with a minute or so to go, and with Hastings having kicked all his team's points to equal Tony Ward's record set in South Africa in 1980, Dean Richards tackled Bunce after a ruck was formed. Kinsey deemed it a penalty, which Grant Fox kicked to win the match 20–18. The Lions could barely contain their disgust with the referee.

'It was the same as the first Test in 1983,' said Winterbottom. 'We didn't play particularly well but did have a chance to win the game – until the referee intervened.'

Gavin Hastings went further: 'I would almost say we were cheated out of victory in the Test series because of what happened in that first Test.'

Ian McGeechan said the decision was a 'killer blow' and added: 'I have watched it a hundred times on video and I am still unable to explain satisfactorily why we were penalized.'

The young raw-boned Martin Johnson came in as a replacement for Wade Dooley, then a serving policeman, whose father sadly died quite suddenly during the tour. Dooley was immediately flown home, but after the funeral and a short period of mourning he wanted to rejoin the tour. However, under the rules of the tour agreement between the home unions and the New Zealand RFU, approved by the IRB, once a player had been replaced he could not rejoin the tour and play. Dooley was invited to return in a non-playing capacity, but declined. This rules fiasco caused a serious outbreak of player disgust, and Bob Weighill, the committee secretary who was blamed for Dooley's plight, bore the brunt of the protests.

Peter Winterbottom said:

What happened to Wade was a disgrace. It really upset the guys that the New Zealand Rugby Union had said it was fine for him to return, and they would pay for everything, but the four home unions said he couldn't go back. It was a bloody disgrace and made us wonder what it was all about. You give up so much to play but then get slapped in the face like that – it definitely affected the guys.

Scott Hastings claimed the bitterness was because the home unions committee reneged on a promise to allow Wade to return, and another Lion, Andy Nicol, also suffered at the hands of the blazered brigade. Nicol had been captaining Scotland on their tour of the South Seas when he got the call from Geoff Cooke to make his way to New Zealand to cover for Rob Jones.

'There had been a lot of injuries, and Geoff and Geech applied to the New Zealand RFU for permission for me to come and help with the training, if nothing else,' said Nicol.

I actually ended up on the bench against Taranaki because Dewi Morris was carrying a knock, and six minutes from the end, with us leading comfortably, Rob Jones 'accidentally' hurt his shoulder and he came off to let me on for that final six minutes. Didn't matter to me how it happened – I got to play for the Lions.

Just like Wade, the home unions then vetoed me staying on the tour as I wasn't actually replacing anybody. I was desperate to stay and the annoying thing is that the host union were happy for me to do so. But I

*watched the Auckland match and flew home that night, despatched by
the blazers who were supposed to be on our side. Still, at least I got my
six minutes and as a 23-year-old I had spent two-and-a-half weeks
training and playing with the Lions – I thought I had won the Lottery.*

The social side of the tour saw the midweek men having a whale of a party
just about all of the time, but for Gavin Hastings the highlight was the
chance to jump off a mountain. He said:

*We were in Invercargill to play Southland and four or five of us,
including Geech, were flown to Queenstown for the day. We were taken
by helicopter up a mountain where we had a go at tandem paraponting,
a form of paragliding. We had a pilot, obviously, but I still managed to
make a hash of my landing and went over on my ankle. Can you imagine
any Lions captain and coach doing that now, far less getting insurance
for it?*

On another occasion, the Lions nearly lost their star flanker Peter Winterbottom. Hastings took up the tale:

*We were at a clay pigeon shooting club in Gisborne and the instructors
were giving their safety talk when Richard Webster, who obviously
hadn't been listening, suddenly fired his gun into the ground. The shot
missed Peter Winterbottom's foot by about three inches. Peter just turned
white. The thing was that Webbo was open side flanker for Wales and
was competing for Peter's place – the lengths some people will go to get a
Test jersey …*

New Zealand wasn't up to scratch for some of the tourists. Rob Andrew,
who was good enough to play first-class cricket as a youngster, found
fewer opportunities to display his talents with bat and ball than he got

in Australia four years previously. Ten years on from his first tour, Winterbottom admitted that New Zealand had modernized a little: 'It had caught up about 30 years and at least the phones worked a bit.'

As soon as Martin Johnson arrived, it was clear that he was going to go straight into the Test side – 'He really was that good,' said Winterbottom.

Despite losing to Auckland and Hawke's Bay, the Lions should have been despondent heading for Wellington and the second Test, yet instead the mood was buoyant.

Winterbottom said: 'The week before against Auckland, even though we got beaten, we started to feel we could win the big games. We felt we had discovered what we were doing wrong and had fixed it.'

Gavin Hastings had suffered a strained hamstring and wanted to leave himself out because he thought only fully fit players should face the All Blacks, but McGeechan would not hear of it. McGeechan was so convinced of the importance of Hastings as captain that he insisted on the full-back playing 'even for ten minutes'. Rob Andrew and Jeremy Guscott also weighed in, telling the captain how necessary he was.

Cooke, McGeechan, Best and Hastings rallied their men and, on the day, the Lions were as pumped up for a match as any side in the red jerseys had been before them. With Fox in devastating form with the boot, the coaching team had drilled into the Lions the need for discipline to keep the penalty count down.

The coach and captain also made a crucial decision: if the Lions won the toss they would play into the infamous Wellington wind, as well as bright sunshine, in the first half. It was a move that seemed to backfire when Hastings himself – going for a high kick from Fox – was blinded by the sun, and the ball bounced to Eroni Clarke for the All Blacks centre to score the opening try, which Fox converted.

With the Lions pack surging forward at every chance, however, Dewi Morris and Rob Andrew at half-back were able to control the match, and two Hastings penalties and a drop goal by Andrew put the tourists 9–7 up at half-time. A stunning try from Rory Underwood early in the second half set the Lions on their way, and Hastings added two penalties either side of that score. The Lions' control of the play was such that not once did Grant Fox get a chance at a kickable penalty.

The Lions won 20–7 and squared the series, but perhaps more importantly, had done so with their highest ever points tally in New Zealand, although previous tourists, such as the 1959 side that lost 17–18 to the All Blacks, would have scored more had the 1993 scoring values been in place back then. Many commentators rightly stated that the All Blacks did not play to their best, but in truth it was a case of the Lions not letting them do so. Rob Andrew in particular turned the All Blacks pack at every opportunity, and even the greatest rugby forwards get sick of having to continually chase back and defend.

Gavin Hastings said:

It should not be forgotten that victory was only the sixth by a Lions side in New Zealand. We gave ourselves a chance of winning the series and scored the most points ever by the Lions against the All Blacks and it was also the biggest margin of victory. By any standards, it was some achievement.

The third and final Test, also the last match of the tour, followed a disappointing loss by the dirt-trackers to Waikato. It was one of the great mysteries of the 1993 tour that the midweek men did not live up to the high standard set by Donal's Doughnuts in Australia in 1989.

Gavin Hastings concluded:

To be fair to them, the standard of opposition in New Zealand was somewhat higher than in Australia, but if you look back through history, all the successful Lions have a good midweek side, and I think it is fair to say that in 1993, one or two players were posted missing once they realized they would not make the Test side.

Peter Winterbottom agreed:

It was not the happiest of touring parties. A big rift developed between the first team and the second team, and the midweek side did not perform and do themselves justice. With any Lions tour you need to have a happy second team with guys all pulling in the same direction. Whether or not you win all the games is not the most important thing; you just have to do your best and provide competition for places, and for some reason that didn't happen in 1993.

In that Waikato game, Will Carling had returned to form and had also captained the side. As Gavin Hastings recalls: 'In the last two midweek games, Will played very well, and he has to be given credit for the way he knuckled down.'

For the deciding Test, the All Blacks made changes to the side, bringing in Lee Stensness, Ian Jones and Arran Pene, and surprisingly leaving out Zinzan Brooke. The introduction of the abrasive Jones and Pene to the pack made a huge difference, and they and their colleagues in the forwards raised their game considerably. Just as the Lions pack had been so dominant the previous week, so the eight All Blacks forwards outplayed their opponents over the 80 minutes. With New Zealand captain Sean Fitpatrick and Fox superbly marshalling their resources, the All Blacks also reduced the number of line-outs they conceded to a minimum, stopping Bayfield and Johnson from terrorizing them.

But at one point it looked as if a different outcome was looming. A try by Scott Gibbs converted by Hastings, plus a penalty from the captain, gave the Lions a 10–0 lead, but that just seemed to annoy the All Blacks and they tore into the Lions. It was frenzied, frenetic stuff, and McGeechan would later admit that the Lions could not match the onslaught from the 'over-psyched' All Blacks.

Tries by Frank Bunce and Fitzpatrick, both converted by Fox, made it 14–10 to New Zealand at half-time, and they went further ahead with another penalty by Fox. Hastings goaled a penalty, but so did Fox, and Preston sold a dummy to land a third try, converted by Fox. The Lions were now playing catch-up rugby, running the ball from deep, a tactic which the All Blacks anticipated and closed down. A final penalty from that man Fox made the final score 30–13 to New Zealand, and it was a very disappointed group of Lions who prepared for the long journey home.

Peter Winterbottom summed up how the players felt:

We just fell away in the last game, which was peculiar really as we knew we had the beating of them, but for some reason it just didn't happen on the day.

It was a disappointing end, and you couldn't blame Geech or Dick Best, or Gav, who had been the right choice as captain. It was just that some players didn't perform, and maybe some were on a different tour to the rest of us.

Gavin Hastings agreed with the 'two tours' theory but added: 'There were a lot of positives that came out of the tour, and for myself I can only say that it was a huge honour and an incredible experience. I was on a high the whole time and thoroughly enjoyed everything.'

Throughout the tour, there had been a lot of sniping at the Lions by the media, mostly by the New Zealand press pack, though there were the usual paparazzi and freelances out to try and find the Lions up to no good when they were off duty. By and large, they did not succeed. In his official report, McGeechan wrote of an 'at times very rugby-illiterate press corps', a clear reference to those journalists who wanted scandal, not views and analysis.

Gavin Hastings enhanced his reputation for dealing with the press, and it was no surprise that, along with his brother Scott, he opened a public relations and marketing agency in his home town of Edinburgh soon afterwards. When the two brothers retired from international rugby, Gavin was Scotland's top points scorer of all time, and Scott was the then most-capped player. They are still working in the PR industry and are in great demand as media pundits. They are also heavily involved with Edinburgh Rugby, one of Scotland's two professional sides, where Gavin is chairman.

Brian Moore recently married for the second time. He is a regular panellist on the BBC's rugby coverage. Nick Popplewell became an auctioneer in Wexford. Dean Richards coached Leicester Tigers to four successive league titles and two consecutive victories in the Heineken Cup before being controversially sacked. He joined Grenoble briefly before taking up his present position as Director of Rugby at Harlequins.

Peter Winterbottom moved to the City from the farm and became a senior executive in the financial services industry. Rob Andrew retired in 1999 after injury, then coached Newcastle Falcons and became Director of Rugby there before being appointed Director of Elite Rugby for the RFU.

Dewi Morris is one of the Sky Sports rugby pundits panel, appearing regularly alongside his 1993 Lions colleague Stuart Barnes. Mick Galwey led Munster to the final of the Heineken Cup, before retiring and moving into club coaching, lifting the All-Ireland title with Shannon RFC.

Will Carling married Julia, and was then divorced after allegedly squiring Princess Diana, though Carling denied any romance. He married his second wife Lisa in 1999. He has a considerable reputation as a management motivational expert.

In the four years after the 1993 tour, rugby union would change beyond recognition when the sport embraced professionalism. It led immediately to speculation that the Lions would not survive in the new era where clubs, district teams or provinces would surely be the driving force, and where the 'tri-nations' of Australia, New Zealand and South Africa would have their own annual tournament. But in rugby, as in so many other sports, often the last people to be heard are the players and the fans. Overwhelmingly, the top players of the four home unions and the three southern hemisphere nations wanted the Lions to continue, and as for the fans – they would give their answer in ever-increasing numbers.

CHAPTER SIXTEEN

MARTIN JOHNSON'S MARVELS

South Africa 1997

In a history that now goes back 120 years, there have been many attempts to kill off the Lions, none more serious than the discussions held by the various home unions in the 1980s and 1990s, when it was felt that tours by individual countries might be the way forward for relations between the northern and southern hemisphere.

The advent of professional rugby in 1995 and the immediate popularity of the tri-nations and super-12 tournaments also seemed to pose a massive threat to the Lions. The rugby season seemed to grow ever longer across the world, so, it was asked, would an extended season be welcomed every four years, especially with player 'burn out' already a concern?

Furthermore, who would now pay the players for taking part in a Lions tour? As professionals, the players surely owed their first loyalty to the people who paid their wages. In the case of England, the paymasters were the big clubs, which fairly swiftly transformed the existing league into what is now the money-spinning Guinness Premiership. The Heineken European Cup also brought in sizeable sums of money, and while the RFU paid players for England duty, it seemed inevitable that there would be conflicts between the clubs and the RFU over the amount of time players would need to spend away from their clubs on duty for their country. Such concerns would come to a head in 1998 and lead to the infamous 'tour from hell' by England to Australia in which a second-string England side were hammered 76–0 by the Wallabies.

All of that was in the future, however, when the South African Rugby Union invited the Lions to tour South Africa in 1997. The home unions may have been in disarray since 1995, but that sporting turmoil was as nothing compared to the changes experienced in South Africa in the early 1990s. The country had been restored to full international relationships, including sport, following the end of apartheid and the election of President Nelson Mandela. The winds of change really had blown through the republic, and South Africa's successful hosting of the 1995 World Cup had shown that the once blinkered sport of rugby could peacefully co-exist with the new democratic structures.

All that remained was for an old relationship to be rekindled, and that meant a visit by the Lions to South Africa. They may have been the world champions, but the Springboks still wanted to test themselves against the ultimate touring team. The worry was that they would be just too good for the Lions and would blow the tourists off the field and perhaps into oblivion.

Several commentators in Britain pointed out that in this new professional era, the Lions would be at a considerable disadvantage as they would be coming together as a scratch team to play against provinces and a national side who all had plenty of time to train together and get to know each other. Very few pundits gave the Lions a chance, and more than a few people predicted the Lions' concept would not survive the tour. The fact that an England XV and Scotland XV went ahead with tours of Argentina and Southern Africa at the same time as the Lions seemed to predict that the future lay in national touring sides rather than the Lions.

All this added to the pressure on the Lions. True, the more perspicacious writers spotted that South Africa might well be in decline after the marvellous high of 1995. They had, after all, lost a series at home to the All Blacks in 1996. But it seemed certain to everyone that if the Lions were to survive in the new transformed sport, they would have to gain successes of some kind – winning perhaps one Test might just about see them able to carry on.

Anyone doubting that becoming a Lion still meant the pinnacle for a player should read Neil Back's words on his reaction. The great Leicester and England flanker, who had struggled for his England place, confessed he cried like a baby when the letter arrived.

> *It was from Fran Cotton, and it congratulated me on my selection. I was a British Lion. For a moment, I just sat there, staring at the sheet of paper. Then I dropped it and burst into tears, sobbing my heart out. A huge reservoir of tension and passion, almost desperation, had built up inside me in my international wilderness years and those few words from Fran burst the dam.*
>
> *All those years of self-denial, of sweat and pain, had finally paid off. There is a special magic associated with the British Lions. To be considered fit to tour with the very best players from these islands and to travel thousands of miles to take on the best that the other side of the world has to offer is a great honour.*

In 1997, there were many other changes to be reckoned with. The laws of the game had been altered to encourage open and more expansive play, and the southern hemisphere nations had seized on these changes with glee. Furthermore, with rugby union having turned professional, there was nothing to stop rugby league players – especially those who had originally started in union – coming back to play in the 15-a-side game. Eventually, no fewer than six players in this category would be part of the 2007 Lions.

Thorny issues regarding payments to players and the cost of expenses were hammered out in the months leading up to the start of the tour. The original idea of paying a reputed sum of £12,000 each plus extra money for the Test side was scrapped as divisive, and instead the players got £15,000 each – the wages were all paid by the host union, who also got all the income. There was an increased back-room squad of coaches, medicos and officials – 12 in all, with one of the most vital additions being specialist kicking coach Dave Alred, making a first Lions appearance fresh from rugby league.

A code of conduct was drawn up for the players to memorize and abide by – in a more image-conscious sport, nothing should be able to tarnish the good name of the Lions, which, after all, was probably the tourists' biggest and most marketable asset. Even the Lions badge was seen as a possible route to earning income – the Home Unions Committee spent a five-figure sum ensuring the famous shield was copyrighted. Despite that, the anticipated income did not match the expenditure and the home unions eventually had to stump up to meet the shortfall, which ran into six figures.

These changes were the result of professionalism, but all the usual old questions remained about the Lions. Who would be the captain? Who would coach them? Who would be the manager? And who would eventually be selected for the tour?

The first three questions were easily answered. Fran Cotton, veteran of the 1977 and 1980 tours and a hugely successful businessman, was asked to be manager and he accepted on the basis that he ran the show. Cotton said:

After I retired from playing I wrote a book like so many international players and duly got banned for about 12 years. But after professionalism came in, myself and Bill Beaumont were reinstated by the RFU at the same time. I got involved with North of England, which was my provincial team at the time, and became chairman of rugby, taking part in selection and so forth, and when I was asked if I would like to be considered as manager of the 1997 Lions I saw it as a fantastic opportunity.

I was just so determined that everything would be done in a professional way and all the lessons I had learned as a player would be heeded and the mistakes rectified.

The biggest job, as always, was selecting the right players and the right management group, and I decided we should go for two hugely experienced Lions.

Ian McGeechan thus broke new ground by becoming coach for the third time, with his old Scotland colleague Jim Telfer as his assistant – 'good cop and bad cop', as one of the players called them.

Cotton said: 'It was very important that they had worked together before and that they got on well together. They had a really united view on how the game should be played.'

Cotton and McGeechan both knew who they wanted as captain, and it was something of a surprise. Ignoring the captains of the home unions, they went for a man who at that point had only captained his club side, and that on a total of nine occasions.

In 1997, Martin Johnson was nearing the peak of his considerable play-ing powers, and had led Leicester when Dean Richards' career began to wind down that season, in which the Tigers won the Pilkington Cup and reached the final of the Heineken European Cup. The captains of Wales, Scotland and Ireland, Ieuan Evans, Rob Wainwright and Keith Wood respectively, were also seen as serious candidates, but in truth any one of a dozen men could have been considered. The problem was that the competition for places was going to be so fierce that several captaincy candidates might not be good enough to start the Tests. One candidate who not considered was England captain Philip De Glanville, who was not even rated good enough to join the initial squad of 62 potential tourists named during the Five Nations championship. He openly admitted to not getting on with Cotton, but the selectors were adamant that playing ability rather than a personality clash was the main reason for leaving him at home.

Johnson got the job because Cotton wanted someone with 'character' while McGeechan was a big admirer of the huge lock, even before he had joined the 1993 tour as a replacement for Wade Dooley. The intimidatory bulk of Johnson at 6ft 7in was a plus for McGeechan, and Jim Telfer came to rely on Johnson's ability to help him motivate a pack that would need to be at its very best to beat the world champions.

Cotton reflected:

It was a choice from left field, it was a risk, but we had done our research. We had good reports of how he captained Leicester, and he was playing really well for England and was guaranteed his spot in the Test side. It was between him and Ieuan Evans, who was both a great player and captain for Wales as well as a great Lion. But we knew the South Africans would be physically big up front and we just thought that a winger might be too far away from the action. I also liked the idea of this huge man leading out the Lions. He was a statement of intent just by standing there. It turned out superbly for the Lions and for Martin.

The man himself would admit that he was not born a great communicator off the pitch or outside the dressing room. Indeed, in one of his first interviews, Johnson confessed he had 'no overwhelming desire' to be captain, but he grew into that communication role as the weeks went on, and his occasionally taciturn appearance actually helped convince the media that he really was putting his heart and soul into the job.

The 35 players finally selected in April to tour South Africa comprised a blend of experienced internationalists, 'returned' former rugby league players such as John Bentley and Alan Tait, and exciting new talents like the uncapped English centre Will Greenwood, son of the former England player and coach Dick.

Against the Lions were a good number of survivors from the 1995 World Cup-winning side, including lanky scrum-half Joost van der Westhuizen, winger James Small, centre Japie Mulder, full-back Andre Joubert, and forwards Os Du Randt, Ruben Kruger, Hannes Strydom and Mark Andrews, though captain Francois Pienaar and the man who kicked South Africa to victory in the final, Joel Stransky, had retired from the scene. Stransky, indeed, moved to England in 1997 to play for Leicester, and there was even talk of him playing for England in the World Cup of 1999, though the player himself eventually ruled that out.

'They were still a side full of great individual players,' said Fran Cotton, 'but I felt they had a weakness in that their coach, Carel du Plessis, was very inexperienced. With Ian and Jim against him, he was totally exposed and I felt that gave us an edge even before we started.'

The stage was set for a memorable tour in front of packed crowds because the South African rugby fans were desperate to see the matches. What truly astonished everyone connected with the Lions, however, was the number of people who travelled from Britain and Ireland to support the Lions. Bedecked in red, a good number of hardy fans went to every match, while there were thousands in the crowds singing their heads off at the Tests. The Lions were certainly not moribund in the hearts of some people, and those fans in South Africa that year helped lay the foundations of the 'Barmy Army' whose numbers have grown to the extent that some predictions say that perhaps as many as 50,000 will follow the Lions at one stage or another in 2009.

'As we kept winning, the numbers kept growing and we had people coming out just for the weekend to see the Tests,' said Ian McGeechan. 'To me, seeing those fans was the watershed. We had kept the traditions going into the professional era, and for the players as well there was no doubt that pulling on a Lions jersey was still very special.'

One of the first surprises for the coaches and players was that they would be accompanied everywhere by a television crew, who were making a documentary entitled *Living with the Lions*. This was later shown on Sky and ITV and became a best-selling video and DVD. Showing how far the various unions had moved since professionalism, the committee gave the go-ahead for the documentary in return for a fee. It was to prove a distraction at times but the material was a revelation, especially to those who had never seen Jim Telfer in full ranting flow. It captured all the behind-the-scenes drama, all the highs and lows, of what became a remarkable tour. The tape recorders also captured some choice language from coaches and players alike – Jim Telfer had to apologize to his mother after it was shown.

As the video illustrated, Jim Telfer's martinet approach to training left players crumpled in heaps of exhaustion. Double Lion John Beattie looked on and knew what Telfer was doing:

In that first week he showed he had learned the lessons from his experience in 1983. He was working with professionals now, and he was able to break them. He bossed them, and broke some of the best players in the world by killing them in training, and then built them up again.

On arrival in South Africa, there was a huge surprise awaiting Fran Cotton and Ian McGeechan as they made their way into the initial press conference of the tour.

'When we arrived in Johannesburg we had to do the conference, but first of all we were taken to meet the sports minister, Steve Tshwete, in a private room at the airport.' Neither man knew that Tshwete had been imprisoned on Robben Island for his campaign against the apartheid regime. Tshwete, who died in 2002 aged 63, had served 15 years on Robben Island alongside Nelson Mandela.

McGeechan recalls:

> *He was sitting there and immediately looked up at Fran and said, '1974, Fran Cotton, Lions loose head, four Test Matches' and then looked at me and said, 'Ian McGeechan, you dropped a goal in the second Test,' adding finally, 'Both of you played in all four Tests, and I know every name of the Lions on that tour because on Robben Island we sat around the radio and we thought the Lions were the best thing that had happened.'*
>
> *I looked at Fran and he looked at me and we just couldn't say anything. The hairs on the back of my neck stood up as I realized what the minister was saying: that on Robben Island, he and Mandela and their colleagues had been listening to us beating the Springboks. I thought of what he had gone through, what he had suffered, to be able to be there talking to us. It was overwhelming.*

Cotton said:

> *I just couldn't believe it when he told us, and of course President Mandela himself had been a Lions fan. It was a big regret that we didn't get the chance to meet him, as it would have been a huge privilege to meet the great, great man.*
>
> *There were huge differences between 1974 and 1997, obviously, but this time we were able to go into the townships and do some coaching, and we saw how the people lived. It was only at that point on that tour that I saw the stark reality of what apartheid meant.*

After all the changes and problems, the hype and the hoopla, the Lions started their tour in tremendous form. They raced through the first eight matches not only unbeaten but playing a style of expansive rugby which had even the South African press purring. There were, however, several nasty injuries and some on-field incidents that were dubious to say the least.

Paul Grayson of England and Rob Howley of Wales were both injured – the latter badly dislocating his shoulder – and had to return home. The pair might well have formed the Test half-back partnership, though Grayson's fitness had been a recurring problem.

It was two nasty incidents, however, that threatened to spoil the friendly atmosphere surrounding the tour. After being outclassed playing for Western Province, Springbok winger James Small alleged that his eyes had been gouged by opposite number John Bentley. Fran Cotton, never a man to call a spade a gardening implement, launched an outspoken attack on Small in defence of Bentley. With no evidence to back up Small's claims, which were in any case made to newspapers some time after the match rather than on the day to officials, no action was taken against Bentley, who protested his innocence.

There was no doubt about the cynical, clinical way in which Doddie Weir was despatched out of the tour. Marius Bosman of Mpumalanga stamped on the Scottish lock's knee, and the damage to his medial ligaments briefly threatened the Newcastle player's career. In the same game, Rob Wainwright was also a victim of foul play with the boot, Elandre van Bergh going in too hard at a ruck – the fact that Wainwright had scored a hat-trick of tries by that point may have upset the South African. Will Greenwood summed up the match:

They were a nasty bunch of bastards, but I didn't think the violence was premeditated. It was more that they couldn't take being utterly humiliated, which is exactly what we did to them. There were no cosy beers with the opposition after that match. In fact, I don't think we mixed much with the South African players at all on tour, because they didn't like us and we didn't much like them. One of them, a big prop, actually spat on me in one match – I just told him to look at the scoreboard.

Fran Cotton let rip with fierce criticism of this sort of foul play:

Doddie had been playing really well when Bosman stood on him and put him out of the tour. I was just fuming that the referee saw the incident and all he did was give a penalty – it should have been a sending-off and Bosman suspended for three to six months.

I felt I had to let the authorities and the referees know how disappointed we were at the lack of protection of the players, who made it clear to me they were not going to be messed around, and I knew what that could mean. By speaking out I got things dealt with, and in fairness there were very few incidents after that.

Jim Telfer felt that the early matches were vital: 'Leading up to the first Test, the Lions had played some scintillating rugby, both by the likely Test team and the second team. That was crucial, because it meant all the players were up to speed.

At the penultimate match one week before the Test, a 42–12 defeat of Natal, there was still no clear division between the Test side and the midweek men, and when the team for the first Test in Cape Town was eventually named there were several surprises. Tom Smith and Paul Wallace were chosen at prop instead of a combination of Jason Leonard, Graham Rowntree and Dai Young. Keith Wood beat Mark Regan and Barry Williams for the hooker's role, while Ireland's Jeremy Davidson joined Martin Johnson in the second row instead of Johnson's England partner Simon Shaw. Davidson kept his place as he was outstanding in the loose play.

The all-England back row of Lawrence Dallaglio, Richard Hill and Tim Rodber was slightly more predictable, as was Matt Dawson's selection at scrum-half. In Grayson's absence, and with his replacement Mike Catt not up to speed, Gregor Townsend gained the No. 10 jersey.

Townsend's selection caused most comment, but McGeechan wanted a man who would play right up in the face of the Springboks. It required courage, because the hits would be hard, but 'Toony' was prepared to take them. 'Geech knew exactly the way we should play to beat South Africa and I wasn't going to argue, especially as I was getting my Lions cap,' said Townsend.

At centre, Scott Gibbs kept his place alongside Jeremy Guscott, who had not even been a certain starter for England during the Five Nations. So important had former league star Alan Tait's defensive qualities become that he was moved to the left wing from his normal centre position, with Ieuan Evans filling the other wing berth. Neil Jenkins was at full-back, largely because his kicking boots would be needed.

Several Lions have told us that they were unaware that the Welshman got horribly nervous before a big Test. 'He started retching up his guts,' said Gregor Townsend, 'but at least it distracted us.' In Will Greenwood's memorable phrase, Jenkins 'sounded like a walrus humping his way up the beach in search of a mate'.

Most people thought South Africa would destroy Smith, Wood and Wallace up front and that would be that. And when the Springboks shunted the Lions' scrum backwards twice in the opening minutes, the outcome looked inevitable, especially when South Africa took the lead with an early penalty. But the Lions' forwards were rampant in the loose and forced an equalizing penalty within a minute of that opening score, and the front row men sorted themselves out, while Johnson and Davidson began to rule the line-out.

Midway through the first half big Os Du Randt scored a try, but Lions pressure told and two further penalties from Jenkins made in 9–8 at half-time, with Jenkins adding another penalty early in the half. South Africa were attacking constantly now. Russell Bennett crashed through a tackle by Jenkins for a second Springbok try and a Henry Honiball penalty put the home side further ahead, though Jenkins brought the Lions back to within one point, which they barely deserved on the play till then.

Once more the Lions raised their game and in the final minutes, Matt Dawson sold three defenders an outrageous dummy for a fine individual try, and when Alan Tait finished off a late move with a try in the corner, the Lions were home and dry by 25–16.

'It was an incredible experience to win in South Africa against the world champions,' said Townsend, 'and we knew we hadn't played that well until late on so it was a question of keeping it going to the next Test.'

The second Test was only a week away, and the midweek men kept up the pressure on the Test incumbents with a fine performance in a high-scoring 52–30 match against the Free State Cheetahs. The match took place in Bloemfontein and Jim Telfer took charge while McGeechan stayed with the Test side in Durban.

Allan Bateman played that day: 'Jim Telfer gave such an emotional speech that I thought we were going to go out onto the field armed with bayonets. It worked and we gave the most complete performance of the tour.'

In that match, Will Greenwood was involved in one of the most shocking incidents on the tour. After a heavy though legal tackle by Jaco Coetzee, he swallowed his tongue and stopped breathing. Austin Healey realized what had happened and took out Greenwood's gumshield, while Rob Wainwright, a qualified doctor, also knew immediately it was very serious and summoned help. Dr Robson was preparing to do a tracheotomy when the player recovered in the dressing room, but had it not been for the quick work of all concerned, Greenwood might have suffered brain damage or worse.

The player himself has no recollection of the incident, which was witnessed from the stand by his mother and father. 'One minute I was taking a pass from Mike Catt, the next I was waking up in a strange bed. The doctor was telling me I had hurt my head, but I told him my shoulder was worse.' And so it was – Greenwood's tour was over.

The selectors kept faith with the first Test heroes, except for Bentley replacing the struggling Evans. All who saw the match in King's Park, Durban, either in the stadium or live on television, will never forget the sheer drama of this pulsating match. At the start, with feelings running high, there were several clashes but none of the mass brawls of yesteryear. Against the run of play, the Lions went ahead with two penalties by Neil Jenkins. But the Springboks were relentless in attack, and scored three tries through Joubert, van der Westhuizen and Percy Montgomery.

All the while the Lions' defence was unbelievably brave, and while South Africa missed no fewer than six attempts at goal by three different kickers, including all three conversions, Jenkins ensured that the Lions punished indiscipline by the Springboks when they were put under pressure. In all, the Welshman goaled five penalties to bring the scores level as the match approached its end.

With just three minutes left on the clock, the Lions mounted perhaps their best attack of the match. Jeremy Davidson took clean ball at the lineout, Townsend took it on, the pack piled in, and from the ruck Dawson spun the ball back to Jeremy Guscott. The Bath and England centre was coolness personified as he slotted a pinpoint drop goal to win the match. Davidson recalled: 'There was nothing on but for Jerry to drop the goal. I didn't see it because I was at the bottom of the ruck. I've watched it on video since and it still gives me shivers down the spine.'

The scenes after the final whistle were some of the most emotional ever seen among the Lions. Not only had they won the series, they might possibly have saved the British and Irish Lions themselves.

Fran Cotton said:

We had beaten the world champions against all the odds. All credit to the coaches and players, because it really was backs to the wall for an hour or so while Neil Jenkins kept us in the game with his kicking. They deserved it because of the unity of effort from all the players.

In 1974, we were better players than the Springboks, but in '97 we were about the same as them. The difference was that we were a better team – that's really what won it.

Jim Telfer, for once, was seen to be emotional:

When you have been beaten in three Test series as a player and coach, to be involved in a winning side – well, let's just say I had begun to think it would never happen. We hadn't played well, but we had hung on and we had beaten the world champions.

Some of the players overdid the celebrations – Neil Back and Keith Wood ended up sleeping on the beach – but all are adamant that the stories which emerged a full two years later of players indulging in 'recreational' drugs after Test Matches were just not true.

The final Test saw the Springboks gain a measure of revenge in Ellis Park, Johannesburg. It was all a bit anti-climactic as the world champions defeated a side which had been much altered because of injuries. Jannie de Beer had come in at fly-half for South Africa and, unfortunately for the Lions, the new chap could kick a goal or two.

Though Neil Jenkins kicked three penalties and converted Matt Dawson's try to set a new Lions series record of 39 points, South Africa turned up the gas after half-time and ran in a total of four tries over the 80 minutes, De Beer adding three penalties and two conversions, with his replacement Honiball also adding a conversion, for a convincing 35–16 scoreline.

Allan Bateman recalled: 'I got my cap when Jerry Guscott broke his arm and I went on for the second half, but it would have meant more to me if I had got it on merit. Still, I had a Lions cap, and I had taken part in a tour which captured the imagination of sports followers in Britain and Ireland.'

Despite that final reverse, Martin Johnson's marvellous Lions had won the series, and the delighted reactions at home showed that the ultimate tourists still very much had a role to play in rugby. They were equally as much in the public consciousness again, and were to remain – several years later, Guscott's drop goal was voted into a poll of the 100 Greatest Moments in Sport.

Guscott is now a full-time BBC correspondent on rugby. Paul Grayson is assistant head coach of Northampton Saints. John Bentley works at Leeds Carnegie and is involved with the Leeds Rugby Foundation in York-shire. Tony Underwood is a commercial airline pilot. A dual Lion in union and league, Allan Bateman qualified as a medical laboratory scientist before taking up his dual code career, and returned to that profession after retiring from international rugby. Rob Wainwright runs a farm on the Isle of Coll off Scotland's west coast. Tim Rodber began in marketing and moved into financial services, at time of writing being the chief operating officer of the investment banking and international operations division of Williams Lea Corporate Information Solutions.

Alan Tait, the first former league player to return to playing for Scotland, had spells as defence coach for the Scottish team and is now assistant coach at Newcastle Falcons. Paul Wallace is a commentator for Sky Sports. Gregor Townsend is the Director of Winning Performance with the Winning Scotland Foundation and is the current backs coach of the Scottish national team.

Ian McGeechan, who will coach the 2009 Lions, reflected:

It is a fantastic experience to win a series. I enjoyed it as a player, but in Australia in '89 and South Africa in '97, I think I enjoyed it more because of the huge satisfaction I got from seeing what it means to the players to win.

The '97 tour changed everything. There had been talk of it being the last Lions tour, basically because we had been seen as no hopers and had been written off. But then we started winning and suddenly there were 20,000 people out there and millions watching on television at home. I don't think you can underestimate the massive impact that tour had.

Fran Cotton, who proved himself one of the best tour managers of them all, if not *the* best, has the final word on the tour:

The record books show what an achievement it was by Ian, Jim and the players. What was really, really satisfying for me was that a good number of the players went on to become all-time greats for their countries, but all of them say the highlight was the '97 Lions. That's what being a Lion should be.

As the Lions prepare to return to South Africa for the first time since Johnson's marvels earned their accolades, they could do worse than look back to 1997 for inspiration. For once again South Africa are world champions – could history repeat itself?

CHAPTER SEVENTEEN

SCRIBBLERS FOR MARTIN JOHNSON'S LIONS

Australia 2001

In the long history of the Lions, there had never been a tour so highly publicized, so controversial and so contentious, at least in the eyes of the media, as the Lions' visit to Australia in 2001. Well, at least until the 2005 tour to New Zealand.

The reasons for the massive attention gained by the 2001 tour are not hard to find. In the few years between the tour to South Africa and the Lions' trip to Australia in 2001, rugby union exploded as a 'big business' in itself. The success of the 1997 squad made the Lions a highly marketable commodity, and the aim of the four home unions was to ensure that while the Lions might not run at a profit, neither should they be a burden on the finances of rugby in Britain and Ireland.

In short, the Lions became a business. With marketing agency Octagon doing the arranging – as they continue to do for the Lions – large-scale sponsorship deals were agreed with several companies, television and internet company NTL paying a reputed seven figure sum to become the main shirt sponsor. Caffrey became the official beer of the tourists, while Adidas were the equipment providers. Land Rover provided transport and Zurich Financial Services complemented their sponsorship of the Premiership in England by adding the Lions to their portfolio.

The popularity of the Lions following the 1997 success meant that the media jumped on the bandwagon. Television rights and the way they are carved up between the various unions have been a bone of contention in the professional era, and perhaps that is why the Lions deals were kept confidential – and still are. But even with kick-off times that hardly suited audiences back in Britain and Ireland, there was still considerable demand from the fans at home to watch the Lions.

The British and Irish press caught on to this new phenomenon, and weighed in with much greater coverage than ever before. As many as 100 journalists from Britain and Ireland covered some or all of the tour. Their newspapers and magazines were only reflecting the public response to the Lions. A slew of books were written on the tour, the best of which is *Up and Down Under* by Jeff Connor whose interviews with players form the basis for this chapter.

Now recognized as, and rejoicing in the title of, the Barmy Army, it is estimated that more than 10,000 people made the journey Down Under for at least some part of the tour, while ex-pats couldn't wait to don their red jerseys. The result was that whole swathes of the stadia that hosted the matches were bedecked in red-jerseyed fans wielding union flags, Irish tricolours, St George's Crosses, Saltires and Dragon flags. They may have been supporting the Lions, but their national origins were not going to be forgotten.

For the second tour running, the Lions would be facing the world champions, Australia having lifted the William Webb-Ellis trophy by beating France 35–12 in the Millennium Stadium in Cardiff. As with South Africa in 1997, the majority of the Australian World Cup-winning side were still playing two years later, and the Wallabies continued to be captained by

John Eales, a survivor of the 1991 and 1999 World Cups and one of the finest people to have graced any sport.

In coach Rod Macqueen, the Wallabies had a man who was seeking a unique treble – the World Cup, a Tri-nations series win (2000) and a series victory over the Lions. Although it was now the professional era, he wasn't doing the job chiefly for money, as he was a rich and successful businessman, importing traits from that role into his coaching. He had also had a brush with cancer, undergoing an operation to remove a tumour from his pituitary gland, so perhaps he had a more philosophical approach to life than most rugby coaches.

The choice of leadership for the 2001 Lions was largely predictable. For captain, the clamour for Martin Johnson to retain the job was unanimous. At 31, if anything he was a more complete player than in 1997, and his leadership of England since 1999 had been inspiring, England having won the Six Nations Championship in 2000 and 2001.

The tour manager, appointed a full 18 months before the party set out, was the wily Irishman Donal Lenihan, who had plenty of experience touring Australia. As a player, he had been the man behind the success of the midweek team in the 1989 tour, the so-called Donal's Doughnuts. Unlike his predecessor Fran Cotton, Cork–born Lenihan had a reputation as a diplomatic type, and while he could state his case as forcefully as anyone, he was one of those rugby administrators who preferred to talk rather than fulminate.

It was perhaps Lenihan's appointment and his way of doing things that ensured that the job of coach did not go to the man who was considered hot favourite, England's manager Clive Woodward, but to Graham Henry, the New Zealand-born coach of Wales. Lenihan, it should be said, had originally wanted Ian McGeechan, but the three-time Lions coach had just begun a new role with Scotland and wanted to concentrate on that.

Woodward was outspoken on any subject that took his fancy and definitely was not everybody's cup of tea, whereas Henry was still dining out on his reputation as 'the Great Redeemer', stemming from Wales's run of 10 victories following his appointment in 1998. His appointment as Lions coach was not greeted with unanimous applause, not least because more than a few people felt that the British and Irish Lions should be coached by someone from the four home unions. It was not a criticism much heard when the tour started so well, but when it went rather disastrously wrong, Henry's nationality became an issue.

The management squad had risen to 13, with England coach Andy Robinson as chief assistant to Henry. This in itself was a major departure for the New Zealander, who is noted for being a one-man band. Robinson was joined by his England backroom colleagues, defensive coach Phil Larder and kicking coach David Alred. From Wales, Henry brought video analyst Alun Carter – who spent so much time on his own preparing tapes that Lenihan nicknamed him 'Terry Waite' after the famous hostage – and fitness advisor Steve Black, who would organize the players' training regimes. Doctor James Robson was on his third tour, phsyiotherapist Mark Davies and masseur Andy Wegrzyk on their second. For the first time there was a media relations manager, Alex Broun, an Australian whose main claim to fame was that in his previous career as an actor he had played Kylie Minogue's boyfriend in the soap opera *Neighbours*. With Joan Moore – the first woman officially in a Lions party – helping with administration and Pat O'Keefe as baggage manager, Lenihan's backroom team was comprehensive, or so most people thought until that command platoon became a full regiment in 2005.

The initial squad of 67 possible Lions was reduced to 37 after a Six Nations Championship disrupted by the outbreak of foot and mouth disease that swept across the UK and Ireland in the early part of 2001. Given England's dominance of the championship, it was no surprise that 18 of the party were English, of whom the most controversial selection was Jason Robinson, a former Great Britain rugby league player who had yet to play a game for England. Robinson was a born-again Christian who was now teetotal after previously having a drink problem, and his main reading material on the tour, by his own admission, was the Bible.

Reflecting Scotland's dire form that year, there were no Scottish backs originally selected though, as you will read, Andy Nicol joined later. Only three Scottish forwards, Tom Smith, Simon Taylor and Scott Murray, were in the original selection, though Gordon Bulloch joined as a replacement. The Scottish media went ballistic, sensing a slight against Ian McGeechan for refusing to coach on the tour, and there was sympathy even from England. Austin Healey said: 'I was surprised Gregor Townsend wasn't taken. Budge Pountney, too. I was surprised *he* didn't go.'

No fewer than four of the selections were carrying injuries when they were named, the hope being that they would be fit by the time of the first Test. Of the four, only Jonny Wilkinson made it to the final match, with Iain Balshaw, Lawrence Dallaglio and Mike Catt all aggravating their injuries on tour.

Some of the dirt-trackers in the party claimed that the Test side had been selected even before the party left for Australia. Certainly there was little doubt that key roles had been decided beforehand, though each of the Test players still had to show their fitness before selection. The front five virtually selected themselves, Tom Smith, Keith Wood, Phil Vickery, Danny Grewcock and, of course, Martin Johnson playing together in all three Tests. Rob Howley of Wales was seen as a certainty for the scrum-half position, but, as had happened in 1997, he was injured in the middle of the tour and Matt Dawson took over for the final Test.

The Lions were blessed with two young men in the back line who would go on to be great stars in the game. Brian O'Driscoll of Ireland and 22-year-old Jonny Wilkinson of Newcastle and England had already made an impact for their own countries, and they greatly enhanced their reputations in Australia. Three men who might have not expected to be in the Test XV – Welsh winger Dafydd James, English full-back Matt Perry and Irish centre Rob Henderson – took their chances and ended up playing in all three Tests.

In the back row, four players shared the duties in the Tests, Scott Quinnell of Wales joining English trio Neil Back, Martin Corry and Richard Hill, who showed just why he was the most underrated player in world rugby with a series of dynamic performances. Back from rugby league, Dai Young captained the midweek men, and while some, such as Scotland hooker Gordon Bulloch and Welsh loose forward Colin Charvis, became somewhat disillusioned with their lot, Young did manage to keep the side ticking over, so that players like Dawson, Austin Healey, Jason Leonard, and Martyn Williams were ready to take their places on the bench in the Tests.

Having seen the documentary on the 1997 tour, some of the Lions were concerned about the way they would be portrayed in a similar film being made about the 2001 tour. Not all, though, were worried. Austin Healey, who was to figure greatly, remarked:

> I had no problems with the filming because it helped brighten up the day. I know if they [the film crew] were a bit stuck they came to me, and I didn't mind that. I was out there to have a bit of fun and try to win a Test series. I tried to have fun like the previous tour. The 1997 tour of South Africa was enjoyable and successful, the second a lot less enjoyable and less successful.

In the weeks running up to the tour, the Australian media was quietly muted, but it did not take them too long to start hurling the brickbats, harking back particularly to the 1989 tour and the violence it had seen. More sensible heads pointed out that such events were unlikely to recur this time as the yellow card and 'sin bin' had arrived in rugby union.

There could not have been a much better start to the tour. A week's preparation at the magnificent Tylney Hall complex in Hampshire involved team-building led by the Impact company. The Impact sessions included dragon boat racing, playing musical instruments, and putting four men on a board on top of a tall post – rugby training with a difference, and the Lions loved it.

After a send-off from hundreds of cheering fans at Heathrow, the Lions set out in optimistic mood. That feeling was soon to be boosted in Perth with their opening fixture against Western Australia. The Lions ran riot as never before, and piled up an astonishing scoreline of 116–10, a new record points score by any Lions team. The tries just kept on coming at the WACA, with 11 players in all touching down. Ronan O'Gara converted 13 of the 18 tries for another record, and even though Western Australia consisted of part-timers and amateurs, it was still a blistering show by the Lions.

There were injury problems, however. Young Scottish back row forward Simon Taylor damaged ligaments in the final minutes after a rousing performance, while Phil Greening never even got to don the red jersey as he had injured a knee in training two days before the opener and missed every match. Martin Corry was sent for from the England XV tour of Canada – Clive Woodward expressed his annoyance – while Scottish hooker Gordon Bulloch replaced Greening.

There also began to be rumblings among the players about the incessant and very tough training sessions that Henry and Robinson were insisting upon. It was a theme that recurred throughout the tour, and it was not just a case of players moaning because they were missing out on what they had hoped would be some relaxing activities. No, this was a genuinely held feeling that, after a long season, some of the squad were in danger of burning out because of the intensity of the work the coaches were demanding.

The points kept on coming, however, the Lions beating Queensland President's XV by 83–6, which included an astonishing 73 points without reply in the second half, and then Queensland Reds were thumped

42–8 at Ballymore – there was a battle or two, of course, but this time there was also a superb performance by what looked like becoming the Test XV.

The supposedly smooth run-up to the first Test all went wrong, however, against Australia's A side. A young uncapped lock forward called Justin Harrison ruled the line-out, and several Lions were plainly carrying knocks. Mike Catt, indeed, had to go off and out of the tour with a recurrence of his leg injury. The result was a disjointed display, even though the Lions came close to snatching victory at the end, going down by just 28–25. Coach Henry made it clear afterwards that the players who had lost to the A side were now the dirt-trackers, though many Lions had already concluded that for themselves: 'The Test team was picked before we got on the plane,' one of them confessed as early as the second week.

In effect, Henry had now abandoned Dai Young and his team, which disheartened many of them. And when he later made the dirt-trackers imitate the Wallabies in practice matches, some of them were livid. Will Greenwood recalled: 'It compounded the suspicion that they had been brought on tour as mere cannon fodder.'

The folly of that decision to create two separate teams was shown the very next day when Dan Luger, England's powerful wing and a Test certainty, sustained a fractured cheekbone in a training accident. Jason Robinson instantly went from dirt-tracker to probable Test player. Still more injuries were to follow in a brutal match against the New South Wales Waratahs.

In an incredible coincidence, Will Greenwood ruptured his ankle ligaments in that match. It was Saturday 23 June, exactly four years to the day since his narrow escape from death in South Africa.

'If I'm ever asked for advice by youngsters, I just say "never play rugby on June 23", and look wise,' said Greenwood.

Ronan O'Gara replaced Greenwood only to be brutally assaulted while lying on the ground by Duncan McRae, the former Saracens player.

O'Gara needed eight stitches in a gaping wound under his left eye, and McRae was both sent off and subsequently banned for seven matches for his offence.

The Lions' forwards gave as good as they got in an ill-tempered encounter, and there were five yellow cards in total, four of them issued after the brawl that followed the O'Gara incident. The Lions eventually won 41–24, but the result's significance was lost in the brouhaha which followed.

The Australian press had decided that the Lions had come Down Under for a fight rather than a game of rugby, and some of the criticism was almost laughable – it was McRae, after all, who had punched O'Gara's face wide open. The beleaguered Lions' management had more worries to cope with other than headlines – Keith Wood was struggling to make the Test, while Will Greenwood and Lawrence Dallaglio were invalided out of the tour altogether. David Wallace of Ireland replaced Dallaglio, making a bit of history as he became the third of three brothers to tour with the Lions in separate tours, Richard and Paul having been with the 1993 and 1997 Lions respectively.

The Lions also received some devastating news. The Australian Rugby Union had loaned Anton Toia to be a liaison officer and baggage handler for the Lions, and he had quickly become a popular member of the party. But on one of the Lions' rare outings, Toia drowned while swimming in the surf. It turned out that he had suffered a heart attack. Many of the players were deeply upset and Martin Johnson would later write: 'It reinforced the feeling that somehow the tour was ill-fated.'

All the signs were that the first Test would be an ordeal for the Lions, but on the night the Lions delivered a stunning performance. They bested the Wallabies in every department in what was a clean match, winning 29–13 with the try count reading 4–2 in the Lions' favour. Jason Robinson brilliantly scored the first try with a wonderful shimmy to announce that he had arrived in international rugby union, with Dafydd James, Brian

O'Driscoll and Scott Quinnell scoring the others. The sight of a demoralized John Eales being substituted said it all about the Lions' dominance.

The gloss was taken off the victory immediately after the match when it was revealed that Matt Dawson had written a column for the *Daily Telegraph*, which had appeared in the morning edition back home. Dawson had been writing a Diary column for the paper, one of 25 Lions who had been contracted by newspapers to write for them. The practice made some administrators uneasy, but since Graham Henry was writing a book about the tour and coaches and managers had done so in the past, there was very little they could do to stop it.

Dawson handed the would-be censors plenty of ammunition. In his ghost-written column he lambasted Graham Henry for his harsh training regime and failing to inspire him – 'I lost faith at our first meeting,' he would later say, and also implied that some players wanted to go home – true, as it happened.

Arriving on the day of victory, Dawson's claims landed like a bombshell on the Lions. Though Dawson apologized to the squad for the timing of his remarks, he never withdrew his criticisms, even after being disciplined for his statements under the tour's code of conduct agreement.

Behind the scenes, Lenihan was livid and Henry and Robinson only marginally less so. But they could not replace the reserve with injury-prone Rob Howley, and Martin Johnson intervened to say that if Dawson went, so would he – so Dawson stayed on tour. Already strained relationships between the Lions' management and the press now began to break down completely, with 'no comment' becoming the mantra after some journalists dared to print what they all knew – that the mood in the Lions camp was divided, edgy and unpleasant. Several other players, such as Colin Charvis and Dan Luger, confirmed the veracity of much of what Dawson said, but only after the tour.

In the second Test in Melbourne's Colonial Stadium, Australia exacted revenge in a thrilling fashion. Just as they had been outplayed in the first

Test, so it was the Wallabies' turn to raise their game to new heights, but only after having been down 11–6 at half-time. In a second half of almost complete control, Australia scored three tries, with Joe Roff grabbing a brace and Matt Burke also going over. Burke converted one and added six penalties, while the Lions only had Neil Back's try and three Jonny Wilkinson penalties to show for their efforts. The 35–14 scoreline meant that Australia had set a new record in points difference over the Lions.

The third and deciding Test looked set to be a classic encounter, but before the ink was even dry on the team sheets, another ghost-written newspaper article caused even more of a furore. This time the culprit was Austin Healey, whose 'ghost' was former Lion Eddie Butler. Earlier in the tour, Healey had been involved in a spat with Justin Harrison of the ACT Brumbies and, in what was probably an ill-advised attempt to wind up Harrison after he was called up for the third Test, Healey referred to the big Australian lock as an 'ape', a 'plod' and a 'plank'. He started the column in *The Guardian* by writing: 'Is that good enough to get in the Sydney Morning Sun Telegraph Herald Load of Shite? If I ever wanted to do something, it was beat you lot.'

Healey then went on to criticize the Australian weather 'to get up your nose' before adding; 'What is it with this country? The females and children are fine, and seem to be perfectly normal human beings, but what are we going to do with this thing called the Aussie male?'

All hell broke loose, particularly in the Australian media. Realizing that Healey had handed the Wallabies a big motivation to beat the Lions, Henry would later describe his actions, and that of Dawson, as a betrayal saying 'it was an age old story – betraying trust and betraying your mates for 30 pieces of silver'. Dawson's reply was that Henry 'was on a different planet'.

In the immediate aftermath, Donal Lenihan announced that Healey would face a disciplinary inquiry on his return home, and later issued a statement saying: 'The Lions' management has expressed considerable concern at the newspaper comments allegedly made by Austin Healey in advance of the Lions' third Test Match against Australia in Sydney last Saturday.' In veiled terms, they were saying they were outraged.

Ironically, although he was in with a chance of playing, Healey succumbed to a back spasm and missed the deciding Test. As if written in the script, Justin Harrison promptly played a blinder.

Healey's absence led to Andy Nicol, scrum-half of Scotland, becoming a double Lion in the most extraordinary circumstances. For the second time in Lions history, a player was called from civvy street to join the Lions on match day, the first being Willie Cunningham back in 1924 in South Africa.

Andy Nicol said:

I was on the official reserve list at one point but I had been asked to lead a supporters' tour and was thoroughly enjoying it. On the evening before the final Test, we were in the bar of the hotel and about to leave to climb Sydney Harbour Bridge when I got a call from Donal Lenihan.

Matt Dawson was first choice scrum-half and the only other cover they had was Austin Healey, as Rob Howley had broken his ribs. Donal explained that Healey had suffered a back spasm when playing on the wing in midweek and was due to get a scan in the morning, so could I be on standby in case the results were bad? Sure enough, the call came to the hotel at 10 o'clock the next morning, the day of the Test, me having been up on the Harbour Bridge at 11 o'clock the previous night – I have a picture of me standing on the bridge, and at least I stayed sober that night because you get breathalysed before you go up the bridge.

Once the call came, I had nine hours to prepare and learn every move and every call – I think the Wallabies knew them better than me. I went down to a park and threw three or four passes to Jonny Wilkinson, so we would have been going in blind if I had got on.

Sitting on the bench during the game, I was in a horrible situation. I had been disappointed not to make the tour, but here was I again a Lion, yet I was praying for every minute to fly by because I knew I would not last more than 15 minutes.

When it got to the last ten minutes I relaxed because I knew that I would make it if I had to go on. I had actually agreed with Matt Dawson beforehand that if we were winning or losing by a lot of points, he would let me on for the last minute because then I would have fulfilled every supporter's dream and been the man who was called from the pub to play for the Lions in the deciding Test. But as we all know, it was a very tight and close match, and Matt stayed on.

Nicol's name is nevertheless listed in most official statistics as having been a member of the 2001 Lions tour. The man himself said: 'I can always look back on those six minutes against Taranaki in 1993 and say I played for the British and Irish Lions.'

The intense emotions of the occasion in Sydney's magnificent Stadium Australia never quite boiled over as both sides went for victory. The first half was enervating stuff, Danny Herbert's try giving the Wallabies a 16–13 lead at half-time. The Lions had failed to capitalize on an earlier try by Robinson, and Wilkinson also missed two kickable penalties, though he goaled the conversion and two other penalties.

Early in the second half, Wilkinson burrowed over for a try, which he converted, but Herbert scored a second try, converted by Burke for a 23–20 lead. Wilkinson equalized with a penalty for a Herbert high tackle on Brian O'Driscoll, but the Lions could not take advantage during the 10 minutes in which Herbert was sin-binned and Burke slotted two more penalties to put the Wallabies 29–23.

With the Lions pressing for a try which, if converted, would win the game and the series, Harrison defied his colleagues to go up against Martin

Johnson and contest a late line-out in touching distance of the Australian line. The 'plank' won the ball, Australia cleared their lines and hung on for victory.

A tour which had promised so much had ended in rancour and defeat. In the dressing room afterwards, the Lions were very quiet. Yet there were moments of solidarity and sportsmanship. Will Greenwood, who had recovered sufficiently to be named as one of the replacements, was presented with his Test jersey by Rob Henderson, who had been his room-mate – 'the worst room-mate in the world', as Greenwood recalled.

'It's a moment I'll always cherish,' said Greenwood. 'It was a brilliant gesture that perfectly captured the spirit of the Lions – an Irishman giving the shirt off his back to an Englishman.' Greenwood had the jersey framed and it hangs on his wall at home.

Inevitably, the blame game began, with Dawson and Healey portrayed as the villains. Just as many people, however, criticized the regime and tactics of Henry. Healey said that both had been 'simple' and added:

> Next time they should make sure there is a collective spirit and that the players have a good time. Professional rugby players don't need to be told where to go on the pitch and don't need to spend so much time beating each other up in training. Camaraderie can take teams beyond where they would normally go.

Hauled before a Lions disciplinary panel, Healey was fined £2,000 for 'bringing the game into disrepute'. On the panel were Lenihan, Henry and Johnson – you don't need to be a human rights lawyer to see how unjust that was. Yet he received a remarkable tribute from his fellow 'miscreant', Matt Dawson:

I don't know how I would have coped with the tour had Austin not been around. Without his presence people would have been slitting their wrists. You need characters like him to lighten the mood. Seeing him getting a bollocking from Henry or whatever provided light relief for everybody else. He knew that. He knew the mood needed to be changed and took it on himself to do it. He was brilliant.

When the storm had first blown up around my diary I'd gone back to the room we were sharing only to find 'Oz' packing my bag for me. 'I thought I'd do this for you because you'll be off tomorrow,' he said. Most other people would have made themselves scarce and left me to fester in my misery. Not him. It was exactly what I needed.

Healey said:

People perceive me as a different character to what I actually am. In my schooldays I tried to be different, whether that was misbehaving or attention-seeking or whatever. I was just trying to be someone else. I didn't want to go through life being like everyone else; I just refused to spend my whole life being one of a crowd. Sometimes I do stupid things on the pitch but that is just me. Don't ask me to explain it because I can't.

Healey made the point that the game was losing touch with people:

The game is too closed off to the public. They should let people in and see how much dedication and enjoyment and friendship there is in the game. That is what I try and do. I try and be honest and let people know what is going on.

He described himself as an 'an easy target' and added:

*I accept that I bring a lot of it on myself. I do things differently and have
to accept the consequences. I admit I have made mistakes.*

*If I had been stony-faced and Jonny Wilkinson-like throughout my life
perhaps I would have got more plaudits, but I play with my heart rather
than my brain.*

In his memoirs, *Finding my Feet*, Jason Robinson wrote of the tour: 'For
me it was a great experience but the hardest two months' rugby of my
life – a lot of travelling, a lot of training, and not enough down time. I
felt like a zombie most of the time, and I was not alone, I can assure you.'
It seems Matt Dawson was spot on with his column.

No one sought to blame the captaincy of Johnson, but the big man
did not spare himself. He later wrote:

*I have to take some of the blame. I think I could have done a better job.
In South Africa I had been very aware of my position as a young and
inexperienced Lions captain, with plenty of more senior players under
me. Four years on, having led England and a very successful Leicester
side for some years, I was more aware of what I wanted and needed from
the players.*

*As a result, I was probably more demanding and harder on the guys
than I had been before. I think a few of the guys thought I was less
interested in them, less caring about their problems than I actually
was. As the tour ended, I couldn't honestly say where I stood with some
of them.*

Johnson didn't need to say that. He could have let others take all the blame,
but as well as being a towering personality the big fellow is as honest
with himself as he is with others. He would show what a class act he was
as a player and a man two years later in the World Cup Final when he led
England to victory over Australia in the same stadium where his Lion's

heart had been broken. Deep down, Johnson could be forgiven then for thinking that he had served up a magnificent riposte to the Aussie baiting of him and his Lions in 2001.

Austin Healey did not play in the World Cup, has retired from playing professionally and is now a businessman. Encouraged by his young daughters – he has four, including twins born in 2008 – he appeared in series six of *Strictly Come Dancing*, reaching the quarter-final. He was not as successful as his friend Matt Dawson, who finished second in the show in 2006. Dawson was at scrum-half in England's World Cup-winning side. He retired from playing in 2006, and has been a team captain on *A Question of Sport* since 2004.

Andy Nicol, who works in banking in Scotland and is a respected pundit for the BBC, as is Scott Gibbs, retired from international rugby after the 2001 tour. Rob Howley retired from playing in 2004 after a serious wrist injury and is now part of the Welsh national coaching team, as is Neil Jenkins. Keith Wood retired after the 2003 World Cup, having far outstripped his father Gordon's 29 Irish caps with 58 for Ireland and 5 for the Lions. He is now an entrepreneur and property developer and works regularly for the BBC and *Daily Telegraph*. Jason Leonard won the World Cup with England and then retired as the most-capped player of all time in 2003 with 114 international appearances for England and 5 for the Lions. He works in the construction industry and is a senior figure in the RFU.

Spinal problems forced Matt Perry's retirement in 2007. He works in management consultancy. Ben Cohen plays for Brive in France, and Dafydd James for Llanelli Scarlets. Scott Murray plays for US Montauban in France's Top-14 league, where Simon Taylor plays for Stade Français. Tom Smith is still playing for Northampton Saints at the age of 37. Dai Young is head coach of Cardiff Blues.

Yet another Lion who showed great bravery on the field and after his career was over was Scott Quinnell, the great No. 8 of Llanelli and Wales, and son of three-time Lion Derek. On this occasion, it was moral courage displayed. Usually a quiet and private individual, The Mighty Quinn has published a book and taken part in a documentary about his long-hidden affliction, dyslexia.

Quinnell publicized his condition in an effort to raise public awareness of dyslexia, which had seen him held back at school and face problems even in such simple tasks as signing autographs for fans. He undertook the DORE programme, which claims to improve the condition, after it was recommended to him by Scotland star Kenny Logan, who had also suffered from dyslexia. Both Logan and Quinell reported remarkable results from the programme, and the screening of the documentary on Quinnell caused considerable debate in Wales. In the House of Commons in May 2008, he was singled out by Kevin Brennan MP for talking 'very bravely' about his dyslexia, and there have subsequently been calls, supported by Quinnell, for large funds to be put into spreading the DORE programme in the UK.

In contrast to Quinnell, some Lions have always had an easy way with words. Among those who criticized the 2001 management was Clive Woodward, unsuccessful candidate for the coaching job. He and Graham Henry began one of those conversations-by-newspaper on just what had gone wrong. Little did they know how their careers would next intertwine.

Woodward, of course, became the successful England manager in the 2003 World Cup, and was knighted for his efforts. There remained afterwards one rugby mountain for Sir Clive to climb, and in the next tour he would be granted the chance to mount a personal summit and coach the British and Irish Lions. But would he be able to reach the top? And would there be someone trying to stop him?

CHAPTER EIGHTEEN

SPEARED BY THE ALL BLACKS: BRIAN O'DRISCOLL

New Zealand 2005

You'd think they would have learned the lessons. In 2001 in Australia, messing about in the media cost the Lions dearly. Yet, on the tour of New Zealand in 2005, the troubles with the media overshadowed almost everything else, not least because the British and Irish Lions suffered a serious reverse in the Test series, never looking like winning and eventually losing 3–0.

It was not quite an unmitigated disaster, not least because the midweek side, coached by Ian McGeechan and captained by Gordon Bulloch, played extremely well at times and did not lose a match. But it was to prove an unhappy, almost wretched tour, for numerous reasons, not all of which could be blamed on the man who eventually came to take the most flak – Sir Clive Woodward.

Nearly four years on, most of the Lions involved in the tour have no wish to revisit it in print – as we shall see, writing memoirs causes problems. The majority of players on that tour are still playing and in contention for 2009, so we felt it would be unfair to ask them to state

309

their views 'on the record' about what happened in 2005. But enough Lions have made their feelings clear about the events in New Zealand for us to form a picture of a tour where life was not a bed of roses but equally not perhaps as All Black as it was painted.

Despite England's stunning triumph in the World Cup in Australia in 2003, no one was in any doubt that the British and Irish Lions would face a monumental task in New Zealand. In the World Cup, the All Blacks had crumpled at the penultimate stage, losing 22–10 to Australia. Coach John Mitchell paid the price for that failure to lift the cup, being replaced by none other than the Great Redeemer himself, former Wales and Lions' coach Graham Henry.

Though his job description and stated aim was to win the 2007 World Cup, his appointment was made with half an eye to the fact that the Lions would be touring New Zealand in 2005, in keeping with the importance which the NZRFU and the All Blacks and their fans placed on the Lions' visit. Having Henry as coach would give the All Blacks a massive insight into the operations of the Lions, no matter who was chosen as the Lions' coach. Henry also recruited former All Blacks coach Wayne Smith to work mainly with the backs.

Henry had a good start in 2004, the All Blacks thrashing the world champions in two matches in Dunedin and Auckland, winning 36–3 and 36–12 respectively. England did not even score a try. It seemed at that stage as though Henry held all the aces for the following year's series with the Lions, but towards the end of 2003 there were signs that New Zealand were becoming at least inconsistent, as they thrashed France 46–5 in Paris but beat Wales by just a single point in a thrilling match in Cardiff.

By then, Henry had known for some time who would be his opposite number, and what an intriguing clash of egos lay in store. Sir Clive Woodward – knighted in the 2004 New Year's Honours List – had been appointed head coach of the 2005 Lions as early as February 2004, so setting up a clash with his immediate predecessor, the man who had surprisingly beaten him to the job for the 2001 tour. To say there was no love lost between the two men would be a considerable understatement.

With Woodward taking over, not a few pundits correctly predicted that the 2005 Lions would attract even more and much bigger headlines than those of 2001 – they seemed to follow Woodward around. That he is a man convinced always of his own correctness is well known, and this has often led him into direct criticism and blunt speaking of the 'I know best' variety.

John Beattie got an interesting insight into the Woodward mindset on their tours to South Africa in 1980 and New Zealand in 1983. During the former tour, Beattie recalled sitting in a hotel with his room-mate Woodward, then an executive with Rank Xerox, when the phone rang.

I answered it and said to him, 'It's for you', and then he picked up the phone and stood for a minute just looking at it before he talked. I asked him, 'What was that all about' and he replied, 'Rank Xerox training – always be in charge of a situation.' It was a first indication of Clive's future approach. I actually really liked him, he was a different sort of bloke.

Woodward may have been a certainty as coach but he was not unanimously popular among officials – he had little time for the blazerati of any union – and players. The same could not be said of the tour manager. Bill Beaumont had led the Lions in 1980, the first Englishman to do so for 50 years, having been called into the 1977 tour as a replacement. By the time of his injury-enforced retirement in 1982, he had already become one of the great figures of English rugby. He was also one of the most famous faces in Britain, due largely to his long stint as a team captain on the BBC's popular quiz show *A Question of Sport* – Beaumont is the longest-serving captain on the programme to date.

There was much more to Beaumont than just the jovial figure 'off the telly', however. He was heavily involved in running the family textile business, and has represented England on the International Rugby Board from 1999 onwards. He also worked hard for rugby charity The Wooden Spoon, and, at that point, he held the OBE, since augmented by the CBE. But even Beaumont's managerial skills and ability to work with the media would be sorely tested in New Zealand.

The first real concerns were over the size of the playing and backroom squads. Apart from the largest ever squad of 45 players, there was a 26-strong management team, which Woodward had agitated for – double the number from 2001. That did not go down well in some quarters of the home unions and in the press. Tony O'Reilly was asked what he would do about the size of the squad: 'Send 14 of them home,' was the great Irish Lion's answer.

All told there were nine coaches, including both Andy Robinson and Ian McGeechan; two video analysts; an expert on refereeing, David McHugh; two doctors, with James Robson back again; a lawyer, Richard Smith; and sundry other physios, masseurs and administrators, including new chief executive John Feehan, who now ran the company that had been set up by the home unions to look after all matters to do with the Lions. The real surprise package was the choice of person to handle press relations – none other than Alastair Campbell, the famously abrasive bagpipe-playing Downing Street spin doctor who had resigned from his government public relations job in 2003. In a sense, Campbell was going back to his roots – the lifelong Burnley fan had started his career in newspapers as a sports reporter, and now he would be back in sport, only on the other side of the fence.

Campbell's appointment in December 2004 caused considerable controversy, some of it no doubt because he was such a political figure, associated with Tony Blair and the Labour Government, and detested by many in the media for his undoubted spin doctoring skills. He was to prove an unpopular figure on the tour, with some players giving him unflattering nicknames, while the New Zealand press reserved their inventiveness for Woodward – the 'King of Smug' was one of the nicer ones.

In all the pre-tour publicity, Woodward was front and centre, and, as had been expected, from the outset he put his stamp on things, including his legendary meticulous preparation which involved spending weeks in the training camps of the Springboks and Australian teams. The extraordinary background to all this was that Woodward was preparing to walk away from rugby, having accepted the job of Director of Football at Southampton FC – not as daft as it sounded, because Woodward had been a talented footballer as a young man and often spoke of his love for the round-ball game.

He desperately wanted to go out of rugby on a high as only the second coach and the first Englishman to lead the Lions to a series victory in New Zealand. But, yet again, Woodward's mouth was his own worst enemy with his prediction that the 2005 Lions would be 'world class'. His words were: 'I have planned for this for so long. Everything is in place and these are the players I want around me when we go into battle. It always takes time for a team to gel but we will. It's the Tests that count. We have to make this a world-class team and I believe we will.'

Former All Blacks coach Laurie Mains replied: 'This is the worst Lions team to arrive in New Zealand that I can remember.' It was clear that one or other group was going to emerge from the tour very badly wounded.

The third member of the triumvirate leading the Lions was Brian O'Driscoll. The Irishman was by common consent the finest centre in the world at that time, and was both a popular and inspirational captain of Ireland. He had been one of the few successes in the 2001 tour, but there was still a feeling that he had been made captain because there was such a preponderance of English players in the squad that something had to be done to offset this.

The reason why there were so many Englishmen in the squad – 22 of them, all told – is not hard to fathom. Woodward had led them to the World Cup just two years previously, and though his great captain Martin Johnson had retired, he still had the core of the team and was prepared to take a risk with players who were less than fully fit – World Cup winning fly-half Jonny Wilkinson was given specially extended time to recover from injury. The Welsh rugby community was incensed that Woodward had clearly decided to ignore the Grand Slam that the principality had just won, and build his team around Ye Olde England, rather than their new star Gavin Henson, the centre who was almost as famous for his rugby as he was for his relationship with singer Charlotte Church. The Scots were incensed that just three players, Chris Cusiter, Simon Taylor and Gordon Bulloch, were considered good enough for the Lions, though Jason White did join them later as a replacement.

Before they left for New Zealand, the Lions took part in what was supposed to be a preparatory match against Argentina at the Millennium Stadium in Cardiff. The Argentineans certainly took it very seriously and were unlucky not to win, the match ending in a 25–25 draw.

The stories of the tour are still too fresh in the memory to need repeating here, yet three crucial events must be analysed. Woodward saw the initial games as merely training exercises, only to see his Test plans blown asunder in the second match of the tour, against Bay of Plenty in Rotorua. About 20 minutes into the match, Lawrence Dallaglio was stretchered off with a broken ankle, the result of a dislocation when he accidentally lost his footing while making a tackle. He was operated on the following day and out of rugby for four months.

Dallaglio had been the man Woodward was counting on to drive the pack to the heights needed to beat the All Blacks. The realization of what his injury meant was best expressed by New Zealand's assistant coach,

Steve Hansen: 'This has robbed the tour of a great player. It will be shattering for the Lions.'

Indeed it was. No one quite stepped up to fill Dallaglio's shoes as an on-field leader, while another English player, giant prop Andrew Sheridan, wasn't at his mighty best either after a great start to the tour – it turned out that he had played for three weeks with a fractured fibula, one of the bones in the lower leg.

The next incident of note was Woodward delivering an almighty blow to the midweek men by telling them they had no chance of being selected for the first Test if they played in the match prior to that Test. Somehow McGeechan managed to maintain their morale and the dirt-trackers won that game against Southland by 26–16.

Prior to that Southland match, there had been outrage in Wales when Gavin Henson had been picked to play in it and it was realized therefore that would not make the Test side. One Welsh fan burned his Lions jersey, and the Welsh media worked themselves into a frenzy. Henson himself believed he'd been 'given the nod' that he'd be selected for the Test, and was furious when he wasn't named.

His demotion would lead directly to an incident that must have unsettled the squad. Trying to spin the story of Henson's exclusion the Lions way, Alistair Campbell had prepared a raft of 'Gavin Henson quotes' for release to the media, who had all been fixated on whether the Welshman would figure in the Test side.

We have Gavin Henson's memoir *My Grand Slam Year* to thank for his account of what happened next. Apparently Campbell told the player, 'It will save you having to talk to the media', but Henson said: 'I read the words that were supposed to have come out of my mouth. I was just stunned, amazed.'

Campbell then secretly arranged for Henson and Woodward to be photographed together, but this backfired as too obvious a piece of spin. In his book, Henson said: 'I've lost any respect I had for Campbell. He was supposed to be part of a team but he was working to his own agenda.' The players now began to question Campbell's role and suggested his presence was dividing the party.

So was someone else, as Josh Lewsey admitted in his memoirs, without naming the person: 'Three days before the Lions Test, I heard one of the coaches say "This is my session." I thought that was wrong.' Put the Henson and Lewsey versions together and you have a tour on which there were indeed differences between players and management and between coaches themselves. Unusually, the splits may have been along nationality lines – Wales's Ryan Jones was also left out of the first Test, and Henson and others were convinced that English players were going to be preferred regardless of form. The Scots were already sure of that – Gordon Bulloch's arrival as a replacement in the dying minutes of the last Test was the only time a Scotsman appeared in the Tests on that tour.

The loss of Dallaglio and the internal ructions were one thing, but the worst incident of the tour – indeed, its defining moment – came a minute into the first Test at Christchurch on Saturday 25 June. In what has subsequently become known as one of the worst rugby tackles of all time, the All Blacks' captain Tana Umaga and hooker Keven Mealamu grabbed Lions' skipper Brian O'Driscoll and upended him, 'spearing' him into the ground. The dreaded 'spear tackle' has always been on the borderline of legality, but this was certainly illegal, as the Irishman did not have the ball in his hands.

The Lions' medical staff worked for 25 minutes to try and pop O'Driscoll's shoulder back into place, but so bad was the dislocation that O'Driscoll was out of the tour from that moment. Another grave loss from that game was Richard Hill, who injured a knee in the first half and was invalided out of the tour – many pundits said he was as big a loss as O'Driscoll and Dallaglio. The Lions were clearly nonplussed by the loss of their captain and star flank forward, and played dismally to lose 3–21 – not quite a record defeat against New Zealand, but the worst since 1983.

O'Driscoll's father Frank, a doctor, witnessed the event: 'People saw what happened and know the truth of the matter. I'm just thankful Brian didn't break his neck. It could easily have happened.'

Clive Woodward described the tackle as 'horrific and horrendous', as a war of words broke out between the Lions and the All Blacks. Campbell took over the spinning of the Lions' undoubted outrage, which deepened when the South African match commissioner Willem Venter refused to cite the two All Blacks for dangerous play, which could have seen them removed from the team for weeks.

Former Labour MP, New Zealand-born Bryan Gould, who was no friend of Campbell, said: 'For him, the spear tackle was manna from heaven.' Woodward played video footage of the tackle at a press conference and said it was an amazing decision to take no further action. O'Driscoll himself said:

There is a huge element of frustration and anger at the way it happened. I have no doubt whatsoever that there was some sort of spear tackle that ended it.

I certainly feel there was plenty in it. I've been on the receiving end before, but I felt this was completely unnecessary and certainly beyond the rules and regulations of the game.

The row rumbled on when Graham Henry then accused Campbell of spinning the tackle story to stop the media focusing on the poor Lions performance: 'The spin doctors have been working overtime to divert attention from the game.' Campbell was so upset he wrote a column in *The Times* denouncing the suggestion.

Not exactly spreading oil on troubled waters, Henry was asked if he would be plastering the headlines on the All Blacks' dressing room to gee them up. 'There wouldn't be enough space to put all that crap on anyway,' said Henry. 'So why bother?'

Interestingly, the spin may have worked, as few people remember the other dreadful incident in that match. Danny Grewcock quite clearly and nastily bit Keven Mealamu on the finger, and the big lock forward promptly drew a suspension of two months for doing so. The loss of Grewcock, added to Dallaglio, Hill and O'Driscoll, had weakened the spine of the team, and it never really recovered.

Meanwhile, Henson was cranking up his anti-Woodward campaign, claiming that the coach 'didn't have a clue' about what he was going to do in the second Test. The All Blacks could have told him – the Lions were going to be thumped. Woodward did admit to making 'a couple of mistakes' – he made 11 personnel and positional changes for the Test in Wellington. He also summoned Alastair Campbell to make a motivational speech to the players – a new career suddenly beckoned for the spin doctor.

It made no difference. The record scoreline of 48–18 in favour of the All Blacks was a true reflection of the game and saw the Lions dismissed as 'a joke' by Laurie Mains. By the end, Woodward had apparently lost track of the score. It was the most points ever scored against the Lions and the biggest-ever points differential, beating by one point the 29–0 defeat suffered in Auckland on 25 July 1908.

The series was lost, and there was worse to come. Usually at such a point in a tour, the Lions would have pulled themselves together and fought the last Test as a matter of pride, but not the 2005 vintage. In Auckland, they collapsed to a miserable 38–19 defeat, and went home licking their wounds. The 'Clivebashing' started immediately and though he defended himself well, Woodward could not deny the fact that his 'world class' Lions had been outplayed, while he had been out-thought by an old adversary.

Bill Beaumont has always been annoyed that the tour was portrayed as a complete disaster, pointing to the 100 per cent record of the midweek side led by Bulloch and coached by McGeechan. Beaumont said: 'Just about every Lions player told me they would not change a thing and that they had a great rugby experience.'

Those players we spoke to confirmed that, apart from the losses, there had been a lot to like about the tour, and all were agreed that Woodward's insistence on using three bases – Auckland, Christchurch and Wellington, and travelling from them rather than going from town to town, had been an inspired idea. But they lost, and many are still hurting.

A senior Lions member said:

It's clear Clive tried to impose what had worked for England on the Lions. He tried to rely on some of the players who had won the World Cup for England, but a Lions tour is totally different. And Clive should have realized that, as he had been on two tours himself as a player. Ultimately, he should not have been given a free rein. Anyone who worked with him with England knew that.

After the series, Woodward did one of his usual tricks by appearing to be magnanimous but at the same time being quite patronizing towards the All Blacks. 'We were beaten by a better side,' he said, 'But I don't think New Zealand fans should be getting too carried away.' At least he got that prediction right, as Graham Henry and the All Blacks went to France in 2007 as firm favourites to win the World Cup for the first time since the inaugural event in 1987, but came away empty-handed. In that tournament, England nearly shocked the world, eventually losing out only to the Springboks in the Final.

Gavin Henson had been the other key figure in the tour, and his 'pop star' presence was resented by some Lions. 'We were there seven weeks and he never had a drink with me,' said one. 'Too busy doing his hair,' said another – and Henson did indeed wear some brightly dyed coiffures.

When Henson brought out his memoirs in late 2005, the whole story of the tour exploded again. He lambasted Woodward as no Lion had dared do on the tour: 'Clive's preparation of the Test team was poor. I also thought his tactics and game plan were outdated, while I was shocked to see how little actual coaching he does. Clive's coaching methods were something new to me and left me a bit bewildered.'

Alastair Campbell also got it in the neck over the speech he gave to the players before the second Test in which he had mentioned that some players had not wanted victory enough in the first Test.

Henson wrote:

The idea that in a Lions Test Match, the pinnacle for any player, people hadn't put their bodies on the line was just insulting. You can take that sort of stuff from ex-internationals. You might disagree with them, but at least they speak from experience. Where was Campbell coming from? What was his rugby experience? A lot of the boys felt very angry listening to that. It was rubbish and it backfired badly.

But Henson also had an unwelcome pop at some of his colleagues, though we understand from sources he may have been right in his view: 'There were too many players who spoke up just for the sake of it. I lost count of the times players went on and on just because they thought it would sound impressive if they talked for a long time. They were in love with the sound of their own voices.'

Strangely, Henson then said the tour had been a 'really, really good experience'. Self-contradiction is the privilege of the young, and as a few Lions pointed out, he was only 23 at the time.

The truth about the 2005 Lions has still to be fully written, but in rugby terms the simple fact is that the All Blacks were at a peak in that year, while the Lions suffered crucial injuries and too many players were not in sufficiently good form to challenge New Zealand. Woodward eventually came to accept he had made mistakes but still felt that he got things mostly right – a view shared by many of the players.

Employing Alastair Campbell was probably his biggest error of judgement, because as any PR person could have told him, when the spin doctor becomes the story himself, your own message gets lost.

The vast majority of the 45 Lions of 2005 are still playing, but Lawrence Dallaglio retired after Wasps won the Premiership title at Twickenham in 2008. He was awarded an OBE to add to his MBE for winning the World Cup. So too was Jason Robinson, who retired from international rugby after that 2005 tour only to be asked back by England coach Brian Ashton and subsequently appear in a second World Cup Final in 2007, after which he did retire. He is now working as a youth coach in rugby league.

Richard Hill fought back from injury but walks now with a permanent limp; he finally retired in May 2008. Denis Hickie retired after the World Cup and is now working for the IRFU. Danny Grewcock, 36, is still playing with Bath.

He and many of the 2005 tourists would like to be selected for the 2009 Lions. They feel they have some unfinished business to attend to ...

CHAPTER NINETEEN

LIONS FOR EVER

It seems incredible, given the history and reputation of the Lions, that there have been several well-meaning but misguided attempts to kill them off over the decades. The British and Irish players who are so desperate to play in South Africa in the summer of 2009, the tens of thousands who will follow them, the people of South Africa and the other southern hemisphere countries, and the millions who will watch them on television, will all tell you that the Lions are too important to die.

Those who in years ahead for selfish financial reasons will look at the Lions as an anachronism and say their time has gone should know this – you will be gainsaying a cause, an ideal, that is very close to the hearts of rugby people, namely that a group of men can come together in friendship from everywhere across Britain and Ireland and play rugby in the common good.

We turned to one of the most famous and finest of rugby players to try and find the words to convey what the Lions mean, what they really are, and why they must continue. Gareth Edwards said:

It is very difficult to explain what it is about the Lions that makes them unique. All I can say is that when you are selected, you become part of a very special family. The friendship and camaraderie I experienced on my tours has stood the test of time. There is also a bond between Lions that transcends countries, and also the years that pass.

It is a very special experience for anybody to be selected to tour with the British and Irish Lions. In any sport there are players who always strive to be the very best and in rugby it doesn't get any better than the Lions. But it is about more than just rugby prowess, more than just making your mark in the sand. It is about being part of a group that has been chosen as the best available at that time.

Some of it is luck, of being in the right place at the right time. Don't forget that the tours are infrequent, and there have been many players who were good enough to be Lions and haven't been able to do it because of injury or loss of form at the time when the touring party was being selected.

But when you are selected, you become part of a history, a heritage. You look back and you see the names of the men who were your heroes when you were growing up, in my case, the Cliff Morgans and the Bleddyn Williamses, and you learn the stories of how they would travel across Africa or sail in a boat for six weeks to New Zealand and suddenly you realize that you are part of something that is very important and very special. You realize that you have been fortunate to fall into an illustrious company. Talk to any of the Lions and they will tell you just what a huge thrill it is.

I am sure that even now when players can get any number of caps and play in World Cups, they still know that to be a Lion is the pinnacle of their career and the ultimate experience for any rugby player in these islands, and that is why they will be striving to be chosen for South Africa 2009.

There has been a lot of talk about why the Lions should not go on, and in the professional world people are always looking to see how they can make more money. But the Lions brand is an extremely strong one and will always be a top draw for rugby crowds.

We know there will be no going back to the three-month-long tours, but there must still be a time set aside in the demanding calendar every four years. For there is no doubt in my mind, space should always be made for the Lions tour. They are just too important to rugby.

Yet the Lions must change, particularly in the face of increased demands from club owners for their players to be their employees first. Driven by television's greed for saturation rugby, clubs are likely to want their players more of the time, and some owners already see tours by nations and the Lions as an unwanted activity.

At the same time, there will be demands for the Lions 'brand', as Gareth Edwards correctly called it, to be exploited by its owners, the four home unions, and there will be demands for tours every two or three years instead of four as at present. The Lions themselves realize the dangers of more tours, and in discussion with them we were persuaded by their strong conviction that the way ahead is for the Lions to stay as a touring party leaving every four years. In other words, leave well alone.

One Lion, who asked to remain anonymous, pointed out that rugby remains the largest team sport, in terms of countries which participate, still absent from the Olympics. There can no longer be demonstration sports at Olympic Games, but, as in Beijing in 2008, a 'national sport' can be demonstrated as part of the cultural Olympiad.

The IRB has called for Rugby Sevens to be included in the Olympics, and will continue to campaign for that to happen. Meanwhile, cricket fans have launched an online petition for a 20–20 contest as part of the Olympiad. But cricket, with all due respect, would hardly unite the four countries of the United Kingdom in support of a British cricket team – it would only be England by another name. So surely the organizers of the London Olympics in 2012 could find some place in the Olympiad for a sport which crosses national barriers in these islands, and which, don't forget, was once an Olympic sport itself. Why not a one-off match at Twickenham between the British and Irish Lions and the Rest of the World? As it would not be part of the competition, the International Olympic Committee would not have to sanction it, and the Olympiad match would be a fitting celebration of the glorious game of rugby and a tribute to the many men who so willingly gave their time and energies for rugby union as British and Irish Lions.

And what of 2009? The general view among the Lions is that they will struggle against the world champions, but every one who ventured an opinion said they had full confidence in Ian McGeechan and Gerald Davies to 'create the conditions for victory', as Jim Telfer put it. 'They don't have a lot of time to get these players together, but they have a lot of experience, and if anyone can do it, they can.'

A key figure in South Africa will be tour manager Davies, who has promised to put some fun back into touring. He and McGeechan have established a warm working relationship and both men will certainly be 'simpatico' with the players, both present and past. Interviewed for this book, Davies gave a genuine insight into the biggest problem, apart from injury and ill-health, that faces most Lions – how do you cope with life after being at the summit of rugby?

After pulling out of the 1977 Lions tour, Davies played one more season for Wales, then had to cope with life after rugby, and while he managed it, becoming a journalist and commentator of renown and racking up honorary degrees and fellowships, he nevertheless has considerable understanding of the plight faced by Barry John and so many others. 'A top sportsman always lives on the edge, up there in the stratosphere, and it can be mind blowing,' said Davies.

The adrenaline flows in response to the demands that are placed upon you, and then suddenly to find that doesn't exist anymore is something that a player has to work out in his mind, and it is not easy. It is quite true what they say of an actor, about the roar of the crowd and the smell of the greasepaint, and I think it's the same for a top rugby player, because you live on a high for so long that it is difficult to come down.

That's one reason why, as we have seen, some Lions have had difficulties in later life. But ask nearly every Lion whether they would have missed out on wearing the red jersey, and the answer is a unanimous no.

They all risked injury by playing, most of them at a time when they were not being paid to play, and did it for the love of the sport. Even those in the professional era who are being paid for playing may well have wondered if prolonging an exhausting season was worth it. They will all tell you that it was, and of course, every player in these islands still wants that red jersey. Why?

We can't better the words of Gerald Davies, who said that Lions want to be Lions because the British and Irish Lions are 'the best of the best, and the Test sides are the best of the best of the best'. We now want to present you with the best of the best of the best of the best, our attempt at describing the list of the Lions' own favourite Lions.

It is entirely typical of the British and Irish Lions that when we sought their views on who were the greatest players ever to fill a Lions jersey, the majority were hesitant to name anybody in case they offended other fellow Lions. A couple steadfastly refused to take part, because they had no wish 'to single out one player from so many greats', as one of them put it, and we respected their wishes.

Assured that the poll was entirely anonymous and that only the authors would ever know how they voted – be assured, we will never reveal individual votes – the Lions gave their verdict.

Some pointed out that only Lions from 1950 onwards could seriously be considered, as no surviving Lion could have seen the pre-war players in the flesh. Others pointed out the difficulty of selecting men from different decades.

It will be no surprise that many of the positions are filled by players from the Golden Era of the Lions in the 1970s. It seemed to us that modern-day players looked back to that age for inspiration, while those from before and during the '70s were clearly happy to name each other for a place. The pre-1960s generation were also less likely to be voted for, on the obvious grounds that there are fewer Lions from that time still around. There is also a clear generational gap in the Lions – those who played before the advent of professionalism in 1995 were less inclined to look favourably on those who were paid to play, though a tinge of jealousy may have applied.

Other Lions felt it was better to name two or three players for each position, pointing out that, in reality, this is how a Lions squad is picked and is supposed to operate. In the end, the voting was so close in most positions that we were unable to differentiate between several players. Therefore we are naming a Lions XV along with 15 replacements to cover the various positions, and there was one tie in the voting (at full-back) so in total the squad numbers 31.

Common denominators were that all of the chosen 31 went on more than one tour, and that being a captain was no guarantee of being chosen – Ciaran Fitzgerald and Mike Campbell-Lamerton being just two examples who were not even mentioned by the players.

The squad (in alphabetical order, with the number of Tests they played in brackets) would thus be:

Props
Fran Cotton (7), Ian McLauchlan (8), Syd Millar (9),
Graham Price (12)

Hookers
John Pullin (7), Bryn Meredith (8)

Second Row
Bill Beaumont (7), Gordon Brown (8),
Willie John McBride (17), Martin Johnson (8)

Flank forwards
Richard Hill (5), Fergus Slattery (4), Jeff Squire (6),
Peter Winterbottom (7)

No. 8
Mervyn Davies (8), Jim Telfer (8)

Scrum-half
Gareth Edwards (10), Dickie Jeeps (13)

Fly-half
Barry John (5), Phil Bennett (8)

Centres
Jeff Butterfield (4), Scott Gibbs (5), Mike Gibson (12),
Jeremy Guscott (8)

Wings
Gerald Davies (5), Ieuan Evans (7), Tony O'Reilly (10),
J.J. Williams (7)

Full-backs
J.P.R. Williams (8), and Gavin Hastings (6)
tied with Andy Irvine (9).

Near misses, i.e. also mentioned, were Tom Smith at prop; Peter Wheeler, Bobby Windsor, Brian Moore and Keith Wood at hooker; Mike Teague, Roger Uttley and Derek Quinnell at flanker; Alun Pask and Dean Richards at No. 8; Cliff Morgan at fly-half; John Dawes, Ian McGeechan, Will Greenwood and Bleddyn Williams at centre; Ken Jones, Peter Jackson and Rory Underwood on the wings, and Neil Jenkins anywhere ('for his kicking alone' as one Lion put it).

For what it's worth, the authors' first choice XV, based on listening to the Lions, would be (from 1 to 15) McLauchlan, Pullin, Price; McBride, Johnson; Slattery, Winterbottom, Davies; Edwards, John; O'Reilly, Gibson, Butterfield, Davies; J.P.R. Williams. Given the obvious fantasy conditions that each man is selected at his best age and in his peak form, we would bet that team against the Rest of the Universe.

When compiling the poll of Lions, it became clear early on that one player was far out in front of the rest in terms of how he was judged on playing ability – Gareth Edwards. By public acclaim some years ago, he was named the Greatest Player Ever, and the Lions have endorsed that view. Some Lions named Jack Kyle, Cliff Morgan, Gerald Davies and Mike Gibson as the best player they saw in a Lions jersey, but by some distance, Gareth Edwards is the Lions' choice as the Lions' Best Ever Player.

Edwards was also named in the second part of our poll to find the man the Lions themselves consider to be the embodiment of what it means to be a British and Irish Lion. Quoting from the Lions themselves: that player has to be 'good in his position', 'work for the team', 'be a squad member', and enjoy 'playing the game for the game's sake'. He also has to 'be a leader on the field and off' and 'work hard and play hard' as well as 'serving the great game of rugby'. Above all that person has to 'understand the history, traditions and uniqueness of the Lions'.

As well as Edwards, there was support for Ian McGeechan, Gerald Davies, Syd Millar, Gavin Hastings and Martin Johnson, with Tony O'Reilly – especially for his decades of support of fellow Lions – and Mike

Gibson given numerous mentions. But there will be no surprise about the name of the man accorded the title of the Greatest Ever Lion by the British and Irish Lions.

His five tours as a player saw him come back from bitter disappointment to triumph in New Zealand in 1971, followed by the ultimate achievement of leading the Lions to an unbeaten series in South Africa in 1974. Since then he has come to embody the best quality of the Lions – he is indomitable.

The British and Irish Lions' choice as the Greatest Ever Lion is Willie John McBride.

To him and all the British and Irish Lions of the last 121 years, the authors owe our thanks for allowing us to tell their stories.

We know that rugby in the southern hemisphere owes all these men, who sacrificed so much for their sport, an unpayable debt of gratitude, not least because the income from tours replenished the coffers of rugby unions in Australia, South Africa and New Zealand and allowed further development of rugby in those countries.

For us, the Lions represent so much that is good in these islands. We have written of Welsh miners, Scottish doctors, English teachers, Irishmen of north and south, and a whole panoply of characters from the rich tapestry of British and Irish rugby. Yes, there were occasional squabbles and serious disappointments at times on tour, and the Lions often expressed to us their strong disgust at the game's administrators over such issues as players being shunned because they went to rugby league. But what was truly remarkable, we found, was how all of them came together, often in only one tour, yet have remained firm friends even four or five decades on.

We hope we have shown a measure of how important the Lions have been to world rugby, and not just rugby in Britain and Ireland. Above all, we hope we have shown how important being a Lion is to the players themselves.

All those Lions, all of them from Stuart Lane who played just 55 seconds to Willie John McBride who played 17 Tests, were special people, and, thankfully, many are still with us to be acknowledged as such. Those who once were Lions and are no longer with us in person can rest in peace in the knowledge that they have earned a kind of immortality. For all those men who once were Lions will never be forgotten.

ROLL OF HONOUR AND ARCHIVE OF RESULTS

1888 – NEW ZEALAND AND AUSTRALIA

Backs: J. Anderton (Lancashire and Salford), H. Brooks (Durham and Edinburgh University), W. Bumby (Lancashire and Swinton), W. Burnett (Roxburgh County and Hawick), J.T. Haslam (Yorkshire and Batley), J. Nolan (Rochdale Hornets), A. Paul (Lancashire and Swinton), H.C. Speakman (Cheshire and Runcorn), A.E. Stoddart [capt, replacing Seddon] (Blackheath and England)

Forwards: T. Banks (Lancashire and Swinton), P. Burnett (Roxburgh County and Hawick), J.P. Clowes (Yorkshire and Halifax), H. Eagles (Lancashire and Swinton), T. Kent (Lancashire and Salford), C. Mathers (Yorkshire and Bramley), A.P. Penketh (Douglas, Isle of Man), R.L. Seddon [capt until deceased] (Lancashire and Swinton), D.J. Smith (Corinthians and Edinburgh University), A.J. Stuart (Yorkshire and Dewsbury), W.H. Thomas (Cambridge University and Wales), S. Williams (Lancashire and Salford)

Managers: A. Shaw and A. Shrewsbury

Results: Dunedin, Sat 28 Apr: Lions 8, Otago 3, Dunedin, Wed 2 May: Lions 4, Otago 3, Christchurch, Sat 5 May: Lions 14, Canterbury 6, Christchurch, Wed 9 May: Lions 4, Canterbury 0, Wellington, Sat 12 May: Lions 3, Wellington 3, Wellington, Mon 14 May: Lions 4, H. Roberts XV 1, New Plymouth, Wed 16 May: Lions 0, Taranaki Clubs 1, Auckland, Sat 19 May: Lions 6, Auckland 3, Auckland, Thu 24 May: Lions 0, Auckland 4, Sydney, Sat 2 Jun: Lions 18, New South Wales 2, Bathurst, Thu 7 Jun: Lions 13, Bathurst 6, Sydney, Sat 9 Jun: Lions 18, New South Wales 6, Sydney, Mon 11 Jun: Lions 11, Sydney Juniors 0, Sydney, Tue 12 Jun: Lions 10, Kings School 10, Adelaide, Mon 16 Jul: Lions 28, Adelaide XV 3, Melbourne, Wed 1 Aug: Lions 9, Victoria 3, Sydney, Sat 4 Aug: Lions 16, New South Wales 2, Sydney, Mon 6 Aug: Lions 2, Sydney Grammar School 2, Bathurst, Wed 8 Aug: Lions 20, Bathurst 10, Sydney, Sat 11 Aug: Lions 8, University Of Sydney 4, Brisbane, Sat 18 Aug: Lions 13, Queensland 6, Brisbane, Tue 21 Aug: Lions 11, Queensland Juniors 3, Ipswich, Thu 23 Aug: Lions 12, Ipswich 1, Brisbane, Sat 25 Aug: Lions 7, Queensland 0, Newcastle, Wed 29 Aug: Lions 14, Newcastle 7, Auckland, Sat 8 Sep: Lions 3, Auckland 0, Auckland, Wed 12 Sep: Lions 1, Auckland 1, Napier, Sat 15 Sep: Lions 3, Hawke's Bay 2, Masterton, Mon 17 Sep: Lions 5, Wairapapa 1, Christchurch, Thu 20 Sep: Lions 8, Canterbury 0, Dunedin, Sat 22 Sep: Lions 0, Otago 0, Dunedin, Wed 26 Sep: Lions 5, South Island 3, Christchurch, Sat 29 Sep: Lions 6, South Island 0 , Hawera, Tue 2 Oct: Lions 7, Taranaki Clubs 1, Wanganui, Wed 3 Oct: Lions 1, Wanganui 1

1891 – SOUTH AFRICA

Backs: R.L. Aston (Blackheath and England), E. Bromet (Cambridge University), P.R. Clauss (Birkenhead Park and Scotland), W.E. Maclagen [capt] (Edinburgh Academicals and Scotland), H. Marshall (Cambridge University), W.G. Mitchell (Richmond and England), B.G. Roscoe (Manchester), A. Rotherham (Cambridge University and England), W. Wotherspoon (Cambridge University and Scotland)

Forwards: W.E. Bromet (Richmond and England), J.H. Gould (Old Leysians), J. Hammond (Cambridge University), P.F. Hancock (Blackheath and England), W. Jackson (Cambridge University), R.G. MacMillan (London Scottish and Scotland), W.E. Mayfield (Cambridge University), C.P. Simpson (Cambridge University), A.A. Surtees (Harlequins), R. Thompson (Cambridge University), W.H. Thomson (Cambridge University), T. Whittaker (Lancashire)

Manager: E. Ash

Results: Cape Town, Thu 9 Jul: Lions 15, Cape Town 1, Cape Town, Sat 11 Jul: Lions 6, Western Province 0, Cape Town, Mon 13 Jul: Lions 14, Cape Colony 0, Kimberley, Sat 18 Jul: Lions 7, Kimberley 0, Kimberley, Mon 20 Jul: Lions 3, Griqualand West 0, Port Elizabeth, Sat 25 Jul: Lions 22, Port Elizabeth 0, Port Elizabeth, Tue 28 Jul: Lions 21, Eastern Province 0, FIRST TEST: Port Elizabeth, Thu 30 Jul: Lions 4, South Africa 0, Grahamstown, Sat 1 Aug: Lions 9, Grahamstown 0, King William's Town, Tue 4 Aug: Lions 18, King William's Town 0, King William's Town, Thu 6 Aug: Lions 16, King William's Town and District 0, Pietermaritzburg, Tue 11 Aug: Lions 25, Pietermaritzburg 0, Johannesburg, Sat 15 Aug: Lions 22, Transvaal Country Districts 0, Johannesburg, Wed 19 Aug: Lions 15, Johannesburg 0, Johannesburg, Sat 22 Aug: Lions 9, Transvaal 0, Kimberley, Wed 26 Aug: Lions 4, Cape Colony 0, SECOND TEST: Kimberley, Sat 29 Aug: Lions 3, South Africa 0, Cape Town, Thu 3 Sep: Lions 7, Cape Colony 0, THIRD TEST: Cape Town, Sat 5 Sep: Lions 4, South Africa 0, Stellenbosch, Wed 9 Sep: Lions 2, Stellenbosch 0

1896 – SOUTH AFRICA

Backs: S.P. Bell (Cambridge University), C.A. Boyd (Dublin University), L.Q. Bulger (Dublin University and Ireland), J.F. Byrne (Moseley and England), O.G. Mackie (Cambridge University and Wakefield Trinity), J.T. Magee (Bective Rangers and Ireland), L.M. Magee (Bective Rangers and Ireland), M.M. Mullineux (Blackheath), C.O. Robinson (Northumberland)

Forwards: W.J. Carey (Oxford University), A.D. Clinch (Dublin University and Ireland), T.J. Crean (Dublin Wanderers and Ireland), J. Hammond [capt] (Cambridge University and Blackheath), P.F. Hancock (Blackheath and Somerset and England), R. Johnston (Dublin Wanderers and Ireland, G.W. Lee (Northumberland), A.W.D. Meares (Dublin University), W. Mortimer (Cambridge University and Marlborough Nomads), R.C. Mullins (Oxford University), J. Sealey (Dublin University and Ireland), A.F. Todd (Blackheath)

Manager: R. Walker

Results: Cape Town, Sat 11 Jul: Lions 14, Cape Town Clubs 9, Cape Town, Mon 13 Jul: Lions 8, Suburban Clubs XV 0, Cape Town, Wed 15 Jul: Lions 0, Western Province 0, Kimberley, Sat 18 Jul: Lions 11, Griqualand West 9, Kimberley, Wed 22 Jul: Lions 16, Griqualand West 0, Port Elizabeth, Sat 25 Jul: Lions 26, Port Elizabeth 3, Port Elizabeth, Tue 28 Jul: Lions 18, Eastern Province 0, FIRST TEST: Port Elizabeth, Thu 30 Jul: Lions 8, South Africa 0, Grahamstown, Sat 1 Aug: Lions 20, Grahamstown 0, King William's Town, Tue 4 Aug: Lions 25, King William's Town 0, East London, Thu 6 Aug: Lions 17, East London 0, Queenstown, Sat 8 Aug: Lions 25, Queenstown 0, Johannesburg, Wed 12 Aug: Lions 7, Johannesburg Country 0, Johannesburg, Sat 15 Aug: Lions 16, Transvaal 3, Johannesburg, Mon 17 Aug: Lions 18, Johannesburg Town 0, Johannesburg, Wed 19 Aug: Lions 15, Transvaal 5, SECOND TEST: Johannesburg, Sat 22 Aug: Lions 17, South Africa 8, Kimberley, Wed 26 Aug: Lions 7, Cape Colony 0, THIRD TEST: Kimberley, Sat 29 Aug: Lions 9, South Africa 3, Cape Town, Thu 3 Sep: Lions 32, Western Province 0, FOURTH TEST: Cape Town, Sat 5 Sep: Lions 0, South Africa 5

1899 – AUSTRALIA

Backs: C.Y. Adamson (Durham), A.M. Bucher (Edinburgh Academicals and Scotland), G. Cookson (Manchester), G.P. Doran (Lansdowne and Ireland), E. Martelli (Dublin University), M.M. Mullineux [capt] (Blackheath), E.G. Nicholls (Cardiff and Wales), E.T. Nicholson (Birkenhead Park), C.E.K. Thompson (Lancashire), A.B. Timms (Edinburgh University and Scotland)

Forwards: A. Ayre-Smith (Guy's Hospital), F.C. Belson (Bath), G.V. Evers (Moseley), J.S. Francombe (Manchester), G.R. Gibson (Northern and England), H.G.S. Gray (Scottish Trialist), J.W. Jarman (Bristol), W. Judkins (Coventry), T.M.W. McGown (North of Ireland and Ireland), F.M. Stout (Gloucester and England), B.I. Swannell (Northampton)

Manager: Rev. M.M. Mullineux

Results: Goulborn, Wed 14 Jun: Lions 11, Central Southern 3, Sydney, Sat 17 Jun: Lions 4, New South Wales 3, Sydney, Tue 20 Jun: Lions 8, Metropolitan 5, FIRST TEST: Sydney, Sat 24 Jun: Lions 3, Australia 13, Toowoomba, Wed 28 Jun: Lions 19, Toowoomba 5, Brisbane, Sat 1 Jul: Lions 3, Queensland 11, Bundaberg, Wed 5 Jul: Lions 36, Bundaberg 3, Rockhampton, Sat 8 Jul: Lions 16, Rockhampton 3, Mount Morgan, Tue 11 Jul: Lions 29, Mount Morgan 3, Rockhampton, Sat 15 Jul: Lions 22, Central Queensland 3, Maryborough, Wed 19 Jul: Lions 27, Maryborough 8, SECOND TEST: Brisbane, Sat 22 Jul: Lions 11, Australia 0, Armidale, Tue 25 Jul: Lions 6, New England 4, Newcastle, Thu 27 Jul: Lions 28, Newcastle 0, Sydney, Sat 29 Jul: Lions 11, New South Wales 5, Sydney, Tue 1 Aug: Lions 5, Metropolitan 8, THIRD TEST: Sydney, Sat 5 Aug: Lions 11, Australia 10, Bathurst, Wed 9 Aug: Lions 19, Western Districts 0, FOURTH TEST: Sydney, Sat 12 Aug: Lions 13, Australia 0, Sydney, Tue 15 Aug: Lions 21, Combined Public Schools 3, Melbourne, Sat 19 Aug: Lions 30, Victoria 0

1903 – SOUTH AFRICA

Backs: G.F. Collett (Gloucestershire), I.G. Davidson (North of Ireland and Ireland), J.I. Gillespie (Edinburgh Academicals and Scotland), L.L. Greig (United Services), P.S. Hancock (Richmond), E.M. Harrison (Guy's Hospital, A.E. Hind (Cambridge University), R.M. Neill (Edinburgh Academicals and Scotland), R.T. Skrimshire (Newport and Wales), E.F. Walker (Lennox)

Forwards: D.R. Bedell-Sivright (Cambridge University and Scotland), W.T. Cave (Cambridge University), T.A. Gibson (Cambridge University), J.C. Hosack (Edinburgh Wanderers), M.C. Morrison [capt] (Royal High School FP and Scotland), W.P. Scott (West of Scotland and Scotland), R.S. Smyth (Dublin University and Ireland), F.M. Stout (Richmond), A. Tedford (Malone and Ireland), James Wallace (Wanderers), Joseph Wallace (Wanderers and Ireland)

Manager: J. Hammond

Results: Cape Town, Thu 9 Jul: Lions 7, Western Province Country 13, Cape Town, Sat 11 Jul: Lions 3, Western Province Towns 12, Cape Town, Mon 13 Jul: Lions 4, Western Province 8, Port Elizabeth, Sat 18 Jul: Lions 15, Port Elizabeth 0, Port Elizabeth, Mon 20 Jul: Lions 12, Eastern Province 0, Grahamstown, Wed 22 Jul: Lions 28, Grahamstown 7, King William's Town, Sat 25 Jul: Lions 37, King William's Town 3, East London, Mon 27 Jul: Lions 7, East London 5, Kimberley, Sat 1 Aug: Lions 0, Griqualand West 11, Kimberley, Tue 4 Aug: Lions 6, Griqualand West 8, Johannesburg, Sat 8 Aug: Lions 3, Transvaal 12, Pretoria, Tue 11 Aug: Lions 15, Pretoria 3, Pietermaritzburg, Thu 13 Aug: Lions 15, Pietermaritzburg 0, Durban, Sat 15 Aug: Lions 22, Durban 0, Johannesburg, Wed 19 Aug: Lions 12, Witwatersrand 0, Johannesburg, Sat 22 Aug: Lions 4, Transvaal 14, FIRST TEST: Johannesburg, Wed 26 Aug: Lions 10, South Africa 10, Bloemfontein, Sat 29 Aug: Lions 17, Orange River County 16, Kimberley, Wed 2 Sep: Lions 11, Griqualand West 5, SECOND TEST: Kimberley, Sat 5 Sep: Lions 0, South Africa 0, Cape Town, Thu 10 Sep: Lions 3, Western Province 3, THIRD TEST: Cape Town, Sat 12 Sep: Lions 0, South Africa 8

1904 – AUSTRALIA AND NEW ZEALAND

Backs: P.F. Bush (Cardiff), J.L. Fisher (Yorkshire), R.T. Gabe (Cardiff and Wales), F.C. Hulme (Birkenhead Park and England), W.F. Jowett (Swansea and Wales), W.M. Llewellyn (Cardiff and Wales), P.F. McEvedy (Guy's Hospital), E.T. Morgan (Guy's Hospital and Wales), A.B. O'Brien (Guy's Hospital), C.F. Stanger-Leathes (Northern), T.H. Vile (Newport)

Forwards: D.R. Bedell-Sivright [capt] (Cambridge University and Scotland), T.S. Bevan (Swansea), S.N. Crowther (Lennox), D.D. Dobson (Oxford University and England), R.W. Edwards (Malone and Ireland), A.F. Harding (London Welsh and Wales), B.F. Massey (Yorkshire), C.D. Patterson (Malone), R.J. Rogers (Bath), S.M. Saunders (Guy's Hospital), J.T. Sharland (Streatham), B.I. Swannell (Northampton), D.H. Trail (Guy's Hospital)

Manager: A.B. O'Brien

Results: Sydney, Sat 18 Jun: Lions 27, New South Wales 0, Bathurst, Wed 22 Jun: Lions 21, Western Districts 6, Sydney, Sat 25 Jun: Lions 29, New South Wales 6, Sydney, Wed 29 Jun, Lions 19, Metropolitan 6, FIRST TEST: Sydney, Sat 2 Jul: Lions 17, Australia 0, Newcastle, Wed 6 Jul: Lions 17, Northern Districts 3, Brisbane, Sat 9 Jul: Lions 25, Queensland 5, Brisbane, Wed 13 Jul: Lions 17, Metropolitan 3, Brisbane, Sat 16 Jul: Lions 18, Queensland 7, Toowoomba, Wed 20 Jul: Lions 12, Toowoomba 3, SECOND TEST: Brisbane, Sat 23 Jul: Lions 17, Australia 0, Armidale, Wed 27 Jul: Lions 26, New England 9, THIRD TEST: Sydney, Sat 30 Jul: Lions 16, Australia 0, Christchurch, Sat 6 Aug: Lions 5, Canterbury, South Canterbury and West Coast 3, Dunedin, Wed 10 Aug: Lions 14, Otago-Southland 8, TEST: Wellington, Sat 13 Aug: Lions 3, New Zealand 9, New Plymouth, Wed 17 Aug: Lions 0, Taranaki-Rarganui-Manawatu 0, Auckland, Sat 20 Aug: Lions 0, Auckland 13, Sydney, Wed 31 Aug: Lions 5, New South Wales 0

1908 – NEW ZEALAND AND AUSTRALIA

Backs: F.E. Chapman (Hartlepool Rovers), J. Davey (Redruth and England), J.C.M. Dyke (Coventry and Wales), R.A. Gibbs (Cardiff and Wales), R.B. Griffiths (Newport), E.J. Jackett (Falmouth and England), J.P. 'Ponty' Jones (Pontypool and Wales), J.P. 'Tuan' Jones (Guy's Hospital), H. Laxon (Cambridge University), P.F. McEvedy (Guy's Hospital), W.L. Morgan (London Welsh), H.H. Vassall (Oxford University and England), G.L. Williams (Liverpool), J.L. Williams (Cardiff and Wales)

Forwards: H.A. Archer (Guy's Hospital), R. Dibble (Bridgewater Albion and England), P.J. Down (Bristol), R.K. Green (Neath), A.F. Harding [capt] (London Welsh and Wales), G.R. Hind (Guy's Hospital), F.S. Jackson (Leicester), G.V. Kyrke (Marlborough Nomads), E. Morgan (Swansea), W.L. Oldham (Coventry and England), J.A.S. Ritson (Northern), T.W. Smith (Leicester), L.S. Thomson (Penarth), J.F. Williams (London Welsh and Wales)

Manager: G.H. Harnett

Results: Masterton, Sat 23 May: Lions 17, Wairapapa 3, Wellington, Wed 27 May: Lions 13, Wellington 19, Dunedin, Sat 30 May: Lions 6, Otago 9, Invercargill, Wed 3 Jun: Lions 14, Southland 8, FIRST TEST: Dunedin, Sat 6 Jun: Lions 5, New Zealand 32, Timaru, Wed 10 Jun: Lions 12, South Canterbury 6, Christchurch, Sat 13 Jun: Lions 8, Canterbury 13, Greymouth, Wed 17 Jun: Lions 22, West Coast-Buller 3, Nelson, Sat 20 Jun: Lions 12, Marlborough-Nelson Bays 0, SECOND TEST: Wellington, Sat 27 Jun: Lions 3, New Zealand 3, Napier, Wed 1 Jul: Lions 25, Hawke's Bay 3, Gisborne, Sat 4 Jul: Lions 26, Poverty Bay 0, Palmerston, Wed 8 Jul: Lions 12, Manawatu-Horowhenua 3, Wanganui, Sat 11 Jul: Lions 9, Wanganui 6, New Plymouth, Wed 15 Jul: Lions 0, Taranaki 5, Auckland, Sat 18 Jul: Lions 0, Auckland 11, THIRD TEST: Auckland, Sat 25 Jul: Lions 0, New Zealand 29, Sydney, Wed 5 Aug: Lions 3, New South Wales 0, Sydney, Sat 8 Aug: Lions 8, New South Wales 0, Bathurst, Wed 12 Aug: Lions 10, Western Districts 15, Sydney, Sat 15 Aug: Lions 16, Metropolitan 13, Newcastle, Wed 19 Aug: Lions 32, Newcastle 0, Sydney, Sat 22 Aug: Lions 3, New South Wales 6, Brisbane, Wed 26 Aug: Lions 20, Queensland 3, Brisbane, Sat 29 Aug: Lions 11, Queensland 8, Brisbane, Wed 2 Sep: Lions 26, Metropolitan 3

1910 – SOUTH AFRICA

Backs: A.M. Baker (Newport and Wales), A.R. Foster (Derry and Ireland), N.F. Humphries (Tynedale), G.A.M. Isherwood (Sale), J.P. Jones (Newport and Wales), A.N. McClinton (North of Ireland and Ireland), A. Melville (Newport), E. Milroy (Watsonians and Scotland), M.E. Neale (Bristol), R.C.S. Plummer (Newport), J.A. Spoors (Bristol), C.G. Timms (Edinburgh University), S.H. Williams (Newport), K.B. Wood (Leicester)

Forwards: W.J. Ashby (Queen's College, Cork), E. O'D Crean (Liverpool), F.G. Handford (Manchester and England), H. Jarman (Newport and Wales), C.H. Pillman (Blackheath and England), O.J.S. Piper (Cork Constitution and Ireland), J. Reid-Kerr (Greenock Wanderers and Scotland), T.J. Richards (Bristol), W.A. Robertson (Edinburgh University), D.F. Smith (Richmond and England), T. Smythe [capt] (Malone and Ireland), L.M. Speirs (Watsonians and Scotland), R. Stevenson (St Andrews University and Scotland), W. Tyrrell (Queen's University Belfast and Ireland), P.D. Waller (Newport and Wales), J. Webb (Abertillery and Wales)

Managers: W. Cail and W.E. Rees

Results: Mossel Bay, Sat 11 Jun: Lions 14, South Western Districts 4, Cape Town, Wed 15 Jun: Lions 9, Western Province Country 3, Cape Town, Sat 18 Jun: Lions 11, Western Provinces Colleges 3, Cape Town, Wed 22 Jun: Lions 11, Western Province Towns 11, Cape Town, Sat 25 Jun: Lions 5, Western Province 3, Kimberley, Wed 29 Jun: Lions 0, Griqualand West 8, Johannesburg, Sat 2 Jul: Lions 8, Transvaal 27, Pretoria, Tue 5 Jul: Lions 17, Pretoria 0, Johannesburg, Thu 7 Jul: Lions 45, Transvaal Country Districts 4, Johannesburg, Sat 9 Jul: Lions 6, Transvaal 13, Pietermaritzburg, Wed 13 Jul: Lions 18, Natal 16, Durban, Sat 16 Jul: Lions 19, Natal 13, Bloemfontein, Wed 20 Jul: Lions 12, Orange River County 9, Kimberley, Sat 23 Jul: Lions 3, Griqualand West 9, Kimberley, Wed 27 Jul: Lions 0, Cape Colony 19, Bulawayo, Sat 30 Jul: Lions 24, Southern Rhodesia 11, FIRST TEST: Johannesburg, Sat 6 Aug: Lions 10, South Africa 14, Burgersdrop, Wed 10 Aug: Lions 8, North-East Districts 8, East London, Sat 13 Aug: Lions 30, Border Bulldogs 10, King William's Town, Wed 17 Aug: Lions 13, Border Bulldogs 13, Port Elizabeth, Sat 20 Aug: Lions 14, Eastern Province 6, SECOND TEST: Port Elizabeth, Sat 27 Aug: Lions 8, South Africa 3, THIRD TEST: Cape Town, Fri 2 Sep: Lions 5, South Africa 21, Cape Town, Tue 6 Sep: Lions 0, Western Province 8

1924 – SOUTH AFRICA

Backs: J.H. Bordass (Cambridge University), W. Cunningham (Lansdowne and Ireland), H.J. Davies (Newport and Wales), D. Drysdale (Heriot's FP and Scotland), W.S. Gainsford (Bart's Hospital), V.M. Griffiths (Newport and Wales), S.W. Harris (Blackheath and England), T.E. Holliday (Aspatria and England), R.M. Kinnear (Heriot's FP), R.B. Maxwell (Birkenhead Park), W. Rowe Harding (Swansea and Wales), I.S. Smith (Oxford University and Scotland), H. Waddell (Glasgow Academicals and Scotland), W. Wallace (Percy Park), H. Whitley (Northern), A.T. Young (Cambridge University and England)

Forwards: A.F. Blakiston (Blackheath and England), M.J. Bradley (Dolphin and Ireland), T.N. Brand (North of Ireland), J.D. Clinch (Dublin University and Ireland), R. Cove-Smith [capt] (Old Merchant Taylors and England), D.S. Davies (Hawick and Scotland), R.G. Henderson (Durham University and Scotland), K.G.P. Hendrie (Edinburgh University and Scotland), R.A. Howie (Edinburgh University and Scotland), N. Macpherson (Newport and Scotland), J. McVicker (Belfast College and Ireland), D. Marsden-Jones (London Welsh and Wales), W.J. Roche (Newport and Ireland), A. Ross (Kilmarnock and Scotland), A.T. Voyce (Gloucester and England)

Manager: H. Packer

Results: Cape Town, Sat 12 Jul: Lions 6, Western Province Town-Country 7, Cape Town, Tue 15 Jul: Lions 9, Western Province Universities 8, Kimberley, Sat 19 Jul: Lions 26, Griqualand West 0, Salisbury, Thu 24 Jul: Lions 16, Rhodesia 3, Potchefstroom, Wed 30 Jul: Lions 8, Western Transvaal 7, Johannesburg, Sat 2 Aug: Lions 12, Transvaal 12, Kroonstad, Wed 6 Aug: Lions 0, Orange Free State Country 6, Bloemfontein, Sat 9 Aug: Lions 3, Orange Free State 6, Pietermaritzburg, Wed 13 Aug: Lions 3, Natal 3, FIRST TEST: Durban, Sat 16 Aug: Lions 3, South Africa 7, Johannesburg, Wed 20 Aug: Lions 6, Witwatersrand 10, SECOND TEST: Johannesburg, Sat 23 Aug: Lions 0, South Africa 17, Pretoria, Wed 27 Aug: Lions 0, Pretoria 6, Kimberley, Sat 30 Aug: Lions 13, Cape Province 3, Aliwal North, Wed 3 Sep: Lions 20, North-East Districts 12, East London, Sat 6 Sep: Lions 12, Border Bulldogs 3, Port Elizabeth, Wed 10 Sep: Lions 6, Eastern Province 14, THIRD TEST: Port Elizabeth, Sat 13 Sep: Lions 3, South Africa 3, Oudtshoorn, Tue 16 Sep: Lions 12, South Western Districts 6, FOURTH TEST: Cape Town, Sat 20 Sep: Lions 9, South Africa 16, Cape Town, Thu 25 Sep: Lions 8, Western Province 6

1930 – NEW ZEALAND AND AUSTRALIA

Backs: C.D. Aarvold (Cambridge University and England), J.A. Bassett (Penarth and Wales), H.M. Bowcott (Cambridge University and Wales), G. Bonner (Bradford), R Jennings (Redruth), T. Jones-Davies (London Welsh and Wales), T.C. Knowles (Birkenhead Park), J.C. Morley (Newport and Wales), P.F. Murray (Wanderers and Ireland), A.L. Novis (Blackheath and England), H. Poole (Cardiff), J.S.R. Reeve (Harlequins and England), W. Sobey (Old Millhillians and England), R.S. Spong (Old Millhillians and England)

Forwards: G.R. Beamish (Leicester and Ireland), B.H. Black (Oxford University and England), M.J. Dunne (Lansdowne and Ireland), J.L. Farrell (Bective Rangers and Ireland), J. McD. Hodgson (Northern), H.C.S. Jones (Manchester), I.E. Jones (Llanelli and Wales), D.A. Kendrew (Leicester and England), S.A. Martindale (Kendal and England), H. O'H. O'Neill (Queen's University Belfast and Ireland), D. Parker (Swansea and Wales), F.D. Prentice [capt] (Leicester and England), H. Rew (Blackheath and England), W.B. Welsh (Hawick and Scotland), H. Wilkinson (Halifax and England)

Manager: James Baxter

Results: Wanganui, Wed 21 May: Lions 19, Wanganui 3, New Plymouth, Sat 24 May: Lions 23, Taranaki 7, Palmerston North, Wed 28 May: Lions 34, Manawhenua 8, Masterton, Sat 31 May: Lions 19, Wairarapa-Bush 6, Wellington, Tue 3 Jun: Lions 8, Wellington 12, Christchurch, Sat 7 Jun: Lions 8, Canterbury 14, Greymouth, Wed 11 Jun: Lions 34, West Coast-Buller 11, Dunedin, Sat 14 Jun: Lions 33, Otago 9, FIRST TEST: Dunedin, Sat 21 Jun: Lions 6, New Zealand 3, Invercargill, Wed 25 Jun: Lions 9, Southland 3, Timaru, Sat 28 Jun: Lions 16, Ashburton, South Canterbury and North Otago 9, SECOND TEST: Christchurch, Sat 5 Jul: Lions 10, New Zealand 13, Wellington, Wed 9 Jul: Lions 19, New Zealand Maori 13, Napier, Sat 12 Jul: Lions 14, Hawke's Bay 3, Gisborne, Wed 16 Jul: Lions 25, Poverty Bay-East Coast 11, Auckland, Sat 19 Jul: Lions 6, Auckland 19, THIRD TEST: Auckland, Sat 26 Jul: Lions 10, New Zealand 15, Whangarei, Wed 30 Jul: Lions 38, North Auckland 5, Hamilton, Sat 2 Aug: Lions 40, Waikato, King Country and Thames Valley 16, FOURTH TEST: Wellington, Sat 9 Aug: Lions 8, New Zealand 22, Blenheim, Tue 12 Aug: Lions 41, Marlborough-Nelson Bays 3, Sydney, Sat 23 Aug: Lions 29, New South Wales 10, TEST: Sydney, Sat 30 Aug: Lions 5, Australia 6, Brisbane, Wed 3 Sep: Lions 26, Queensland 16, Sydney, Wed 10 Sep: Lions 3, New South Wales 28, Melbourne, Sat 13 Sep: Lions 41, Victoria 36, Perth, Mon 22 Sep: Lions 71, Western Australia 3 (unofficial fixture)

1938 – SOUTH AFRICA

Backs: C.V. Boyle (Dublin University and Ireland), W.H. Clement (Llanelli and Wales), G.E. Cromey (Queen's University Belfast and Ireland), J.L. Giles (Coventry and England), C.F. Grieve (Oxford University and Scotland), V.G.J. Jenkins (London Welsh and Wales), E.L. Jones (Llanelli), R. Leyland (Waterloo and England), H.R. McKibbin (Queen's University Belfast and Ireland), D.J. Macrae (St Andrews University and Scotland), G.J. Morgan (Clontarf and Ireland), B.E. Nicholson (Harlequins and England), F.J. Reynolds (Army and England), H. Tanner (Swansea and Wales), E.J. Unwin (Rosslyn Park and England)

Forwards: R. Alexander (North of Ireland and Ireland), S.R. Couchman (Old Cranleighans), G.T. Dancer (Bedford), P.L. Duff (Glasgow Academicals and Scotland), C.R.A. Graves (Wanderers and Ireland), W.G. Howard (Old Birkonians), R.B. Mayne (Queen's University Belfast and Ireland), M.E. Morgan (Swansea and Wales), A.G. Purchas (Coventry), A.R. Taylor (Cross Keys and Wales), W.H. Travers (Newport and Wales), S. Walker [capt] (Instonians and Ireland), J.A. Waters (Selkirk and Scotland), I. Williams (Cardiff)

Manager: B.C. Hartley

Assistant manager: H.A. Haig-Smith

Results: East London, Sat 11 Jun: Lions 11, Border Bulldogs 8, Kimberley, Wed 15 Jun: Lions 22, Griqualand West 9, Cape Town, Sat 18 Jun: Lions 8, Western Province Town and Country 11, Oudtshoorn, Wed 22 Jun: Lions 19, South Western Districts 10, Cape Town, Sat 25 Jun: Lions 11, Western Province 21, Potchefstroom, Wed 29 Jun: Lions 26, Western 9, Bloemfontein, Sat 2 Jul: Lions 21, Orange Free State 6, Kroonstad, Wed 6 Jul: Lions 18, Orange Free State (Country) 3, Johannesburg, Sat 9 Jul: Lions 9, Transvaal 16, Pretoria, Wed 13 Jul: Lions 20, North East Transvaal 12, Kimberley Sat 16 Jul: Lions 10, Cape Province 3, Salisbury, Wed 20 Jul: Lions 25, Rhodesia 11, Bulawayo, Sat 23 Jul: Lions 45, Rhodesia 11, Johannesburg, Sat 30 Jul: Lions 17, Transvaal 9, FIRST TEST: Johannesburg, Sat 6 Aug: Lions 12, South Africa 26, Durban, Sat 13 Aug: Lions 8, Northern Province 26, Pietermaritzburg, Wed 17 Aug: Lions 15, Natal 11, East London, Sat 20 Aug: Lions 19, Border Bulldogs 11, Burgersdrop, Wed 24 Aug: Lions 42, North-East Districts 3, Port Elizabeth, Sat 27 Aug: Lions 6, Eastern Province 5, SECOND TEST: Port Elizabeth, Sat 3 Sep: Lions 3, South Africa 12, THIRD TEST: Cape Town, Sat 10 Sep: Lions 21, South Africa 16, Cape Town, Sat 17 Sep: Lions 19, Western Province Universities 16, Cape Town, Wed 21 Sep: Lions 7, Western Province Country 12

1950 – NEW ZEALAND AND AUSTRALIA

Backs: A.W. Black (Edinburgh University and Scotland), W.B. Cleaver (Cardiff and Wales), N.J. Henderson (Queen's University Belfast and Ireland), B.L. Jones (Llanelli and Wales), K.J. Jones (Newport and Wales), J.W. Kyle (Queen's University Belfast and Ireland), M.F. Lane (University College Cork and Ireland), R. Macdonald (Edinburgh University and Scotland), J. Matthews (Cardiff and Wales), G.W. Norton (Bective Rangers and Ireland), I. Preece (Coventry and England), G. Rimmer (Waterloo and England), D.W.C. Smith (London Scottish and Scotland), M.C. Thomas (Newport and Wales), B.L. Williams (Cardiff and Wales), W.R. Willis (Cardiff and Wales)

Forwards: G.M. Budgc (Edinburgh Wanderers and Scotland), T. Clifford (Munster and Ireland), C. Davies (Cardiff and Wales), D.M. Davies (Somerset Police and Wales), R.T. Evans (Newport and Wales), D.J. Hayward (Newbridge and Wales), E.R. John (Neath and Wales), P.W. Kininmonth (Richmond and Scotland), J.S. McCarthy (Dolphin and Ireland), J.W. McKay (Queen's University Belfast and Ireland), K.D. Mullen [capt] (Old Belvedere and Ireland), J.E. Nelson (Malone and Ireland), V.G. Roberts (Penryn and England), J.D. Robins (Birkenhead Park and Wales), J.R.G. Stephens (Neath and Wales)

Manager: L.B. Osborne

Results: Nelson, Wed 10 May: Lions 24, Marlborough, Nelson Bay, Golden Bay and Motueka 3, Westport, Sat 13 May: Lions 24, Buller 9, Greymouth, Tue 16 May: Lions 32, West Coast 3, Dunedin, Sat 20 May: Lions 9, Otago 23, Invercargill, Tue 23 May: Lions 0, Southland 11, FIRST TEST: Dunedin, Sat 27 May: Lions 9, New Zealand 9, Timaru, Wed 31 May: Lions 27, South Canterbury 3, Christchurch, Sat 3 Jun: Lions 16, Canterbury 5, Ashburton, Tue 6 Jun: Lions 29, Ashburton County-North Otago 6, SECOND TEST: Christchurch, Sat 10 Jun: Lions 0, New Zealand 8, Masterton, Wed 14 Jun: Lions 27, Wairarapa-Bush 13, Napier, Sat 17 Jun: Lions 20, Hawke's Bay 0, Gisborne, Wed 21 Jun: Lions 27, East Coast, Poverty Bay and Bay of Plenty 3, Wellington, Sat 24 Jun: Lions 12, Wellington 6, THIRD TEST: Wellington, Sat 1 Jul: Lions 3, New Zealand 6, Wanganui, Wed 5 Jul: Lions 31, Wanganui 3, New Plymouth, Sat 8 Jul: Lions 25, Taranaki 3, Palmerston North, Wed 12 Jul: Lions 13, Manawatu-Horowhenua 8, Hamilton, Sat 15 Jul: Lions 30, Waikato, King Country and Thames Valley 0, Whangarei, Wed 19 Jul: Lions 8, North Auckland 6, Auckland, Sat 22 Jul: Lions 32, Auckland 0, FOURTH TEST: Auckland, Sat 29 Jul: Lions 8, New Zealand 11, Wellington, Wed 2 Aug: Lions 14, New Zealand Maori 9, Canberra, Wed 9 Aug: Lions 47, New South Wales Country 3, Sydney, Sat 12 Aug: Lions 22, New South Wales 6, FIRST TEST: Brisbane, Sat 19 Aug: Lions 19, Australia 6, SECOND TEST: Sydney, Sat 26 Aug: Lions 24, Australia 3, Sydney, Wed 30 Aug: Lions 26, Metropolitan 17, Newcastle, Mon 4 Sep: Lions 12, New South Wales 17, Colombo, Wed 16 Sep: Lions 44, Ceylon (Sri Lanka) 6 (unofficial fixture)

1955 – SOUTH AFRICA

Backs: D.G.S. Baker (Old Merchant Taylor and England), J. Butterfield (Northampton and England), A. Cameron (Glasgow HSFP and Scotland), W.P.C. Davies (Harlequins and England), G.M. Griffiths (Cardiff and Wales), R.E.G. Jeeps (Northampton), T. Lloyd (Maesteg and Wales), C.I. Morgan (Cardiff and Wales), H.T. Morris (Cardiff and Wales), A.J.F. O'Reilly (Old Belvedere and Ireland), A.C. Pedlow (Queen's University Belfast and Ireland), J.P. Quinn (New Brighton and England), A.R. Smith (Cambridge University and Scotland), F.D. Sykes (Northampton and England), A.G. Thomas (Llanelli and Wales), J.E. Williams (Old Millhillians and England)

Forwards: T. Elliot (Gala and Scotland), J.T. Greenwood (Dunfermline and Scotland), R. Higgins (Liverpool and England), H.F. McLeod (Hawick and Scotland), B.V. Meredith (Newport and Wales), C.C. Meredith (Neath and Wales), E.T.S. Michie (Aberdeen University and Scotland), T.E. Reid (Garryowen and Ireland), R.J. Robins (Pontypridd and Wales), R. Roe (Lansdowne and Ireland), R.C.C. Thomas (Swansea and Wales), R.H. Thompson [capt] (Instonians and Ireland), R.H. Williams (Llanelli and Wales), W.O.G. Williams (Swansea and Wales), D.S. Wilson (Metropolitan Police and England)

Manager: J.A.E. Siggins

Assistant manager: D.E. Davies

Results: Potchefstroom, Wed 22 Jun: Lions 6, Western Transvaal 9, Kimberley, Sat 25 Jun: Lions 24, Griqualand West 14, Johannesburg, Wed 29 Jun: Lions 32, Transvaal Universities 6, Kroonstad, Sat 2 Jul: Lions 31, Orange Free State 3, Windhoek, Tue 5 Jul: Lions 9, South West Africa 0, Cape Town, Sat 9 Jul: Lions 11, Western Province 3, Oudtshoorn, Wed 13 Jul: Lions 22, South Western Districts 3, Port Elizabeth, Sat 16 Jul: Lions 0, Eastern Province 20, Aliwal North, Wed 20 Jul: Lions 34, North-East Districts 6, Johannesburg, Sat 23 Jul: Lions 36, Transvaal 13, Kitwe, Wed 27 Jul: Lions 27, Rhodesia 14, Salisbury, Sat 30 Jul: Lions 16, Rhodesia 12, FIRST TEST: Johannesburg, Sat 6 Aug: Lions 23, South Africa 22, Durban, Wed 10 Aug: Lions 21, Central Universities 14, Wellington, Sat 13 Aug: Lions 11, Boland 0, Cape Town, Tue 16 Aug: Lions 20, Western Province 17, SECOND TEST: Cape Town, Sat 20 Aug: Lions 9, South Africa 25, Springs, Wed 24 Aug: Lions 17, Eastern Transvaal 17, Pretoria, Sat 27 Aug: Lions 14, Northern Transvaal 11, THIRD TEST: Pretoria, Sat 3 Sep: Lions 9, South Africa 6, Durban, Sat 10 Sep: Lions 11, Natal 8, Bloemfontein, Wed 14 Sep: Lions 15, Junior Springboks 12, East London, Sat 17 Sep: Lions 12, Border Bulldogs 14, FOURTH TEST: Port Elizabeth, Sat 24 Sep: Lions 8, South Africa 22, Nairobi, Kenya, Wed 28 Sep: Lions 39, East Africa 12

1959 – AUSTRALIA, NEW ZEALAND and CANADA

Backs: N.H. Brophy (University College Dublin and Ireland), J. Butterfield (Northampton and England), S. Coughtrie (Edinburgh Academicals and Scotland), T.J. Davies (Llanelli and Wales), M.A.F. English (Bohemians and Ireland), D. Hewitt (Queen's University Belfast and Ireland), J.P. Horrocks-Taylor (Leicester and England), P.B. Jackson (Coventry and England), R.E.G. Jeeps (Northampton and England), A.A. Mulligan (Wanderers and Ireland), A.J.F. O'Reilly (Old Belvedere and Ireland), W.M. Patterson (Sale), M.J. Price (Pontypool and Wales), A.B.W. Risman (Manchester and England), K.J.F. Scotland (Cambridge University and Scotland), M.C. Thomas (Newport and Wales), G.H. Waddell (Cambridge University and Scotland), J.R.C. Young (Harlequins and England)

Forwards: A. Ashcroft (Waterloo and England), A.R. Dawson [capt] (Wanderers and Ireland), W.R. Evans (Cardiff and Wales), J. Faull (Swansea and Wales), H.F. McLeod (Hawick and Scotland), R.W.D. Marques (Harlequins and England), B.V. Meredith (Newport and Wales), S. Millar (Ballymena and Ireland), H.J. Morgan (Abertillery and Wales), W.A. Mulcahy (University College Dublin and Ireland), N.A.A. Murphy (Cork Constitution and Ireland), T.R. Prosser (Pontypool and Wales), G.K. Smith (Kelso and Scotland), R.H. Williams (Llanelli and Wales), B.G.M. Wood (Garryowen and Ireland)

Manager: A.W. Wilson

Assistant manager: O.B. Glasgow

Results: Melbourne, Sat 23 May: Lions 53, Victoria 18, Sydney, Sat 30 May: Lions 14, New South Wales 18, Brisbane, Tue 2 Jun: Lions 39, Queensland 11, FIRST TEST: Brisbane, Sat 6 Jun: Lions 17, Australia 6, Tamworth, Tue 9 Jun: Lions 27, New South Wales Country 14, SECOND TEST: Sydney, Sat 13 Jun: Lions 24, Australia 3, Napier, Sat 20 Jun: Lions 52, Hawke's Bay 12, Gisborne, Wed 24 Jun: Lions 23, Poverty Bay-East Coast 14, Auckland, Sat 27 Jun: Lions 15, Auckland 10, Christchurch, Wed 1 Jul: Lions 25, New Zealand Universities 13, Dunedin, Sat 4 Jul: Lions 8, Otago 26, Timaru, Wed 8 Jul: Lions 21, South and Mid Canterbury and North Otago 11, Invercargill, Sat 11 Jul: Lions 11, Southland 6, FIRST TEST: Dunedin, Sat 18 Jul: Lions 17, New Zealand 18, Greymouth, Wed 22 Jul: Lions 58, West Coast-Buller 3, Christchurch, Sat 25 Jul: Lions 20, Canterbury 14, Blenheim, Wed 29 Jul: Lions 64, Marlborough-Nelson Bays 5, Wellington, Sat 1 Aug: Lions 21, Wellington 6, Wanganui, Wed 5 Aug: Lions 9, Wanganui 6, New Plymouth, Sat 8 Aug: Lions 15, Taranaki 3, Palmerston North, Tue 11 Aug: Lions 26, Manawatu-Horowhenua 6, SECOND TEST: Wellington, Sat 15 Aug: Lions 8, New Zealand 11, Taumarunui, Wed 19 Aug: Lions 25, King Country-Counties 5, Hamilton, Sat 22 Aug: Lions 14, Waikato 0, Masterton, Tue 25 Aug: Lions 37, Wairarapa-Bush 11, THIRD TEST: Christchurch, Sat 29 Aug: Lions 8, New Zealand 22, Wellington, Wed 2 Sep: Lions 29, New Zealand Juniors 9, Auckland, Sat 5 Sep: Lions 12, New Zealand Maori 6, Rotorua, Wed 9 Sep: Lions 26, Bay Of Plenty-Thames Valley 24, Whangarei, Sat 12 Sep: Lions 35, North Auckland 13, FOURTH TEST: Auckland, Sat 19 Sep: Lions 9, New Zealand 6, Vancouver, Sat 26 Sep: Lions 16, British Columbia 11, Toronto, Tue 29 Sep: Lions 70, Eastern Canada 6

1962 – SOUTH AFRICA

Backs: D.I.E. Bebb (Swansea and Wales), N.H. Brophy (University College Dublin and Ireland), H.J.C. Brown (Blackheath and RAF), R.C. Cowan (Selkirk and Scotland), J.M. Dee (Hartlepool Rovers and England), D. Hewitt (Queen's University Belfast and Ireland), W.R. Hunter (Church of Ireland Young Mens Society and Ireland), R.E.G. Jeeps (Northampton and England), T.J. Kiernan (University College Cork and Ireland), D.K. Jones (Llanelli and Wales), A. O'Connor (Aberavon and Wales), R.A.W. Sharp (Oxford University and England), A.R. Smith [capt] (Edinburgh Wanderers and Scotland), G.H. Waddell (London Scottish and Scotland), M.P. Weston (Durham City and England), J.G. Wilcox (Oxford University and England)

Forwards: M.J. Campbell-Lamerton (Army and Halifax and Scotland), G.D. Davidge (Newport and Wales), J. Douglas (Stewart's College FP and Scotland), H.O. Godwin (Coventry and England), S.A.M. Hodgson (Durham City and England), K.D. Jones (Cardiff and Wales), W.J. McBride (Ballymena and Ireland), B.V. Meredith (Newport and Wales), S. Millar (Ballymena and Ireland), H.J. Morgan (Abertillery and Wales), W.A. Mulcahy (Bohemians and Ireland, D. Nash (Ebbw Vale and Wales), A.E.I. Pask (Abertillery and Wales), D.P. Rogers (Bedford and England), D.M.D. Rollo (Howe of Fife and Scotland), K.A. Rowlands (Cardiff and Wales), T.P. Wright (Blackheath and England)

Manager: D.B. Vaughan

Assistant manager: H.R. McKibbin

Results: Bulawayo, Sat 26 May: Lions 38, Rhodesia 9, Kimberley, Wed 30 May: Lions 8, Griqualand West 8, Potchefstroom, Sat 2 Jun: Lions 11, Western Transvaal 6, Cape Town, Wed 6 Jun: Lions 14, Western Province Universities 11, Wellington, Sat 9 Jun: Lions 25, Boland 8, Windhoek, Tue 12 Jun: Lions 14, South West Africa 6, Pretoria, Sat 16 Jun: Lions 6, Northern Transvaal 14, FIRST TEST: Johannesburg, Sat 23 Jun: Lions 3, South Africa 3, Durban, Wed 27 Jun: Lions 13, Natal 3, Port Elizabeth, Sat 30 Jun: Lions 21, Eastern Province 6, Bloemfontein, Wed 4 Jul: Lions 14, Orange Free State 14, Pretoria, Sat 7 Jul: Lions 16, Junior Springboks 11, Potchefstroom, Wed 11 Jul: Lions 20, Combined Services 6, Cape Town, Sat 14 Jul: Lions 21, Western Province 13, Oudtshoorn, Tue 17 Jul: Lions 11, South Western Districts 3, SECOND TEST: Durban, Sat 21 Jul: Lions 0, South Africa 3, Springs, Wed 25 Jul: Lions 6, Northern Universities 6, Johannesburg, Sat 28 Jul: Lions 24, Transvaal 3, THIRD TEST: Cape Town, Sat 4 Aug: Lions 3, South Africa 8, Burgersdrop, Wed 8 Aug: Lions 34, North-East Districts 8, East London, Sat 11 Aug: Lions 5, Border Bulldogs 0, Port Elizabeth, Wed 15 Aug: Lions 14, Central Universities 6, Springs, Sat 18 Aug: Lions 16, Eastern Transvaal 19, FOURTH TEST: Bloemfontein, Sat 25 Aug: Lions 14, South Africa 34, Nairobi, Tue 28 Aug: Lions 50, East Africa 0

1966 – AUSTRALIA, NEW ZEALAND and CANADA

Backs: D.I.E. Bebb (Swansea and Wales), F.B.K. Bresnihan (Wanderers and Ireland), C.M.H. Gibson (Cambridge University and Ireland), A.J.W. Hinshelwood (London Scottish and Scotland), D.K. Jones (Cardiff and Wales), A.R. Lewis (Newport and Wales), C.W. McFadyean (Moseley and England), T.G. Price (Llanelli and Wales), D. Rutherford (Gloucester and England), K.F. Savage (Northampton and England), J.C. Walsh (Sunday's Well and Ireland), D. Watkins (Newport and Wales), S.J. Watkins (Newport and Wales), M.P. Weston (Durham City and England), S. Wilson (London Scottish and Scotland), R.M. Young (Queen's University Belfast and Ireland)

Forwards: M.J. Campbell-Lamerton [capt] (London Scottish and Scotland), D. Grant (Hawick and Scotland), K.W. Kennedy (Church of Ireland Young Mens Society and Ireland), F.A.L. Laidlaw (Melrose and Scotland), R.A. Lamont (Instonians and Ireland), W.J. McBride (Ballymena and Ireland), R.J. McLoughlin (Gosforth and Ireland), N.A.A. Murphy (Cork Constitution and Ireland), C.H. Norris (Cardiff and Wales), A.E.I. Pask (Abertillery and Wales), D.L. Powell (Northampton and England), B. Price (Newport and Wales), G.J. Prothero (Bridgend and Wales), J.W. Telfer (Melrose and Scotland), W.D. Thomas (Llanelli), D. Williams (Ebbw Vale and Wales)

Manager: D.J. O'Brien

Coach: J.D. Robins

Results: Perth, Sat 7 May: Lions 60, Western Australia 3, Adelaide, Wed 11 May: Lions 38, South Australia 11, Melbourne, Sat 14 May: Lions 24, Victoria 14, Canberra, Wed 18 May: Lions 6, New South Wales Country 3, Sydney, Sat 21 May: Lions 6, New South Wales 6, FIRST TEST: Sydney, Sat 28 May: Lions 11, Australia 8, Brisbane, Tue 31 May: Lions 26, Queensland 3, SECOND TEST Brisbane Sat 4 Jun: Lions 31, Australia 0, Invercargill, Sat 11 Jun: Lions 8, Southland 14, Timaru, Wed 15 Jun: Lions 20, South and Mid Canterbury and North Otago 12, Dunedin, Sat 18 Jun: Lions 9, Otago 17, Christchurch, Wed 22 Jun: Lions 24, New Zealand Universities 11, Wellington, Sat 25 Jun: Lions 6, Wellington 20, Nelson, Wed 29 Jun: Lions 22, Marlborough-Nelson Bays 14, New Plymouth, Sat 2 Jul: Lions 12, Taranaki 9, Rotorua, Wed 6 Jul: Lions 6, Bay of Plenty 6, Whangarei, Sat 9 Jul: Lions 6, North Auckland 3, FIRST TEST: Dunedin, Sat 16 Jul: Lions 3, New Zealand 20, Westport, Wed 20 Jul: Lions 25, West Coast-Buller 6, Christchurch, Sat 23 Jul: Lions 8, Canterbury 6, Palmerston North, Wed 27 Jul: Lions 17, Manawatu-Horowhenua 8, Auckland, Sat 30 Jul: Lions 12, Auckland 6, Masterton, Tue 2 Aug: Lions 9, Wairarapa-Bush 6, SECOND TEST: Wellington, Sat 6 Aug: Lions 12, New Zealand 16, Wanganui, Wed 10 Aug: Lions 6, Wanganui-King Country 12, Auckland, Sat 13 Aug: Lions 16, Maoris 14 , Gisborne, Wed 17 Aug: Lions 9, Poverty Bay-East Coast 6, Napier, Sat 20 Aug: Lions 11, Hawke's Bay 11, THIRD TEST: Christchurch, Sat 27 Aug: Lions 6, New Zealand 19, Wellington, Wed 31 Aug: Lions 9, New Zealand Juniors 3, Hamilton, Sat 3 Sep: Lions 20, Waikato 9, Papakura, Tue 6 Sep: Lions 13, Counties-Thames Valley 9, FOURTH TEST: Auckland, Sat 10 Sep: Lions 11, New Zealand 24, Vancouver, Wed 14 Sep: Lions 3, British Columbia 8, Toronto, Sat 17 Sep: Lions 19, Canada 8

1968 – SOUTH AFRICA

Backs: F.P.K. Bresnihan (University College Dublin and Ireland), G.C. Connell (London Scottish and Scotland), T.G.R. Davies (Cardiff and Wales), G.O. Edwards (Cardiff and Wales), C.M.H. Gibson (North of Ireland and Ireland), R. Hiller (Harlequins and England), A.J.W. Hinshelwood (London Scottish and Scotland), K.S. Jarrett (Newport and Wales), B. John (Cardiff and Wales), W.K. Jones (Cardiff and Wales), T.J. Kiernan [capt] (Cork Constitution and Ireland), W.H. Raybould (London Welsh and Wales), M.C.R. Richards (Cardiff and Wales), K.F. Savage (Northampton and England), J.W.C. Turner (Gala and Scotland), R.M. Young (Queen's University Belfast and Ireland)

Forwards: R.J. Arneil (Edinburgh Academicals and Scotland), M.J. Coulman (Moseley and England), M.G. Doyle (Blackrock College and Ireland), K.G. Goodall (City of Derry and Ireland), A.L. Horton (Blackheath and England), P.J. Larter (Northampton and England), W.J. McBride (Ballymena and Ireland), S. Millar (Ballymena and Ireland), J.P. O'Shea (Cardiff and Wales), J.V. Pullin (Bristol and England), P.K. Stagg (Sale and Scotland), J. Taylor (London Welsh and Wales), R.B. Taylor (Northampton and England), J.W. Telfer (Melrose and Scotland), W.D. Thomas (Llanelli and Wales), B.R. West (Northampton and England), J. Young (Harrogate and Wales)

Manager: D.K. Brooks

Coach: A.R. Dawson

Results: Potchefstroom, Sat 18 May: Lions 20, Western Transvaal 20, Cape Town, Wed 22 May: Lions 10, Western Province 6, Mossel Bay, Sat 25 May: Lions 24, South Western Districts 6, Port Elizabeth, Wed 29 May: Lions 23, Eastern Province 14, Durban, Sat 1 Jun: Lions 17, Natal 5, Salisbury, Mon 3 Jun: Lions 32, Rhodesia 6, FIRST TEST: Pretoria, Sat 8 Jun: Lions 20, South Africa 25, Upington, Wed 12 Jun: Lions 25, North-West Cape 5, Windhoek, Sat 15 Jun: Lions 23, South West Africa 0, Johannesburg, Tue 18 Jun: Lions 6, Transvaal 14, SECOND TEST: Port Elizabeth, Sat 22 Jun: Lions 6, South Africa 6, Springs, Sat 29 Jun: Lions 37, Eastern Transvaal 9, Pretoria, Wed 3 Jul: Lions 22, Northern Transvaal 19, Kimberley, Sat 6 Jul: Lions 11, Griqualand West 3, Wellington, Mon 8 Jul: Lions 14, Boland 0, THIRD TEST: Cape Town, Sat 13 Jul: Lions 6, South Africa 11, East London, Wed 17 Jul: Lions 26, Border Bulldogs 6, Bloemfontein, Sat 20 Jul: Lions 9, Orange Free State 3, Cradock, Mon 22 Jul: Lions 40, North-East Districts 12, FOURTH TEST: Johannesburg, Sat 27 Jul: Lions 6, South Africa 19

1971 – NEW ZEALAND AND AUSTRALIA

Backs: J.C. Bevan (Cardiff College of Education and Wales), A.G. Biggar (London Scottish and Scotland), T.G.R. Davies (London Welsh and Wales), S.J. Dawes [capt] (London Welsh and Wales), D.J. Duckham (Coventry and England), G.O. Edwards (Cardiff and Wales), C.M.H. Gibson (North of Ireland and Ireland), R. Hiller (Harlequins and England), R. Hopkins (Maesteg and Wales), B. John (Cardiff and Wales), A.J.L. Lewis (Ebbw Vale and Wales), C.W.W. Rea (Headingley and Scotland), J.S. Spencer (Headingley and England), J.P.R. Williams (Bridgend and Wales)

Forwards: R.J. Arneill (Leicester and Scotland), G.L. Brown (West of Scotland and Scotland), A.B. Carmichael (West of Scotland and Scotland), T.M. Davies (London Welsh and Wales), P.J. Dixon (Harlequins and England), T.G. Evans (London Welsh and Wales), M.L. Hipwell (Terenure College and Ireland), F.A.L. Laidlaw (Melrose and Scotland), J.F. Lynch (St Mary's College and Ireland), W.J. McBride (Ballymena and Ireland), I. McLauchlan (Jordanhill College and Scotland), R.J. McLoughlin (Blackrock College and Ireland), J.V. Pullin (Bristol and England), D.L. Quinnell (Llanelli), M.G. Roberts (London Welsh and Wales), J.F. Slattery (University College Dublin and Ireland), C.B. Stevens (Harlequins and England), J. Taylor (London Welsh and Wales), W.D. Thomas (Llanelli and Wales)

Manager: Dr D.W.C. Smith

Coach: C.R. James

Results: Brisbane, Wed 12 May: Lions 11, Queensland 15, Sydney, Sat 15 May: Lions 14, New South Wales 12, Pukekohe, Sat 22 May: Lions 25, Counties-Thames Valley 3, Wanganui, Wed 26 May: Lions 22, King Country-Wanganui 9, Hamilton, Sat 29 May: Lions 35, Waikato 14, Auckland, Wed 2: Lions 23, New Zealand Maoris 12, Wellington, Sat 5 Jun: Lions 47, Wellington 9, Timaru, Wed 9 Jun: Lions 25, South Canterbury-North Otago 6, Dunedin, Sat 12 Jun: Lions 21, Otago 9, Greymouth, Wed 16 Jun: Lions 39, West Coast-Buller 6, Christchurch, Sat 19 Jun: Lions 14, Canterbury 3, Blenheim, Tue 22 Jun: Lions 31, Marlborough-Nelson 12, FIRST TEST: Dunedin, Sat 26 Jun: Lions 9, New Zealand 3, Invercargill, Wed 30 Jun: Lions 25, Southland 3, New Plymouth, Sat 3 Jul: Lions 14, Taranaki 9, Wellington, Tue 6 Jul: Lions 27, New Zealand Universities 6, SECOND TEST: Christchurch, Sat 10 Jul: Lions 12, New Zealand 22, Masterton, Wed 14 Jul: Lions 27, Wairarapa-Bush 6, Napier, Sat 17 Jul: Lions 25, Hawke's Bay 6, Gisborne, Wed 21 Jul: Lions 18, East Coast-Poverty Bay 12, Auckland, Sat 24 Jul: Lions 19, Auckland 12, THIRD TEST: Wellington, Sat 31 Jul: Lions 13, New Zealand 3, Palmerston North, Wed 4 Aug: Lions 39, Manawatu-Horowhenua 6, Whangarei, Sat 7 Aug: Lions 11, North Auckland 5, Tauranga, Tue 10 Aug: Lions 20, Bay of Plenty 14, FOURTH TEST: Auckland, Sat 14 Aug: Lions 14, New Zealand 14

1974 – SOUTH AFRICA

Backs: P. Bennett (Llanelli and Wales), R.T.E. Bergiers (Llanelli and Wales), G.O. Edwards (Cardiff and Wales), G.W. Evans (Coventry and England), C.M.H. Gibson (North of Ireland and Ireland), T.O. Grace (St Mary's College and Ireland), A.R. Irvine (Heriot's FP and Scotland), I.R. McGeechan (Headingley and Scotland), R.A. Milliken (Bangor and Ireland), J.J. Moloney (St Mary's College and Ireland), A.J. Morley (Bristol and England), A.G.B. Old (Leicester and England), C.F.W. Rees (London Welsh and Wales), W.C.C. Steele (Bedford and RAF and Scotland), J.J. Williams (Llanelli and Wales), J.P.R. Williams (London Welsh and Wales)

Forwards: G.L. Brown (West of Scotland and Scotland), M.A. Burton (Gloucester and England), A.B. Carmichael (West of Scotland and Scotland), F.E. Cotton (Coventry and England), T.P. David (Llanelli and Wales), T.M. Davies (Swansea and Wales), K.W. Kennedy (London Irish and Ireland), W.J. McBride [capt] (Ballymena and Ireland), S.A. McKinney (Dungannon and Ireland), J. McLauchlan (Jordanhill College and Scotland), A. Neary (Broughton Park and England), C.W. Ralston (Richmond and England), A.G. Ripley (Rosslyn Park and England), J.F. Slattery (Blackrock College and Ireland), R.M. Uttley (Gosforth and England), R.W. Windsor (Pontypool and Wales)

Manager: A.G. Thomas

Assistant manager and coach: S. Millar

Results: Potchefstroom, Wed 15 May: Lions 59, Western Transvaal 13, Windhoek, Sat 18 May: Lions 23, South West Africa 16, Wellington, Thu 23 May: Lions 33, Boland 6, Port Elizabeth, Sun 26 May: Lions 28, Eastern Province 14, Mossel Bay, Wed 29 May: Lions 97, South Western Districts 0, Cape Town, Sat 1 Jun: Lions 17, Western Province 8, Cape Town, Tue 4 Jun: Lions 37, SAR Federation XV 6, FIRST TEST: Cape Town, Sat 8 Jun: Lions 12, South Africa 3, Cape Town, Tue 11 Jun: Lions 26, Western Province Universities 4, Johannesburg, Sat 15 Jun: Lions 23, Transvaal 15, Salisbury, Tue 18 Jun: Lions 42, Rhodesia 6, SECOND TEST: Pretoria, Sat 22 Jun: Lions 28, South Africa 9, Johannesburg, Thu 27 Jun: Lions 20, Quaggas 16, Bloemfontein, Sat 29 Jun: Lions 11, Orange Free State 9, Kimberley, Wed 3 Jul: Lions 69, Griqualand West 16, Pretoria, Sat 6 Jul: Lions 16, Northern Transvaal 12, East London, Tue 9 Jul: Lions 56, SA Africans (Leopards) 10, THIRD TEST: Port Elizabeth, 13 Jul: Lions 26, South Africa 9, East London, Wed 17 Jul: Lions 26, Border Bulldogs 6, Durban, Sat 20 Jul: Lions 34, Natal 6, Springs, Tue 23 Jul: Lions 33, Eastern Transvaal 10, FOURTH TEST: Sat 27 Jul: Lions 13, South Africa 13

1977 – NEW ZEALAND AND FIJI

Backs: P. Bennett [capt] (Llanelli and Wales), J.D. Bevan (Aberavon and Wales), D.H. Burcher (Newport and Wales), G.L. Evans (Newport and Wales), S.P. Fenwick (Bridgend and Wales), C.M.H. Gibson (North of Ireland and Ireland), B.H. Hay (Boroughmuir and Scotland), A.R. Irvine (Heriot's FP and Scotland), A.D. Lewis (Cambridge University and London Welsh), I.R. McGeechan (Headingley and Scotland), D.W. Morgan (Stewart's Melville FP and Scotland), H.E. Rees (Neath), P.J. Squires (Harrogate and England), D.B. Williams (Cardiff), J.J. Williams (Llanelli and Wales)

Forwards: W.B. Beaumont (Fylde and England), G.L. Brown (West of Scotland and Scotland), T.J. Cobner (Pontypool and Wales), F.E. Cotton (Coventry and England), W.P. Duggan (Blackrock College and Ireland), T.P. Evans (Swansea and Wales), A.G. Faulkner (Pontypool and Wales), N.E. Horton (Moseley and England), M.I. Keane (Lansdowne and Ireland), A.J. Martin (Aberavon and Wales), A. Neary (Broughton Park and England), P.A. Orr (Old Wesley and Ireland), G. Price (Porthcawl and Wales), D.L. Quinnell (Llanelli and Wales), J. Squire (Newport and Wales), P.J. Wheeler (Leicester and England), C. Williams (Aberavon and Wales), R.W. Windsor (Pontypool and Wales)

Manager: G. Burrell

Assistant manager and coach: J. Dawes

Results: Masterton, Wed 18 May: Lions 41, Wairarapa Bush 13, Napier, Sat 21 May: Lions 13, Hawke's Bay 11, Gisborne, Wed 25 May: Lions 25, Poverty Bay-East Coast 6, New Plymouth, Sat 28 May: Lions 21, Taranaki 13, Taumaranui, Wed 1 Jun: Lions 60, King Country-Wanganui 9, Palmerston North, Sat 4 Jun: Lions 18, Manawatu-Horowhenua 12, Dunedin, Wed 8 Jun: Lions 12, Otago 7, Invercargill, Sat 11 Jun: Lions 20, Southland 12, Christchurch, Tue 14 Jun: Lions 9, New Zealand Universities 21, FIRST TEST: Wellington, Sat 18 Jun: Lions 12, New Zealand 16, Timaru, Wed 22 Jun: Lions 45, Hanan Shield Districts 6, Christchurch, Sat 25 Jun: Lions 14, Canterbury 13, Westport, Wed 29 Jun: Lions 45, West Coast-Buller 0, Wellington, Sat 2 Jul: Lions 13, Wellington 6, Blenheim, Tue 5 Jul: Lions 40, Marlborough-Nelson 23, SECOND TEST: Christchurch, Sat 9 Jul: Lions 13, New Zealand 9, Auckland, Wed 13 Jul: Lions 22, New Zealand Maori 19, Hamilton, Sat 16 Jul: Lions 18, Waikato 13, Wellington, Wed 20 Jul: Lions 19, New Zealand Juniors 9, Auckland, Sat 23 Jul: Lions 34, Auckland 15, THIRD TEST: Dunedin, Sat 30 Jul: Lions 7, New Zealand 19, Pukekohe, Wed 3 Aug: Lions 35, Counties-Thames Valley 10, Whangarei, Sat 6 Aug: Lions 18, North Auckland 7, Rotorua, Tue 9 Aug: Lions 23, Bay of Plenty 16, FOURTH TEST, Auckland, Sat 13 Aug: Lions 9, New Zealand 10, Suva, Tue 16 Aug: Lions 21, Fiji 25

1980 – SOUTH AFRICA

Backs: S.O. Campbell (Old Belvedere and Ireland), J. Carleton (Orrell and England), W.G. Davies (Cardiff and Wales), P.W. Dodge (Leicester and England), R.W.R. Gravell (Llanelli and Wales), B.H. Hay (Boroughmuir and Scotland), T.D. Holmes (Cardiff and Wales), A.R. Irvine (Heriot's FP and Scotland), P.J. Morgan (Llanelli and Wales), R.C. O'Donnell (St Mary's College and Ireland), C.S. Patterson (Instonians and Ireland), H.E. Rees (Neath and Wales), J.M. Renwick (Hawick and Scotland), D.S. Richards (Swansea and Wales), J.C. Robbie (Greystones and Ireland), M.A.C. Slemen (Liverpool and England), S.J. Smith (Sale and England), A.J.P. Ward (Garryowen and Ireland), C.R. Woodward (Leicester and England)

Forwards: J.R. Beattie (Glasgow Academicals and Scotland), W.B. Beaumont [capt] (Fylde and England), P.J. Blakeway (Gloucester and England), M.J. Colclough (Angouleme and England), F.E. Cotton (Sale and England), S.M. Lane (Cardiff and Wales), A.J. Martin (Aberavon and Wales), J.B. O'Driscoll (London Irish and Ireland), P.A. Orr (Old Wesley and Ireland), A.J. Phillips (Cardiff and Wales), G. Price (Pontypool and Wales), D.L. Quinnell (Llanelli and Wales), J. Squire (Pontypool and Wales), I. Stephens (Bridgend and Wales), A.J. Tomes (Hawick and Scotland), C.C. Tucker (Shannon and Ireland), P.J. Wheeler (Leicester and England), C. Williams (Swansea and Wales), G.P. Williams (Bridgend and Wales)

Manager: S. Millar

Assistant manager and coach: N. Murphy

Results: Port Elizabeth, Sat 10 May: Lions 28, Eastern Province 16, East London, Wed 14 May: Lions 28 S.A.R.A. XV 6, Durban, Sat 17 May: Lions 21, Natal 15, Potchefstroom, Wed 21 May: Lions 22, SA Invitation 19, Bloemfontein, Sat 24 May: Lions 21, Orange Free State 17, Stellenbosch, Tue 27 May: Lions 15, SAR Federation XV 6, FIRST TEST: Cape Town, Sat 31 May: Lions, 22, South Africa 26, Windhoek, Wed 4 Jun: Lions 27, South African Country 7, Johannesburg, Sat 7 Jun: Lions 32, Transvaal 12, Springs, Tue 10 Jun: Lions 21, Eastern Transvaal 15, SECOND TEST: Bloemfontein, Sat 14 Jun: Lions 19, South Africa 26, Johannesburg, Wed 18 Jun: Lions 17, Junior Springboks 6, Pretoria, Sat 21 Jun: Lions 16, Northern Transvaal 9, THIRD TEST: Port Elizabeth, Sat 28 Jun: Lions 10, South Africa 12, Durban, Wed 2 Jul: Lions 25, SA Barbarians 14, Cape Town, Sat 5 Jul: Lions 37, Western Province 6, Kimberley, Tue 8 Jul: Lions 23, Griqualand West, FOURTH TEST: Pretoria, Sat 12 Jul: Lions 17, South Africa 13

1983 – NEW ZEALAND

Backs: R.A. Ackerman (London Welsh and Wales), G.R.T. Baird (Kelso and Scotland), S.O. Campbell (Old Belvedere and Ireland), J. Carleton (Orrell and England), G. Evans (Maesteg and Wales), W.H. Hare (Leicester and England), T.D. Holmes (Cardiff and Wales), D.G. Irwin (Instonians and Ireland), M.J. Kiernan (Dolphin and Ireland), R.J. Laidlaw (Jedforest and Scotland), H.P. MacNeill (Oxford University and Ireland), N.D. Melville (Wasps), T.M. Ringland (Ballymena and Ireland), J.Y. Rutherford (Selkirk and Scotland), S.J. Smith (Sale and England), C.R. Woodward (Leicester and England)

Forwards: S.J. Bainbridge (Gosforth and England), J.R. Beattie (Glasgow Academicals and Scotland), S.B. Boyle (Gloucester and England), E.T. Butler (Pontypool and Wales), J.H. Calder (Stewart's Melville FP and Scotland), M.J. Colclough (Angouleme and England), C.T. Deans (Hawick and Scotland), C.F. Fitzgerald ([capt] (St Mary's College and Ireland), N.C. Jeavons (Moseley and England), S.T. Jones (Pontypool and Wales), D.G. Lenihan (Cork Constitution and Ireland), G.A.J. McLoughlin (Shannon and Ireland), I.G. Milne (Heriot's FP and Scotland), R.L. Norster (Cardiff and Wales), J.B. O'Driscoll (London Irish and Ireland), I.A.M. Paxton (Selkirk and Scotland), G. Price (Pontypool and Wales), J. Squire (Pontypool and Wales), I. Stephens (Bridgend and Wales), P.J. Winterbottom (Headingley and England)

Manager: W.J. McBride

Assistant manager and coach: J.W. Telfer

Results: Wanganui, Sat 14 May: Lions 47, Wanganui 15, Auckland, Wed 18 May: Lions 12, Auckland 13, Rotorua, Sat 21 May: Lions 34, Bay of Plenty 16, Wellington, Wed 25 May: Lions 27, Wellington 19, Palmerston North, Sat 28 May: Lions 25, Manawatu 18, Ashburton, Tue 31 May: Lions 26, Mid Canterbury 6, FIRST TEST: Christchurch, Sat 4 Jun: Lions 12, New Zealand 16, Greymouth, Wed 8 Jun: Lions 52, West Coast 16, Invercargill, Sat 11 Jun: Lions 41, Southland 3, Masterton, Tue 14 Jun: Lions 57, Wairarapa-Bush 10, SECOND TEST: Wellington, Sat 18 Jun: Lions 0, New Zealand 9, Whangarei, Sat 25 Jun: Lions 21, North Auckland 12, Christchurch Tue 28 Jun: Lions 20, Canterbury 22, THIRD TEST: Dunedin, Sat 2 Jul: Lions 8, New Zealand 15, Napier, Wed 6 Jul: Lions 25, Hawke's Bay 19, Pukekohe, Sat 9 Jul: Lions 25, Counties-Manukau 16, Hamilton, Tue 12 Jul: Lions 40, Waikato 13, FOURTH TEST: Auckland, Sat 16 Jul: Lions 6, New Zealand 38

1989 – AUSTRALIA

Backs: C.R. Andrew (Wasps and England), G. Armstrong (Jedforest and Scotland), C.M. Chalmers (Melrose and Scotland), A. Clement (Swansea and Wales), P.M. Dean (St Mary's College and Ireland), J.A. Devereux (Bridgend and Wales), P.W. Dods (Gala and Scotland), I.C. Evans (Llanelli and Wales), J.C. Guscott (Bath and England), M.R. Hall (Bridgend and Wales), A.G. Hastings (London Scottish and Scotland), S. Hastings (Watsonians and Scotland), R.N. Jones (Swansea and Wales), B.J. Mullin (London Irish and Ireland), C. Oti (Wasps and England), R. Underwood (Leicester and RAF and England)

Forwards: P.J. Ackford (Harlequins and England), F. Calder [capt] (Stewart's Melville FP and Scotland), G.J. Chilcott (Bath and England), W.A. Dooley (Preston Grasshoppers and England), M. Griffiths (Bridgend and Wales), J. Jeffrey (Kelso and Scotland), D.G. Lenihan (Cork Constitution and Ireland), B.C. Moore (Nottingham and England), R.L. Norster (Cardiff and Wales), D. Richards (Leicester and England), R.A. Robinson (Bath and England), S.J. Smith (Ballymena and Ireland), D.M.B. Sole (Edinburgh Academicals and Scotland), M.C. Teague (Gloucester and England), D.B. White (London Scottish and Scotland), D. Young (Cardiff and Wales)

Manager: D.C.T Rowlands

Coaches: I.R. McGeechan and R.M. Uttley

Results: Perth, Sat 10 Jun: Lions 44, Western Australia 0, Melbourne, Wed 14 Jun: Lions 23, Australia B 18, Brisbane, Sat 17 Jun: Lions 19, Queensland 15, Cairns, Wed 21 Jun: Lions 30, Queensland 6, Sydney, Sat 24 Jun: Lions 23, New South Wales 21, Dubbo, Tue 27 Jun: Lions 39, New South Wales B 19, FIRST TEST: Sydney, Sat 1 Jul: Lions 12, Australia 30, Canberra, Tue 4 Jul: Lions 41, Australian Capital Territory 25, SECOND TEST: Brisbane, Sat 8 Jul: Lions 19, Australia 12, THIRD TEST: Sydney, Sat 15 Jul: Lions 19, Australia 18, Newcastle, Wed 19 Jul: Lions 72, New South Wales Country 13, Brisbane, Sun 23 Jul: Lions 19, Anzac XV 15

1993 – NEW ZEALAND

Backs: C.R. Andrew (Wasps and England), S. Barnes (Bath and England), W.D.C. Carling (Harlequins and England), A. Clement (Swansea and Wales), V.J.G. Cunningham (St Mary's College and Ireland), I.C. Evans (Llanelli and Wales), I.S. Gibbs (Swansea and Wales), J.C. Guscott (Bath and England), A.G. Hastings [capt] (Watsonians and Scotland), S. Hastings (Watsonians and Scotland), I. Hunter (Northampton and England), R.N. Jones (Swansea and Wales), C.D. Morris (Orrell and England), A.D. Nicol (Dundee HS FP and Scotland), R. Underwood (Leicester and RAF and England), T. Underwood (Leicester and England), R.M. Wallace (Garryowen and Ireland)

Forwards: M.C. Bayfield (Northampton and England), A.P. Burnell (London Scottish and Scotland), B.B. Clarke (Bath and England), D.F. Cronin (London Scottish and Scotland), W.A. Dooley (Preston Grasshoppers and England), M.J. Galwey (Shannon and Ireland), M.O. Johnson (Leicester and England), J. Leonard (Harlequins and England), K.S. Milne (Heriot's FP and Scotland), B.C. Moore (Harlequins and England), N.J. Popplewell (Greystones and Ireland), A.I. Reed (Bath and Scotland), D. Richards (Leicester and England), M.C. Teague (Moseley and England), R.E. Webster (Swansea and Wales), P.J. Winterbottom (Harlequins and England), P.H. Wright (Boroughmuir and Scotland)

Manager: G. Cooke

Coach: I.R. McGeechan

Assistant coach: R. Best

Results: Whangarei, Sat 22 May: Lions 30, North Auckland 17, Auckland, Wed 26 May: Lions 29, North Harbour 13, Wellington, Sat 29 May: Lions 24, New Zealand 20, Christchurch, Wed 2 Jun: Lions 28, Canterbury 10, Dunedin, Sat 5 Jun: Lions 24, Otago 37, Invercargill, Tue 8 Jun: Lions 34, Southland 16, FIRST TEST: Sat 12 Jun: Lions 18, New Zealand 20, New Plymouth, Wed 16 Jun: Lions 49, Taranaki 25, Auckland, Sat 19 Jun: Lions 18, Auckland 23, Napier, Tue 22 Jun: Lions 17, Hawke's Bay 29, SECOND TEST: Wellington, Sat 26 Jun: Lions 20, New Zealand 7, Hamilton, Tue 29 Jun: Lions 10, Waikato 38, THIRD TEST: Auckland, Sat 3 Jul: Lions 13, New Zealand 30

1997 – SOUTH AFRICA

Backs: A. Bateman (Richmond and Wales), N. Beal (Northampton and England), J. Bentley (Newcastle and England), K. Bracken (Saracens and England), M. Catt (Bath and England), M. Dawson (Northampton and England), I. Evans (Llanelli and Wales), S. Gibbs (Swansea and Wales), P. Grayson (Northampton and England), W. Greenwood (Leicester and England), J. Guscott (Bath and England), A. Healey (Leicester and England), R. Howley (Cardiff and Wales), N. Jenkins (Pontypridd and Wales), A.G. Stanger (Hawick and Scotland), T. Stimpson (Newcastle and England), A. Tait (Newcastle and Scotland), G. Townsend (Northampton and Scotland), T. Underwood (Newcastle and England)

Forwards: N. Back (Leicester and England), L. Dallaglio (Wasps and England), J. Davidson (London Irish and Ireland), T. Diprose (Saracens and England), R. Hill (Saracens and England), M. Johnson [capt] (Leicester and England), J. Leonard (Harlequins and England), E. Miller (Leicester and Ireland), S. Quinnell (Richmond and Wales), N. Redman (Bath and England), M. Regan (Bristol and England), T. Rodber (Northampton and England), G. Rowntree (Leicester and England), S. Shaw (Bristol and England), T. Smith (Watsonians and Scotland), R. Wainwright (Watsonians and Scotland), P. Wallace (Saracens and Ireland), G. Weir (Newcastle and Scotland), B. Williams (Neath and Wales), K. Wood (Harlequins and Ireland), D. Young (Cardiff and Wales)

Manager: F. Cotton

Coach: I.R. McGeechan

Assistant coach: J.W. Telfer

Results: Port Elizabeth, Sat 24 May: Lions 39, Eastern Province Inv XV 11, East London, Wed 28 May: Lions 18, Border Bulldogs 14, Cape Town, Sat 31 May: Lions 38, Western Province 21, Witbank, Tue 3 Jun: Lions 64, Mpumalanga 14, Pretoria, Sat 7 Jun: Lions 30, Northern Transvaal 35, Johannesburg, Wed 11 Jun: Lions 20, Gauteng Lions 14, Durban, Sat 14 Jun: Lions 42, Natal 12, Wellington, Tue 17 Jun: Lions 51, Emerging Springboks 22, FIRST TEST: Cape Town, Sat 21 Jun: Lions 25, South Africa 16, Bloemfontein, Tue 24 Jun: Lions 52, Free State Cheetahs 30, SECOND TEST: Durban, Sat 28 Jun: Lions 18, South Africa 15, Welkom, Tue 1 Jul: Lions 67, Northern Free State 39, THIRD TEST: Johannesburg, Sat 5 Jul: Lions 16, South Africa 35

2001 – AUSTRALIA

Backs: I. Balshaw (Bath and England), M. Perry (Bath and England), B. Cohen (Northampton and England), D. James (Llanelli and Wales), D. Luger (Saracens and England), J. Robinson (Sale and England), T. Howe (Ulster and Ireland), M. Catt (Bath and England), W. Greenwood (Harlequins and England), R. Henderson (Wasps and Ireland), B. O'Driscoll (Blackrock College and Ireland), M. Taylor (Swansea and Wales), S. Gibbs (Swansea and Wales), N. Jenkins (Cardiff and Wales), R. O'Gara (Cork Constitution and Ireland), J. Wilkinson (Newcastle and England), M. Dawson (Northampton and England), A. Healey (Leicester and England), R. Howley (Cardiff and Wales), A. Nicol (Glasgow and Scotland)

Forwards: J. Leonard (Harlequins and England), D. Morris (Swansea and Wales), T. Smith (Brive and Scotland), P. Vickery (Gloucester and England), D. Young (Cardiff and Wales), P. Greening (Wasps and England), R. McBryde (Llanelli and Wales), K. Wood (Harlequins and Ireland), G. Bulloch (Glasgow and Scotland), D. West (Leicester and England), J. Davidson (Castres and Ireland), D. Grewcock (Saracens and England), M. Johnson [capt] (Leicester and England), S. Murray (Saracens and Scotland), M. O'Kelly (St Mary's College), N. Back (Leicester and England), C. Charvis (Swansea and Wales), L. Dallaglio (Wasps and England), R. Hill (Saracens and England), S. Quinnell (Llanelli and Wales), S. Taylor (Edinburgh and Scotland), M. Williams (Cardiff and Wales), M. Corry (Leicester and England), D. Wallace (Munster and Ireland)

Manager: D. Lenihan

Coach: G. Henry

Assistant coaches: A. Robinson, P. Larder, S. Black

Results: Perth, Fri 8 Jun: Lions 116, Western Australia 10, Townsville, Tue 12 Jun: Lions 83, Queensland President's XV 6, Brisbane, Sat 16 Jun: Lions 42, Queensland Reds 8, Gosford, Tue 19 Jun: Lions 25, Australia A 28, Sydney, Sat 23 Jun: Lions 41, New South Wales Waratahs 24, Coffs Harbour, Tue 26 Jun: Lions 46, New South Wales Country 3, FIRST TEST: Brisbane, Sat 30 Jun: Lions 29, Australia 13, Canberra, Tue 3 Jul: Lions 30, ACT Brumbies 28, SECOND TEST: Melbourne, Sat 7 Jul: Lions 14, Australia 35, THIRD TEST: Sydney, Sat 14 Jul: Lions 23, Australia 29

2005 – NEW ZEALAND

Backs: I. Balshaw (Leeds Tykes and England), G. Cooper (Newport Gwent Dragons and Wales), M. Cueto (Sale Sharks and England), C. Cusiter (The Borders and Scotland), G. D'Arcy (Leinster and Ireland), M. Dawson (Wasps and England), W. Greenwood (Harlequins and England), G. Henson (Ospreys and Wales), D. Hickie (Leinster and Ireland), C. Hodgson (Sale Sharks and England), S. Horgan (Leinster and Ireland), S. Jones (Clermont Auvergne and Wales), J. Lewsey (Wasps and England), G. Murphy (Leicester Tigers and Ireland), B. O'Driscoll [capt] (Leinster and Ireland), R. O'Gara (Munster and Ireland), D. Peel (Llanelli Scarlets and Wales), J. Robinson (Sale Sharks and England), T. Shanklin (Cardiff Blues and Wales), O. Smith (Leicester Tigers and England), G. Thomas (Toulouse and Wales), S. Williams (Ospreys and Wales), J. Wilkinson (Newcastle Falcons and England)

Forwards: N. Back (Leicester Tigers and England), G. Bulloch (Glasgow and Scotland), S. Byrne (Leinster and Ireland), B. Cockbain (Ospreys and Wales), M. Corry (Leicester Tigers and England), L. Dallaglio (Wasps and England), S. Easterby (Llanelli Scarlets and Ireland), D. Grewcock (Bath and England), J. Hayes (Munster and Ireland), R. Hill (Saracens and England), G. Jenkins (Cardiff Blues and Wales), R. Jones (Ospreys and Wales), B. Kay (Leicester Tigers and England), L. Moody (Leicester Tigers and England), D. O'Callaghan (Munster and Ireland), P. O'Connell (Munster and Ireland), M. O'Kelly (Leinster and Ireland), M. Owen (Newport Gwent Dragons and Wales), G. Rowntree (Leicester Tigers and England), A. Sheridan (Sale Sharks and England), S. Shaw (Wasps and England), M. Stevens (Bath and England), S. Taylor (Edinburgh and Scotland), S. Thompson (Northampton Saints and England), A. Titterrell (Sale Sharks and England), Jason White (Sale Sharks and Scotland), Julian White (Leicester Tigers and England), M. Williams (Cardiff Blues and Wales)

Manager: W.B. Beaumont

Head coach: C.R. Woodward

Coaches: A. Robinson, E. O'Sullivan, P. Larder, I.R. McGeechan, G. Jenkins, M. Ford

Results: Cardiff, Mon 23 May: Lions 25, Argentina 25, Rotorua, Sat 4 Jun: Lions 34, Bay of Plenty 20, New Plymouth, Wed 8 Jun: Lions 36, Taranaki 14, Hamilton, Sat 11 Jun: Lions 13, New Zealand Maori 19, Wellington, Wed 15 Jun: Lions 23, Wellington 6, Dunedin, Sat 18 Jun: Lions 30, Otago 19, Invercargill, Tue 21 Jun: Lions 26, Southland 16, FIRST TEST: Christchurch, Sat 25 Jun: Lions 3, New Zealand 21, Palmerston North, Tue 28 Jun: Lions 109, Manawatu 6, SECOND TEST: Wellington, Sat 2 Jul: Lions 18, New Zealand 48, Auckland, Tue 5 Jul: Lions 17, Auckland 13, THIRD TEST: Auckland, Sat 9 Jul: Lions 19, New Zealand 38

INDEX